Frommer's

Walt Disney World® & Orlando

by Rena Bulkin

Macmillan • USA

ABOUT THE AUTHOR

Rena Bulkin began her travel writing career in 1964 when she set out for Europe in search of adventure. She found it writing about hotels and restaurants for the *New York Times* International Edition. She has since authored dozens of magazine articles and 15 travel guides to far-flung destinations.

MACMILLAN TRAVEL

A Prentice Hall Macmillan Company
1633 Broadway
New York, NY 10019

ISBN 0-028-60649-3
ISSN 1082-2615

Editor: Alice K. Thompson
Map Editor: Douglas Stallings
Design by Michele Laseau
Digital Cartography by Jim Moore and Ortelius Design

SPECIAL SALES

Bulk purchases (10+ copies) of Frommer's travel guides are available to corporations at special discounts. The Special Sales Department can produce custom editions to be used as premiums and/or for sales promotion to suit individual needs. Existing editions can be produced with custom cover imprints such as corporate logos. For more information write to: Special Sales, Simon & Schuster 1230 Avenue of the Americas, New York, NY 10020.

Manufactured in the United States of America

Contents

List of Maps

AN INVITATION TO THE READER

In researching this book, I discovered many wonderful places—hotels, restaurants, shops, and more. I'm sure you'll find others. Please tell us about them, so we can share the information with your fellow travelers in upcoming editions. If you were disappointed with a recommendation, we'd love to know that, too. Please write to:

Rena Bulkin
Frommer's Walt Disney World & Orlando '96
Macmillan Travel
1633 Broadway
New York, NY 10019

AN ADDITIONAL NOTE

Please be advised that travel information is subject to change at any time—and this is especially true of prices. We therefore suggest that you write or call ahead for confirmation when making your travel plans. The authors, editors, and publisher cannot be held responsible for the experiences of readers while traveling. Your safety is important to us, however, so we encourage you to stay alert and be aware of your surroundings. Keep a close eye on cameras, purses, and wallets, all favorite targets of thieves and pickpockets.

WHAT THE SYMBOLS MEAN

✪ Frommer's Favorites

Hotels, restaurants, attractions, and entertainments you should not miss.

⑤ Super-Special Values

Hotels and restaurants that offer great value for your money.

The following abbreviations are used for credit cards:

AE	American Express	ER	enRoute
CB	Carte Blanche	JCB	Japan Credit Bank
DC	Diners Club	MC	MasterCard
DISC	Discover	V	Visa

Introducing Walt Disney World & Orlando

Orlando was a sleepy Southern town ringed with sparkling lakes, pine forests, and citrus groves until Walt Disney waved his pixie-dusted paintbrush over 43 square miles of swampland and turned it into a Magic Kingdom. He literally "animated" the area, sparking an unprecedented building boom, as hotels, restaurants, and scores of additional attractions arose to take advantage of the tourist traffic Disney had generated.

The world's most famous mouse changed central Florida forever. Though the citrus industry still exists here, orange groves have largely given way to high-rise apartment complexes, vast hotels and resorts, and shopping malls. Many national firms have relocated their headquarters to this thriving sunbelt region, and it has also become one of the fastest-growing high-technology centers in the country. Recently, *Newsweek* named Orlando one of the 10 best U.S. cities in which to live and work.

For travelers, Orlando represents a vacation from stressful reality to a gossamer world of make-believe—one where there are parades every day and fireworks every night. Forget all your problems but one: How are you possibly going to cram so many attractions into one short vacation?

1 Frommer's Favorite Orlando Experiences

Splash Mountain   This Magic Kingdom attraction combines gorgeous scenery with Disney magic and a theme park thrill—a five-story splashdown! Don't chicken out. It's great.

The Daily Parade and SpectroMagic   The daily 3pm parade at the Magic Kingdom is enchanting. And SpectroMagic, which takes place after dark and adds high-tech dazzle to Disney's genius for spectacle, is simply awe-inspiring.

The Making of Me   Martin Short teaches the facts of life in this delightful and very charming 15-minute film at Epcot's Wonders of Life pavilion.

Cranium Command   Another Wonders of Life feature, this hilarious multimedia attraction is one of Epcot's best. It stars a handful of "Saturday Night Live" actors and other comedians.

Wonders of China   This 360-degree Circle-Vision™ film at Epcot's China pavilion explores 6,000 years of Chinese history and ranges the country's landscape in stunning cinematography.

Jim Henson's Muppet Vision 3D   High-tech 3-D Muppets, with lots of special-effects wizardry. A delight. At Disney-MGM Studios.

Aladdin's Royal Caravan   Disney-MGM Studio's exotic version of the Magic Kingdom parade, complete with scimitar dancers, fire-eaters, and snake charmers.

Universal Studios   Steven Spielberg is the park's creative consultant. How can you go wrong? Not-to-be-missed attractions here: Back to the Future, Jaws, Kongfrontation, and Earthquake: The Big One.

Mermaids, Myths & Monsters   A thrilling nighttime multimedia spectacular at Sea World that features fireworks and hologram-like imagery against a towering 60-foot screen of illuminated water.

Cypress Gardens   Two hundred acres of gorgeous botanical gardens punctuated by lakes and lagoons, waterfalls, and sculpture.

Harry P. Leu Gardens   A delightful 56-acre botanical garden in Orlando on the shores of Lake Rowena.

2 A Look at the Past

It would almost seem that the history of Orlando could be condensed into two terse sentences. 1. There were orange groves. 2. Walt Disney came. There is, however, considerably more juice to be squeezed from the story. The modern metropolis of Orlando began as a rough-and-tumble Florida frontier town.

Dateline

- 1513 Spanish explorer Ponce de León, in search of the fabled Fountain of Youth, discovers and names Florida.
- 1817–18 The First Seminole War. Aligned with refugee Creeks from Georgia, native Apalachees, and runaway slaves, the Seminoles

SETTLERS VS. SEMINOLES: THE ROAD TO STATEHOOD

Florida history dates back to 1513—more than a century before the Pilgrims landed at Plymouth Rock—when Ponce de León, in search of the fabled "fountain of youth," spied the beaches and lush greenery of Florida's Atlantic coast. He named it La Florida—"the Flowery Land." After years of alternating Spanish, French, and British rule, the territory was ceded (by Spain) to the United States in 1821. Lost in the international shuffle were the Seminoles, who, after migrating from Georgia and the Carolinas in the late 18th century to settle on some of Florida's richest farmlands, were viewed by the Americans as an obstacle to white settlement. After a series of compromise treaties that left both sides dissatisfied, the federal government threw down the

continues

final gauntlet with the Indian Removal Act of 1830, stipulating that all eastern tribes be removed to reservations west of the Mississippi. This cruel edict sparked the Second Seminole War (1835–42). At a treaty conference at Payne's Landing in 1832, a young warrior named Osceola strode up to the bargaining table, slammed his knife into the papers on it, and pointing to the quivering blade, proclaimed, "The only treaty I will ever make is this!"

Guerilla warfare thwarted the U.S. army's attempt to remove the Seminoles for almost eight years, during which time many of the resisters drifted south into the interior of central Florida. In what is today the Orlando area—on a small triangular parcel of land formed by Lake Gatlin, Lake Gem Mary, and Lake Jennie Jewell—the Americans built Fort Gatlin in 1838 to offer protection to pioneer homesteaders. The fort, sited near an ancient oak tree where followers of Osceola frequently met to discuss strategies, was the scene of many skirmishes. The Seminoles kept up a fierce rebellion until 1842, when, undefeated, they accepted a treaty whereby their remaining numbers (about 300) were given land and left in peace. The same year, the Armed Occupation Act offered 160 acres to any pioneers willing to settle here for a minimum of five years. The land was fertile, wild turkeys and deer abounded in the woods, grazing for cattle was equally plentiful, and dozens of lakes provided fish and watering for livestock. In 1843, what had been Mosquito County was more invitingly renamed Orange County. And with the Seminoles more or less out of the way (though sporadic cattle rustling and bloody uprisings still occurred), the Territorial General Legislature petitioned Congress for statehood. On March 3, 1845, Pres. John Tyler signed a bill making Florida the 27th state in the Union.

Settlements and statehood notwithstanding, at the middle of the 19th century the Orlando area (named Jernigan for one of its first settler families) was comprised largely of pristine lakes and pine-forested wilderness. There were no roads, and you could ride all day (if you could find a trail) without meeting a soul. The Jernigans successfully raised cattle, and their home and stockade, which was granted a post office in 1850, became a waystop for travelers and the seat of

battle Andrew Jackson's troops while Florida is still a Spanish territory.

- **1821** After centuries of European struggle for supremacy in the New World, Spain cedes the territory of Florida to the United States.

- **1835–42** Resistance to white settlement results in the Second Seminole War. Many Native Americans migrate south to central Florida.

- **1843** Mosquito County is renamed Orange County.

- **1845** Florida becomes the 27th state in the Union.

- **1856** Orlando becomes the official seat of Orange County.

- **1861** Florida secedes from the Union. The demise of slavery sounds the death knell for the area's burgeoning cotton industry.

- **1870** Cattle ranching and citrus growing replace cotton as the bulwark of Orlando's economy.

continues

■ **1875** Orlando is officially incorporated as a municipality under state law.

■ **1880** The South Florida Railroad facilitates the expansion of Orlando's agricultural markets.

■ **1884** Fire rages out of control, destroying much of Orlando's fledgling business district.

■ **1894–95** Freezing temperatures destroy two years of citrus crops and wreck orchards. Many growers lose everything.

■ **1910–25** A land boom hits Florida. Fortunes are made overnight.

■ **1926** The land boom goes bust. Fortunes are lost overnight.

■ **1929** An invasion of Mediterranean fruit flies devastates Orlando's citrus industry. Its ruined economy is capped by the stock market crash.

■ **1939–45** World War II revives Orlando's ailing economy.

continues

future development. Farmers and cattle ranchers were drawn to the area's verdant grasslands. Before long a sawmill went up (on the site of today's Orlando Public Library) and a trading post was opened. Other merchants followed, and farms and ranches—which would grow to vast agricultural dynasties—were carved out of the wilderness. In 1856, the boundaries of Orange County were revised, and, thanks to the manipulations of resident James Gamble Speer, a member of the Indian Removal Commission, Fort Gatlin (Jernigan) became its official seat. How the fledgling town came to be named Orlando is a matter of some speculation. Some say Speer renamed the town after a dearly loved friend, while other sources say he named it after one of his favorite Shakespearean characters from *As You Like It*. But the most accepted version is that the town was named for prominent plantation owner Orlando Reeves (or Rees), who died in battle with the Seminoles in 1835. The site where he was buried on the shores of Lake Eola came to be known as "Orlando's Grave." Speer is reported to have said, "This place is often spoken of as 'Orlando's Grave.' Let's drop the word 'grave' and let the county seat be called Orlando."

THE 1860S: CIVIL WAR/CATTLE WARS

Throughout the early 1860s, cotton plantations and cattle ranches became the hallmarks of central Florida. Orlando was ringed by a vast cotton empire. Log cabins went up along the lakes, and the pioneers eked out a somewhat lonely existence separated from each other by miles of farmland. But there were troubles brewing in the 31-state nation that would soon devastate Orlando's planters. The institution of slavery was a major issue of the day. In his 1858 debate with Stephen Douglas, Abraham Lincoln declared, "This government cannot endure permanently half slave and half free." A year later it was obvious that only a war would resolve the issue. In 1861, Florida became the third state to secede from the Union, and the modest progress it had achieved came to a standstill. The Stars and Bars flew from every flagpole, and local men enlisted in the Confederate army, leaving the fledgling town in poverty. A Federal blockade made it difficult to obtain necessities, and many slaves fled. In 1866, the Confederate troops of Florida surrendered, the remaining slaves were freed, and a ragtag group of defeated soldiers returned to Orlando. They found a dying cotton industry, unable to function without slave labor or transport to markets. In 1868 Florida was readmitted into the Union.

Its untended cotton fields having gone to seed, Orlando now concentrated on cattle ranching, a business plagued by heavy taxation on herds by the occupation government and one that ushered in an era of lawlessness and violence. Cattle rustling, widely practiced, generated vicious feuds, clogging courtroom calendars and igniting long-running hostilities between warring parties. Like frontier cattle towns out west, post–Civil War Orlando was short on civilized behavior; gunfights, brawls, and murders were commonplace. But as the 1860s drew to a close, large herd owners from other parts of the state moved into the area and began organizing the industry in a less chaotic fashion. Branding and penning greatly reduced rustling, though it never totally eliminated the problem; even a century later soaring beef prices brought on a rash of cattle thievery as late as 1973!

AN ORANGE TREE GROWS IN ORLANDO

In the 1870s, articles in national magazines began luring large numbers of Americans to central Florida with promises of arable land and a warm climate. In Orlando, public roads, schools, and churches appeared to serve the newcomers, many of whom replanted defunct cotton fields with citrus groves. Orlando was officially incorporated under state law in 1875, setting up definitive boundaries, a city government complete with a mayor, laws and ordinances, a city hall, a jail, and other adjuncts of a municipality. New settlers poured in from all over the country, businesses flourished, and by the end of the year, the town had its first newspaper, the *Orange County Reporter*. The first locomotive of the South Florida Railroad chugged into town in 1880, representing a major step toward growth and prosperity and sparking a building and land boom—the first of many. Orlando got sidewalks and its first bank in 1883—the same year the town voted itself "dry" in hopes of averting the fistfights and brawls that ensued when cowboys crowded into local saloons every Saturday night for rowdy

The city becomes "Florida's Air Capital."

- **1955** Nearby Cape Canaveral becomes a focal point for the space program.
- **1964** Walt Disney begins surreptitiously buying up central Florida farmland, purchasing more than 28,000 acres at a cost of nearly $5.5 million.
- **1965** Disney announces his plan to build the world's most spectacular theme park in Orlando.
- **1968** Kennedy Space Center becomes the launch site for American manned space missions.
- **1971** The Magic Kingdom opens its gates.
- **1972** A new one-day attendance mark is set on December 27, when 72,328 people visit the Magic Kingdom. It will be broken almost every year thereafter.
- **1973** Shamu ventures into Orlando waters. Sea World opens.
- **1979** Mickey Mouse welcomes

continues

R&R. For many years the city continued to vote itself alternately wet and dry, but in actuality, it made very little difference. Legal or not, liquor was always readily available.

FIRE & ICE

In January of 1884, a grocery fire that started at 4am wiped out blocks of businesses, including the offices of the *Orange County Reporter*. But 19th-century Orlando was a bit like a Frank Capra movie. The town rallied round, providing a new location for the paper and presenting its publisher, Mahlon Gore, with $1,200 in cash to help defray losses and $300 in new subscriptions. The paper not only survived but flourished. And the city, realizing the need, created its first fire brigade. By August of 1884, a census revealed that the population had grown to 1,666. That same year 600,000 boxes of oranges were shipped from Florida to points north—most of those boxes originating in Orlando. By 1885, Orlando was a viable town boasting as many as 50 businesses. It was dubbed the "Phenomenal City" after a South Florida Railroad booklet called the city's growth "phenomenal." Which is not to say it was New York. Razorback hogs roamed the streets, and alligator wrestling was a main form of entertainment.

Disaster struck a week after Christmas in 1894, when the temperature plummeted to an unseasonal 24 degrees. Water pipes burst, and orange blossoms froze, blackened, and died. The freeze continued for three days, wrecking the citrus crop for the year. Karl H. Abbott, son of the owner of the San Juan Hotel, where northern buyers met to bid on citrus crops, later described the pandemonium that broke out as the thermometer began dipping shortly after noon:

". . . The buyers hurriedly left the lunch tables and went out of doors to view the weather. The big thermometer in front of the hotel indicated unusual cold. By 2:00 p.m. the San Juan was in an uproar. Prices had dropped to 'no sale.' Commission merchants were frantically trying to get out of options and heated debates and fist fights started in the lobby. . . . About nine that night a fine looking grey haired gentleman in a black coat and Stetson hat walked up the street in front of the hotel and looked at the thermometer, groaned 'Oh my God!' and shot himself through the head . . ."

Many grove owners went bust, and those who remained were hit with a second devastating freeze the following year. Tens of thousands of trees died in the killing frost. Small growers were wiped out, but large conglomerates that could afford to buy up their properties at bargain prices and wait for new groves to mature assured the survival of the industry.

encounters with E.T. and King Kong.

■ 1993 Sea World continues a major expansion. And Universal Studios unleashes the fearsome *Jaws*.

SPECULATION FEVER: GOOD DEALS, BAD DEALS . . .

As Orlando entered the 20th century, citrus and agriculture had surpassed cattle ranching as the mainstay of the local economy. Stray cows no longer had to be shooed from the railway tracks. Streets were being paved and electricity and telephone service installed. The population at the turn of the century was 2,481. In 1902, the city passed its first automobile laws, which included an in-town speed limit of five miles per hour. In 1904, the city flooded. And in 1905 it suffered a drought that ended—miraculously or coincidentally—on a day when all faiths united at the local First Baptist Church to pray for rain. By 1910, prosperity had returned, and Orlando, with a population of nearly 4,000, was becoming a tourism and convention center. World War I brought further industrial growth and a real estate boom, not just to Orlando but to all of Florida. Millions of immigrants, speculators, and builders descended on the state in search of a quick buck. As land speculation reached a fever pitch, and property was bought and resold almost overnight, many citrus groves gave way to urbanization. Preeminent Orlando builder and promoter Carl Dann described the action thusly: "It finally became nothing more than a gambling machine, each man buying on a shoestring, betting dollars a bigger fool would come along and buy his option."

Quite suddenly, the bubble burst. A July 1926 issue of the *Nation* provided the obituary for the Florida land boom: "The world's greatest poker game, played with lots instead of chips, is over. And the players are now . . . paying up." Construction slowed to a trickle, and many newcomers who had arrived in Florida to jump on the bandwagon returned to their homes in the north. Though Orlando was not quite as hard hit as Miami—scene of the greediest land grabs—some belt-tightening was in order. The city even managed to build a municipal airport in 1928. Then came a Mediterranean fruit fly infestation that crippled the citrus industry. Hundreds of thousands of acres of land in quarantined areas had to be cleared of fruit and vast quantities of boxed fruit destroyed. The 1929 stock market crash that precipitated the Great Depression seemed almost an afterthought to Florida's ruined economy.

. . . AND NEW DEALS

President Franklin D. Roosevelt's New Deal helped the state climb back on its feet. The Works Progress Administration (WPA) put 40,000 unemployed Floridians back to work—work that included hundreds of public projects in Orlando. Of these, the most important

Florida

was the expansion and resurfacing of the city's airport. By 1936, the tourist trade had revived somewhat, construction was up once again, and the state began attracting a broader range of visitors than ever before. But the event that finally lifted Florida—and the nation—out of the Depression was World War II.

Orlando had weathered the Great Depression. Now it prepared for war with the construction of army bases, housing for servicemen, and training facilities. Almost all new business was geared toward defense. Enlisted men poured into the city, and the airport was again enlarged and equipped with barracks, a military hospital, administration buildings, and mess halls. By 1944, Orlando had a second airport and was known as "Florida's Air Capital"—home to major aircraft and aviation-parts-manufacturing factories. Thousands of U.S. servicemen did part of their hitch in Orlando, and when the war ended, many returned to settle there.

In the Words of Walt Disney

"I only hope we never lose sight of one thing . . . that it was all started by a mouse."

POSTWAR PROSPERITY

By 1950, Orlando—with a population of 51,826—was the financial and transportation hub of central Florida. The city shared the bullish economy of the 1950s with the rest of the nation. In the face of the cold war, the Orlando air force base remained and grew, funneling millions of dollars into the local economy. Florida's population increased by a whopping 78.7% during the decade—making it America's 10th most-populous state—and tourists came in droves, nearly 4.5 million in 1950 alone. One reason for the influx was the advent of the air conditioner, which made life in Florida infinitely more pleasant. Also fueling Orlando's economy was a brand-new industry arriving in nearby Cape Canaveral in 1955—the government-run space program. Cape Canaveral became NASA's headquarters for the Apollo rocket program that eventually blasted Neil Armstrong heavenward toward his famous "giant leap." During the same decade, the Glenn L. Martin Company (later Martin Marietta), builder of the Matador Missile, purchased 10 square miles for a plant site four miles south of Orlando. Its advent sparked further industrial growth, and property values soared. More than 60 new industries located in the area in 1959 alone. But even the most optimistic Orlando boosters could not foresee the glorious future that was the city's ultimate destiny.

THE DISNEY DECADES

In 1964, Walt Disney began secretly buying up millions of dollars worth of central Florida farmland. As vast areas of land were purchased in lots of 5,000 acres here, 20,000 there—at remarkably high prices—rumors flew as to who needed so much land and had so much money to acquire it. Some thought it was Howard Hughes; others, the space program. Speculation was rife almost to the very day, November 15, 1965 ("D" Day for Orlando), when Disney himself arrived in town and announced his plans to build the world's most spectacular theme park ("bigger and better than Disneyland"). In a two-year construction effort, Disney employed 9,000 people. Land speculation reached unprecedented heights, as hotel chains and restaurateurs grabbed up property near the proposed parks. Mere swampland sold for millions. Total cost of the project by its October 1971 opening was $400 million. Mickey Mouse personally led the first visitor into the Magic Kingdom, and numerous celebrities—everyone from Bob Hope to Julie Andrews—took part in the opening ceremonies. In Walt Disney World's first two years, the attraction drew 20 million visitors and employed 13,000 people. The sleepy citrus-growing town of Orlando had become the "Action Center of Florida" and the fastest-growing city in the state. A 1972 referendum revitalized downtown Orlando. Additional attractions multiplied faster than fruit flies, and hundreds of firms relocated their businesses in the area. Sea World, a major theme park, came to town in 1973. Walt Disney World has continued to grow and expand, adding Epcot in 1982 and Disney-MGM Studios in 1989, along with water parks, over a dozen "official" resorts, a shopping/restaurant village, campgrounds, a vast array of recreational facilities, and several other adjuncts thoroughly described farther on in this book. Universal Studios, which also continues to expand, opened in 1990.

ORLANDO TODAY

In the 1990s, Orlando enjoys the best overall business climate in the state. In addition to tourism, its dynamic economy thrives on diverse industry, thousands of technology-related companies, and agriculture. The only remnant of Orlando's slow-paced pre-Disney southern image is its down-home friendliness. This burgeoning sunbelt metropolis looks forward to the future with unbounded optimism.

3 Famous Orlandoans

Walter Elias (Walt) Disney   (1901–66). Animation impresario Walt Disney created world-famous cartoon characters Mickey Mouse, Donald Duck, Pluto, and Goofy, among many others. His first full-length cartoon feature was *Snow White and the Seven Dwarfs* (1938). In 1955 he built the 250-acre Disneyland Park in Anaheim, California, which became one of the major tourist attractions in the United States. Many of his plans were realized after his death—among them Orlando's Magic Kingdom, Epcot, and Disney-MGM Studios Theme Park.

Donald Duck   (b. 1934). Member of a prominent thespian family (which includes nephews Huey, Dewey, and Louie, billionaire Uncle Scrooge, and Grandma Duck), Donald has starred in more than 170 cartoons and movies since his 1930s debut as an extra in *The Wise Little Hen*. As recorded in Disney archives, "he bellowed and strutted his way into that production until, bit part or no, he was practically the star of the piece." Though Disney directors have always liked working with the superbly gifted "mad mallard," his career has been somewhat hindered by his terrible temper—most notably his public tantrums when Mickey got his own television show, "The Mickey Mouse Club," in the 1950s. The bellicose duck's most memorable line of dialogue, "Wanna fight?" is said to have inspired Clint Eastwood's "Make my day."

Christian (Buddy) Ebsen   (b. 1908). American actor and dancer specializing in countrified characters. He played second fiddle to Fess Parker in the Davy Crockett movies and was a lead character in the television series "The Beverly Hillbillies." At 64 he became Barnaby Jones. Ebsen has appeared in many movies, including *Breakfast at Tiffany's*.

Michael Dammann Eisner   (b. 1942). Chairman and CEO of the entire Walt Disney Company since 1984. Though his father made him read for two hours each day before watching TV, Eisner started climbing the corporate ladder in the programming departments of CBS, NBC, and ABC. Prior to taking over the helm at Disney, Eisner was president and CEO of Paramount Pictures. In his first decade at the firm, Eisner revitalized Disney's motion picture, television, and theme park operations; opened Disney-MGM Studios Theme Park; moved into commercial television, magazines, and book publishing; and expanded to Europe with Euro Disney.

Goofy   (b. 1932). Goofy first appeared along with Mickey Mouse in a cartoon called *Mickey's Revue.* Though his original name was Dippy Dawg, which later evolved into Dippy the Goof, and finally, Goofy, there has been, over the years, an ongoing controversy as to exactly what kind of animal he is. The claim of Disney representatives that he is supposed to be a human being has never been adequately substantiated. And Goofy himself fueled speculation when he answered a reporter's question about his species in 1992 with the words "Gawrsh! I dunno." Tabloid rumors notwithstanding, this dumb but likable toon is the living embodiment of Murphy's Law—whatever can go wrong will go wrong. But he continues to laugh ("hyuk, hyuk") in the face of adversity.

Mahlon Gore   (1837–1917). Editor and proprietor of the *Orange County Reporter,* businessman, and tireless city booster, Gore came to Orlando from Iowa in 1880 when, he later reported, there were only "200 inhabitants, three stores, a livery stable, and a saloon." Today an Orlando avenue bears his name.

Mickey Mouse   (b. 1928). A prominent Orlando resident since 1971, Mickey also maintains a home in Anaheim, California. Star of more than 120 cartoons and movies, he made his film debut the year of his birth in *Steamboat Willie.* His significant other, Minnie Mouse (no relation), also appeared in the film. Mickey's dad almost named him Mortimer, but his mom (Mrs. Disney) persuaded her husband that Mortimer was too pompous a moniker for a mouse and suggested Mickey. Mickey considers the 1940s, when he starred in *Fantasia,* as his "Golden Decade." And he's especially proud that during World War II his name was used as the password of Allied forces on D-Day. Having reached the age of retirement, Mickey has no plans to stop working. "Better to wear out than rust out," says the still teenlike toon.

James Gamble Speer   (1820–93). A prominent early settler, Judge Speer took a leading role in securing the county seat for Orlando. He is also credited with naming the city. Today an Orlando avenue is named in his honor.

Jacob Summerlin   (1820–93). Dubbed "King of the Crackers" and "Cattle King of Florida," Summerlin was the first child born in the new state—in a fort where his parents had sought refuge from Seminole attack. He organized Florida cattle owners to supply the Confederate army with beef during the Civil War, engaged in blockade-running, financed free public schools, built Orlando's first luxury hotel, and donated his property for parkland around Lake Eola.

Joe Tinker   (1880–1948). Florida building developer, former star shortstop of the Chicago Cubs, and manager of the Cincinnati Reds,

In the Words of Walt Disney

"Why be a governor or a senator when you can be king of Disneyland?"

"You can dream, create, design, and build the most wonderful place in the world . . . but it required people to make the dream a reality."

Tinker created a baseball team for Orlando that won the 1921 Florida State League championship. He also convinced the Cincinnati Reds to sign a three-year contract to play in Orlando at the new $15,000 Tinker Field completed in 1923—a ballpark larger than the New York Yankee Field. Tinker was immortalized in Franklin P. Adams's verse *Baseball's Sad Lexicon,* better known as "Tinker to Evers to Chance."

W. W. Yothers   (1879–1971). An entomologist who worked for a quarter of a century in the Orlando area, Yothers is credited with stopping the Mediterranean fruit fly epidemic of 1929–30 and helping control diseases that threatened the citrus industry.

2

Planning a Trip to Walt Disney World & Orlando

In attraction-rich Orlando, advance planning is the sure key to optimum enjoyment. In addition to the information below, see Chapters 5 (accommodations) and 7 (attractions) for "how-to" hints.

1 Information & Money

As soon as you know you're going to Orlando, write or call the **Orlando/Orange County Convention & Visitors Bureau,** 8445 International Dr. (in the Mercado Shopping Village), Orlando, FL 32819 (☎ 407/363-5871). The bureau can answer all your questions and will be happy to send you maps, brochures (including the informative *Official Visitors Guide,* the *Area Guide* to local restaurants, and the *Official Accommodations Guide*), and the "Magicard," good for discounts of 10% to 50% on accommodations, attractions, car rentals, and more.

For general information about Walt Disney World—and a copy of the informative *Walt Disney World Vacations*—write or call the **Walt Disney World Co.,** Box 10,000, Lake Buena Vista, FL 32830-1000 (☎ 407/934-7639).

Also contact the **Kissimmee–St. Cloud Convention & Visitors Bureau,** 1925 E. Irlo Bronson Blvd. (U.S. 192)—or P.O. Box 422007—Kissimmee, FL 34742-2007 (☎ 407/847-5000, or 800/ 327-9159). They'll send maps, brochures, discount books, and the *Kissimmee–St. Cloud Vacation Guide,* which details the area's accommodations and attractions.

2 When to Go—Climate & Events

WHEN TO GO

Orlando is essentially a theme park destination, and its busiest seasons are whenever kids are out of school—summer (early June to about August 20), holiday weekends, Christmas season (mid-December to mid-January), and Easter. Obviously, the whole experience is more enjoyable when the crowds are thinnest and the weather most

What Things Cost in Orlando	U.S. $
Taxi from airport to WDW area	38.00
Bus from airport to WDW area (adult fare)	23.00
Double room at Disney's Grand Floridian Beach Resort (very expensive)	245.00–345.00
Double room at Marriott's Orlando World Center (expensive)	155.00–199.00
Double room at Disney's Port Orleans Resort (moderate)	89.00–121.00
Double room at Disney's All-Star Music Resort (inexpensive)	69.00–79.00
Double room at Ramada Ltd., Kissimmee (inexpensive)	27.95–45.00
Seven-course prix-fixe dinner for one at Victoria & Albert's, not including tip or wine (very expensive)	80.00
Three-course dinner at L'Originale Alfredo di Roma in Epcot, not including tip or wine (expensive)	30.00
All-you-can-eat buffet dinner at Akershus in Epcot, not including tip or wine (inexpensive)	17.95
Bottle of beer (restaurant)	2.25
Coca-Cola (restaurant)	.95
Cup of coffee	1.25
Roll of ASA 100 Kodacolor film, 36 exposures purchased at Walt Disney World	7.37
Adult Four-Day Value Pass admission to Walt Disney World	124.00
Four-Day Value Pass admission to Walt Disney World for children 3–9	97.00
Adult one-day admission to Sea World	35.95
One-day admission to Sea World for children 3–9	30.95
Adult one-day admission to Universal Studios	36.00
One-day admission to Universal Studios for children 3–9	29.00

Central Florida Average Temperatures

	Jan	Feb	Mar	Apr	May	June	July	Aug	Sept	Oct	Nov	Dec
High F°	71.7	72.9	78.3	83.6	88.3	90.6	91.7	91.6	89.7	84.4	78.2	73.1
C°	22.0	22.7	25.7	28.7	31.3	32.5	33.2	33.1	32.0	29.1	25.7	22.8
Low F°	49.3	50.0	55.3	60.3	66.2	71.2	73.0	73.4	72.5	65.4	56.8	50.9
C°	9.6	10.0	12.5	15.7	19.0	21.8	22.7	23.0	22.5	18.6	13.8	10.5

temperate. Hotel rooms are also lower priced off-season. Best times: the week after Labor Day until Thanksgiving, the week after Thanksgiving until mid-December, and the six weeks before and after school spring vacations. Worst time: summer, when crowds are very large and weather oppressively hot and humid. I probably shouldn't say this, but I would pull the kids out of school for a few days around an off-season weekend to avoid long lines.

ORLANDO CALENDAR OF EVENTS

January

○ **Florida Citrus Bowl Classic**   This annual college football game, featuring two of the year's top national teams, usually plays to a full house.

> **Where:** The Florida Citrus Bowl Stadium. 1610 W. Church St., at Tampa Street. **When:** On or close to New Year's Day. **How:** Call 407/849-2020 for information, 407/839-3900 for tickets. Tickets go on sale late October/early November. Tickets are $40.

• **Scottish Highland Games.** Featuring Scottish dancing, caber tossing, antique British car shows, dog shows, bagpipe playing, and food and crafts vendors, this event takes place on a Saturday or Sunday during the last weekend of the month at the Central Florida Fairgrounds, 4603 W. Colonial Dr., between Mercy and Pine Hills roads. Tickets are $10 for adults, $3 for children 6 to 12, under 6 free. Call 407/422-8226 for details.

• **Walt Disney World Marathon.** This 26.2-mile marathon winding through the resort and theme park areas is open to all comers, including the physically challenged. There is a $50 entry fee, which is included in room price with some Disney resort packages. Pre-registration is required. Call 407/824-4321 for details.

February

○ **Silver Spurs Rodeo**   A major event on the professional circuit, this is one of the top 20 PRCA rodeos in the nation, featuring professional cowboys and cowgirls in a wide variety of competitions—calf roping, bull and bronc riding, barrel racing, and more. The Silver Spurs Quadrille performs their famous dance on horseback.

> **Where:** At the Silver Spurs Arena, 1875 E. Irlo Bronson Memorial Hwy. (U.S. 192) in Kissimmee. **When:** On the third weekend in February. **How:** Call 407/847-5000 for details. 407/67-RODEO for tickets. All seats are $15.

• **Kissimmee Valley Livestock Show and Osceola County Fair.** This down-home-style county fair—complete with agricultural exhibits, livestock judging, rides, and crafts—takes place for six days during the third week of the month at the Kissimmee Valley Agricultural Center, 1901 E. Irlo Bronson Memorial Hwy. (U.S. 192), next to the Silver Spurs Arena. Admission is $3 for adults, $1 for children 4 to 12, under 4 free. Midway rides are extra. Call 407/846-6046 for details.

- **Mardi Gras Celebration at Pleasure Island,** Walt Disney World. This rollicking Mardi Gras revel is a street party with food, drink, costumes, parades, and entertainment. Call 407/824-4321 for details.

March

- **Houston Astros Spring Training.** Training begins in late February and there are games through March or early April at Osceola County Stadium, 1000 Bill Beck Blvd., in Kissimmee. Tickets are $5 to $6. Call 407/933-2520 for details and tickets.

- **Kissimmee Bluegrass Festival.** Bluegrass and gospel entertainers from all over the country, including the Lewis Family, perform at this four-day festival beginning the first weekend of the month. It takes place at the Silver Spurs Arena, 1875 E. Irlo Bronson Memorial Hwy. (U.S. 192). Tickets are $10 to $17. Multi-day packages are available. Call 800/473-7773 for details.

- **Central Florida Fair.** During 11 days in early March, the fair features rides, entertainers, 4-H and Future Farmers of America exhibits, livestock exhibits, a monkey show, and food booths. The Orange County District School Science and Engineering Fair takes place here at the same time. At the Central Florida Fairgrounds, 4603 W. Colonial Dr., between Mercy and Pine Hills roads. Tickets cost $5 for adults, $2 for children 6 to 10, under 6 free. Call 407/295-3247 for details.

- **Bay Hill Invitational.** Arnold Palmer hosts this seven-day, mid-month PGA Tour event at the Bay Hill Club, 9000 Bay Hill Blvd., just north of Sand Lake Rd. Daily admission is $28, week-long admission $50. Call 407/876-2888 for details.

- **Spring Flower Festival.** More than 88,000 brightly colored bedding plants, including pansies, impatiens, and begonias, create beautiful floral topiaries shaped as butterflies, birds, and animals. March through May at Cypress Gardens, FL 540 at Cypress Gardens Boulevard, in Winter Haven. Entry included with park admission. Call 813/324-2111 for details.

- **Sidewalk Art Festival.** This major arts festival in Winter Park, drawing artists and artisans from all over North America, takes place along Park Avenue. Third weekend in March. Call 407/672-6390, 407/623-3234, or 407/644-8281 for details.

April

- **Orlando Cubs Baseball Season.** The Chicago Cubs farm team plays at Tinker Field, 287 Tampa Ave. South, from April through early September. Admission is $3 to $5. Call 407/872-7593 for details.

- **Easter Sunrise Service.** An interdenominational service, with music, is presented at the Atlantis Theatre at Sea World, 7007 Sea World Dr. It is hosted by a well-known person each year, most recently Elizabeth Dole. Admission is free. Call 407/351-3600 for details.

- **Easter Sunday,** Walt Disney World. The holiday is celebrated with an old-fashioned Easter Parade. All areas of the park open early and stay open late during the Easter season. Call 407/824-4321 for details.

May

- **Epcot International Flower and Garden Festival.** Themed gardens, topiary characters, special floral displays, and speakers and seminars are part of this month-long floral celebration.

June

- **Walt Disney World Wine Festival.** More than 60 wineries from all over the United States participate. Events include wine tastings, seminars, food, and celebrity-chef cooking demonstrations at Disney's Yacht and Beach Club Convention Center. Call 407/827-7200 or 407/824-4321 for details.
- **Walt Disney World All-American College Orchestra and College Band.** The best collegiate musical talent in the country performs at Epcot and the Magic Kingdom throughout the summer. Call 407/824-4321 for details.

July

- **Independence Day.** Walt Disney World's Star-Spangled Spectacular brings bands, singers, dancers, and unbelievable fireworks displays to all the Disney parks, which stay open late. Call 407/824-4321 for details. **Sea World,** 7007 Sea World Dr., also features a dazzling laser/fireworks spectacular. Call 407/351-3600 for details.
- ✪ **Silver Spurs Rodeo**   Big-time rodeo returns to Kissimmee (see details above in February listings).

  Where: At the Silver Spurs Arena, 1875 E. Irlo Bronson Memorial Hwy. (U.S. 192) in Kissimmee. **When:** On a weekend in early July. **How:** Call 417/847-5000 for details, 407/67-RODEO for tickets. All seats are $15. Children 12, and under pay half price.

September

- ✪ **Nights of Joy**   The Magic Kingdom hosts a festival of contemporary Christian music featuring top artists.

  When: Over several weekends, selected annually. **How:** This is a very popular event; obtain tickets early. Admission is about $25 to $30 per night. Exclusive use of Magic Kingdom attractions is included. Call 407/824-4321 for details.

October

- **Florida State Air Fair.** Sponsored by the Rotary Club of Kissimmee, this is one of the biggest air shows in the southeast, featuring aerobatics, static displays, wing walking, and jet and piston aircraft demonstration teams. On a selected weekend in October each year. At the Kissimmee Municipal Airport, 301 N. Dyer Blvd. Tickets are $12 for adults, $7 for children 7 to 12, under 7 free. Call 407/933-8922 for details.
- **Halloween Horror Nights.** Universal Studios Florida, 1000 Universal Studios Plaza, off Kirkman Road, transforms its studios and attractions for a gigantic "spooktacular" nighttime Halloween party

during several long weekends prior to Halloween. Attractions include haunted attractions, live bands, a psychopath maze, special shows, and hundreds of ghouls and goblins roaming the studio streets terrifying the populace. Special admission is charged. Call 407/363-8000 for details.

- **Shamu's Halloween Spooktacular,** Sea World, 7007 Sea World Dr., hosts a "kooky, spooky" Halloween bash on the holiday weekend with eerie events, a shark tunnel, costume judging, special shows, and more. Call 407/351-3600 for details.

- **Walt Disney World Oldsmobile Golf Classic.** Top PGA tour players compete for a total purse of $1 million at WDW golf courses. The event is preceded by the world's largest golf tournament, the Oldsmobile Scramble, on the same courses. Admission for Scramble is free. For the Golf Classic, daily ticket prices range from $8 to $15. Call 407/824-4321 for details.

- **Walt Disney World Village Boat Show.** Central Florida's largest in-the-water boat show featuring the best of new watercraft takes place at the Village Marketplace over a three-day weekend early in the month. Call 407/824-4321 for details.

November

- **Annual Chrysanthemum Festival.** A month-long event featuring displays of over two million multicolored mums—in flower beds, "blooming" gazebos, poodle baskets, and bonsais. At Cypress Gardens, FL 540 at Cypress Gardens Boulevard, in Winter Haven. Entry included with park admission. Call 813/324-2111 for details.

- **Walt Disney World Festival of the Masters.** One of the largest art shows in the south takes place at the Village Marketplace for three days including the second weekend of November. It features top artists, photographers, and craftspeople, winners of juried shows throughout the country. No admission. Call 407/824-4321 for details.

- **Walt Disney World Doll and Teddy Bear Convention.** The top doll and teddy bear designers from around the world travel to WDW to meet with enthusiasts and collectors. Special editions and one-of-a-kind auctions highlight the event, which takes place in a selected Disney resort and throughout the parks. Call 407/824-4321 or 407/560-7232 for details.

- **Walt Disney World Jolly Holidays Dinner Shows.** Late November through mid-December, all-you-can-eat dinner shows are offered at the Contemporary Resort's Fantasia Ballroom. A cast of over 100 Disney characters, singers, and dancers performs in a delightful old-fashioned Christmas extravaganza. Call 407/W-DISNEY for details and ticket prices.

- **Magic Basketball.** Shaquille O'Neal and his teammates on the Orlando Magic do battle against visiting teams between October and April at the Orlando Arena, 600 W. Amelia St. Ticket prices range from about $12 to $32. Call 407/896-2442 for details, 407/839-3900 for tickets.

December

- **Annual Poinsettia Festival.** A spectacular floral showcase of more than 40,000 red, white, and pink poinsettias (including topiary reindeer). From early December through mid-January at Cypress Gardens, FL 540 at Cypress Gardens Boulevard, in Winter Haven. Entry included with park admission. Call 813/324-2111 for details.
- **Florida Citrus Sports Half-Marathon and Hooter's 5K Run.** This annual race, early in December, takes place in downtown Orlando, beginning at Church Street Market, 200 S. Orange Ave. It begins at 8am. Anyone can participate. An entry fee is charged. The event kicks off the Citrus Bowl season. Call 407/423-2476 for information.
- **Walt Disney World Christmas Festivities.** For the holiday season, Main Street is lavishly decked out with lights and holly, and visitors are greeted by carolers. An 80-foot tree is illuminated by thousands of colored lights. Epcot and MGM Studios also offer special embellishments and entertainments throughout the holiday season, as do all Disney resorts. Holiday highlights include: **Mickey's Very Merry Christmas Party,** an after-dark ticketed event weekends at the Magic Kingdom with a traditional Christmas parade and a breathtaking fireworks display. Admission price includes free cookies and cocoa and a souvenir photo. The **Glory and Pageantry of Christmas** at the Walt Disney Village Marketplace, including several shows nightly, tells the story of the birth of Jesus. Admission is free. The **Candlelight Procession** at Epcot features hundreds of candleholding carolers, a celebrity narrator telling the Christmas story, and a 450-voice choir.

  Call 407/824-4321 for details about all of the above—and more, 407/W-DISNEY to inquire about hotel/events packages.
- **Walt Disney World New Year's Eve Celebration.** The **Magic Kingdom** is open until 2am for a massive fireworks exhibition. Other New Year's festivities in the WDW parks include: a big bash at **Pleasure Island** featuring music headliners, a special *Hoop-Dee-Doo Musical Revue* show, and guest performances by well-known musical groups at **Disney-MGM Studios and Epcot.** Call 407/824-4321 for details.
- **Sea World Holiday Events.** Sea World, 7007 Sea World Dr., features a special Shamu show and a luau show called *Christmas in Hawaii.* The 400-foot sky tower is lit like a Christmas tree nightly. Call 407/351-3600 for details.
- **The Citrus Bowl Parade.** On December 31, lavish floats—including some from Disney and Sea World—join with local high school bands for a nationally televised parade beginning at 1pm. Reserved seats in the bleachers are $12. Call 407/423-2476 for details.
- **New Year's Citrus Eve.** The official New Year's Eve celebration of the Florida Citrus Bowl takes place at Sea World, 7007 Sea World Dr. Events include headliner concerts (featuring artists such as Miami Sound Machine, Lee Greenwood, and Tanya Tucker), a

laser and fireworks spectacular, a countdown to midnight, and special shows throughout the park. Admission is charged. Call 407/351-3600 for details.

3 What to Pack

Most of the year, the ideal Orlando ensemble is sneakers, shorts, and a T-shirt—in other words, the least amount of clothing you can wear in public without causing a commotion. You might, however, wish to pack jeans and a light jacket for the occasional cooler day. Since interior spaces are always frigidly air-conditioned—even at indoor theme park attractions—carry a sweater if you tend to feel chilly. And a fold-up umbrella is always a good idea, even in Florida. If you don't ever use it, so much the better.

Packing evening wear is optional, though I do suggest that men pack at least one jacket and women one evening outfit for dinners at upscale establishments. However, even at better Orlando restaurants, not everyone dresses up. Especially casual are restaurants at the Disney parks, where most of the clientele is a come-as-you-are crowd, having spent the day on rides.

One thing I like to pack is a 100-watt light bulb, especially if I'm staying at an inexpensive hotel where bedside lamps seldom provide adequate wattage for reading. You don't need to pack a travel iron. Almost all hotels these days provide irons at the front desk, albeit usually with those tiny boards that make ironing even more hateful than usual. Find out if your hotel offers hair dryers before you pack one. And, finally, don't forget sunscreen.

4 Tips for the Disabled, Seniors, Singles, Students & Families

FOR THE DISABLED   Write or call **The Florida Department of Commerce,** Division of Tourism, Visitor Inquiry, 126 Van Buren St., Tallahassee, FL 32399-2000 (☎ 904/487-1462), for a free copy of the *Physically Challenged Guide to Florida.* It offers valuable information on accessibility at tourist facilities throughout the state.

An Orlando-based organization called **Friends of the Family,** 7380 Sand Lake Rd., Orlando, FL 32819 (☎ 407/856-7676 or 800/741-2282), provides help with transportation, accommodations, medical care, and other aspects of travel for the disabled. They can also refer you to travel agents who offer packages tailored to the disabled.

At Walt Disney World: WDW does everything possible to facilitate disabled guests. Its many services are detailed in the *Guidebook for Guests with Disabilities.* To obtain a copy prior to your visit, write Guest Letters, P.O. Box 10,040, Lake Buena Vista, FL 32830-0040, or call 407/824-4321. Also call that number for answers to any questions regarding special needs. Some examples of Disney services: Almost all Disney resorts have rooms for those with disabilities; there are braille directories inside the Magic Kingdom in front of the Main Street train station and in a gazebo in front of the Crystal Palace restaurant; there are special parking lots at all three parks; complimentary guided-tour audiocassette tapes and recorders are available at Guest Services to assist visually impaired guests; personal translator units are available to amplify the audio at selected Epcot attractions (inquire at Earth Station); and wheelchairs can be rented at all of the Disney parks. For information about Telecommunications Devices for the Deaf (TDDs) call 407/827-5141.

Some nationwide resources: Mobility International USA, P.O. Box 10767, Eugene, OR 97440 (☎ 503/343-1284), offering accessibility information and has many interesting travel programs for the disabled. They also publish a quarterly newsletter called *Over the Rainbow* ($15 per year to subscribe). Help (accessibility information and more) is also available from the **Travel Information Service** (☎ 215/456-9600) and the **Society for the Advancement of Travel for the Handicapped** (SATH), 347 Fifth Ave., Suite 610, New York, NY 10016 (☎ 212/447-7284).

Accessible Journeys (☎ 610/521-0339 or 800/TINGLES) and **Flying Wheels Travel** (☎ 507/451-5005 or 800/535-6790) offer tours for people with physical disabilities. **The Guided Tour Inc.** (☎ 215/782-1370) has tours for people with physical or mental disabilities, the visually impaired, and the elderly.

Recommended books: A publisher called **Twin Peaks Press,** Box 129, Vancouver, WA 98666 (☎ 360/694-2462), specializes in books for people with disabilities. Write for their *Disability Bookshop Catalog,* enclosing $4.

Amtrak (☎ 800/USA-RAIL) provides redcap service, wheelchair assistance, and special seats with 72 hours' notice. The disabled are also entitled to a 25% discount on one-way regular coach fares. Disabled children ages 2 to 15 can also get a 50% discount on already discounted one-way disabled adult fares. Documentation from a doctor or an ID card proving your disability is required. Amtrak also provides wheelchair-accessible sleeping accommodations on long-distance trains, and service dogs are permissible and travel free of charge. Write for a free booklet called *Amtrak's America* from Amtrak Distribution Center, P.O. Box 7717, Itasca, IL 60143, which has a chapter detailing services for passengers with disabilities.

Greyhound (☎ 800/752-4841) allows a disabled person to travel with a companion for a single fare and, if you call 48 hours in advance, they will arrange help along the way.

FOR SENIORS   Always carry some form of photo ID so that you can take advantage of discounts wherever they're offered. And it never hurts to ask.

If you haven't already done so, consider joining the **American Association of Retired Persons** (AARP), 601 E. St. NW, Washington, DC 20049 (☎ 202/434-2277). Annual membership costs $8 per person or per couple. You must be at least 50 to join. Membership entitles you to many discounts. Write to Purchase Privilege Program, AARP Fulfillment, 601 E St. NW, Washington, DC 20049, to receive AARP's Purchase Privilege brochure—a free list of hotels, motels, and car-rental firms nationwide that offer discounts to AARP members.

Elderhostel is a national organization that offers low-priced educational programs for people over 55 (your non-spouse companion must be at least 50). Programs are generally a week long, and prices average about $325 per person, including room, board, and classes. For information on programs in Florida call or write Elderhostel headquarters, 75 Federal St., Boston, MA 02110-1941 (☎ 617/426-7788) and ask for a free U.S., catalog. Or call the Florida office at 813/864-8312.

Amtrak (☎ 800/USA-RAIL) offers a 15% discount off the lowest available coach fare (with certain travel restrictions) to people 62 or over.

Greyhound also offers discounted fares for senior citizens. Call your local Greyhound office for details.

FOR SINGLE TRAVELERS   The best nightlife choices for meeting up with others are **Church Street Station** (in downtown Orlando) and **Pleasure Island** (see details on both, and other clubs, in Chapter 9).

Want a fellow traveler? Contact **Travel Companion,** P.O. Box P-833, Amityville, NY 11701-0833 (☎ 516/454-0880), an organization that matches up single travelers with compatible partners. For a fee, you'll be listed in and receive the organization's newsletter, which provides a list of potential companions (you can request same sex or opposite sex).

FOR STUDENTS   The key to securing discounts is valid student ID. Be sure to carry such and keep your eyes open for special student prices.

FOR FAMILIES   No city in the world is more geared to family travel than Orlando. In addition to its theme parks, recreational facilities provide abundant opportunities for family fun. Every restaurant in town has a low-priced children's menu, and many hotels maintain children's activity centers (see details in Chapter 5). A few general suggestions to make traveling with kids easier:

Get the Kids Involved   Let them, if they're old enough, write to the tourist offices for information and color brochures. If you're driving, give them a map on which they can outline the route. Let them help decide your sightseeing itinerary.

Packing   Although your home may be toddler-proof, hotel accommodations are not. Bring blank plugs to cover outlets and whatever else is necessary.

Accommodations   Children under 12, and in many cases even older, stay free in their parents' rooms in most hotels. Look for establishments that have pools and other recreational facilities.

Ground Rules   Set up ground rules before leaving home about issues such as bedtime and spending money on souvenirs.

Publications   Contact **Travel With Your Children (TWYCH)**, 45 W. 18th St., New York, NY 10011 (☎ 212/206-0688), to subscribe to the *Family Travel Times,* a newsletter about traveling with children. It's packed with useful information, and subscribers can call in for travel advice on Wednesdays between 10am and 1pm.

5 Getting There

BY PLANE

THE MAJOR AIRLINES **Delta,** the official airline of Walt Disney World, has the most flights—over 25%—into Orlando International Airport. It offers service from 200 cities and has a Fantastic Flyer program for kids. Other carriers include Aero Costa Rica, Aeropostal, Air Jamaica, All Nippon Airways, America West, American, American Trans Air, British Airways, ComAir, Continental, Icelandair, Kiwi, Martinair, Midway, Northwest, Spirit, Transbrasil, TWA, United, USAir, Valuejet, and Virgin Atlantic.

AIRFARES Since advance-purchase fares are almost always the lowest available, it's a good idea to book your flight as far in advance as possible. Advance-purchase fares can be as much as 75% lower than fares booked the last minute!

When you call to reserve your flight, you might also inquire about money-saving packages. **Delta Dream Vacations,** in several price ranges, include: round-trip air transport; accommodations (state and hotel room tax/baggage gratuities included); an air-conditioned intermediate rental car with unlimited mileage or round-trip airport transfer; a "Magic Passport" that provides unlimited admission to all WDW parks for the length of your stay; one breakfast (which can be a character breakfast); and entry into a selected theme park one hour before regular opening time. Since the packages utilize Walt Disney World Resorts, you get all the advantages accruing to guests at these properties (see Chapter 5 for details). If you put all of those components together on your own, the cost would be much, much higher. Delta also has Orlando packages for which WDW tickets are optional. For details, call 800/872-7786 or consult your local travel agent. *Note:* Though it also offers packages using non-WDW accommodations, Delta is the only airline authorized to use Disney resorts in its packages.

ORLANDO'S AIRPORT Serving over 22 million passengers each year, **Orlando International Airport** (☎ 407/825-2001) is a thoroughly modern and user-friendly facility with restaurants, shops, a 450-room on-premises Hyatt Regency Hotel, and centrally located information kiosks. All major car-rental companies are located at the airport; see "Getting Around" in Chapter 4 for more information on rentals.

The airport is 25 miles from Walt Disney World. **Mears Transportation Group** (☎ 407/423-5566) buses ply the route from the airport (board outside baggage claim) to all Disney resorts and official hotels as well as most other area properties. Their comfortable, air-conditioned shuttle vans operate around the clock, departing every 15 to 25 minutes in either direction. Rates vary with your destination. Round-trip cost for adults is $19 between the airport and downtown Orlando or International Drive, $23 for Walt Disney World / Lake Buena Vista or Kissimmee/Hwy. 192. Children ages 4 to 11 pay $14 and $17, respectively. Children 3 and under ride free.

Note: It's always a good idea to ask about transportation options between the airport and your hotel when you make your reservations, or, if you're planning to rent a car, for driving directions from the airport.

BY TRAIN

Amtrak trains (☎ 800/USA-RAIL) pull into stations at 1400 Sligh Blvd., between Columbia and Miller streets in downtown Orlando (about 23 miles from Walt Disney World), and 111 Dakin Avenue, at Thurman Street in Kissimmee (about 15 miles from Walt Disney World).

From the Orlando station, you can catch **LYNX** bus no. 34, which departs weekdays at least once an hour between 10:25am and 5:25pm (weekends take bus nos. 7 or 11 from the stop at the corner of Orange and Columbia avenues, two blocks away). All trips involve a transfer at the downtown bus station—not too much of a hassle because the bus will usually be right there when you arrive. This connecting bus (no. 8) makes stops about every $1^1/_2$ blocks along International Drive, culminating at Sea World where you can get a taxi ($17 to $20) to Walt Disney World–area hotels. For further details about bus transportation from the Orlando Amtrak station call 407/841-8240. A taxi from the Orlando Amtrak station to Walt Disney World–area hotels is $30 to $35.

From the Kissimmee Amtrak station a taxi ($20 to $25 to WDW-area hotels) is your only option.

FARES   A limited number of seats on reserved trains are set aside for discount fares. Many people reserve fares months in advance, so the minute you know the dates of your trip, make your reservations so that you can increase your chance of getting a discount. There may be some restrictions on travel dates for discounted fares, mostly around very busy holiday times. To inquire about Amtrak's money-saving packages—including hotel accommodations (some at WDW resorts), car rentals, tours, etc., with your train fare—call 800/321-8684.

AMTRAK'S AUTO TRAIN   Amtrak's Auto Train offers the convenience of having a car in Florida without driving it there. The Auto Train begins in Lorton, Virginia—about a four-hour drive from New York, two hours from Philadelphia—and ends up at Sanford, Florida, about 23 miles northeast of Orlando. Once again, reserve early for the lowest fares. The Auto Train departs Lorton and Sanford at 4:30pm daily, arriving at its destination at 9am the next morning. *Note:* You have to arrive one or two hours before departure time so they can board your car. Call 800/USA-RAIL for details.

BY BUS

Greyhound buses connect the entire country with Orlando. They pull into a terminal at 555 N. Magruder Blvd. (John Young Parkway), between West Colonial Drive and Winter Garden Road, a few miles west of downtown Orlando (☎ 407/292-3422), or in Kissimmee at 16 N. Orlando Ave., between Emmett and Mabbette streets, about 14 miles from Walt Disney World (☎ 407/847-3911). There is van transport from the Kissimmee terminal to most area hotels and motels.

It's Better with the Bahamas

Premier Cruise Lines (the Big Red Boat) offers three- and four-night luxury ocean cruises to the Bahamas (Nassau and Port Lucaya) in conjunction with three- or four-day Orlando theme-park vacations. Cruises depart from and return to Port Canaveral, 45 minutes from Walt Disney World. You can add the island segment before or after your stay in Orlando. Participating hotels include Disney resorts. Ships are equipped with swimming pools, Jacuzzis, health clubs, jogging tracks, movie theaters, beauty salons, casinos, bar/lounges, video-game arcades, shops, and nightclubs. Looney Tunes characters (Bugs Bunny, Porky Pig, Daffy Duck) are your on-board hosts. Package price includes all meals on board ship, an Alamo rental car with unlimited mileage for seven days, round-trip airfare to/from Orlando, and admission to varied attractions. Rates depend on stateroom and hotel category and the season you're traveling. At this writing, seven-night packages with New York departure start at about $899 per person, based on double occupancy, $529 for children under 12. Call 800/726-5678 for details. Cruises can only be booked through a travel agent.

From Orlando, a taxi ($25 to $30 to Walt Disney area hotels) is the only viable option. Greyhound's fare structure tends to be complex, but the good news is that when you call to make a reservation, the agent will always give you the lowest-fare options. Once again, advance-purchase fares booked three to 21 days prior to travel represent vast savings. Check your phone book for a local Greyhound listing or call 800/231-2222.

BY CAR

Orlando is 436 miles from Atlanta, 1,312 miles from Boston, 1,120 miles from Chicago, 1,009 miles from Cleveland, 1,170 miles from Dallas, 1,114 miles from Detroit, 1,105 miles from New York City, and 1,261 miles from Toronto.

From Atlanta take I-75 south to the Florida Turnpike to I-4 west. From Boston, New York, and other points northeast, take I-95 south to I-4 west. From Chicago take I-65 south to Nashville, then I-24 south to I-75 south to the Florida Turnpike to I-4 west. From Cleveland take I-77 south to Columbia, South Carolina, then I-26 east to I-95 south to I-4 west. From Dallas take I-20 east to I-49 south to I-10 east to I-75 south to the Florida Turnpike to I-4 west. From Detroit take I-75 south to the Florida Turnpike to I-4 west. From Toronto take Canadian Route 401 south to Queen Elizabeth Way south to I-90 (New York State Thruway) east to I-87 (New York State Thruway) south to I-95 over the George Washington Bridge, and continue south on I-95 to I-4 west. AAA and some other automobile club members can call local offices for maps and optimum driving directions.

For Foreign Visitors

Although American fads and fashions have spread across Europe and other parts of the world so that America may seem like familiar territory before your arrival, there are still many peculiarities and uniquely American situations that any foreign visitor will encounter.

1 Preparing for Your Trip

ENTRY REQUIREMENTS

DOCUMENT REGULATIONS Canadian citizens may enter the United States without visas; they need only proof of residence.

Citizens of the U.K., New Zealand, Japan, and most western European countries traveling on valid passports may not need a visa for fewer than 90 days of holiday or business travel to the United States, providing that they hold a round-trip or return ticket and enter the United States on an airline or cruise line participating in the visa waiver program.

(Note that citizens of these visa-exempt countries who first enter the United States may then visit Mexico, Canada, Bermuda, and/or the Caribbean islands and then reenter the States, by any mode of transportation, without needing a visa. Further information is available from any U.S. embassy or consulate.)

Citizens of countries other than those stipulated above, including citizens of Australia, must have two documents: a valid **passport,** with an expiration date at least six months later than the scheduled end of the visit to the United States; and a **tourist visa,** available without charge from the nearest U.S. consulate. To obtain a visa, the traveler must submit a completed application form (either in person or by mail) with a $1^1/_2$-inch square photo and demonstrate binding ties to a residence abroad.

Usually you can obtain a visa at once or within 24 hours, but it may take longer during the summer rush from June to August. If you cannot go in person, contact the nearest U.S. embassy or consulate for directions on applying by mail. Your travel agent or airline office may also be able to provide you with visa applications and instructions. The U.S. consulate or embassy that issues your visa will determine whether you will be issued a multiple- or single-entry visa and any restrictions regarding the length of your stay.

MEDICAL REQUIREMENTS   No inoculations are needed to enter the United States unless you are coming from, or have stopped over in, areas known to be suffering from epidemics, particularly cholera or yellow fever.

If you have a disease requiring treatment with medications containing narcotics or drugs requiring a syringe, carry a valid signed prescription from your physician to allay any suspicions that you are smuggling drugs.

CUSTOMS REQUIREMENTS   Every adult visitor may bring in free of duty: one liter of wine or hard liquor; 200 cigarettes or 100 cigars (but no cigars from Cuba) or three pounds of smoking tobacco; $100 worth of gifts. These exemptions are offered to travelers who spend at least 72 hours in the United States and who have not claimed them within the preceding six months. It is altogether forbidden to bring into the country foodstuffs (particularly cheese, fruit, cooked meats, and canned goods) and plants (vegetables, seeds, tropical plants, and so on). Foreign tourists may bring in or take out up to $10,000 in U.S. or foreign currency with no formalities; larger sums must be declared to Customs on entering or leaving.

INSURANCE

There is no national health system in the United States. Because the cost of medical care is extremely high, we strongly advise every traveler to secure health coverage before setting out.

You may want to take out a comprehensive travel policy that covers (for a relatively low premium) sickness or injury costs (medical, surgical, and hospital); loss or theft of your baggage; trip-cancellation costs; guarantee of bail in case you are arrested; and costs of accident, repatriation, or death. Such packages (for example, "Europe Assistance" in Europe) are sold by automobile clubs at attractive rates, as well as by insurance companies and travel agencies.

MONEY

CURRENCY & EXCHANGE   The U.S. monetary system has a decimal base: one American **dollar ($1)** = 100 **cents** (100¢).

Dollar bills commonly come in $1 ("a buck"), $5, $10, $20, $50, and $100 denominations (the last two are not welcome when paying for small purchases and are not accepted in taxis or at subway ticket booths). There are also $2 bills (seldom encountered).

There are six denominations of coins: 1¢ (one cent or "penny"), 5¢ (five cents or "a nickel"), 10¢ (ten cents or "a dime"), 25¢ (twenty-five cents or "a quarter"), 50¢ (fifty cents or "a half dollar"), and the rare $1 piece.

The "foreign-exchange bureaus" so common in Europe are rare even at airports in the United States, and nonexistent outside major cities. Try to avoid having to change foreign money, or traveler's checks denominated other than in U.S. dollars, at a small-town bank, or even a branch in a big city.

You can exchange foreign currency at Guest Services windows in all three Disney parks, or at City Hall in the Magic Kingdom and Earth Station at Epcot. Currency can also be exchanged at Walt Disney

World resorts and at the Sun Bank just across from the Village Marketplace. There are also exchange services at the Orlando International Airport.

TRAVELER'S CHECKS   Traveler's checks denominated in U.S. dollars are readily accepted at most hotels, motels, restaurants, and large stores. But the best place to change traveler's checks is at a bank. Do not bring traveler's checks denominated in other currencies.

CREDIT CARDS   The method of payment most widely used is the credit card: Visa (BarclayCard in Britain), MasterCard (EuroCard in Europe, Access in Britain, Chargex in Canada), American Express, Diners Club, Discover, and Carte Blanche. You can save yourself trouble by using "plastic money" rather than cash or traveler's checks in most hotels, motels, restaurants, and retail stores. American Express, MasterCard, and Visa are accepted for admission to, and all restaurants within, the Disney Parks. You must have a credit card to rent a car. It can also be used as proof of identity (often carrying more weight than a passport), or as a "cash card," enabling you to draw money from banks that accept them.

SAFETY

While the Walt Disney World/Orlando area in general—and the theme parks in particular—are extremely safe, there are some general precautions you can take to minimize your chances of being the victim of crime.

GENERAL   While tourist areas are generally safe, crime is on the increase everywhere, and U.S. urban areas tend to be less safe than those in Europe or Japan. Visitors should always stay alert. This is particularly true of large U.S. cities. It is wise to ask the city's or area's tourist office if you're in doubt about which neighborhoods are safe. Avoid deserted areas, especially at night. Don't go into any city park at night unless there is an event that attracts crowds. Generally speaking, you can feel safe in areas where there are many people, and many open establishments.

Avoid carrying valuables with you on the street, and don't display expensive cameras or electronic equipment. Hold on to your pocketbook, and place your billfold in an inside pocket. In theaters, restaurants, and other public places, keep your possessions in sight.

Remember also that hotels are open to the public, and in a large hotel, security may not be able to screen everyone entering. Always lock your room door—don't assume that once inside your hotel you are automatically safe and no longer need be aware of your surroundings.

DRIVING   Safety while driving is particularly important. Question your rental agency about personal safety, or ask for a brochure of traveler safety tips when you pick up your car. Obtain written directions, or a map with the route marked in red, from the agency showing how to get to your destination. And, if possible, arrive and depart during daylight hours.

Recently more and more crime has involved cars and drivers. If you drive off a highway into a doubtful neighborhood, leave the area as quickly as possible. If you have an accident, even on the highway, stay in your car with the doors locked until you assess the situation or until the police arrive. If you are bumped from behind on the street or are involved in a minor accident with no injuries and the situation appears to be suspicious, motion to the other driver to follow you. *Never* get out of your car in such situations. You can also keep a pre-made sign in your car which reads: PLEASE FOLLOW THIS VEHICLE TO REPORT THE ACCIDENT. Show the sign to the other driver and go directly to the nearest police precinct, well-lighted service station, or all-night store.

If you see someone on the road who indicates a need for help, do *not* stop. Take note of the location, drive on to a well-lighted area, and telephone the police by dialing 911.

Park in well-lighted, well-traveled areas if possible. Always keep your car doors locked, whether attended or unattended. Look around you before you get out of your car, and never leave any packages or valuables in sight. If someone attempts to rob you or steal your car, do *not* try to resist the thief/carjacker—report the incident to the police department immediately.

2   Getting To & Around the U.S.

GETTING TO THE U.S.   Travelers from overseas can take advantage of the **APEX (Advance Purchase Excursion) fares** offered by all the major U.S. and European carriers. Aside from these, attractive values are offered by **Icelandair** on flights from Luxembourg to New York and by **Virgin Atlantic Airways** from London to New York/Newark.

British Airways (☎ 081/897-4000 from within the U.K.) offers direct flights from London to Miami and Orlando, as does **Virgin Atlantic** (☎ 01/293-74-77-47 from within the U.K.). Canadian readers might book flights with **Air Canada** (☎ 800/776-3000), which offers service from Toronto and Montréal to Miami and Tampa.

Some large American airlines (for example, TWA, American Airlines, Northwest, United, and Delta) offer travelers on their transatlantic or transpacific flights special discount tickets under the name **Visit USA,** allowing travel between any U.S. destinations at minimum rates. They are not on sale in the United States, and must, therefore, be purchased before you leave your foreign point of departure. This system is the best, easiest, and fastest way to see the United States at low cost. You should obtain information well in advance from your travel agent or the office of the airline concerned, since the conditions attached to these discount tickets can be changed without advance notice.

The visitor arriving by air, no matter what the port of entry, should cultivate patience and resignation before setting foot on U.S. soil. Getting through Immigration control may take as long as two hours on some days. Add the time it takes to clear Customs and you'll see that you should make very generous allowance for delay in planning connections between international and domestic flights—an average of two to three hours at least.

In contrast, travelers arriving by car or by rail from Canada will find border-crossing formalities streamlined to the vanishing point. And air travelers from Canada, Bermuda, and some places in the Caribbean can sometimes go through Customs and Immigration at the point of departure, which is much quicker and less painful.

GETTING AROUND THE U.S.   International visitors can buy a **USA Railpass,** good for 15 or 30 days of unlimited travel on Amtrak, the national rail passenger corporation. The pass is available through many foreign travel agents. Prices in 1995 for a 15-day pass were $229 off-peak, $340 peak; a 30-day pass cost $339 off-peak, $425 peak. (With a foreign passport, you can also buy passes at some Amtrak offices in the United States, including locations in San Francisco, Los Angeles, Chicago, New York, Miami, Boston, and Washington, D.C.) Reservations are generally required and should be made for each part of your trip as early as possible.

Visitors should be aware of the limitations of long-distance rail travel in the United States. With a few notable exceptions (for instance, the Northeast Corridor line between Boston and Washington, D.C.), service is rarely up to European standards: Delays are common, routes are limited and often infrequently served, and fares are rarely significantly lower than discount airfares. Thus, cross-country train travel should be approached with caution.

Bus travel in the United States can be both slow and uncomfortable, so this option is not for everyone. Although ticket prices for short hops between cities are often the most economical form of public transit, at this writing bus passes are priced slightly higher than similar train passes. Greyhound, the sole nationwide bus line, offers an **Ameripass** for unlimited travel for 7 days ($259), 15 days ($459), and 30 days ($559).

For further information about travel to Florida, see "Getting There" in Chapter 2.

FAST FACTS: For the Foreign Traveler

Automobile Organizations   Auto clubs will supply maps, suggested routes, guidebooks, accident and bail-bond insurance, and emergency road service. The major auto club in the United States, with 983 offices nationwide, is the **American Automobile Association (AAA).** Members of some foreign auto clubs have reciprocal arrangements with the AAA and enjoy its services at no charge. If you belong to an auto club, inquire about AAA reciprocity before you leave. The AAA can provide you with an International Driving Permit validating your foreign license. You may be able to join the AAA even if you are not a member of a reciprocal club. To inquire, call 800/222-4357. In addition, some automobile rental agencies now provide these services, so you should inquire about their availability when you rent your car.

Automobile Rentals   To rent a car you need a major credit card. A valid driver's license is required, and you usually need to be at least 25. Some companies do rent to younger people but add a daily surcharge. Be sure to return your car with the same amount of gas you started out with; rental companies charge excessive prices for gasoline. All the major car-rental companies are represented in Florida (see "Getting Around" in Chapter 4).

Business Hours   Banks are open weekdays from 9am to 3 or 4pm, although there's 24-hour access to the automatic tellers (ATMs) at most banks and other outlets. Generally, offices are open weekdays from 9am to 5pm. Stores are open six days a week, with many open on Sunday, too; department stores usually stay open until 9pm at least one day a week.

Climate   See "When to Go" in Chapter 2.

Currency & Exchange   See "Money" in "Preparing for Your Trip," earlier in this chapter.

Drinking Laws   See "Liquor Laws" in "Fast Facts" in Chapter 4.

Electricity   The United States uses 110–120 volts, 60 cycles, compared to 220–240 volts, 50 cycles, as in most of Europe. In addition to a 100-volt converter, small appliances of non-American manufacture, such as hair dryers or shavers, will require a plug adapter, with two flat, parallel pins.

Embassies and Consulates   All embassies are located in the national capital, Washington, D.C.; some consulates are located in major cities, and most nations have a mission to the United Nations in New York City. Foreign visitors can obtain telephone numbers for their embassies and consulates by calling "Information" in Washington, D.C. (☎ 202/555-1212).

The Canadian consulate closest to Orlando is at 200 S. Biscayne Blvd., Suite 1600, Miami, FL 33131 (☎ 305/579-1600). There's a British consulate located at 1001 S. Bayshore Dr., Miami, FL 33131 (☎ 305/374-1522); for emergency situations there is an office in Orlando at the Sun Bank Tower, Suite 2110, 200 S. Orange Ave. (☎ 407/426-7855).

Emergencies   Call **911** to report a fire, call the police, or get an ambulance.

Gasoline (Petrol)   One U.S. gallon equals 3.75 liters, while 1.2 U.S. gallons equals one Imperial gallon. You'll notice there are several grades (and price levels) of gasoline available at most gas stations. And you'll also notice that their names change from company to company. The unleaded ones with the highest octane are the most expensive (most rental cars take the least expensive "regular" unleaded) and leaded gas is the least expensive, but only older cars can take this any more, so check if you're not sure.

Holidays   On the following legal national holidays, banks, government offices, post offices, and many stores, restaurants, and museums are closed:

January 1 (New Year's Day)
Third Monday in January (Martin Luther King Day)
Third Monday in February (Presidents Day, Washington's Birthday)
Last Monday in May (Memorial Day)
July 4 (Independence Day)

First Monday in September (Labor Day)
Second Monday in October (Columbus Day)
November 11 (Veteran's Day/Armistice Day)
Last Thursday in November (Thanksgiving Day)
December 25 (Christmas).

Finally, the Tuesday following the first Monday in November is Election Day, and is a legal holiday in presidential-election years like 1996.

Languages   Major hotels may have multilingual employees. Unless your language is very obscure, they can usually supply a translator on request. Especially in southern Florida, many people are fluent in Spanish.

Legal Aid   The foreign tourist will probably never become involved with the American legal system. If you are pulled up for a minor infraction (for example, of the highway code, such as speeding), never attempt to pay the fine directly to a police officer; you may wind up arrested on the much more serious charge of attempted bribery. Pay fines by mail, or directly into the hands of the clerk of the court. If accused of a more serious offense, it's wise to say and do nothing before consulting a lawyer. Under U.S. law, an arrested person is allowed one telephone call to a party of his or her choice. Call your embassy or consulate.

Mail   If you want your mail to follow you on your vacation and you aren't sure of your address, your mail can be sent to you, in your name, c/o General Delivery at the main post office of the city or region where you expect to be. The addressee must pick it up in person and produce proof of identity (driver's license, credit card, passport, etc.).

Generally to be found at intersections, mailboxes are blue with a red-and-white stripe and carry the inscription U.S. MAIL. If your mail is addressed to a U.S. destination, don't forget to add the five-figure postal code, or ZIP (Zone Improvement Plan) Code, after the two-letter abbreviation of the state to which the mail is addressed (CA for California, FL for Florida, NY for New York, and so on).

Newspapers and Magazines   National newspapers include the *New York Times, USA Today,* and the *Wall Street Journal.* National news weeklies include *Newsweek, Time,* and *U.S. News & World Report.* All over Florida, you'll be able to purchase the *Miami Herald,* one of the most highly respected dailies in the country. The local newspaper is the *Orlando Sentinel,* and there's a monthly city magazine called *Orlando.*

Radio and Television   Audiovisual media, with four coast-to-coast networks—ABC, CBS, NBC, and Fox—joined in recent years by the Public Broadcasting System (PBS) and the cable network CNN, play a major part in American life. In big cities, televiewers have a choice of about a dozen channels (including the UHF channels), most of them transmitting 24 hours a day, without counting the pay-TV channels showing recent movies or sports events. All options are usually indicated on your hotel TV set. You'll also find a wide choice of local radio stations, each broadcasting particular kinds of talk shows and/or music—classical, country, jazz, pop, gospel—punctuated by news broadcasts and frequent commercials.

Safety   See "Safety" in "Preparing for Your Trip," above.

Taxes   In the United States there is no VAT (Value-Added Tax) or other indirect tax at a national level. Every state, and each city in it, has the right to levy its own local tax on all purchases, including hotel and restaurant checks, airline tickets, and so on. In Florida, sales tax is 6%. Hotel tax in Orlando is 10%, in Kissimmee 11%.

Telephone, Telegraph, and Telex   The telephone system in the United States is run by private corporations, so rates, especially for long distance service, can vary widely—even on calls made from public telephones. Local calls in the United States usually cost 25¢.

Generally, hotel surcharges on long-distance and local calls are astronomical. You are usually better off using a public pay telephone, which you will find clearly marked in most public buildings and private establishments as well as on the street. Outside metropolitan areas, public telephones are more difficult to find. Stores and gas stations are your best bet.

Most **long-distance** and **international calls** can be dialed directly from any phone. For calls to Canada and other parts of the United States, dial 1 followed by the area code and the seven-digit number. For international calls, dial 011 followed by the country code, city code, and the telephone number of the person you wish to call.

For **reversed-charge or collect calls,** and for **person-to-person calls,** dial 0 (zero, *not* the letter "O") followed by the area code and number you want; an operator will then come on the line, and you should specify that you are calling collect, or person-to-person, or both. If your operator-assisted call is international, ask for the overseas operator.

For local **directory assistance** ("information"), dial 411; for **long-distance information,** dial 1, then the appropriate area code and 555-1212.

Like the telephone system, **telegraph** and **telex** services are provided by private corporations like ITT, MCI, and above all, Western Union, the most important. You can bring your telegram in to the nearest Western Union office (there are hundreds across the country), or dictate it over the phone (a toll-free call, 800/325-6000). You can also telegraph money, or have it telegraphed to you, very quickly over the Western Union system.

Telephone Directory   There are two kinds of telephone directories available to you. The general directory is the so-called **white pages,** in which private and business subscribers are listed in alphabetical order. The inside front cover lists the emergency number for police, fire, and ambulance, and other vital numbers (like the Coast

Guard, poison-control center, crime-victims hotline, and so on). The first few pages are devoted to community-service numbers, including a guide to long-distance and international calling, complete with country codes and area codes.

The second directory, printed on yellow paper (hence its name, *yellow pages*), lists all local services, businesses, and industries by type of activity, with an index at the back. The listings cover not only such obvious items as automobile repairs by make of car, or drugstores (pharmacies), often by geographical location, but also restaurants by type of cuisine and geographical location, bookstores by special subject and/or language, places of worship by religious denomination, and other information that the tourist might otherwise not readily find. The yellow pages also include city plans or detailed area maps, often showing postal ZIP Codes and public transportation routes.

Time   The United States is divided into four time zones (six, if Alaska and Hawaii are included). From east to west, these are: eastern standard time (EST), central standard time (CST), mountain standard time (MST), Pacific standard time (PST), Alaska standard time (AST), and Hawaii standard time (HST). Always keep changing time zones in mind if you are traveling (or even telephoning) long distances in the United States. For example, noon in New York City (EST) is 11am in Chicago (CST), 10am in Denver (MST), 9am in Los Angeles (PST), 8am in Anchorage (AST), and 7am in Honolulu (HST).

Orlando, like most of Florida, observes eastern standard time; the western part of the state's Panhandle region is on central standard time (its clocks are set an hour earlier). Daylight saving time is in effect from the first Sunday in April through the last Saturday in October (actually, the change is made at 2am on Sunday) except in Arizona, Hawaii, part of Indiana, and Puerto Rico. Daylight saving time moves the clock one hour ahead of standard time.

Tipping   This is part of the American way of life, on the principle that you must expect to pay for any service you get. Here are some rules of thumb:

Bartenders: 10% to 15%.
Bellhops: at least 50¢ per piece; $2 to $3 for a lot of baggage.
Cab drivers: 15% of the fare.
Cafeterias, fast-food restaurants: no tip.
Chambermaids: $1 a day.
Checkroom attendants (restaurants, theaters): $1 per garment.
Cinemas, movies, theaters: no tip.
Doormen (hotels or restaurants): not obligatory.
Gas-station attendants: no tip.
Hairdressers: 15% to 20%.
Redcaps (airport and railroad station): at least 50¢ per piece,
    $2 to $3 for a lot of baggage.
Restaurants, nightclubs: 15% to 20% of the check.

Sleeping-car porters: $2 to $3 per night to your attendant.

Valet parking attendants: $1.

Toilets   Foreign visitors often complain that public toilets are hard to find in most U.S. cities. True, there are none on the streets, but the visitor can usually find one in a bar, restaurant, hotel, museum, department store, or service station—and it will probably be clean (although the last-mentioned sometimes leaves much to be desired). Note, however, a growing practice in some restaurants and bars of displaying a notice that "toilets are for the use of patrons only." You can ignore this sign, or better yet, avoid arguments by paying for a cup of coffee or soft drink, which will qualify you as a patron. The cleanliness of toilets at railroad stations and bus depots may be more open to question, and some public places are equipped with pay toilets, which require you to insert one or more coins into a slot on the door before it will open.

THE AMERICAN SYSTEM OF MEASUREMENTS

Length

1 inch (in.)	=	2.54 cm				
1 foot (ft.)	=	12 in.	=	30.48cm	=	.305m
1 yard	=	3 ft.			=	.915m
1 mile (mi.)	=	5,280 ft.			=	1.609km

To convert miles to kilometers, multiply the number of miles by 1.61 (for example, 50 mi. × 1.61 = 80.5km). Note that this conversion can be used to convert speeds from miles per hour (m.p.h.) to kilometers per hour (km/h).

To convert kilometers to miles, multiply the number of kilometers by .62 (for example, 25km × .62 = 15.5 mi.). Note that this same conversion can be used to convert speeds from kilometers per hour to miles per hour.

Capacity

1 fluid ounce (fl. oz.)			=	.03 liter		
1 pint	=	16 fl. oz.	=	.47 liters		
1 quart	=	2 pints	=	.94 liters		
1 gallon (gal.)	=	4 quarts	=	3.79 liters	=	.83 Imperial gal.

To convert U.S. gallons to liters, multiply the number of gallons by 3.79 (example, 12 gal. × 3.79 = 45.58 liters).

To convert U.S. gallons to Imperial gallons, multiply the number of U.S. gallons by .83 (example, 12 U.S. gal. × .83 = 9.95 Imperial gal.).

To convert liters to U.S. gallons, multiply the number of liters by .26 (example, 50 liters × .26 = 13 U.S. gal.).

To convert Imperial gallons to U.S. gallons, multiply the number of Imperial gallons by 1.2 (example, 8 Imperial gal. × 1.2 = 9.6 U.S. gal.).

Weight

1 ounce (oz.)	=	28.35 grams			
1 pound (lb.)	=	16 oz.	=	453.6 grams	=	.45 kilograms
1 ton	=	2,000 lb.	=	907 kilograms	=	.91 metric ton

To convert pounds to kilograms, multiply the number of pounds by .45 (example, 90 lb. × .45 = 40.5kg).

To convert kilograms to pounds, multiply the number of kilos by 2.2 (example, 75kg × 2.2 = 165 lb.).

Area

1 acre			=	.41 hectare		
1 square mile (sq. mi.)	=	640 acres	=	259 hectares	=	2.6km²

To convert acres to hectares, multiply the number of acres by .41 (example, 40 acres × .41 = 16.4ha).

To convert square miles to square kilometers, multiply the number of square miles by 2.6 (example, 80 sq. mi. × 2.6 = 208km²).

To convert hectares to acres, multiply the number of hectares by 2.47 (example, 20ha × 2.47 = 49.4 acres).

To convert square kilometers to square miles, multiply the number of square kilometers by .39 (example, 150km² × .39 = 58.5 sq. mi.).

Temperature

To convert degrees Fahrenheit to degrees Celsius, subtract 32 from °F, multiply by 5, then divide by 9 (example, 85°F - 32 × 5/9 = 29.4°C).

To convert degrees Celsius to degrees Fahrenheit, multiply °C by 9, divide by 5, and add 32 (example, 20°C × 9/5 + 32 = 68°F).

4

Getting to Know Walt Disney World & Orlando

Many visitors to the area never venture beyond the Disney World area, except perhaps to Sea World and Universal Studios, which are close by. For those who do, almost all area hotels offer transportation to the airport and city attractions.

1 Orientation

VISITOR INFORMATION

Contact the **Orlando/Orange County Convention & Visitors Bureau,** 8445 International Dr. (in the Mercado Shopping Village), Orlando, FL 32819 (☎ 407/363-5871). They can answer all your questions and will be happy to send you maps, brochures (including the informative *Official Visitors Guide,* the *Area Guide* to local restaurants, and the *Official Accommodations Guide*), and the "Magicard," good for discounts of 10% to 50% on accommodations, attractions, car rentals, and more. Discount tickets to attractions other than Disney parks are sold on the premises, and the multilingual staff can also make dining reservations and hotel referrals. The bureau is open daily except Christmas from 8am to 8pm.

For general information about Walt Disney World—and a copy of the informative *Walt Disney World Vacations*—write or call the **Walt Disney World Co.,** Box 10,000, Lake Buena Vista, FL 32830-1000 (☎ 407/934-7639).

If you're driving, you can stop at the Disney/AAA Travel Center in Ocala, Florida, at the intersection of I-75 (exit 68) and FL 200, about 90 miles north of Orlando. Here you can purchase tickets and Mickey ears, get help planning your park itinerary, and make hotel reservations. Hours are 9am to 6pm, 7pm June through August.

And at the Orlando International Airport, arriving passengers can stroll over to **Greetings from Walt Disney World Resort** (☎ 407/825-2301), a shop and information center on the third floor in the main lobby just behind the Northwest counter. This facility sells WDW park tickets, makes dinner show and hotel reservations at Disney properties, and provides brochures and assistance. Open daily from 6am to 10pm.

Radio: Upon entering WDW grounds you can tune your radio to 1030 AM when you're approaching the Magic Kingdom, 850 AM when approaching Epcot. Tune to 1200 AM when departing from the Magic Kingdom, 910 AM when departing Epcot. TVs in all Disney resorts and official Disney hotels also have park information stations.

Also contact the **Kissimmee–St. Cloud Convention & Visitors Bureau,** 1925 E. Irlo Bronson Blvd. (P.O. Box 422007), Kissimmee, FL 34742-2007 (☎ 407/847-5000, or 800/327-9159. They'll send maps, brochures, discount books, and the *Kissimmee–St. Cloud Vacation Guide,* which details the area's accommodations and attractions.

CITY LAYOUT

Orlando's major artery is I-4, which runs diagonally across the state from Tampa to Daytona Beach. Exits from I-4 take you to Walt Disney World, Sea World, International Drive, U.S. 192, Kissimmee, Lake Buena Vista, Church Street Station, downtown Orlando, and Winter Park. The Florida Turnpike crosses I-4 and links up with I-75 to the north. U.S. 192, a major east-west artery, stretches from Kissimmee (along a major motel strip) to U.S. 27, crossing I-4 near the Walt Disney World entrance road. Farther north, a toll road called the Beeline Expressway (FL 528) goes east from I-4 past Orlando International Airport to Cape Canaveral. Walt Disney World property is bounded roughly by I-4 and FL 535 to the east (the latter also north), World Drive (the entrance road) to the west, and U.S. 192 to the south. Epcot Center Drive (Hwy. 536/the south end of International Drive) and Buena Vista Drive cut across the complex in a more-or-less east-west direction; the two roads cross at Bonnet Creek Parkway. Excellent highways and explicit signage make it very easy to find your way around. *Note:* The Disney parks are actually much closer to Kissimmee than to downtown Orlando.

NEIGHBORHOODS IN BRIEF

Walt Disney World   A city unto itself, WDW sprawls over more than 26,000 acres containing theme parks, resorts, hotels, shops, restaurants, and recreational facilities galore. Copious details below.

Lake Buena Vista   This area centers on a hotel village/marketplace owned and operated by Walt Disney World on the eastern edge of Disney property. However, though Disney owns all the real estate, many of the hotels, and some shops and restaurants here, are independently owned. Lake Buena Vista is a charming area of manicured lawns and verdant thoroughfares with traffic islands shaded by towering oak trees.

International Drive   This is another attractive area extending 7 to 10 miles north of the Disney parks between FL 535 and the Florida Turnpike. It, too, centers—for a long way—on a wide thoroughfare with a tree-shaded traffic island. It contains numerous hotels, restaurants, shopping centers, and the Orange County Convention Center, and offers easy access to Sea World and Universal Studios. *Note:* Locally, this road is always referred to as I-Drive.

Kissimmee   South of the Disney parks, Kissimmee centers on U.S. 192/Irlo Bronson Memorial Highway—a strip as archetypical of American cities as Main Street. U.S. 192 is lined with budget motels, lesser attractions, and every fast-food restaurant you can name.

Downtown Orlando   Reached via I-4 east, this burgeoning sunbelt metropolis is 17 miles northeast of Walt Disney World. Though many tourists never venture downtown, it does have a number of attractions, including noteworthy nightlife.

2 Getting Around

In a city that thrives on its visitor attractions, you won't find it difficult to get around. All hotels offer transport to and from theme parks and other tourist destinations. It's not difficult getting places, but it can be expensive. If you don't have a car, one way to avoid many transportation costs is to stay at a Disney resort or official hotel.

Disney resorts and official hotels offer unlimited complimentary transportation via bus, monorail, ferry, and water taxi to all three parks from two hours prior to opening until two hours after closing; also to Disney Village Marketplace, Typhoon Lagoon, Pleasure Island, Fort Wilderness, and other Disney resorts. Disney properties offer transportation to other area attractions as well, though it's not complimentary.

BY BUS

Mears Transportation Group (☎ 407/423-5566) operates buses to all major attractions, including Cypress Gardens, Kennedy Space Center, Universal Studios, Sea World, Busch Gardens (in Tampa), and Church Street Station, among others. Call for details.

BY TAXI

Taxis line up in front of major hotels, and at smaller properties the front desk will be happy to call you a cab. Or call **Yellow Cab** (☎ 407/699-9999). Charge is $2.45 for the first mile, $1.40 per mile thereafter.

BY CAR

Though you can get to and around Walt Disney World and other major attractions without a car, it's always handy to have one.

RENTALS   All major companies are represented in Orlando and maintain desks at the airport. The best rates I've found are offered by Alamo (☎ 800/327-9633) and Value Rent-A-Car (☎ 800/GO-VALUE), both of them open for pick up and return 24 hours a day. Some other handy phone numbers: Avis (☎ 800/331-1212), Budget (☎ 800/527-0700), Dollar (☎ 800/800-4000), Hertz (☎ 800/654-3131), and Thrifty (☎ 800/367-2277).

FAST FACTS: Walt Disney World & Orlando

Ambulances   See "Emergencies," below.

Area Code   The area code for Orlando is 407.

Walt Disney World/ Orlando Area Orientation

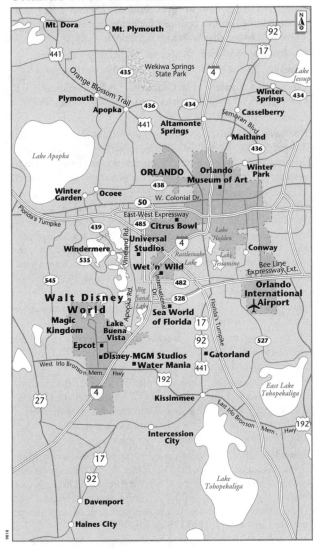

Babysitters In this child-oriented town almost every hotel provides babysitting services, and several Disney properties have marvelous child-care facilities with counselor-supervised activity programs on the premises. Disney properties use KinderCare sitters (☎ 407/ 827-5444), so you can be sure they've been very carefully checked out. If you're not staying at a Disney accommodation, you can call them on your own. Rates for in-room service are: $9 per hour for one child, $10 per hour for two children, $11 per hour for three children, $14 per hour for four children. There is a four-hour minimum, the first half hour of which is travel time for the sitter. Twenty-four-hour advance notice is required.

Car Rentals   See "Getting Around," earlier in this chapter.

Climate   See "When to Go," in Chapter 2.

Convention Center   The Orange County Convention/Civic Center is located at 9800 International Dr. (☎ 407/345-9800).

Crime   See "Safety," below.

Doctors and Dentists   Inquire at your hotel desk. Or call Dental Referral Service (☎ 800/917-6453); they can tell you the nearest dentist who meets your needs. Phones are manned from 5:30am to 6pm daily. Check the yellow pages for 24-hour emergency services.

Disney has first-aid centers in all three major parks. There's also a very good 24-hour service in the area called HouseMed (☎ 407/396-1195). HouseMed doctors—who can dispense medication—make "house calls" to all area hotels. HouseMed also operates the Medi-Clinic, a walk-in medical facility (not for emergencies) at the intersection of I-4 and Hwy. 192 open daily from 9am to 9pm (same phone). Call for directions from your hotel. See also "Hospitals" and "Pharmacies," below.

Emergencies   Dial **911** to contact the police or fire department or to call an ambulance.

Florist   Floral and fruit arrangements can be delivered anywhere on Walt Disney World Resort property by calling 407/827-3505 between 8am and 8pm.

Hospitals   Sand Lake Hospital, 9400 Turkey Lake Rd., is about two miles south of Sand Lake Road (☎ 407/351-8550). From the WDW area, take Exit 27A (Sea World exit) off I-4, make a left at the stop sign at the end of the exit ramp, and bear right onto Turkey Lake Road; the hospital is ahead on your left.

Kennels   All of the major theme parks offer animal-boarding facilities at reasonable fees. At Walt Disney World, there are kennels at Fort Wilderness, Epcot, the Magic Kingdom, and Disney-MGM Studios. If you're traveling with a pet, don't leave it in the car—even with a window cracked—while you enjoy the park. Many pets have perished this way in the hot Florida sun.

Kosher Food   It can be arranged at restaurants at Disney parks and resorts with 24 hours' advance notice. Call 407/WDW-DINE.

Liquor Laws   Minimum drinking age is 21. No liquor is served in the Magic Kingdom at Walt Disney World; however, drinks are available at the other parks.

Lockers   You can rent lockers at all of the Disney parks. Most other theme parks also offer this service. Inquire at Guest Relations.

Lost Children   Every theme park has a designated spot for parents to meet up with lost children. Find out where it is when you enter any park and instruct your children to ask park personnel to take them there if they are lost. Young children should have name tags.

Newspapers and Magazines   The *Orlando Sentinel* is the major local newspaper, but you can also purchase papers of major cities (most notably the *New York Times*) in most hotel gift shops. Also informative is a city magazine called *Orlando*.

Pharmacies   Walgreen Drug Store, 1003 W. Vine St. (Hwy. 192), just east of Bermuda Avenue (☎ 407/847-5252), operates a 24-hour pharmacy. They can deliver to hotels for a charge ($10 from 7am to 5pm, $15 at all other times).

Photography   Two-hour film processing is available at all three major Disney parks. Look for the Photo Express sign. You can also buy film and rent or buy 35mm, disc, and video cameras in all three parks.

Post Office   The main post office in Lake Buena Vista is at 12541 FL 535 near TGI Friday's in the Crossroads Shopping Center (☎ 407/828-2606). It's open Monday through Friday from 9am to 4pm, Saturday from 9am to noon.

Religious Services   Hotel desks invariably keep a list of local churches and synagogues. You can also check the yellow pages.

Safety   Whenever you're traveling in an unfamiliar city, stay alert. Be aware of your immediate surroundings. It's a good idea to keep your valuables in a safety-deposit box (inquire at the front desk), though some hotels nowadays are equipped with in-room safes. Do keep a close eye on your valuables when you're in a public place— restaurant, theater, even airport terminal. And don't leave valuables in your car, even in the trunk.

Taxes   Hotel tax in Orlando is 10%, in Kissimmee 11%; both of those rates include a state sales tax (6%) that is charged on all goods except most grocery store items and medicines.

Time   Call 407/646-3131 for the correct time and temperature.

Tourist Information   See "Orientation," above.

Travel Information   The Delta Air Lines Travel Desk at Disney's Contemporary Resort (on the ground floor of the Tower) provides information on buses, airline reservations, rental cars, and tours to other central Florida attractions.

Weather   Call 407/851-7510 for a weather recording.

5

Accommodations

You'll find a wealth of hotel options in the Walt Disney World area. Beautifully landscaped multifacility resorts are the rule, but there's something to suit every taste and pocketbook. Do, of course, reserve as far in advance as possible—the minute you've decided on the dates of your trip.

In some hotel listings below, I've mentioned **concierge levels.** In these "hotels within a hotel" guests enjoy a luxurious private lounge (usually with spectacular views) that is the setting for complimentary continental breakfast, hot and cold hors d'oeuvres at cocktail hour, and late-night cordials and pastries. Rooms are usually on high floors and room decor upgraded. Guests are cosseted with special services (private registration and checkout, a personal concierge, nightly bed turndown) and amenities (upgraded toiletries, bathroom scales, terry robes, hair dryers). Ask for specifics when you reserve.

Also mentioned under "Facilities" in some cases are **counselor-supervised child-care/activity centers.** Very popular in Orlando, these are marvelous, creatively run facilities where kids enjoy Disney movies, video games, arts and crafts, storytelling, puppet shows, indoor and outdoor activities, and much more. Some centers provide meals and/or have beds where a child can go to sleep while you're out on the town. Check individual hotel listings for these facilities and call to find out exactly what is offered.

Note: If you don't have a car, be sure to ask the price of hotel shuttle buses to and from Walt Disney World parks and other area attractions you plan to visit before reserving a room. Compute these charges—which can be as high as $12 per person per day—in determining hotel price value. All Disney-owned properties and Disney "official" hotels offer complimentary transportation to and from WDW parks (see details below).

Reservations Services

Most Kissimmee hotels listed below can be booked by calling the **Kissimmee–St. Cloud Convention & Visitors Bureau** at 800/333-KISS.

Also consider using the services of an Orlando-based organization called **Check-In** (☎ 813/756-4880, or 800/237-1033; fax 813/739-2703). A central booking agency, it has listings for hundreds of condos, resorts, hotels, villas, and luxurious private homes in all price ranges. A minimum stay of three nights is required. Check-In doesn't accept credit cards, but it does take personal checks. There's no fee for the service.

How to Read the Listings

The hotels listed below are first divided by location, then by price category alphabetically within a given district. All of the properties I've selected offer easy access to the Walt Disney World parks and other nearby major attractions.

Hotels listed in the **inexpensive** category are those charging $80 or less for a double room (don't blame me, I didn't invent inflation). Properties with $80 to $150 rooms make up the **moderate** category, $150 to $225 I've listed as **expensive,** and anything above that ranks as **very expensive.** Any extras included in the rates (for example, breakfast or other meals) are listed for each property. Categories are approximate, because hotel rates do vary considerably, depending on whether you visit in peak or off-seasons.

1 Best Bets

Best for Families: All of the Disney properties cater to families, with special menus for kids and character meals, video-game arcades, free transport to the parks, and many, many recreational facilities. Camping at woodsy Fort Wilderness makes for a special family experience.

Best Moderately Priced Hotel: Disney's Dixie Landings and Port Orleans Resorts, offering magnificently landscaped grounds and extensive facilities, are worthy of much higher prices.

Best Inexpensive Hotel: Disney's All-Star Music and All-Star Sports Resorts. You can't beat 'em with a stick.

Best for Business Travelers: Marriott's Orlando World Center offers full concierge service, 24-hour room service, fine restaurants and spacious lounges, and an extensive array of business services—plus full resort facilities should you find time to relax.

Best for a Romantic Getaway: The 1,500-acre grounds of the Hyatt Regency Grand Cypress are a veritable botanic garden surrounding a swan-filled lake. Couples enjoy stunning accommodations, great service, first-rate restaurants, and every imaginable facility. Also consider the luxurious lodgings—with fireplaces and whirlpool tubs—at the adjoining Villas of Grand Cypress.

Best Location: Disney's Grand Floridian Beach Resort, Polynesian Resort, or Contemporary Resort—all right on the monorail to whisk you straight to the parks for early opening.

Best Service: The elegant Peabody Orlando offers 24-hour concierge and room service, nightly bed turndown, and other attentive pampering.

Best Pools: All of the Walt Disney World resorts have terrific swimming pools—generally Olympic-size and often themed (the Caribbean Beach pool, for instance, replicates a Caribbean fort with stone walls and cannons; it also has a water slide). Outside the Disney complex the Hyatt Regency Grand Cypress pool is notable: a half-acre lagoonlike affair, it flows through rock grottos, is spanned by a rope bridge, and has 12 waterfalls and two steep water slides.

Best Health Club: The Walt Disney World Dolphin has a fully equipped Body By Jake club complete with a weight room overlooking a lake. It contains a full complement of Polaris, Lifestep, Lifecycle, and Liferower equipment; offers aerobics classes throughout the day, personal training, massage, and body wraps; and includes saunas and a large whirlpool.

2 Disney Properties & "Official" Hotels

Described below are the 14 Disney-owned properties (hotels, resorts, villas, wilderness homes, and campsites) and 9 privately owned properties designated as "official" hotels. All are within the Walt Disney World complex.

In addition to location (they all offer close proximity to the parks), there are a number of advantages to staying at a Disney property or official hotel, especially the former. At all Disney resorts and official hotels these include:

- Unlimited complimentary transportation via bus, monorail, ferry, and water taxi to and from all three parks from two hours prior to opening until two hours after closing. Unlimited complimentary transport is also provided to and from Disney Village Marketplace, Typhoon Lagoon, Pleasure Island, Fort Wilderness, and other Disney resorts. Three properties—the Polynesian, Contemporary, and Grand Floridian—are stops on the monorail. This free transport can save a lot of money you'd otherwise have to spend on a rental car or expensive hotel shuttle buses. It also means you're guaranteed admission to all parks, even during peak times when parking lots sometimes fill up.
- Free parking at WDW parking lots (other visitors pay $5 a day).
- Reduced-price children's menus in almost all restaurants.
- Character breakfasts and/or dinners at many restaurants.
- TVs equipped with the Disney channel and Walt Disney World information stations.
- A guest services desk where you can purchase tickets to all WDW theme parks and attractions and obtain general information.
- Use of—and in some cases complimentary transport to—the five Disney-owned golf courses and preferred tee times at them (these can be booked up to 30 days in advance).
- Access to most recreational facilities at other Disney resorts.
- Service by the Mears airport shuttle.

Additional perks at Disney-owned hotels, resorts, villas, and campgrounds—as well as at the Walt Disney World Swan and Dolphin, but not at other official hotels—include the following:

- Charge privileges at restaurants and shops throughout Walt Disney World.
- Early admission, prior to public opening, to the Magic Kingdom, Epcot, and Disney-MGM on specific days (except at the Dolphin).
- On-premises National Car Rental desk.

WALT DISNEY WORLD CENTRAL RESERVATIONS OFFICE   To reserve a room at Disney hotels, resorts, and villas; official hotels; or Fort Wilderness homes and campsites, contact: the **Central Reservations Office,** P.O. Box 10,100, Lake Buena Vista, FL 32830-0100 (☎ 407/W-DISNEY), open Monday to Friday 8am to 10pm, Saturday and Sunday 9am to 6pm. Have your dates and credit card ready when you call.

CRO can recommend accommodations that will suit your specific needs as to price, location (perhaps you wish to be closest to Epcot, Magic Kingdom, or Disney-MGM Studios), and facilities such as counselor-supervised child-care centers, a pool large enough for lap swimming, a state-of-the-art health club, on-premises golf or tennis (or other recreational facilities), a kitchen, and so on.

Be sure to inquire about their numerous package plans, which include meals, tickets, recreation, and other features. The right package plan can save you money and time (more of your vacation is planned in advance), and a comprehensive plan is helpful in computing the cost of your vacation in advance.

CRO can also give you information about various park ticket options and make dinner show reservations for you at the *Hoop-Dee-Doo Musical Revue* or the *Polynesian Luau Dinner Show* when you book your room.

OTHER SOURCES FOR PACKAGES   In addition to the CRO, there are other sources for Disney packages. **Delta** is the official airline of Walt Disney World and the only airline permitted to use Disney resorts and campgrounds in its packages. Delta offers accommodations in different price ranges at your choice of any Disney resort as well as other area hotels. At this writing, three-night midweek packages, including round-trip airfare, accommodations, a rental car with unlimited mileage or round-trip airport transfer, and much more, begin at $369–$409, per person (based on double occupancy and New York departure; range reflects season). A pass for unlimited admission to all parks is an additional option. For details call 800/872-7786. **American Express Vacations** is also officially authorized to use Disney properties in its packages. For details call 800/241-1700. Most hotels listed below also offer packages; inquire when you call. And finally, check with your travel agent.

DISNEY RESORTS IN THE WORKS   Disney resorts have proven so successful that the company is expanding its accommodations offerings. Coming soon are the following:

The **Walt Disney World Boardwalk,** themed after plush seaside resorts of the 1920s and 1930s, will offer 375 luxurious rooms and 525 villas on 45 acres along the shores of Lake Crescent near Epcot. Two- to four-story buildings with shingled rooftops will surround private courtyards and New England–style gardens; a quarter-mile boardwalk on the premises will feature two dozen shops and restaurants; and facilities will include a sports bar, 1920s-style dance club, two dinner theaters, two waterside restaurants, a carnival-themed swimming pool with a roller-coaster slide, and a 15,000-square-foot conference center designed to resemble a New England town hall.

The moderately priced 1,980-room **Disney's Coronado Springs Resort** will be themed after the American Southwest. Its four- and five-story hacienda-like buildings will have terra-cotta tile roofs and palm-shaded courtyards. The property will encompass a major 95,000-square-foot convention center and the largest ballroom in the Southeast. Additional facilities will include a white-sand beach, boat rentals, and four swimming pools.

Shades of Green on Walt Disney World Resort will be a 288-room accommodation for vacationing military personnel from all branches of the armed forces. It will replace the current Disney Inn.

Disney's Mediterranean Resort, a deluxe 1,000-room property on the Seven Seas Lagoon, will be right on the monorail line. Designed to evoke the sunny resorts of the Greek Islands, it will provide a luxurious new convention facility and a marina.

And, finally, the 575-room **Disney's Wilderness Junction Resort** will be a rustic log-sided hotel in the Fort Wilderness woods at the end of a nature trail.

DISNEY RESORTS
VERY EXPENSIVE

⊙ Disney's Beach Club Resort

1800 Epcot Resorts Blvd., off Buena Vista Dr. (P.O. Box 10,100), Lake Buena Vista, FL 32830-0100. ☎ **407/W-DISNEY** or 934-8000. Fax 407/354-1866. 584 rms, 23 suites. A/C MINIBAR TV TEL. $215–$295 single or double, depending on view and season. Extra person $15. Children under 18 free. Inquire about packages. AE, MC, V. Free self- and valet parking.

With its pristine exterior, palm-fringed entranceway, quarter-mile-long white-sand beach, and manicured gardens, the Beach Club (which lies within walking distance of Epcot) evokes a luxurious Victorian Cape Cod resort. The sun-dappled lobby, done up in beachy pastels, has upholstered wicker and rattan furnishings amid big potted palms. Charming rooms, furnished in bleached woods, are decorated in seafoam green with peach and coral accents. Some rooms have widow's walk balconies. Amenities include ceiling fans, extra phones in the bath, safes, and game tables.

Stormalong Bay—a huge, free-form swimming pool/waterpark—sprawls over three acres. It includes a 150-foot water slide, a smaller slide for little kids, shallow wading areas, and a sand strip.

Dining/Entertainment: There are several restaurants, including Ariel's and the Cape May Café (see complete reviews in Chapter 6). There are also two bars, a casual grill serving light fare, and an ice-cream parlor.

Services: 24-hour room service, babysitting, guest services desk, complimentary daily newspaper, boat transport to Disney-MGM theme park.

Facilities: Large secluded swimming pool, Jacuzzi, boat rentals, two hard-surface night-lit tennis courts, state-of-the-art health club (including indoor whirlpool, sauna, and steam), massage, volleyball/croquet/bocci ball courts, two-mile jogging trail, coin-op washers/dryers, unisex hair salon, shops, full business center, car-rental desk, large video-game arcade, and the Sandcastle Club (a counselor-supervised children's activity center).

✪ Disney's Grand Floridian Beach Resort

4401 Floridian Way, right near the Magic Kingdom (P.O. Box 10,100), Lake Buena Vista, FL 32830-0100. ☎ **407/W-DISNEY** or 824-3000. Fax 407/354-1866. 839 rms, 34 suites. A/C MINIBAR TV TEL. $245–$345 single or double, depending on view and season; $430–$465 concierge floors; $500–$1,500 suite. Extra person $15. Children under 18 free. Inquire about packages. AE, MC, V. Free self- and valet parking.

The Grand Floridian is magnificent from the moment you step into its opulent five-story lobby under triple-domed stained-glass skylights. The lacy white wrought-iron balustrades, potted palms, glittering chandeliers, white birdcage elevators, and the Chinese Chippendale aviary housing Australian parrots are all reminiscent of a bygone era of luxury and leisure. A pianist entertains during afternoon tea, and an orchestra plays big-band music every evening from 5 to 10:30pm. Sunny rooms, some with dormer windows, are decorated in muted greens and pinks and furnished with Victorian-style daybeds or convertible sofas and bleached oak two-poster beds made up with lovely floral-chintz spreads. In-room amenities include safes and plantation-style ceiling fans. In the bath, you'll find a cosmetic mirror, extra phone, hair dryer, and terry robe. And private latticed balconies or verandas overlook formal gardens, the pool, or a 200-acre lagoon.

Dining/Entertainment: Victoria & Albert's, Orlando's finest restaurant, is described at length in Chapter 6. There's also the lovely Grand Floridian Cafe, overlooking formal gardens and serving American fare; southern specialties such as battered fried catfish are featured. The festive 1900 Park Fare is the setting for buffet character breakfasts and dinners. Flagler's offers northern Italian fare while a strolling guitarist entertains. Narcoossee's overlooks the lagoon near the boat landing; grilled meats and seafood are prepared in an exhibition kitchen. The 24-hour Gasparilla Grill proffers sandwiches, snacks, and ice cream, as well as continental breakfasts. Intimate and very Victorian, Mizner's Lounge offers an international selection of ports, brandies, and appetizers. The light and airy Garden View Lounge is the setting for elegant afternoon teas complete with crumpets and scones with Devonshire cream. And frozen drinks and snacks are available from the Summerhouse Pool Bar.

Services: 24-hour room service, nightly turndown with Belgian chocolates, babysitting, on-premises monorail, boat transport to Magic Kingdom and Polynesian Resort, free trolley transport around property, shoeshine, massage, guest services desk, complimentary daily newspaper.

Facilities: Large swimming pool, children's wading pool, whirlpool, two night-lit clay tennis courts, boat rental, waterskiing, croquet, volleyball, children's playground, jogging trails, fishing excursions, white-sand beach, full business center, unisex hair salon, car-rental desk, wedding pavilion, coin-op washers/dryers, shops, extensive state-of-the-art health club, video-game arcade, organized children's activities in summer and peak seasons, the Mouseketeer Clubhouse (a counselor-supervised child-care/activity center).

Disney's Polynesian Resort

1600 Seven Seas Dr., just below the Magic Kingdom (P.O. Box 10,100), Lake Buena Vista, FL 32830-0100. ☎ **407/W-DISNEY** or 824-2000. Fax 407/354-1866. 841 rms, 12 suites. A/C TV TEL. $200–$295 single or double, depending on view and season; $305–$370 concierge floors; $385–$1,100 suite. Extra person $15. Children under 18 free. Inquire about packages. AE, MC, V. Free self- and valet parking.

Designed to complement Adventureland in the Magic Kingdom, the 25-acre Polynesian is fronted by lush tropical foliage, waterfalls, palms, and koi ponds. At night lava-rock walkways are illuminated by flaming torchiers. A private white-sand beach—dotted with canvas cabanas, hammocks, umbrella tables, and large swings—looks out on a 200-acre lagoon. One of the swimming pools is immense, with waterfalls, grottoes, and a waterslide. And the skylit lobby is a virtual rain forest of ferns, orchids, and hibiscus, with colorful resident macaws and a rushing waterfall cascading into a stream stocked with goldfish. Large, beautiful rooms—most with balconies or patios—have canopied beds made up with gorgeous batik spreads, daybed sofas, ceiling fans, bamboo and rattan furnishings, and walls hung with Gauguin prints. All overlook tropical gardens or the lagoon. Concierge-level guests enjoy a stunning private lounge (setting for complimentary continental breakfasts, afternoon snacks, and evening hors d'oeuvres), nightly turndown, private check-in/check-out, services of a private concierge, and upgraded amenities.

Dining/Entertainment: The O'Hana at Papeete is the setting for a daily breakfast buffet featuring Disney characters; it also features elegant all-you-can-eat dinners with open-pit rock-grilled specialties. Luau Cove hosts Mickey's Tropical Luau for kids each afternoon and a Polynesian Luau dinner twice nightly. There are several other restaurants and bars, including a 24-hour ice-cream parlor and the Barefoot Pool Bar, with a beautiful setting on the beach overlooking the lagoon.

Services: Room service from 6:30am to midnight, babysitting, on-premises monorail, boat transport (to Magic Kingdom, Discovery Island, Fort Wilderness, and River Country), guest services desk, complimentary daily newspaper.

Facilities: Two swimming pools, children's wading pool, boat rental, waterskiing, volleyball, children's playground, 1.5-mile jogging trail, fishing excursions, coin-op washers/dryers, car-rental desk, shops, large video-game arcade, the Neverland Club (a counselor-supervised evening activity center for children).

✪ Disney's Yacht Club Resort

1700 Epcot Resorts Blvd., off Buena Vista Dr. (P.O. Box 10,100), Lake Buena Vista, FL 32830-0100. ☎ **407/W-DISNEY** or 934-7000. Fax 407/354-1866. 625 rms, 12 suites. A/C MINIBAR TV TEL. $215–$295 single or double, depending on view and season; $360–$395 concierge level. Extra person $15. Children under 18 free. Inquire about packages. AE, MC, V. Free self- and valet parking.

This beautiful resort shares a 25-acre lake, facilities, and gorgeous landscaping with the adjacent Beach Club Resort (details above). Grounds are planted with Japanese elms, Bradford pear trees, magnolias, crape myrtles, and lush tropical foliage; and gardenias and roses bloom in charming brick courtyards. The main five-story clapboard building evokes a luxurious turn-of-the-century New England yacht club. It's

Walt Disney World Accommodations

Buena Vista Palace 16	Disney's Polynesian Resort 2	Hyatt Regency
Courtyard by Marriott 20	Disney's Port Orleans Resort 7	Grand Cypress 11
Cypress Pointe Resort 9	Disney's Vacation Club Resort 8	Marriott's Orlando
Disney's All-Star Music Resort 30	Disney's Village Resort/	World Center 23
Disney's All-Star Sports Resort 29	Disney Institute 15	Residence Inn by Marriott 22
Disney's Beach Club Resort 24	Disney's Wilderness Lodge 4	Royal Plaza 18
Disney's Caribbean Beach Resort 28	Disney's Yacht Club Resort 25	Summerfield Suites
Disney's Contemporary Resort 3	Wyndham Garden Hotel 12	Lake Buena Vista 10
Disney's Dixie Landings Resort 6	Grosvenor Resort 17	Travelodge Hotel 13
Disney's Fort Wilderness	Guest Quarters Suite Resort 14	Vistana Resort 21
Resort & Campground 5	Hilton at Walt Disney	Walt Disney World Dolphin 26
Disney's Grand Floridian 1	World Village 19	Walt Disney World Swan 27

entered via a magnificent lobby, furnished with plush leather wing chairs and sofas amid potted palms in Chinese porcelain pots.

The nautical theme carries over to very inviting rooms, decorated in snappy blue and white, with brass sconces and ship lights, maps and paintings of ship captains on the walls, and crisp floral-chintz drapes, valances, and bed ruffles. French doors open onto porches or balconies. Amenities include ceiling fans, extra phones in the bath, safes, and game tables.

Dining/Entertainment: The plush Yachtsman Steakhouse is reviewed in Chapter 6. The Yacht Club Galley is the resort's comfortable family restaurant, offering American regional fare. Crew's Cup Lounge, its pine-paneled walls hung with Ivy League rowing-team memorabilia, serves up light fare and frosted mugs of international ales and beers; the cozy Ale and Compass Lounge, a lobby bar with working fireplace, features specialty coffees and cocktails.

Services: 24-hour room service, babysitting, guest services desk, complimentary daily newspaper, boat transport to Disney-MGM theme park, tram transport to Epcot.

Facilities: Yacht Club facilities are identical to those of the Beach Club Resort (details above).

EXPENSIVE

Disney's Contemporary Resort

4600 N. World Dr. (P.O. Box 10,100), Lake Buena Vista, FL 32830-0100, ☎ **407/ W-DISNEY** or 407/824-1000. Fax 407/354-1865. 1,041 rms. 80 suites. A/C TV TEL. $195–$240 single or double. $260–$280 tower room. Extra person $15. Children under 17 free. Inquire about packages. AE, MC, V. Free self- and valet parking.

When it opened in 1971 to complement the Magic Kingdom's futuristic Tomorrowland, the Contemporary's aesthetic was cutting-edge. Today its dramatic angular planes, free-form furnishings, and abstract paintings appear, rather charmingly, retro-modern. The property—centering on a sleek 15-story, A-frame Tower flanked by two Garden Wings—occupies 26 acres bounded by a natural lake and the Disney-made Seven Seas Lagoon. Kids are thrilled that the monorail whizzes right through the hotel. Tennis buffs appreciate the six night-lit hard-surface tennis courts (lessons are available and there's a pro shop). Rooms are quite nice, with art deco furnishings, ceiling fans, and cheerful Matisse prints. The 14th floor of the Tower comprises a concierge level where guests enjoy a more sumptuous decor, plus upgraded amenities (hair dryers, live plants, toiletries) and services (nightly turndown, concierge). They also have balconies and a private lake-view lounge—the setting for complimentary breakfast buffets, hot and cold hors d'oeuvres with beer and wine every afternoon, and late-night cordials and petit fours.

Dining/Entertainment: The California Grill provides panoramic vistas of the Magic Kingdom and Seven Seas Lagoon and centers on a full exhibition kitchen with a wood-burning pizza oven, bakery oven, and rotisserie. Guests mingle with chefs and enjoy Asian-nuanced West Coast cuisine; a comfortable lounge and adjoining bar feature a tasting menu and premium wines by the glass. This is a prime venue for viewing nightly fireworks. There's also the Concourse Steakhouse; the garden-themed Contemporary Café, serving prime rib buffet dinners

In the Words of Walt Disney

"My operations are based on experience, thoughtful observation, and warm fellowship with my neighbors at home and around the world."

and character breakfast buffets; and several other spots for drinks and light fare.

Services: 24-hour room service, guest services desk, daily newspaper delivery, babysitting, boat transport (to Discovery Island, Fort Wilderness, and River Country), direct monorail link to the Polynesian and Grand Floridian resorts.

Facilities: Two swimming pools; children's wading pool; white-sand beach with volleyball court; shuffleboard; boat rentals; unisex hair salon; six tennis courts; shops; Delta Air Lines desk; car-rental desk; coin-op washers/dryers; full business center; extensive health club; sauna/ massage/tanning rooms; vast 24-hour video-game arcade; the Mouseketeer Clubhouse (a counselor-supervised child-care/activity center).

Disney's Vacation Club Resort

1510 North Cove Rd., off Community Dr. (P.O. Box 10,100), Lake Buena Vista, FL 32830-0100. ☎ **407/W-DISNEY** or 407/827-7700. Fax 407/354-1866. 709 villas. A/C TV TEL. $190–$205 deluxe room; $250–$275 one-bedroom vacation home; $355–$375 two-bedroom vacation home; $755 three-bedroom Grand Villa. Range reflects high and low seasons. Inquire about packages. AE, MC, V. Free self-parking.

Its architecture evocative of Key West at the turn of the century, the Vacation Club is a "vacation ownership" (time-share) property. If you're interested in purchasing a vacation villa here, they'll be happy to give you a presentation. For nonowners, however, this is just like any other luxurious Disney resort; you rent accommodations when not in use by owners. The 156-acre property is beautifully landscaped. Tree-lined brick walkways are edged by white picket fences, palms sway softly in the breeze, shorebirds swoop lazily over lagoons, and the air is scented with honeysuckle.

Gorgeous residential-style accommodations offer home-away-from-home comfort, with fully equipped kitchens and furnished patios and amenities including bedroom ceiling fans, full laundry rooms, large-screen remote-control cable TVs with VCRs in the living room (smaller sets in bedrooms), and phones in each bedroom and living room. Many units contain whirlpool tubs in the master suite, and Grand Villas have stereo systems. *Note:* Deluxe rooms do not offer kitchens, patios, VCRs, or laundry rooms.

Dining/Entertainment: Olivia's Cafe is a pleasant plant-filled dining room that also offers al fresco seating on a patio overlooking the Trumbo Canal. There are a few other spots for drinks and light fare, including the Gurgling Suitcase pool bar, where you can sit out and watch the sunset while sipping a piña colada.

Services: Babysitting, guest services desk, ferry service to Disney Village Marketplace and Pleasure Island, free bus transport around property, food shopping for a minimal charge.

Facilities: Two hard-surface night-lit tennis courts, lighted basketball court, white-sand play area, boardwalk, four swimming pools, whirlpool, kiddie pool, bicycle rental, car-rental, boat rentals, children's playground, extensive health club, sauna, shuffleboard, horseshoes, volleyball, complimentary use of washers/dryers, general store, small video-game arcade, and complimentary video library. The Community Hall, a recreation center, shows Disney movies nightly and offers activities such as Monday-night football, Ping-Pong tournaments, bingo, Pictionary, and arts and crafts for adults and children.

❂ Disney's Village Resort/Disney Institute

1901 Buena Vista Dr., adjacent to the Disney Village Marketplace (P.O. Box 10,100), Lake Buena Vista, FL 32830-0100. ☎ **407/W-DISNEY** or 407/827-1100. Fax 407/ 354-1866. 324 suites. A/C TV TEL. $345–$365 Treehouse Villa (for up to 6 people); $365–$390 2-bedroom Fairway unit (for up to 8 people); $185–$205 Club Suite (for up to 5 people); $275–$295 1-bedroom Vacation Villa (for up to 4 people); $310– $330 2-bedroom Vacation Villa (for up to 6 people); $750 2-bedroom Grand Vista home; $975 3-bedroom Grand Vista home. Range reflects view and season. Inquire about discounted package rates and Disney Institute packages. AE, MC, V. Free self-parking.

Sprawled over 265 acres of lakes, woodlands, and streams, and offering a wealth of sports facilities, the Village Resort is a great choice for golfers and families. Peacocks roam the grounds, and your accommodations might overlook a verdant golf course, gurgling river, or a forest of towering pines, magnolias, cypress, and live oaks draped with Spanish moss. The Disney Institute, an exciting new WDW concept, will be opening on Village grounds shortly after we go to press (see box below).

Accommodations include the following. Octagonal Treehouse Villas, elevated on stilts, have large outdoor patios and balconies amid the treetops. Decorated in earth tones, with plushly upholstered twig and branch furnishings, these rustic two-story lodgings each contain a fully equipped kitchen, dining area, living room, three bedrooms, and two baths. Similarly equipped two-bedroom Fairway Villas, just off the golf course, are elegant ski lodge–style cedar townhouses (the upstairs units have beamed cathedral ceilings). The most inexpensive accommodations are one-bedroom lakeside Club Suites with kitchenettes and balconies or porches. One- and two-bedroom Vacation Villas, in two-story town houses, overlook woodlands or waterways; their Early American furnishings include spool beds and two-posters. All have country kitchens, dining areas, large living rooms with convertible sofas, and patios. And for total luxury there are two- and three-bedroom Grand Vista homes that sleep six to eight people. They're beautiful residential accommodations with full kitchens, two big screened porches (one set up for dining), upscale furnishings, marble whirlpool tubs in the bath, and homey touches such as live plants, shelves of books, and objets d'art. Each is supplied with its own electric golf cart, bicycles, and barbecue grill. Grand Vista guests also enjoy special services, such as nightly bed turndown and daily newspaper delivery.

Dining/Entertainment: The elegant Seasons—with four dining rooms, each of them evocative of a season—features nightly changing international menus ranging from Polynesian to California cuisine. Serving-staff attire, music, and other elements also vary nightly to reflect the evening's theme. A vast bar/lounge with a veranda adjoins.

Services: Room service, babysitting, guest services desk, free bus transport around property, free grocery delivery from the Gourmet Pantry.

The Disney Institute

Opening shortly after presstime, the Disney Institute is an exciting new concept that will allow guests to custom-design unique Walt Disney World vacations outside the theme park areas. It will feature interactive programs in dozens of diverse areas (animation, gourmet cooking, lifestyles, the arts, organic gardening, rock climbing, storytelling, landscape design, wilderness adventure, and many more). The property will also offer extensive sporting facilities (see the listing for Disney Village Resort/Disney Institute) and group fitness activities such as morning nature walks. A luxurious spa vacation will be another option here. Nightly performances and recitals will take place in an 800-seat open-air amphitheater and a 200-seat performance center, and films will be screened every evening in a 400-seat state-of-the-art movie theater. An artist-in-residence program will enable guests to meet, and attend workshops led by, noted artists, writers, and performers. And a counselor-supervised youth center will offer a full roster of daytime programs and activities for children 10 to 13 and teens as well as evening activities for the latter. All Disney Institute vacations will be sold as packages. Call 800/746-5858 for information, 800/282-9282 for reservations.

Facilities: Four tennis courts, 18-hole, par-72 championship golf course, golf/tennis pros/pro shops, electric cart rentals, six swimming pools, five whirlpools, kiddie pool, bike rental/bike trails, three sand volleyball courts, softball/multipurpose sports field, rock-climbing wall, boat rentals, state-of-the-art health club, extensive spa services/facilities, two children's playgrounds, 3.4-mile jogging course with 32 exercise stations, open-air amphitheater, performance center, movie theater, car-rental desk, free washers/dryers, BBQ grills and picnic tables scattered throughout property, counselor-supervised youth center, video game arcade. A footbridge connects to Disney's Village Marketplace.

✪ Disney's Wilderness Lodge

901 Timberline Dr., on the southwest shore of Bay Lake just east of the Magic Kingdom (mailing address P.O. Box 10,100), Lake Buena Vista, FL 32830-0100. ☎ **407/ W-DISNEY** or 407/824-3200. Fax 407/354-1866. 697 rms, 25 junior suites, 6 suites. A/C TV TEL. $149–$195 single or double, depending on view and season; junior suites $250–$270; suites $480–$580. Extra person $15; children under 18 free. Inquire about packages. AE, MC, V. Free self- and valet parking.

Evocative of rustic turn-of-the-century national park lodges, this 56-acre Disney resort is surrounded by towering oak and pine forests. The imposing lobby houses floor-to-ceiling eagle- and raven-motif totem poles and an equally massive stone fireplace embedded with replicas of fossils. A geothermal spring flows under a picture-window wall into Silver Creek, which itself empties into beautiful 340-acre Bay Lake. There's a lakefront Sand beach, as well as an immense serpentine swimming pool—seemingly excavated out of the rocks. "Volcanic" meadow landscaping is punctuated by bubbling craters, a babbling brook, a cascading waterfall, and a spewing geyser.

Guest rooms—off hallways with Native American-motif carpeting and buffalo-themed lighting fixtures—are decorated with reddish mahogany woodwork and coffee-hued walls, the latter adorned with tribal friezes and landscape paintings of the Northwest. Furnishings are Mission style. Amenities include remote-control cable TVs (in handsome maple armoires stenciled with Yellowstone scenes), ceiling fans, and safes. Furnished patios or balconies overlook the lake, woodlands, or meadow. Junior suites offer living rooms with queen-size sleeper sofas, wet bars, and small refrigerators.

Dining/Entertainment: Artist's Point is reviewed in Chapter 6; it offers fine dinners and character breakfasts. The rustic western-themed Whispering Canyon Cafe serves up hearty all-you-can-eat prix-fixe family-style meals (breakfast, lunch, and dinner) in iron skillets. And there are additional spots for drinks and light fare. Five-minute geyser shows take place in the meadow periodically throughout the day, and nightly electric water pageants can be viewed from the shores of Bay Lake.

Services: Room service after 4pm; guest services desk; babysitting; Mears airport shuttle; boat transport to Magic Kingdom; bus transport to Disney-MGM, Epcot, and other park areas.

Facilities: Swimming pool, kiddie pool with water slide, lakefront sand beach, hot and cold spa pools, boat rentals, children's playground/recreation area, bicycle rental, two-mile jogging/bike trail with exercise stations, large video-game arcade, gift shop, Cub's Den (a counselor-supervised activity center for children 4–12).

MODERATE

❸ Disney's Caribbean Beach Resort

900 Cayman Way, off Buena Vista Dr. (P.O. Box 10,100), Lake Buena Vista, FL 32830-0100. ☎ **407/W-DISNEY** or 407/934-3400. Fax 407/354-1866. 2,112 rms. A/C MINIBAR TV TEL. $94–$124 single or double. Extra person $12. Children under 17 free. Inquire about packages. AE, MC, V. Free self-parking.

The Caribbean Beach occupies 200 lush, palm-fringed tropical acres. The main swimming pool replicates a Spanish-style Caribbean fort with pirate's cannon and stone walls (it has a water slide, kiddie pool, and whirlpool). Upon registering in the Custom House lobby—where potted palms and overhead fans set the island mood—guests are issued helpful informational newsletters. Accommodations surround a large, duck-filled lake in five "villages," each with metal-roofed stucco buildings painted in bright tropical hues. Room interiors are charming; all have attractive oak furnishings with pineapple motifs. In-room amenities include coffee makers and ceiling fans; refrigerators are available at $5 per night. And all rooms have verandas, many of them overlooking the lake. In addition, 16 beautifully landscaped public courtyards furnished with umbrella tables dot the property.

Dining/Entertainment: There's a festive food court, the nautically themed Captain's Tavern, and a pool bar serving snacks and frozen tropical drinks.

Services: Room service (pizza delivery only) from 4pm to midnight, guest services desk, babysitting, complimentary shuttle around grounds.

Facilities: Video-game arcade, shops, boat rentals, bicycle rental, car rental, coin-op washers/dryers in each village. In addition to the main swimming pool, there are nice-sized pools, children's playgrounds, and lakefront white-sand beaches in each village. A 1.4-mile promenade circles the lake. An arched wooden bridge leads to Parrot Cay Island, where there is a short nature trail, an aviary of tropical birds, a picnic area, and a playground.

⑤ Disney's Dixie Landings Resort

1251 Dixie Dr., off Bonnet Creek Pkwy. (P.O. Box 10,100), Lake Buena Vista, FL 32830-0100. ☎ **407/W-DISNEY** or 407/934-6000. Fax 407/934-5777. 2,048 rms. A/C TV TEL. $89–$121 for up to four in a room. Children under 18 free. Inquire about packages. AE, MC, V. Free self-parking.

Nestled on the banks of the Disney-made Sassagoula River and dotted with bayous, Dixie Landings shares its magnificently landscaped 325-acre site with the Port Orleans Resort, described below. Ol' Man Island, a woodsy 3^1/$_2$-acre recreation area, centers on an ancient live oak tree with a 78-foot branch spread. On the island are an immense rustically themed free-form pool with waterfalls cascading from a broken bridge and a water slide entered via a pump house, a playground, children's wading pool, whirlpool, sun deck, and fishin' hole (rent bait and poles and angle for catfish and bass). Themed after the Louisiana countryside, it is divided into "parishes" with accommodations housed in stately colonnaded plantation homes (fronted by brick courtyards and manicured lawns with vine-covered trellises) or rustic Cajun-style dwellings (set amid bayous and stands of cypress and towering pine). Rooms in the former are elegantly decorated in Federalist blue and gold, with brass-trimmed maple furnishings. Cajun rooms, on the other hand, feature bed frames made of bent branches, patchwork quilts, and calico-print drapes. In-room amenities throughout include ceiling fans and double sinks in the bath; and many accommodations offer river views.

Dining/Entertainment: Boatwright's Dining Hall is reviewed in Chapter 6. There's also a food court, a pool bar, and the Cotton Co-op lounge—with a beautiful pressed-copper ceiling and plush couches before a blazing fireplace.

Services: Room service (pizza delivery only), guest services desk, babysitting; boat transport to Port Orleans, Village Marketplace, and Pleasure Island.

Facilities: Six large swimming pools, coin-op washers/dryers, children's playground, vast video-game arcade, bicycle rental, car-rental desk, boat rentals, 1.7-mile riverfront jogging/biking path, Fulton's General Store.

⑤ Disney's Port Orleans Resort

2201 Orleans Dr., off Bonnet Creek Pkwy. (P.O. Box 10,100), Lake Buena Vista, FL 32830-0100. ☎ **407/W-DISNEY** or 407/934-5000. Fax 407/934-5353. 1,008 rms. A/C TV TEL. $89–$121 for up to four in a room. Children under 18 free. Inquire about packages. AE, MC, V. Free self-parking.

This beautiful resort, themed after turn-of-the-century New Orleans, shares a site on the banks of the "mighty" Sassagoula River, with Dixie Landings, described above. The charming glass-walled lobby under a vaulted ceiling replicates a New Orleans mint; guests register at old-fashioned bank teller windows. Cheerful three-story buildings, painted in variegated pastels with shuttered windows and lacy wrought-iron balconies, house lovely rooms. Decorated in mocha, rust, and teal, they have pretty cherrywood furnishings, walls hung with gilt-framed botanical prints and family photographs, and ceiling fans. Accommodations buildings are fronted by lovely flower gardens opening onto fountained courtyards. And landscaping throughout the property is a delight, with stately oaks, formal boxwood hedges, azaleas, and fragrant jasmine.

Dining/Entertainment: Bonfamille's Café is reviewed in Chapter 6. There are a few other restaurants and bars, including Scat Cat's Club, a cocktail lounge off the lobby, with family-oriented live entertainment (rock, country, New Orleans jazz, sing-alongs).

Services: Room service (pizza delivery only), guest services desk, babysitting; boat transport to Dixie Landings, Village Marketplace, and Pleasure Island.

🔵 Family-Friendly Hotels

All Disney Properties and "Official" Hotels   *(see pp. 46)* The many advantages for kids include proximity to Walt Disney World parks, complimentary transportation between hotels and the parks, and reduced-price children's menus and Disney character appearances in hotel restaurants. Extensive facilities might include lakefront beaches, boating, waterskiing, bike rentals, playgrounds, video-game arcades, swimming pools with waterfalls and slides, and/or organized children's activities. See listings for details.

Disney's Fort Wilderness Resort and Campground   *(see p. 60)* All of the above and more is offered here—plus you get to go camping.

Residence Inns   *(see p. 71)* Residence Inns not only have swimming pools, children's playgrounds, and other recreational facilities, but accommodations with fully equipped kitchens—a potential money-saver when traveling with family. Rates include breakfast. The Lake Cecile property *(see p. 76)* has on-premises barbecue grills and picnic tables and offers boating and waterskiing on a scenic lake.

Holiday Inn Sunspree Resort Lake Buena Vista   *(see p. 73)* This hotel has a special check-in desk for kids and on-premises mascots to welcome them. Rooms are equipped with kitchenettes, but it doesn't cost much to feed your family here. Kids under 12 eat free in their own restaurant where movies and cartoons are shown. Numerous organized children's activities are free.

Holiday Inn Maingate East   *(see p. 75)* The inn offers children's facilities identical to its Lake Buena Vista counterpart.

Facilities: Larger-than-Olympic-size Doubloon Lagoon swimming pool, with an enormous sea serpent–shaped water slide (an "alligator jazz band" plays in a pink clamshell near the pool); whirlpool, children's wading pool, coin-op washers/dryers, vast video-game arcade, bicycle rental, car-rental desk, boat rentals, croquet court, 1.7-mile riverfront jogging/biking path, shop.

INEXPENSIVE

Disney's All-Star Music Resort

1801 W. Buena Vista Dr., at World Dr. and Osceola Pkwy. (P.O. Box 10,100), Lake Buena Vista, FL 32830-0100. ☎ **407/W-DISNEY** or 407/939-6000. Fax 407/354-1866. 1,920 rms. A/C TV TEL. $69–$79 single or double, depending on view and season. Extra person $8. Children under 18 free. Inquire about packages. AE, MC, V. Free self-parking.

Nestled among pristine pine forests southwest of Disney-MGM Studios, this Disney property—part of a 246-acre complex that also includes the adjacent All-Star Sports Resort (see below)—offers extensive facilities at low prices. Its ten buildings are musically themed around country, jazz, rock, calypso, or Broadway show tunes. The calypso building, for instance, has a palm-fringed roof frieze and balconies adorned with tropical birds and musical notes, while a convoy of 18-wheelers travels around the country building, which is adorned with fiddles and banjos. There are oversized "icons" in public areas throughout the property, such as three-story cowboy boots, a conga drum–shaped stairway, and a walk-through jukebox (these are lit by neon and fiber optics at night). Small ponds dot the property, and building courtyards are attractively landscaped. Attractive rooms have musically themed bedspreads, paintings, and wall friezes.

Dining/Entertainment: There's a cheerful food court and an adjoining bar.

Services: Room service (pizza only), babysitting, guest services desk, Mears airport shuttle.

Facilities: Two vast swimming pools (one grand piano–shaped, the other guitar-shaped, with three caballeros at the center shooting water from guns), kiddie pool, themed children's playground, coin-op washers/dryers, large retail shop, car-rental desk, state-of-the-art video game arcade with kid-sized bowling alley.

Disney's All-Star Sports Resort

1701 W. Buena Vista Dr., at World Dr. and Osceola Pkwy. (P.O. Box 10,100), Lake Buena Vista, FL 32830-0100. ☎ **407/W-DISNEY** or 407/939-5000. Fax 407/354-1866. 1,920 rms. A/C TV TEL. $69–$79 single or double, depending on view of season. Extra person $8. Children under 18 free. Inquire about packages. AE, MC, V. Free self-parking.

Adjacent to and sharing facilities with the above-listed All-Star Music Resort, this 82-acre property is elaborately sports themed. Lobby walls are covered with sports photographs, and rooms are housed in buildings themed around football, baseball, basketball, tennis, and surfing. For instance, the turquoise surf buildings have waves along their rooflines, surfboards mounted on exterior walls, and a courtyard encompassing a swimming pool; pink fish swim along wavy balcony railings. Public-area "icons" here include oversized tennis-can stairways, four-story football helmets and whistles, a baseball scoreboard, and a tennis umpire chair. Cheerful rooms, with painted furniture, feature sports-action-motif bedspreads, paintings, and wall friezes.

Dining/Entertainment: There's a brightly decorated food court and an adjoining bar.

Services: Room service (pizza only), babysitting, guest services desk, Mears airport shuttle.

Facilities: Two vast swimming pools (one surfing-themed with two 38-foot shark fins, the other shaped like a baseball diamond with an "outfield" sundeck), kiddie pool, themed children's playground, coin-op washers/dryers, large sports arena–themed shop, car-rental desk, state-of-the-art video game arcade.

A DISNEY CAMPGROUND

Disney's Fort Wilderness Resort and Campground

3520 N. Fort Wilderness Trail (P.O. Box 10,100), Lake Buena Vista, FL 32830-0100. ☎ **407/W-DISNEY** or 407/824-2900. Fax 407/354-1866. 784 campsites, 408 wilderness homes. AC TV. $35–$52 campsite per night (range depends on season, number of people, location, size, and extent of hookup); $180–$195 wilderness home. Inquire about packages. AE, MC, V. Free self-parking at your campsite or wilderness home.

This woodsy 780-acre camping resort—shaded by towering pines and cypress trees and crossed by fish-filled streams, lakes, and canals—makes an ideal venue for family vacations, with extensive sports facilities (even horseback riding and pony rides are available). Secluded **campsites** (most of them set up for tent campers, the others for trailers), offer 110/220-volt outlets, barbecue grills, picnic tables, and children's play areas. Another option here is **wilderness homes**—rustic one-bedroom cabins with piney interiors. Accommodating two adults and up to four children, these have cozy living rooms with Murphy beds, baths, fully equipped eat-in kitchens, and on-premises telephones, picnic tables, and barbecue grills. Amenities include remote-control cable TVs (with WDW information channels) and alarm-clock radios. Guests here enjoy a lot of extras, including extensive recreational facilities and a nightly campfire program hosted by Chip 'n' Dale and featuring Disney movies, cartoons, and sing-alongs.

Dining/Entertainment: There are two full-service restaurants, Trails End and Crockett's Tavern, which features Texas fare. During summer months, guests enjoy a dazzling electrical water pageant from the beach here nightly at 9:45pm. Following the pageant, the beach is a great place to view Magic Kingdom fireworks. And the rambunctious *Hoop-Dee-Doo Musical Revue* takes place in Pioneer Hall nightly (details in Chapter 9).

Services: Guest services desk, babysitting; boat transport to Discovery Island, Magic Kingdom, and Contemporary Resort.

Facilities: Comfort station in each campground area (with restrooms, private showers, ice machines, telephones, and laundry rooms), two large swimming pools, white-sand beach, Circle D Ranch horseback riding (trail rides), petting farm, pony rides, fishing, three sand volleyball courts, ball fields, tetherball, shuffleboard, bike rentals, boat rentals, 1.5-mile nature trail, 1.5-mile jogging path, two 18-hole championship golf courses, two night-lit hard-surface tennis courts, shops, kennel, car-rental desk, two video-game arcades.

LAKE BUENA VISTA/OFFICIAL HOTELS

These properties, designated "official" WDW hotels, are located on and around Hotel Plaza Boulevard. Guests at the below-listed hotels enjoy many privileges (see above). And the location is a big plus—close to the Disney parks and within walking distance of Disney Village Marketplace and Crossroads shops and restaurants as well as Pleasure Island nightlife.

Note: In addition to the addresses and toll-free phone numbers provided in each listing below, you can also make reservations at any of these official hotels through the Central Reservations Office, P.O. Box 10,100, Lake Buena Vista, FL 32830-0100 (☎ 407/W-DISNEY).

EXPENSIVE

Buena Vista Palace

1900 Buena Vista Dr., just north of Hotel Plaza Blvd., Lake Buena Vista, FL 32830. ☎ **407/827-2727**, or 800/327-2990. Fax 407/827-6034. 887 rms, 127 suites. A/C MINIBAR TV TEL. $145–$235 single or double; $219–$250 Crown Level; $245–$290 one-bedroom suite, $390–$455 two-bedroom suite. Range reflects view and season. Extra person $15. Children under 18 stay free. Inquire about packages. AE, CB, DC, MC, Optima, V. Free self-parking, valet parking $6 per night.

This 27-acre waterfront resort in Walt Disney World Village flies the flags of all Epcot countries at its entrance. There are extensive boating facilities here at an on-premises marina and at the nearby Disney Village Marina. And travelers who want serious pampering will love the European-style spa. Accommodations, in four handsome stucco towers with gleaming mirrored balconies, are decorated in earth tones, with dark oak furnishings. All but a few have balconies or patios, many of them overlooking Lake Buena Vista. Amenities include remote-control cable TVs (with Spectravision movie options), safes, bedroom and bath phones, and ceiling fans. Luxurious residential-style one- and two-bedroom suites—with living rooms, dining rooms, private balconies or patios, minibars, microwave ovens, and refrigerators—are housed in a building on the property's Recreation Island; it connects to a tower building via tropically landscaped walkways. Crown rooms on the 10th floor comprise a concierge level.

Dining/Entertainment: The hotel's spot for haute cuisine, Arthur's 27 offers panoramic views of Walt Disney World parks and has an award-winning wine cellar; there's an adjoining bar with live jazz and piano-bar entertainment. In the Outback Restaurant (complete with a three-story indoor waterfall), an Australian storyteller entertains during dinner. Character breakfasts are offered in the Watercress Cafe, and there are a number of other venues for dining and drinking, including a 24-hour pastry shop and the Kookaburra Good Time Bar, which boasts a selection of 99 beers and offers live bands for dancing nightly.

Services: 24-hour room service, babysitting, 24-hour guest services desk (sells tickets to WDW parks and all other nearby attractions), complimentary newspaper at guest services, shoeshine/shoe repair.

Facilities: Two large swimming pools, whirlpool, children's wading pool, three night-lit hard-surface tennis courts, on-premises marina (offering water bikes, fling jet boats, and suncat electric boats), additional boat rental at nearby Disney Village Marina, mile jogging path, two- and three-mile jogging paths, bike rental, sand volleyball, children's playground, car-rental desk, full business center, shops, coin-op washers/dryers, large video-game arcade, oversize speaker phone phone booths for family or group calls, Kids Stuff (a counselor-supervised child-care program. A European-style spa offers massage, herbal wraps, a fully equipped health club, sauna, whirlpools, a unisex beauty salon, and more.

Hilton at Walt Disney World Village

1751 Hotel Plaza Blvd., just east of Buena Vista Dr., Lake Buena Vista, FL 32830. ☎ **407/827-4000**, or 800/782-4414. Fax 407/827-3890. 787 rms, 27 suites, A/C MINIBAR TV TEL. $145–$250 single or double. Tower rooms $40 additional. Range reflects season. Extra person $20. Children of any age stay free in parents' room. Inquire about packages and weekend rates. AE, CB, DC, DISC, ER, JCB, MC, V. Free self-parking, valet parking $6 per night.

Heralded by a palm-fringed circular driveway leading up to an imposing waterfall and fountain, the Hilton occupies 23 beautifully landscaped acres including two large lakes. Accommodations, in a vast 10-story main building with a plant-filled skylit lobby, include remote-control cable TVs with HBO and Spectravision movie options and phones with voicemail and computer jacks. The ninth and 10th floors comprise The Towers, a concierge level with a gorgeous lake-view lounge.

Dining/Entertainment: There's Finn's Grill, a Key West–themed steak and seafood restaurant; Benihana Japanese Steakhouse; a cheerful coffee shop; and several other spots. John T's Plantation Bar features light fare, exotic tropical drinks, and nighttime entertainment for dancing. Kids love the Old Fashioned Soda Shoppe for pizzas, burgers, hot dogs, not to mention malts, shakes, and sundaes; it even has video games. And a cedar gazebo is the scene of frequent live poolside entertainment.

Services: Room service from 6:30am to midnight; babysitting, concierge on duty from 7am to 10pm (sells tickets and arranges transport to all other nearby attractions/airport; WDW tickets available at the Disney shop on the lobby level), nightly bed turndown on request.

Facilities: Two very large swimming pools, two-tiered whirlpool in tropical/rock garden setting, children's spray pool, two night-lit hard-surface tennis courts, golf privileges at—and free transportation to—WDW courses, boat rental at nearby Disney Village Marina, volleyball, water volleyball, badminton, children's playground, car-rental desk, unisex beauty salon, full business center, fully equipped health club, sauna, shops, coin-op washers/dryers, large high-tech video-game arcade, Vacation Station Kids Hotel (a counselor-supervised child-care center).

MODERATE

Courtyard by Marriott, WDW Village

1805 Hotel Plaza Blvd. (between Lake Buena Vista Dr. and Apopka-Vineland Rd./FL 535), Lake Buena Vista, FL 32830. ☎ **407/828-8888,** or 800/223-9930. Fax 407/ 827-4623. 321 rms, 2 suites. A/C TV TEL. $105–$145 single or double, depending on view and season. Inquire about packages. AE, CB, DC, DISC, JCB, MC, V. Free self-parking.

This property recently underwent a $4.5 million renovation. Public areas were upgraded and rooms were refurbished and redecorated. Rooms have in-room safes, cable TVs with pay-movie options and interactive Nintendo, and coffee makers; most have balconies, and refrigerators are available on request.

Dining/Entertainment: There's a full-service restaurant serving American fare at all meals; a lobby lounge; a poolside tiki bar open in season; and an on-premises deli featuring pizza and frozen yogurt.

Services: Room service, babysitting, guest services desk (sells tickets and arranges transport to all nearby attractions; WDW park tickets are available at an on-premises shop), complimentary transport to/ from all major WDW parks and Pleasure Island.

Facilities: Two swimming pools, whirlpool, children's wading pool, boat rental at nearby Disney Village Marina, children's playground, car-rental desk, exercise room, shops, coin-op washers/dryers, large video-game arcade.

Grosvenor Resort

1850 Hotel Plaza Blvd., just east of Buena Vista Dr., Lake Buena Vista, FL 32830. ☎ **407/828-4444,** or 800/624-4109. Fax 407/828-8192. 626 rms, 7 suites. A/C TV TEL. $99–$160 for up to four people in a room. Range depends on view and season. Inquire about packages. AE, CB, DC, DISC, ER, JCB, MC, Optima, V. Free self-parking, valet parking $5 per night.

The British colonial–themed Grosvenor, on 13 lakeside acres, centers on a 19-story peach stucco building fronted by towering palms. The guest rooms have been attractively decorated in seafoam green or muted blue color schemes with splashy print bedspreads, light oak furnishings, and marble-topped desks. Walls are adorned with decorative friezes and pleasant paintings of tropical resorts. Amenities include remote-control cable TVs with VCRs (movie tapes can be rented), coffee makers (tea and coffee supplied), safes, and minibars (stocked on request); small refrigerators can be rented.

Dining/Entertainment: The rather elegant Baskervilles Restaurant, on the mezzanine, displays 19th-century Sherlock Holmes book illustrations on its walls and even has a Sherlock Holmes museum—a re-creation of his Baker Street headquarters—on the premises. Windowed walls overlook the lake. Saturday nights, Baskervilles is the scene of mystery dinner theater productions ($30 for adults, $15 for children 3 to 9). The restaurant also features buffet breakfasts and dinners (including a Disney character breakfast every Tuesday, Thursday, and Saturday morning, and a character dinner every Wednesday night). There's also a pub (with live entertainment in high season), a 24-hour food court, a pool bar, and a lounge with a large-screen TV.

Services: Room service from 7am to midnight, babysitting, guest services from 7am to 10pm (sells tickets and arranges transport to all nearby attractions; WDW park tickets are available at the Disney shop), stocked minibar on request, free newspaper delivered to your room daily on request.

Facilities: Two swimming pools (one of them quite large), whirlpool, children's wading pool, two hard-surface night-lit tennis courts, exercise room, boat rental at nearby Disney Village Marina, children's playground, lawn games (shuffleboard, volleyball, basketball, handball, horseshoes), car-rental desk, coin-op washers/dryers, shops, video-game arcade.

Guest Quarters Suite Resort

2305 Hotel Plaza Blvd., just west of Apopka-Vineland Rd./FL 535, Lake Buena Vista, FL 32830. ☎ **407/934-1000,** or 800/424-2900. Fax 407/934-1011. 229 suites. A/C TV TEL. $129–$235 for up to four people in a one-bedroom suite. Extra person $20. Children under 18 free. Range depends on view and season. $275–$395 two-bedroom suite. Inquire about packages and rates including breakfast. AE, CB, DC, DISC, JCB, MC, V. Free self-parking.

Entered via a cheerful skylit atrium lobby with an aviary of tropical birds and theme park murals, this seven-story all-suite hotel is a great choice for families. Children have their own check-in desk where they receive a free gift. Large one-bedroom suites (643 square feet)—which can sleep up to six people—are delightfully decorated with light wood furnishings and pretty floral-print fabrics. They include a full living room with a convertible sofa, dining area, and a separate bedroom. Among your in-room amenities are a wet bar, refrigerator, coffee maker (free coffee and tea supplied), microwave oven, remote-control cable TVs with pay-movie options in the living room and bedroom, a smaller black-and-white TV in the bath, two phones, and a hair dryer.

Dining/Entertainment: The festive Streamers—part of a massive renovation of public areas that took place in 1994—serves buffet and à la carte breakfasts and dinners featuring American fare with Southwestern specialties. A bar lounge adjoins, as does a theater where kids can watch Disney movies on a large-screen TV and play with toys while Mom and Dad linger over coffee. And the Cool Pool Deli & Market—comprising an awninged terrace, ice-cream parlor interior, small convenience store, and poolside bar—serves light fare and drinks.

Services: Room service from 6:30am to 11pm, babysitting, guest services desk (sells tickets to WDW parks and all other nearby attractions; also arranges transport to latter).

Facilities: Beautifully landscaped sun deck with large swimming pool, whirlpool, children's wading pool with fountain, and hammocks; two night-lit hard surface tennis courts; boat rental at nearby Disney Village Marina; jogging path; volleyball; children's playground; car-rental desk; exercise room; shops; coin-op washers/dryers; video-game arcade.

Royal Plaza

1905 Hotel Plaza Blvd., between Buena Vista Dr. and Apopka-Vineland Rd./FL 535, Lake Buena Vista, FL 32830. ☎ **407/828-2828,** or 800/248-7890. Fax

407/827-6338. 386 rms, 10 suites. A/C TV TEL. $97–$197 for up to four people in a room; $304–$550 suite. Range depends on view and season. Inquire about packages. AE, Barclaycard, CB, DC, DISC, ER, JCB, MC, Optima, V. Free self- and valet parking.

As we go to press, the 17-story Royal Plaza is a multimillion-dollar renovation and upgrade—adding two executive floors and a concierge level, and refurbishing all accommodations and public areas. By the time you read this, it should be looking great. You can watch Magic Kingdom fireworks from your furnished balcony here. And amenities include cable TVs and VCRs (movie tapes can be rented), safes, and Mickey Mouse phones; refrigerators are available on request, and deluxe rooms have wet bars. Two of the suites here are unique; they were decorated, respectively, by Barbara Mandrell and Burt Reynolds, who supplied family photographs, platinum records/acting awards, and other personal memorabilia for display.

Dining/Entertainment: A new upscale restaurant and lounge, plus a lobby bar, are in the works at this writing. There's also a lounge and a pool bar (open in season).

Services: Room service from 6am to midnight, babysitting, guest services (sells tickets and arranges transport to all nearby attractions; WDW park tickets are available at the Disney shop), overnight film developing.

Facilities: Large swimming pool, whirlpool, four hard-surface night-lit tennis courts, boat rental at nearby Disney Village Marina, sauna, shuffleboard, Ping-Pong, car-rental desk, coin-op washers/dryers, shops, video-game arcade.

Travelodge Hotel

2000 Hotel Plaza Blvd., between Buena Vista Dr. and Apopka-Vineland Rd./FL 535, Lake Buena Vista, FL 32830. ☎ **407/828-2424**, or 800/348-3765. Fax 407/828-8933. 321 rms, 4 suites. A/C MINIBAR TV TEL. $99–$169 for up to four people in a room. Range depends on room size and season. Inquire about packages. AE, CB, DC, DISC, ER, JCB, MC, Optima, V. Free self-parking.

This 12-acre lakefront property is spiffy and immaculate, with more upscale rooms and public areas than you might expect at a Travelodge. This is the company's flagship hotel. Designed to evoke a Barbados plantation manor house, it has a Caribbean resort ambience with tropical foliage and colorful floral-print fabrics and carpeting. Rooms are particularly inviting, with light-bleached wood furnishings. All accommodations have furnished balconies, many of them overlooking Lake Buena Vista. Corner king rooms with chaise lounges and convertible sofas are especially desirable. Amenities include cable TVs with Spectravision movie options, coffee makers (tea and coffee supplied), and hair dryers. Free local phone calls and in-room safes are a plus.

Dining/Entertainment: Traders is open for breakfast and dinner, the latter featuring steak and seafood. On the 18th floor, Toppers, a beautiful nightclub with windows all around, offers magnificent views of Lake Buena Vista and beyond. It's a great vantage point for watching nightly laser shows and fireworks. A DJ or live band plays Top 40s dance music. There's also a cocktail bar and a casual cafe.

Services: Room service from 7am to midnight, babysitting, guest services (sells tickets and arranges transport to all nearby attractions; WDW park tickets are available at the Disney shop), free newspaper delivered to your room weekdays.

Facilities: Large swimming pool, children's wading pool, boat rental at nearby Disney Village Marina, children's playground, car-rental desk, coin-op washers/dryers, shops, video-game arcade.

THE DOLPHIN & THE SWAN

The Dolphin and Swan, both within walking distance of Epcot, occupy some kind of middle ground between Disney properties and official hotels. They offer almost all the perks of Disney-owned properties, such as advance reservations at WDW restaurants and shows, including Epcot establishments, via the hotel concierge. Both are also distinctive for Michael Graves's fantastical architectural style, which people tend to adore or detest.

VERY EXPENSIVE

Walt Disney World Dolphin

1500 Epcot Resorts Blvd., off Buena Vista Dr., Lake Buena Vista, FL 32830-2653. ☎ **407/934-4000,** or 800/227-1500. Fax 407/934-4099. 1,370 rms, 140 suites; A/C MINIBAR TV TEL. $230–$350 single or double, depending on view and season: $310–$365 Dolphin Towers floors; $450–$2,400 suite. Extra person $15. Up to 2 children under 18 free. Inquire about packages. AE, CB, DC, DISC, ER, JCB, MC, V. Free self-parking, valet parking $6.

Designed by whimsical architect Michael Graves, the Dolphin overlooks Crescent Lake and has a beachy coral and turquoise facade centered on a 27-story pyramid. This triangular tower is flanked by two 11-story wings painted with giant banana leaves and crowned by 56-foot twin dolphin sculptures. Graves dubs his more-Disneyesque-than-Disney creations "entertainment architecture." Close to a dozen cascading fountains on the property range from a seven-dolphin extravaganza at the entrance to waters rushing across rock-faced grottoes in a fiber-optic "starlit" foyer.

A free-form rock-sculpted grotto pool—with waterfalls, a water slide, rope bridge, and three secluded whirlpools—sprawls over two acres between the Dolphin and the adjoining Swan. Both properties also share a white sandy beach on Crescent Lake. And serious sports enthusiasts will appreciate the extensive health club, boat rentals, and tennis facilities.

There are thousands of works of art in public areas. In the rooms, pastel-hued walls are hung with prints by Picasso, Matisse, Hockney, and other artists, and painted wood furnishings are stenciled with palm trees and pineapples. Amenities include cable TVs with HBO and pay-movie options, desk and bedside phones, safes, coffee makers, hair dryers, and irons/ironing boards. The Dolphin Towers comprise a 77-room concierge level where guests are greeted with chilled champagne and enjoy complimentary continental breakfast, cocktail-hour hors d'oeuvres, and late-night desserts in a private lounge. Other Towers perks include a private concierge, express check-in/checkout, complimentary health club use, upgraded bath amenities, and terry robes.

Dining/Entertainment: The elegant Sum Chows serves haute-cuisine Chinese, Japanese, Vietnamese, and Thai dinners. There are a number of other venues, including Juan and Only's Bar & Jail for moderately priced Tex-Mex fare; Harry's Safari Bar & Grille, open for dinner nightly and for Sunday character brunch buffets; and a casual cafe; an ice-cream shop; a 24-hour cafeteria; Copa Banana, with a DJ spinning tunes for nightly dancing; a lobby lounge; and a poolside bar.

Services: 24-hour room service, water launch transport to Epcot and Disney-MGM Studios, concierge, guest services desk (sells tickets and arranges transport to all nearby attractions), Japanese tour desk, babysitting, complimentary daily newspaper.

Facilities: See also facilities at the Swan, below. Water volleyball, boat rentals, eight hard-surface night-lit tennis courts, tennis pro shop, fully equipped Body by Jake health club (including sauna, whirlpool, massage, personal training, aerobics classes, body wraps), two beach volleyball courts, three-mile jogging trail, coin-op washers/dryers, unisex hair salon, shops, full business center, car-rental desk, Delta Air Lines desk, large video-game arcade, Camp Dolphin (a counselor-supervised children's activity center, open daily).

Walt Disney World Swan

1200 Epcot Resorts Blvd., off Buena Vista Dr. (P.O. Box 22786), Lake Buena Vista, FL 32830-2786. ☎ **407/934-3000**, or 800/248-SWAN or 800/228-3000. Fax 407/934-4499. 702 rms, 56 suites. A/C MINIBAR TV TEL. $260–$380 single or double, depending on view and season; $330–$380 concierge floors; $300–$1,700 suite. Extra person $25. Children under 18 free. Inquire about packages. AE, CB, DC, DISC, ER, JCB, MC, V. Free self-parking, valet parking $7.

Operated by Westin Hotels & Resorts, this 12-story aquamarine and adobe-peach hotel—its rooftop flanked by 45-foot swan statues and seashell fountains—is adjacent to, and shares a white-sand lakeside beach and facilities with, the above-mentioned Dolphin. The hotels are connected by a canopied walkway. Here Michael Graves has created a festive interior replete with swan fountains, sea horse–motif chandeliers, hallway walls painted with beach scenes, and striped room doors evocative of cabanas. Luxurious accommodations, decorated in cheerful pastels, have Drexel Heritage furnishings stenciled with parrots and pineapples, swan- and palm-tree motif lamps, and walls hung with prints by Matisse, Cézanne, and other artists. In-room amenities include cable TVs with HBO and pay-movie options, desk and bedside phones, safes, and baths with double sinks. King-bedded rooms have pullout sleeper sofas. The 11th and 12th floors comprise the Royal Beach Club, a concierge level.

Dining/Entertainment: The casually elegant Italian-*moderne* Palio has large windows that overlook scenic canals; strolling musicians entertain while you dine. An exhibition kitchen affords an appetizing view of pizzas being placed in a wood-fired brick oven. Open for dinner nightly. There's also a casual cafe with twice-weekly character breakfasts and character dinners Monday and Thursday nights. Evenings the Grove serves steaks and prime rib, and in the morning, a traditional Japanese breakfast is an option. The handsome Kimono's serves a wide selection of sushi; open from 4pm daily, it becomes a karaoke bar after 8:30pm. There's also a lobby lounge, a grill and deli overlooking the pool, and a poolside bar.

Services: 24-hour room service, babysitting, complimentary water launch to Epcot and Disney-MGM Studios, guest services desk, concierge, complimentary daily newspaper; nightly turndown on request.

Facilities: See also facilities at the Dolphin, above. Olympic-size lap pool, children's wading pool, fully equipped health club with sauna and massage therapy, full business center, car-rental desk, unisex hair salon, children's playground, shops, video-game arcade, Camp Swan (a counselor-supervised child-care/activity center).

3 Other Lake Buena Vista Area Hotels

All of the below-listed are within a few minutes' drive of WDW parks.

VERY EXPENSIVE

✪ Hyatt Regency Grand Cypress/Villas of Grand Cypress

1 Grand Cypress Blvd., off FL 535, Orlando, FL 32836. ☎ **407/239-1234**, or 800/ 233-1234. Fax 407/239-3800. For villas ☎ 407/239-4700, or 800/835-7377. Fax 407/239-7219. 676 rms, 74 suites, 146 villas. A/C MINIBAR TV TEL. $185–$325 for up to five people in a room; $350–$420 Regency Club; $150–$1,120 villa. Range reflects room size, view, and season. Inquire about packages. AE, CB, DC, DISC, ER, JCB, MC, V. Free self-parking, valet parking $8 per night.

This dazzling multifacility resort is in a class by itself. With a beautiful swimming pool with waterfalls and waterslides, incredible golf and tennis facilities, and an equestrian center, it's the perfect place for an active vacation. The tropical plantings of the atrium lobby comprise a small rain forest with stone-bedded streams and live birds in brass cages. Outside, the Hyatt's gardeners have created an Edenic 1,500-acre botanic garden, dotted with babbling brooks, beautiful flower beds, charming outdoor sculpture, and rock gardens ablaze with bougainvillea and hibiscus. Colorful sailboats and swans glide serenely on 21-acre Lake Windsong. Thousands of palms sway in the breeze; dogwood, trumpet trees, and crape myrtle bloom in season; and native oaks, pines, and cypresses create canopies of shade.

Accommodations are deluxe, with grasspaper wall coverings and oak armoires that house cable TVs with Spectravision movie options. Amenities include ceiling fans, safes, and, in the bath, hair dryers, cotton robes, bathroom scales, and fine toiletries. Two floors comprise the Regency Club, a concierge level with a gorgeous lake-view lounge.

And especially luxurious are one- to four-bedroom Mediterranean-style **Villas of Grand Cypress** accommodations, with fully equipped kitchens, patios, living rooms, and dining rooms. Many have working fireplaces and whirlpool bathtubs. Large picture windows overlook the golf course. Villa guests enjoy deluxe services and amenities.

Dining/Entertainment: Hemingway's and the Black Swan are reviewed in Chapter 6. There are 11 other venues as well—from the elegant La Coquin, where a harpist entertains diners while they enjoy Asian-influenced French cuisine, to the Rock Hyatt Club, which offers movies, music, and games for teens 13 to 17.

Services: 24-hour room service, babysitting, concierge (sells tickets to WDW parks and other nearby attractions), free transportation around property via shuttle buses and restored Victorian trolleys, hourly shuttle between the hotel and all WDW parks (round-trip fare is $5 a day), Mears airport shuttle.

Facilities: Half-acre lagoonlike swimming pool spanned by a rope bridge and flowing through rock grottoes (with 12 waterfalls and two steep water slides), three secluded whirlpools, white-sand beach, 12 tennis courts (eight clay, four hard-surface, six lit for night play), award-winning 45-hole/par-72 Jack Nicklaus–designed golf course, nine-hole pitch-and-putt golf course, golf and tennis instruction/pro shops, equestrian center (lessons, trail rides), bicycle rental, boat rental, 4.7-mile jogging path, 45-acre Audubon nature walk through pristine marshland with elevated boardwalks and descriptive signage, racquetball/volleyball/shuffleboard courts, croquet, children's playground, car-rental desk, unisex beauty salon, full business center, state-of-the-art health club (offering sauna, steam, massage, and aerobics classes), shops, helicopter landing pad, large high-tech video-game arcade, counselor-supervised child-care center/Camp Hyatt activity center, teen activities program.

EXPENSIVE

Cypress Pointe Resort

8651 Treasure Cay Lane, off Apopka-Vineland Rd. (FL 535), Lake Buena Vista, FL 32830. ☎ **407/238-2300,** or 800/749-8651. Fax 407/238-2886. 104 2- and 3-bedroom suites. A/C TV TEL. $175 two-bedroom suite for up to six people; $225 three-bedroom suite for up to nine people. Inquire about packages. AE, CB, DC, DISC, MC, V. Free self-parking.

This luxurious top-level vacation-ownership resort property is entered via a plant-filled lobby, with cages of tropical birds and an aquarium of colorful fish behind the registration desk. Very spacious accommodations (three-bedroom suites are 1,490 square feet) are housed in dormer-windowed stucco buildings painted in pleasing pastels with white trim—a very Caribbean look. They're simply gorgeous, with plushly furnished living rooms (equipped with large-screen TVs, VCRs, and CD/cassette players), large dining areas, additional dining set-ups on screened patios, fully equipped kitchens, whirlpools big enough for two in master bedrooms, and baths for each bedroom. Amenities abound—washers dryers, irons and ironing boards, TVs and phones in living room and two bedrooms, and ceiling fans in all rooms (including the patio). Cypress Pointe is just minutes from Disney's main gate and adjacent to the Disney Village Marketplace.

Dining/Entertainment: Breakfast and light lunches are available poolside from a cabana bar, and beer and pizza are options during free movies shown nightly in an upstairs recreation room. Numerous restaurants are close by, many of which deliver food to the premises; you'll find a menu roster in your room.

Services: Guest services desk (sells tickets to WDW parks and other nearby attractions, most of them discounted), airport shuttle, babysitting. Round-trip fare to WDW parks is $7.

Facilities: Vast swimming pool with waterfall and "erupting volcano" whirlpool, sand volleyball court, basketball/shuffleboard courts,
tennis court, children's playground and ball crawl, well-equipped health
club, game room (Ping-Pong, darts, football), organized resort activities (movie nights, pool games, etc.), 24-hour convenience store (with
movie rentals), small video-game arcade.

❂ Marriott's Orlando World Center

8701 World Center Dr., on FL 536 between I-4 and FL 535, Orlando, FL 32821.
☎ **407/239-4200,** or 800/621-0638. Fax 407/238-8777. 1,504 rms, 85 suites.
A/C MINIBAR TV TEL. $155–$199 for up to five people in a room (range reflects
season). Pool-view room $10 additional per night. 14-day advance-purchase rates are
$124–$154, subject to availability. $265–$2,400 suite. Inquire about packages and
rates including full buffet breakfast. AE, CB, DC, DISC, ER, JCB, MC, Optima, V. Free
self-parking, valet parking $8 per night.

This sprawling 230-acre resort, just two miles from WDW parks, is
one of Florida's top venues for meetings and conventions. And the excellent service and array of facilities that make it so popular with corporate executives also make it a great choice for tourists—especially for
travelers who are serious about their golf or tennis game. It's terrific for
families, too, with lots of children's activities available. A grand
palm-lined driveway, flanked by rolling golf greens, leads to the main
building—a massive 27-story tower fronted by flower beds and fountains. In its 12-story atrium lobby, tropical plants and palms flourish
in sunlight streaming through a lofty skylight, museum-quality 16th-
and 17th-century chinoiseries and fine paintings set an elegant tone,
and the sound of splashing fountains blends with soft piano music.

The tower houses spacious guest rooms cheerfully decorated in pastel
hues with bamboo and rattan furnishings. All have desks, sofa beds,
large closets (in which you'll find an iron and ironing board), and
patios or balconies. Amenities include safes, cable TVs (with HBO,
extensive pay-movie options, and video account review/message
retrieval), and hair dryers in the bathrooms. Step outside the tower and
you'll find magnificently landscaped grounds, with shaded groves of
pines and magnolias and cascading waterfalls; black and white swans
and ducks inhabit over a dozen lakes and lagoons spanned by graceful
arched bridges.

Dining/Entertainment: Mikado Japanese Steak House and
Tuscany are reviewed in Chapter 6. JW's Steakhouse is one of my
favorite places in town for breakfast or lunch on a screened balcony that
yields beautiful views of the lagoon and golf greens or for cozy dinners
in the rustic pine interior. There's also Allie's American Grille for
family dining; Champion's, a sports bar; nightly piano-bar entertainment; and several other spots for light fare.

Services: 24-hour room service, babysitting, concierge from 7am
to 11pm, shoeshine, nightly bed turndown on request, newspaper
delivered to your room weekdays, Mears transportation/sightseeing
desk (sells tickets to all nearby attractions, including WDW parks; also
provides transport, by reservation, to WDW, other attractions, and airport), one-hour film developing. Round-trip fare between hotel and
WDW parks is $5 per day, free for children under 12.

Facilities: Three swimming pools (including a vast indoor pool, a larger-than-Olympic free-form pool with water slides and waterfalls, and a smaller pool with a volleyball net), four whirlpools, large children's wading pool, eight night-lit hard-surface tennis courts, 18-hole/par-71 Joe Lee–designed championship golf course, golf and tennis pro shops/instruction, 18-hole miniature golf course, two-mile jogging path, two volleyball courts, car-rental desk, unisex beauty salon, very extensive business center, state-of-the-art health club (offering sauna, massage therapy, and aerobics classes), coin-op washers/dryers, shops video-game arcade, Lollipop Lounge (a counselor-supervised child-care/activities center). Inquire as well about organized children's activities—games, movies, nature walks, and more.

✪ Residence Inn by Marriott

8800 Meadow Creek Dr., just off FL 535, between Hwy. 536 and I-4, Orlando, FL 32821. ☎ **407/239-7700**, or 800/331-3131. Fax 407/239-7605. 688 suites. A/C TV TEL. $159–$179 one-bedroom suite accommodating up to four people, $179–$209 two-bedroom suite accommodating up to six people. Range reflects season. Inquire about packages. (Rates include full breakfast.) AE, CB, DC, DISC, ER, JCB, MC, V. Free self-parking.

This delightful all-suite property, a converted luxury apartment complex, occupies 50 magnificently landscaped acres, with neatly manicured lawns, duck-filled ponds, fountains, and flower beds shaded by tall palms, pine trees, live oaks, and magnolias. Guests enjoy the seclusion of a private community (you have to drive through a security gate to enter) and can avail themselves of the extensive facilities at the adjoining Marriott Orlando World Center (see details above) with room-charge privileges. A lighted walkway connects the two properties via a gorgeous golf course.

Accommodations, housed in 86 two-story cream stucco buildings with Spanish-style terra-cotta roofs, are tastefully decorated. All offer fully equipped eat-in kitchens (some with washing machines and dryers), private balconies or patios, very ample closet space, and large, comfortable living rooms with sleeper sofas. Amenities include cable TVs (with HBO, Spectravision movie options, and VCRs; movie tapes can be rented), two phones (kitchen and bedroom), ceiling fans, and safes. Two-bedroom units have two baths.

Dining/Entertainment: Breakfast is available in the gatehouse each morning. Many guests enjoy this meal al fresco on a covered open-air veranda overlooking the pool. A Pizza Hut is on the premises. Local restaurants also deliver food (there are menus in each room), and, of course, there are quite a few restaurants at the adjoining Marriott.

Services: Guest services desk (sells tickets and provides transport to all nearby theme parks and attractions; round-trip to Disney parks costs $6), babysitting, complimentary daily newspaper, free shuttle transport around the property, next-day film developing, free food-shopping service from an in-house store, Mears airport shuttle.

Facilities: Three large swimming pools (one with a rock waterfall), two beautiful secluded whirlpools, sports court (basketball, badminton, volleyball, paddle tennis, shuffleboard), one night-lit hard-surface tennis court, children's playground, coin-op washers/dryers, shops, two small video-game arcades. Do note all the additional facilities available to guests here at Marriott's Orlando World Center (see listing above).

Summerfield Suites Lake Buena Vista

8751 Suiteside Dr., off Apopka-Vineland Rd. (FL 535), Lake Buena Vista, FL 32836. ☎ **407/238-0777**, or 800/833-4353. Fax 407/238-0778. 150 suites. A/C TV TEL. $169–$209 one-bedroom suite for up to four people; $199–$249 two-bedroom suite for up to eight people. Range reflects season. Inquire about packages. (Rates include continental breakfast.) AE, CB, DC, DISC, MC, V. Free self-parking.

This all-suite property, just minutes from Disney's main gate and adjacent to the Disney Village Marketplace, is an excellent choice for families. Immaculate accommodations in three-story terra-cotta–roofed stucco buildings surround a palm-fringed brick courtyard with fountains, big pots of flowering plants, umbrella tables, and gazebos. Spacious residential-style suites are attractively decorated in peach and teal with bleached oak furnishings. They contain fully equipped eat-in kitchens, comfortable living rooms with convertible sofas, big walk-in closets, and large dressing areas. Two-bedroom units have two baths, and all bedrooms have doors (ensuring privacy). Amenities include irons and ironing boards, phones in each bedroom and the kitchen (with two lines, computer hookup, and voice-mail messaging), cable TVs in each bedroom and the living room (with free HBO, attraction-information stations, and pay-movie options), and VCRs (a wide selection of movies can be rented). In-room safes are available for a nominal charge.

Dining/Entertainment: Guests enjoy continental breakfast in the pleasant dining room or at umbrella tables in the courtyard. An on-premises deli (which sells liquor as well as light fare) has a service window on the courtyard to serve swimmers and sunbathers. Local restaurants deliver food to the premises; you'll find a menu in your room.

Services: Room service from in-house deli, guest services desk (sells tickets to WDW parks and other nearby attractions, many of them discounted), shuttle available to airport and nearby attractions, free newspaper delivered to your room daily, complimentary grocery shopping, babysitting. Most important: There's free scheduled transport to and from the Disney parks throughout the day, representing a big savings for families.

Facilities: Large swimming pool, whirlpool, children's wading pool, car-rental desk, full business services, exercise room, coin-op washers/dryers, convenience shop, small video-game arcade.

Vistana Resort

8800 Vistana Center Dr., off FL 535, between I-4 and FL 536, Lake Buena Vista, FL 32830. ☎ **407/239-3100**, or 800/877-8787. Fax 407/239-3062. 972 1- and 2-bedroom villas. A/C TV TEL. $115–$275 for up to six to eight people, range depending on season. Inquire about packages and weekly rates. AE, CB, DC, DISC, MC, Optima, V. Free self-parking.

This deluxe property offers stunning one- and two-bedroom, two-bath villas and extensive resort facilities on 135 beautifully landscaped acres encompassing shimmering lakes (home to ducks and black swans) and cascading waterfalls. There are fabulous swimming pools and outstanding tennis facilities. Accommodations are individually furnished and decorated, though most utilize beachy resort pastels, bleached woods, wicker, and bamboo. All offer full living rooms (with convertible sofas and cable TVs equipped with VCRs), full dining areas (often there's a second dining set-up on the patio), two bedrooms (each with a TV and phone) fully equipped kitchens, washers and dryers, and patios or balconies (some screened, many overlooking scenic waterways). Some master bedroom baths have whirlpool tubs, and there are ceiling fans in many rooms.

Dining/Entertainment: The gardenlike Flamingo Cafe & Lounge—with seating at canvas umbrella tables and windows overlooking a weeping willow–shaded pond—specializes in steak, seafood, and pasta entrées. It's open for buffet breakfasts and à la carte lunches and dinners. Kids love the Flamingo's create-your-own-sundae bar. There's also a casual spot called Zimmie's and a poolside bar.

Services: Babysitting, overnight photo processing, grocery shopping (you can have your room prestocked with food on request). Two guest services desks provide conciergelike assistance, also sell tickets (many of them discounted), and arrange transportation to/from all nearby attractions. Transportation to/from Disney parks is free.

Facilities: Six swimming pools (one of them an immense free-form affair with a rock waterfall, water volleyball, and water slide), five children's wading pools, seven outdoor whirlpools (some secluded), 13 tennis courts (nine clay, four hard-surface, all lit for night play), tennis pro shop/instruction, 18-hole/par-38 miniature golf course, basketball/sand volleyball/shuffleboard courts, bicycle rental, raft rental, children's playgrounds, full health club and recreation center (including sauna, steam, tanning salon, massage), game library, outdoor barbecue grills, $1^1/2$-mile/12-station jogging path, general store (includes movie-rental library), three video-game arcades. A comprehensive daily activities schedule for adults and children includes nature walks, casino nights, Ping-Pong tournaments, arts and crafts, barbecues, karaoke, and much, much more.

MODERATE

⑤ Holiday Inn Sunspree Resort Lake Buena Vista

13351 FL 535, between FL 536 and I-4, Lake Buena Vista, FL 32821. ☎ **407/ 239-4500,** or 800/FON-MAXX. Fax 407/239-7713. 507 rms. A/C TV TEL. $89–$129 for up to four people in a room, depending on the season. Inquire about packages. AE, CB, DC, DISC, JCB, MC, V. Free self-parking.

About a mile from Disney parks, this Holiday Inn caters to children in a big way. Kids "check-in" at their own pint-size desk and receive a free fun bag containing a video-game token coupon, a lollipop, and a small gift. And they're personally welcomed by animated raccoon mascots (Max and Maxine). Camp Holiday activities—magic shows, clowns, bingo, movies, sing-alongs, video games, arts and crafts, storytelling, and much more—cost $3 for up to four hours, $5 for five to eight hours, for kids 2 to 12. And parents can arrange (by reservation) for Max to come tuck a child into bed. Accommodations—in a six-story peach stucco building—are decorated in aqua, peach, and teal, with bleached oak furnishings, tropically themed paintings, and shell-motif lamps. All rooms have kitchenettes with refrigerators, microwave ovens, and coffee/tea makers. Amenities include cable TVs with local attraction-information channels, VCRs (tapes can be rented), hair dryers, and safes. Local calls are free. Open-air hallways add to the resort ambience.

Dining/Entertainment: Max's Funtime Parlor, serving free hot and cold hors d'oeuvres during happy hour, offers nightly bingo (with prizes) and karaoke; it also airs sporting events on a large-screen TV. There's also Maxine's, Pinky's Diner, and a poolside bar and grill. Kids 12 and under eat all meals free, either in a hotel restaurant with parents or in Kid's Kottage—a cheerful facility where movies and cartoons are shown on a large-screen TV and dinner includes a make-your-own-sundae bar.

Services: Room service from 7am to 2pm and 5pm to midnight, babysitting, guest services desk (sells tickets to all nearby attractions, including Walt Disney World parks), free scheduled transport to the Magic Kingdom/Epcot/Disney-MGM Studios (there's a charge for transport to other nearby attractions), telephone grocery shopping, Mears airport shuttle.

Facilities: Large free-form swimming pool with lovely palm-fringed sun deck, two whirlpools, children's wading pool, poolside Ping-Pong and billiards, innovative children's playground, fitness center, coin-op washers/dryers, shops, car-rental desk, video-game arcade, Camp Holiday (a counselor-supervised child-care/activity center for ages 2 to 12, open from 8am to midnight; parents can rent beepers to keep in touch with kids).

Wyndham Garden Hotel

8688 Palm Pkwy., between FL 535 and I-4, Lake Buena Vista, FL 32830. ☎ **407/239-8500,** or 800/228-2846. Fax 407/239-8591. 164 rms. 3 suites. A/C TV TEL. $69–$99 single or double, depending on season; $125–$150 suites. Extra person $10. Children under 12 free. AE, CB, DC, DISC, ER, Optima, MC, V. Free self-parking.

Located on a pleasant tree-lined parkway and overlooking a lake out back, the Wyndham Garden is completing a massive renovation as we go to press. All public areas have been given a fresh new look, and rooms have been redecorated with bleached pine furnishings and cheerful resort-themed prints. All are equipped with cable TVs (with pay movies, a tourism-information station, and Nintendo), hair dryers, and coffee makers; some have convertible sofas. The Crossroads Shopping Center and Walt Disney World Village put dozens of shops, services, and restaurants in easy walking distance. And to compete with nearby "official" hotels, the Wyndham offers free shuttle transport to/from Disney parks.

Dining/Entertainment: The Garden Café, serving American fare at breakfast and dinner, has an outdoor poolside seating area with white canvas umbrella tables. A bar/lounge adjoins.

Services: Room service, complimentary shuttle to/from Disney parks, guest services desk (sells tickets, many of them discounted, and arranges transport to all nearby attractions), babysitting, complimentary daily newspaper.

Facilities: Nice-sized swimming pool and whirlpool, coin-op washers/dryers, exercise room, business center, small video game arcade.

INEXPENSIVE

⑤ Comfort Inn

8442 Palm Pkwy., between FL 535 and I-4, Lake Buena Vista, FL 32830. ☎ **407/239-7300** or 800/999-7300. Fax 407/239-7740. 640 rms. A/C TV TEL. $39–$69 for up to four people. Range reflects season. Inquire about packages. AE, CB, DC, DISC, MC, V. Free self-parking.

This is an ideally located, large, and attractively landscaped property with two small manmade lakes amid expanses of manicured lawn and lush greenery. It offers great value for your hotel dollar, including free transport to/from Disney parks which are just two miles away. Immaculate rooms are housed in five-story stucco buildings. The Boardwalk Buffet, a sunny restaurant with windows all around, offers reasonably priced buffet meals at breakfast and dinner; kids 11 and under eat free. The Comfort Zone, a bar/lounge, adjoins. And complimentary tea and coffee are served in the lobby every afternoon. The guest services desk sells tickets (most of them discounted) and provides transport to all nearby theme parks, dinner shows, and the airport. On-premises facilities include two nice-sized swimming pools, coin-op washers/dyers, a snack-vending machine area, a gift shop, and video-game arcade. Pets are permitted.

4 Accommodations on U.S. 192/Kissimmee Area

This very American stretch of highway dotted with fast-food eateries isn't what you'd call scenic, but it does contain many inexpensive hotels within one to eight miles of WDW parks.

MODERATE

⑤ Holiday Inn Maingate East

5678 Irlo Bronson Memorial Hwy. (U.S. 192), between I-4 and Poinciana Blvd., Kissimmee, FL 34746. ☎ **407/396-4488,** or 800/FON-KIDS. Fax 407/396-8915. 670 rms. A/C TV TEL. $75–$105 for up to four people in a room, depending on the season. Inquire about packages. AE, CB, DC, DISC, JCB, MC, V. Free self-parking.

Just three miles from the entrance to the Magic Kingdom, Holiday Inn Maingate East, occupying 23 attractively landscaped acres, offers identical facilities to the Holiday Inn Sunspree Resort Lake Buena Vista described above—including its own Camp Holiday and all the kid-pleaser features (here the welcoming mascots are Holiday and Holly Hound). There's even a small merry-go-round in the lobby. Accommodations, in two-story motel-style buildings enclosing courtyard swimming pools, are decorated in muted blue and peach. Pets are permitted at this location.

Dining/Entertainment: There's a casual cafe, a food court, and a pool bar. Kids 12 and under eat all meals free, either in a hotel restaurant with parents or in the Gingerbread House—a cheerful facility where movies and cartoons are shown on a large-screen TV and dinner includes a make-your-own-sundae bar.

Services: Room service from 7am to 2pm and 5:30 to 10pm, baby-sitting, guest services desk (sells tickets to all nearby attractions, including Walt Disney World parks), free scheduled transport to the Magic Kingdom/Epcot/Disney-MGM Studios (there's a charge for transport to other nearby attractions), telephone grocery shopping, Mears airport shuttle.

Facilities: Two Olympic-size swimming pools, two whirlpools, children's wading pool, children's playground, two night-lit hard-surface tennis courts, sand volleyball, basketball court, coin-op washers/dryers, shops, car-rental desk, two video-game arcades, Camp Holiday (a counselor-supervised child-care/activity center for ages 3 to 12, open from 2 to 10pm; cost is $1 per hour per child, and parents can rent beepers to keep in touch with kids).

☺ Residence Inn by Marriott on Lake Cecile

4786 W. Irlo Bronson Memorial Hwy., between FL 535 and Siesta Lago Dr., Kissimmee, FL 34746. ☎ **407/396-2056,** or 800/468-3027. Fax 407/396-2909. 159 suites. A/C TV TEL. $115–$119 studio accommodating up to four people; $125–$129 studio double (up to four people); $169–$189 bi-level penthouse (up to six people). Range reflects season. (Rates include extended continental breakfast.) AE, CB, DC, DISC, ER, JCB, MC, Optima, V. Free self-parking.

This all-suite property has attractively landscaped grounds on the banks of beautiful 223-acre Lake Cecile. Like many Residence Inns, its accommodations are in two-story residential-looking cream stucco buildings fronted by neatly manicured lawns. Suites have fully equipped eat-in kitchens (the maid does your dishes) and comfortable living room areas with sleeper sofas. All but studio doubles have wood-burning fireplaces (logs are available), and cathedral-ceilinged penthouses have full baths upstairs and down. Many suites offer balconies overlooking the lake. Amenities include cable TVs (VCRs are available on request) and in-room safes.

Dining/Entertainment: The lovely gatehouse lounge off the lobby, with big, comfy sofas facing a working fireplace, is the setting for an extended continental breakfast each morning. And an al fresco bar serves light fare and frosty drinks poolside on a canopied wooden deck with umbrella tables. Local restaurants deliver food (there are menus in each room).

Services: Guest services desk (sells tickets—most of them discounted—and provides transport to all nearby theme parks and attractions), complimentary daily newspaper, free food-shopping service. Round-trip fare to WDW parks is $7.

Facilities: Small swimming pool, whirlpool, sports court (basketball, volleyball, badminton, paddle tennis), children's playground, coin-op washers/dryers, 24-hour food shop, picnic tables, barbecue grills. Lake activities include fishing, jet skiing, bumper rides, and waterskiing.

INEXPENSIVE

Colonial Motor Lodge

1815 W. Vine St. (U.S. 192), between Bermuda and Thacker aves., Kissimmee, FL 34741. ☎ **407/847-6121,** or 800/325-4348. Fax 407/847-0728. 83 rms, 40 apts. A/C TV TEL. $22.95–$50 for up to four people. $44.95–$89.95 for up to six people

Kissimmee Area Accommodations

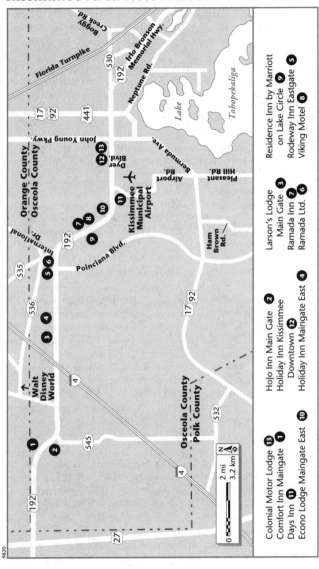

Colonial Motor Lodge ⑬
Comfort Inn Maingate ①
Days Inn ⑪
Econo Lodge Maingate East ⑩

Hojo Inn Main Gate ②
Holiday Inn Kissimmee Downtown ⑫
Holiday Inn Maingate East ④

Larson's Lodge Main Gate ③
Ramada Inn ⑦
Ramada Ltd. ⑥

Residence Inn by Marriott on Lake Circle ⑨
Rodeway Inn Eastgate ⑧
Viking Motel ⑤

Airport ✈

in a two-bedroom apt. Range reflects season. (Rates include continental breakfast.) AE, DC, DISC, MC, V. Free self-parking.

This well-run motor lodge is entered via a white colonial-style building with peach columns and shutters and a Federalist eagle over the door. The pleasantly furnished lobby is the setting for a free continental breakfast each morning. Snacks and fruit juices are sold in vending machines. Standard motel rooms offer cable TVs with HBO.

Two-bedroom apartments, in two-story white buildings fronted by small gardens, represent a good choice for families. In addition to two full bedrooms, they have living rooms and fully equipped eat-in kitchens.

Facilities include two Junior Olympic-size outdoor pools and a kiddie pool. Adjacent to the Colonial are an International House of Pancakes and a shopping center with a dry cleaner and coin-op laundry. The Black Angus, a steak and seafood restaurant, is across the street. And a supermarket, 7-Eleven, Hardy's, and Kentucky Fried Chicken are a block away. Guest services sells tickets to all Disney parks and nearby attractions (some of them discounted) and offers paid transportation to/from them and the airport. Round-trip transport to Disney parks is $12 per person.

Comfort Inn Maingate

7571 W. Irlo Bronson Memorial Hwy. (U.S. 192), between Reedy Creek Blvd. and Sherbeth Rd., Kissimmee, FL 34747. ☎ **407/396-7500,** or toll free 800/221-2222. Fax 407/396-7497. 281 rms. A/C TV TEL. $33–$65 for up to four people, depending on the season. Garden rooms $6–$10 additional. AE, CB, DC, DISC, ER, JCB, MC, V. Free self-parking.

Just one mile from Disney parks, this Comfort Inn houses clean, spiffy-looking standard motel accommodations in two-story peach stucco buildings. More upscale are garden rooms facing a lawn with a gazebo; they're equipped with small refrigerators, coffee makers, and hair dryers. The Royal Palms Restaurant on the premises serves low-priced buffets and à la carte meals. A comfortable bar/lounge adjoins. And right next door are a 7-Eleven and an International House of Pancakes. The guest services desk sells tickets (most of them discounted) and provides transport to all nearby attractions and the airport; round-trip fare to WDW parks is $7. Facilities include a medium-sized swimming pool, children's playground, coin-op washers/dryers, and a small video-game arcade.

Days Inn

4104 and 4125 W. Irlo Bronson Memorial Hwy. (U.S. 192), at Hoagland Blvd. N., Kissimmee, FL 34741. ☎ **407/846-4714,** or 800/647-0010 or 800/DAYS-INN. Fax 407/932-2699. 194 rms, 32 efficiency units. A/C TV TEL. $29–$59 for up to four people, depending on season; $37–$63 efficiency unit; $55–$75 Jacuzzi room (for one or two people). Rates may be higher during major events. (Rates include continental breakfast.) AE, CB, DC, DISC, ER, MC, V. Free self-parking.

These two Days Inn properties on either side of U.S. 192 share facilities, which include coin-op washers and dryers, a gift shop, two swimming pools, and a small video-game arcade. Several restaurants (which deliver food), a large shopping mall with a 12-theater movie house, and a supermarket are in close walking distance. Rooms at both locations are clean and attractive standard motel units. Best bet are efficiency units with fully equipped kitchenettes (two-burner stoves, sinks, small refrigerators) at 4104. On the other hand, at 4125 you can ask for a room with a large Jacuzzi, a refrigerator, and a microwave oven. All accommodations offer cable TVs (with free HBO and pay-movie options) and in-room safes, and both locations serve a free continental breakfast in their lobbies each morning. Guest services at 4104 sells tickets (many of them discounted) and arranges transport to all nearby attractions, including WDW parks. Round-trip fare to WDW parks $9. Airport transfers can also be arranged.

⑤ Econo Lodge Maingate East

4311 W. Irlo Bronson Memorial Hwy. (U.S. 192), between Hoagland Blvd. and FL 535, Kissimmee, FL 34746. ☎ **407/396-7100,** or 800/ENJOY-FL. Fax 407/239-2636. 173 rms. A/C TV TEL. $29–$79 for up to four people in a room, depending on the season. AE, CB, DC, DISC, JCB, MC, V. Free self-parking.

At this attractively landscaped Econo Lodge, accommodations are set well back from the highway in rustic two- and three-story buildings with cedar balconies and roofing. Well-maintained standard motel rooms are equipped with cable TVs and safes; small refrigerators can be rented. Snacks and soft drinks are sold in the lobby, and the pool bar serves light fare, including full breakfasts and lunches at umbrella tables under towering live oaks. The guest services desk sells tickets (most of them discounted) and provides transport to all nearby attractions and the airport. And a big plus: scheduled round-trip transport to/from WDW parks is free. On-premises facilities include a large swimming pool, children's pool, volleyball, shuffleboard, horseshoes, coin-op washers/dryers, picnic tables, barbecue grills, and a small video-game arcade. Guests' children under 12 eat free at all meals at a nearby International House of Pancakes. This is one of six area hotels under the same ownership, all of which can be booked via the above toll-free number.

Hojo Inn Main Gate

6051 W. Irlo Bronson Memorial Hwy. (U.S. 192), just east of I-4, Kissimmee, FL 34747. ☎ **407/396-1748,** or 800/288-4678. Fax 407/649-8642. 358 rms, 9 family suites. A/C TV TEL. $60–$75 for up to four people, depending on the season. Children under 19 stay free. Add $10 for an efficiency unit with a kitchenette. $80–$95 family suite. Inquire about packages. AE, CB, DC, DISC, JCB, MC, V. Free self-parking.

This Howard Johnson's property just two miles from the Magic Kingdom offers attractive accommodations housed in pristine white stucco two- and three-story buildings. Completely renovated in 1992, they're nicely decorated with quilted bedspreads and beach-themed paintings on the walls. In-room amenities include cable TVs (with pay-movie options) and safes. Efficiency units have fully equipped kitchenettes with small refrigerators, two-burner stoves, and sinks. And family suites have both full kitchens and living rooms with convertible sofas.

Facilities here include a medium-sized swimming pool, whirlpool, kiddie pool, children's playground, coin-op washers/dryers, small 24-hour video-game arcade, car-rental desk, and pool table. Adjoining the property is a large water park called Watermania and an International House of Pancakes open from 7am to 11pm (where kids under 12 with an adult eat free). On premises, a pool bar serves light fare and drinks, and coffee and tea are served each morning, in the lobby. Guest services sells tickets to all Disney parks and nearby attractions (some of them discounted) and offers transportation to/from them and the airport. Transport to Disney parks is $7 per person round-trip. *Note:* You can call guest services at 800/TOUR-FLA in advance of your trip to arrange attractions tickets, paid transportation, car rental, and other vacation needs.

⑤ Holiday Inn Kissimmee Downtown

2009 W. Vine St. (U.S. 192), at Thacker Ave., Kissimmee, FL 34741. ☎ **407/846-2713**, or 800/624-5905. Fax 407/846-8695. 200 rms. A/C TV TEL. $39–$79 for up to four people, depending on the season. Add $10 for an efficiency unit with a kitchenette. AE, CB, DC, DISC, MC, V. Free self-parking.

Just eight miles from Walt Disney World, this Holiday Inn offers immaculate motel units equipped with cable TVs and in-room safes. There are also efficiency units here with living room areas and fully equipped kitchens. Pets are permitted. There's a steakhouse and a bar lounge on the premises.

Services: Room service during restaurant hours, guest services desk (sells tickets, many of them discounted, to all nearby theme parks, including WDW), scheduled shuttle bus between the property and all WDW parks (round-trip fare is $10); transport is also available to other nearby attractions and the airport.

Facilities: Two swimming pools (one very large), kiddie pool, whirlpool, children's playground, night-lit hard-surface tennis court, gift/sundries shop, coin-op washers/dryers, video-game arcade.

⑤ Larson's Lodge Main Gate

6075 W. Irlo Bronson Memorial Hwy. (U.S. 192), just east of I-4, Kissimmee, FL 34747. ☎ **407/396-6100**, or 800/327-9074. Fax 407/396-6965. 128 rms. A/C TV TEL. $39–$79 single or double, depending on the season. Extra person $8. Children under 18 stay free. Add $15 for an efficiency unit with a kitchenette. AE, CB, DC, DISC, MC, V. Free self-parking.

With its large, on-premises water park (Watermania), children's playground, and poolside picnic tables and barbecue grills, Larson's Lodge is a good choice for families. It has a cheerful on-site Shoney's restaurant (open from 6am to midnight). Accommodations are standard motel units with bleached oak furnishings. They're equipped with cable TVs (VCRs and movie tapes can be rented), coffee makers, and in-room safes. Efficiency units have fully equipped kitchenettes with sinks, two-burner stoves, small refrigerators, and microwave ovens. A supermarket is just a few minutes away by car.

The guest services desk sells tickets to all nearby theme parks, including WDW (many of them discounted), and a shuttle bus plies the route between the property and all WDW parks at scheduled times throughout the day (round-trip fare is $8). Transport is also available to other nearby attractions and the airport. On-premises facilities include a large swimming pool and whirlpool, shops, 24-hour photo developing, coin-op washers/dryers, and a small video-game arcade. Guests enjoy free use of the tennis court at the above-mentioned Holiday Inn Kissimmee Downtown. Pets are permitted.

Ramada Inn

4559 W. Irlo Bronson Memorial Hwy. (U.S. 192), between Siesta Lago Dr. and Bass Rd./Old Vineland Rd., Kissimmee, FL 34746. ☎ **407/396-1212**, or 800/446-5669. Fax 407/396-7926. 114 rms. A/C TV TEL. $23.95–$40.95 for up to four people, depending on season; $6 per night additional for efficiency unit. AE, DC, DISC, MC, V. Free self-parking.

This Ramada offers standard motel rooms equipped with cable TVs (with free HBO) and safes; refrigerators are available on request for $6 a night. Efficiency units offer two-burner stoves, extra sinks, and small refrigerators (no eating or cooking utensils are provided). Facilities include coin-op washers/dryers, a swimming pool, children's playground, and picnic tables. The 1950s-style Hollywood Diner—which has an adjoining bar/lounge—serves American fare at all meals; one child under 12 per paying adult eats free. Shuttle service to WDW parks is available for $9 per person, round-trip. Pets are accepted.

Ramada Ltd.

5055 W. Irlo Bronson Memorial Hwy. (U.S. 192), between Poinciana Blvd. and FL 535, Kissimmee, FL 34746. ☎ **407/396-2212,** or 800/446-5669. Fax 407/396-0253. 107 rms. A/C TV TEL. $27.95–$45 for up to four people, depending on season. (Rates include continental breakfast.) AE, DC, DISC, MC, V. Free self-parking.

Less than four miles from Walt Disney World parks, this Ramada houses its rooms in a three-story stucco building. Accommodations are standard motel rooms with oak furnishings, splashy floral-print bedspreads, cable TVs (with Disney channel and free HBO movies), and safes; refrigerators are available on request for $6 a night. Facilities include a swimming pool and coin-op washers/dryers. Continental breakfast is served in the lobby each morning. Shuttle service to WDW parks is available for $8 per person, round-trip. Pets are accepted.

Rodeway Inn Eastgate

5245 W. Irlo Bronson Memorial Hwy. (U.S. 192), between Poinciana and Polynesian Isle blvds., Kissimmee, FL 34746. ☎ **407/396-7700,** or 800/423-3864. Fax 407/396-0293. 200 rms. A/C TV TEL. $31–$55 for up to four people. Range reflects view and season. Rates may be higher during major events. AE, CB, DC, DISC, ER, JCB, MC, V. Free self-parking.

The Rodeway's U-shaped configuration of two-story pink stucco buildings form an attractively landscaped courtyard around a large swimming pool. There are picnic tables and a children's play area on the lawn. Rooms are nicely decorated in teal, aqua, and mauve, with oak furnishings.

The on-site Terrace Restaurant serves buffet breakfasts, and the comfy Half Time Lounge, where sporting events are aired on a seven-by-seven-foot screen, has a pool table and dart boards. Other facilities include a small video-game arcade off the lobby, coin-op washers/dryers, and a shop selling gifts and sundries. Guest services sells tickets to all Disney parks and nearby attractions (many of them discounted) and offers transportation to/from them and the airport. Transport to Disney parks is $7.50 per person round-trip.

Viking Motel

4539 W. Irlo Bronson Memorial Hwy. (U.S. 192), between FL 535 and Hoagland Blvd. N., Kissimmee, FL 34746. ☎ **407/396-8860,** or 800/396-8860. Fax 407/396-2088. 49 rms. A/C TV TEL. $25–$60 single or double, depending on season. Extra person $5. Add $10 for kitchenette units. AE, DISC, MC, V. Free self-parking.

Kids love this family-owned property housed in a fantasy castle, with towers topped by little Viking ships. Owners Bert and Christine Langenstroer are from Germany, and they've prettified their motel's

Alpine-style balconies with neat flower boxes. Immaculate rooms have peach stucco walls hung with old-fashioned lithograph portraits in oval frames and kitschy landscape paintings. All are equipped with cable TVs (with free HBO), safes, and Magic Fingers bed massagers, and some have refrigerators. A few units offer kitchenettes with two-burner stoves, small refrigerators, sinks, microwave ovens, toasters, and coffee makers; these units also have cozy breakfast nooks. On-premises facilities include coin-op washers/dryers, a shuffleboard court, a Viking-themed playground and sandbox, and a small free-form swimming pool with outdoor tables under thatched umbrellas and barbecue grills on the sun deck. A Waffle House restaurant and a miniature golf course are next door. The guest services desk sells tickets, many of them discounted, to nearby attractions, though it does not carry WDW park tickets. Transportation is, however, available to WDW parks (round-trip fare is $8 per person), other area attractions, and the airport. The Viking is six miles from the Magic Kingdom.

5 Accommodations on International Drive

Properties listed here are 7 to 10 miles north of WDW parks and close to Universal Studios and Sea World.

EXPENSIVE

✪ The Peabody Orlando

9801 International Dr., between Beeline Expy. and Sand Lake Rd. (across from the Civic Center), Orlando, FL 32819. ☎ **407/352-4000,** or 800/PEABODY. Fax 407/351-0073. 834 rms, 57 suites. A/C MINIBAR TV TEL. $210–$250 for up to three people in a room; $270 Peabody Club; $375–$1,300 suite. Children under 18 free. Seniors 50 and over pay $89. Inquire about packages as well as holiday and summer discounts. AE, CB, DC, DISC, ER, JCB, MC, V. Free self-parking, valet parking $6 per night.

This deluxe 27-story resort hotel—its porte-cochère facade fronted by splashing fountains, waterfalls, and lush tropical plantings—has some especially famous avian residents. Every morning at 11am, five fluffy ducks proudly parade along a red carpet to the beat of John Philip Sousa's *King Cotton* march, their journey culminating at a marble fountain in the lobby. They frolic there throughout the day, until the duckmaster directs them back to their "Royal Duck Palace" at 5pm. But ducks are just a fillip here. The Peabody, in the grand hotel tradition, pampers guests with sumptuous surroundings and attentive service. Its skylit atrium lobby and other public areas are enhanced by stunning displays of live orchids, towering palms, bamboo, ficus, and magnolia trees. Luxurious rooms have bamboo and bleached wood furnishings and walls hung with quality artwork. Amenities include two phones (bedroom and bath) with two lines and modern capacity, cable TVs with Spectravision and laser-disc movie set-ups (more than 500 movies are available from a video library), and, in the bath, cosmetic lights, fine European toiletries, a hair dryer, and a small TV. The concierge-level Peabody Club, with rooms on the top three floors, offers individualized concierge service and a beautiful lounge.

Dining/Entertainment: Dux, Capriccio, and the 24-hour B-Line Diner are reviewed in Chapter 6. A singer and trio perform jazz, blues, and show tunes in the atrium Lobby Bar nightly from 8pm to 1:30am. The lobby is also the setting for weekday afternoon teas with petit fours, pastries, scones with Devonshire cream, and finger sandwiches. There are two other bars as well, and al fresco jazz concerts take place on the fourth-floor recreation level spring and fall.

Services: 24-hour room service, babysitting, 24-hour concierge, shoeshine, nightly bed turndown on request, free newspaper delivered to your room daily, "Double Ducker" shuttle bus making round-trip runs between the hotel and all WDW parks throughout the day (unlimited daily round-trips cost $6), Mears transportation/sightseeing desk (sells tickets to all nearby attractions, including WDW parks and dinner shows; also provides transport, by reservation, to attractions and airport).

Facilities: Olympic-length swimming pool, indoor and outdoor whirlpools, large children's wading pool with waterfall fountain, four hard-surface night-lit tennis courts, golf privileges at four nearby courses, seven-mile jogging path, car-rental desk, Delta Air Lines desk, unisex beauty salon, full business center, state-of-the-art health club (offering tanning, sauna, steam, massage therapy, Nautilus, and aerobics classes), shops, small video-game arcade. Hot-air balloon rides, deep-sea fishing, scuba lessons, and other amusements/excursions can be arranged.

MODERATE

Courtyard by Marriott

8600 Austrian Court, off International Dr. between Sand Lake Rd. and Beeline Expy. (Hwy. 528), Orlando, FL 32819. ☎ **407/351-2244,** or 800/321-2211. Fax 407/351-1933. 140 rms, 11 suites. A/C TV TEL. $89 single, $99 double (for up to four people); suite $119 single, $129 double (for up to four people). Extra person $10. AE, CB, DC, DISC, MC, V. Free self-parking.

Located in a secluded complex of hotels and restaurants off International Drive, the Courtyard is fronted by lush tropical plantings, and most of its rooms overlook a landscaped central courtyard with a gazebo that is ideal for picnics. Courtyard is a moderately priced link in the Marriott chain, with lower prices achieved via limited services (for instance, there's no bellman, though you can get a luggage cart). But don't envision a Spartan, no-frills atmosphere. The rooms are furnished in mahogany pieces and equipped with cable TVs (with HBO, Spectravision movie, and visitor-information channels), nice-sized dressing area, and boiling-water dispensers for making tea or coffee (both available free at the front desk). King- bedded rooms have sleeper couches. And spacious suites have full sofa-bedded living rooms with extra phones and TVs plus small refrigerators. Accommodations facing the courtyard have patios.

Dining/Entertainment: A plant-filled lobby restaurant serves full and continental buffet breakfasts daily. The adjoining plushly furnished lounge, which has a working fireplace and a TV, serves overstuffed subs and frozen tropical drinks from 4 to 10pm Monday through Friday.

In addition, several local eateries deliver food (there are menus in each room).

Services: The guest services desk sells tickets (most of them discounted) and provides transport to all nearby theme parks and attractions and the airport. Round-trip fare to WDW parks costs $10.

Facilities: Swimming pool, whirlpool, exercise room, small video-game arcade, coin-op washers/dryers.

⑤ Heritage Inn Orlando

9861 International Dr., between Beeline Expy. and Sand Lake Rd., Orlando, FL 32819. ☎ **407/352-0008**, or 800/447-1890. Fax 407/352-5449. 150 rms. A/C TV TEL. $59–$139 single or double, depending on view and season. Extra person $10. Up to two children under 18 free. Inquire about packages. AE, CB, DC, DISC, ER, MC, V. Free self-parking.

Centered on a white-trimmed pale-peach octagonal building crowned by a windowed cupola, the Heritage Inn evokes 19th-century Florida—the leisurely era of riverboat travel and gracious plantations. Ceiling fans whirr slowly over verandas and balconies furnished with wicker rocking chairs, and a charmingly landscaped courtyard with neat lawns and flower beds encompasses a large free-form swimming pool backed by verdant woodlands and a wide canal. The balustraded Victorian lobby, flanked by graceful staircases and housing an elegant dining room, is handsomely furnished in period pieces. Overhead, you'll view the beautiful cupola—painted peach and Wedgwood green—from within. Charming guest rooms are housed in two-story peach buildings on either side of the octagon. Furnished in handsome maple or mahogany pieces, they have dark teal carpeting and ecru walls adorned with floral friezes and 19th-century folk art. French doors open onto patios, balconies, or courtyards, and baths have art nouveau lighting fixtures. In-room amenities include cable TVs with free HBO and Spectravision movie options, phones with modem jacks, wood-bladed chandelier ceiling fans, safes, and small refrigerators. Larger deluxe rooms offer sleeper sofas, microwave ovens, and hair dryers.

Dining/Entertainment: The Plantation Dining Room is open for all meals, including a Sunday champagne brunch, at which a pianist entertains; it offers a moderately priced American menu. The Victorian-look Front Porch Lounge, with oak parquet floors, a pressed-tin ceiling, and lace-curtained French doors, is popular with locals. It features happy hour buffets weekdays from 5:30 to 7pm.

Services: Room service from 7 to 10:30am and 6 to 10pm, guest services desk (sells tickets, many of them discounted, and arranges transport to all nearby attractions, including WDW parks), babysitting, Mears airport shuttle. Round-trip fare to WDW parks costs $9.

⑤ Orlando Marriott

8001 International Dr., at Sand Lake Rd., Orlando, FL 32819. ☎ **407/351-2420**, or 800/421-8001. Fax 407/351-5016. 1,060 rms, 16 suites. A/C TV TEL. $79–$120 single or double, depending on view and season; $110–$300 suite. Extra person $10. Children under 18 stay free. Inquire about packages. AE, DC, DISC, MC, V. Free self-parking.

This verdant 48-acre resort contrasts neatly manicured lawns and flower beds with dense stands of palm, fern gullies, lush tropical foliage, sprightly fountained pools, and serene lagoons. Accommodations, housed in pale pink stucco bi-level villas, are attractively decorated in resort mode, with light wood and bamboo/rattan furnishings. Half have balconies or patios, and about a fifth offer full kitchens. In-room amenities include TVs with free HBO and pay-movie stations, safes, and desk and bedside phones. Many are also equipped with hair dryers, electric shoeshine machines, and irons/ironing boards.

Dining/Entertainment: There are several restaurants and bars, including a 24-hour Pizza Hut to satisfy late-night cravings. At Illusions, a DJ plays Top 40 tunes. If you don't feel like dancing, there's a blackjack table (you can't win money; it's just for fun), a pool table, and an electric dart board. Complimentary hors d'oeuvres are served daily from 5 to 7pm.

Services: Room service from 6am to 11pm (pizza available 24 hours), babysitting, guest services desk (sells tickets, many of them discounted, and arranges transportation to/from Disney parks and all other nearby attractions), 24-hour free tram service around the property, Mears airport shuttle. Round-trip fare to WDW parks costs $8.

Facilities: Three swimming pools (one quite large), two children's wading pools, whirlpool, four hard-surface night-lit tennis courts, sand volleyball court, children's playground, exercise room, 1.4-mile jogging trail, coin-op washers/dryers, car rental, unisex hair salon, shops, two video-game arcades.

Residence Inn by Marriott

7975 Canada Ave., just off Sand Lake Rd. a block east of International Dr., Orlando, FL 32819. ☎ **407/345-0117,** or 800/227-3978. Fax 407/352-2689. 176 suites. A/C TV TEL. $94 studio accommodating up to four people, $105 studio double (up to four people); $144 bi-level penthouse (up to six people). Inquire about packages. (Rates include extended continental breakfast.) AE, MC, V. Free self-parking.

Marriott's Residence Inns are designed to offer home-away-from-home comfort. Accommodations, in two-story residential-looking brick and stucco buildings with weathered pine trim, are surrounded by neatly manicured lawns, shrubbery, and beds of geraniums. Staying here is like having your own Orlando apartment, with a private entrance and a large, fully equipped eat-in kitchen. Suites are handsomely decorated. All have comfortable living room areas with convertible sofas; all but studio doubles have wood-burning fireplaces, and penthouses have full baths upstairs and down. Amenities include cable TVs with free HBO, alarm clocks, and in-room safes.

Dining/Entertainment: The comfortably furnished gatehouse, off the lobby, is the setting for an extended continental breakfast daily, and complimentary beer, wine, soft drinks, and hors d'oeuvres Monday to Thursday from 5 to 7pm. Guests can also enjoy breakfast and snacks outdoors at umbrella tables by the pool. Local restaurants deliver food (there are menus in each room).

Services: Guest services desk (sells tickets—most of them discounted—and provides transport to all nearby theme parks and attractions), complimentary daily newspaper, free food-shopping service, Mears airport shuttle. Round-trip fare to WDW parks costs $7.

Facilities: Swimming pool, whirlpool, basketball court, sand volleyball court, free use of Bally health club nearby, coin-op washers/dryers, food shop, picnic tables, barbecue grills.

⊙ Summerfield Suites

8480 International Dr., between Beeline Expy. and Sand Lake Rd. (near the Civic Center), Orlando, FL 32819. ☎ **407/352-2400,** or 800/833-4353. Fax 407/352-4631. 146 suites. A/C TV TEL. $149–$189 one-bedroom suite (for up to four people), $169–$229 two-bedroom suite (for up to eight people). Range reflects room size and season. Inquire about packages. (Rates include continental breakfast.) AE, CB, DC, DISC, MC, V. Free self-parking.

This delightful five-story cream stucco hotel is built around a nicely landscaped central courtyard. Open-air balconies adorned with potted plants serve as hallways, creating a welcoming resort ambience. Spacious, neat-as-a-pin residential-style suites, very attractively decorated, contain fully equipped eat-in kitchens, comfortable living rooms, big walk-in closets, and large dressing areas. Two-bedroom units have two baths, and you'll find a large desk in the master bedroom. Amenities include irons and ironing boards, phones (with two lines, computer hookup, and voice-mail messaging) in each bedroom and the kitchen, and satellite TVs (with free HBO, attraction-information station, and pay-movie options) in each bedroom and the living room (the latter with a VCR; rent your choice of 200 movies downstairs). A large shopping center is across the street, WDW parks are about 15 minutes away by car, Sea World and Universal Studios are very close, and numerous restaurants are in the area. This is a great choice for families.

Dining/Entertainment: Continental buffet breakfast is served in a charming dining room. In addition, made-to-order omelets and Belgian waffles can be purchased. The cozy lobby bar is a popular gathering place evenings. And local restaurants (you'll find a menu roster in your room) deliver food to the premises.

Services: Babysitting, concierge/tour desk (sells tickets to WDW parks and other nearby attractions), newspapers delivered to your room daily, transport between the hotel and all WDW parks (round-trip fare is $7), shuttle available to airport and nearby attractions, complimentary grocery shopping.

Facilities: Nice-sized swimming pool with fountain and bilevel sun deck, whirlpool, children's wading pool, car-rental desk, full business services, exercise room, coin-op washers/dryers, 24-hour shop, small video-game arcade.

INEXPENSIVE

⊙ Fairfield Inn by Marriott

8342 Jamaican Court, off International Dr. between Sand Lake Rd. and Beeline Expy. (Hwy. 528), Orlando, FL 32819. ☎ **407/363-1944,** or 800/228-2800. Fax 407/363-1944. 134 rms. A/C TV TEL. $35–$70 for up to four people. Range reflects season. (Rates include continental breakfast.) AE, CB, DC, DISC, JCB, MC, V. Free self-parking.

Jamaican Court, in a secluded area off International Drive, is a neatly landscaped complex of hotels and restaurants, including this handsome three-story property. It has spiffy-looking rooms decorated in rust, tan, and Federalist blue with oak furnishings. In-room amenities include cable TVs with free HBO and attractions-information channels, and phones equipped with 25-foot cords and modem jacks. Daily newspapers and local calls are free. A continental breakfast is served in the lobby each morning. In addition, there are many freestanding and hotel restaurants right in Jamaican Court, and several local eateries deliver food (there are menus in each room).

The guest services desk sells tickets (most of them discounted) and can arrange transport to all nearby theme parks and attractions and the airport; round-trip to Disney parks costs $10. There's a small swimming pool and a video-game room on the premises, and the lobby has a microwave oven for guests' use.

6 At the Airport

Hyatt Regency Orlando International Airport

9300 Airport Blvd., Orlando, FL 32827. ☎ **407/825-1234,** or 800/233-1234. Fax 407/856-1672. 420 rms, 23 suites. A/C TV TEL. $165 single, $190 double; $225–$450 suite. Extra person $25. Children under 18 free. AE, CB, DC, DISC, ER, JCB, MC, V. Self-parking $8, valet parking $11.

If you have to catch an early-morning flight out of Orlando, treat yourself to a night at this gorgeous multifacility hotel right in the airport's main terminal. It's luxurious from the moment you set foot in the plush 40,000-square-foot palm court atrium lobby. Large, resort-style rooms—off balconies bordered by planters of bougainvillea or philodendrons—are attractively decorated and equipped with large desks, three phones (desk, bedside, and bath), cable TVs (with Spectravision movie, tourism-information, and flight arrival/departure channels), full-size ironing boards/irons, and hair dryers. Rooms are soundproofed so you don't hear planes taking off and landing.

Dining/Entertainment: The elegant Hemisphere Restaurant serves sophisticated American fare at lunch, northern Italian specialties at dinner; a pianist entertains weekend nights. McCoy's Bar & Grill centers on a display kitchen with an oak-burning pizza oven. You can also avail yourself of all the airport eateries, including a food court.

Services: 24-hour concierge/room service, shoeshine, car rental, babysitting, full business center, currency exchange.

Facilities: Airport shopping mall, airline desks, unisex hair salon, swimming pool, fully equipped health club, travel agency.

6

Dining

Since most Orlando visitors spend the majority of their time in the Walt Disney World area, I've focused on the best dining choices there. Also listed are some worthwhile restaurants beyond the realm. Parents will be pleased to note that just about every place in town offers a low-priced children's menu and usually provides some kind of kid's activity (mazes, coloring books, paper dolls) as well. *Note:* Since the clientele at even the fanciest Epcot World Showcase restaurants are coming directly from the parks, you don't have to dress up for dinner. See also listings for dinner shows in Chapter 9.

Listings are divided by the following price categories: **very expensive** (dinner, typically, is more than $40 per person for a full meal, including a glass of wine, tip, and tax), **expensive** ($30 to $40), **moderate** ($20 to $30), **inexpensive** ($20 and under). Keep in mind that the above categories refer to dinner prices, and some very expensive restaurants offer affordable lunches. Also, I'm going by the assumption that you're not stinting when you order. Some restaurants, for instance, have entrées ranging from $12 to $20. In most cases, you can dine for less if you order carefully. My favorite restaurants are marked with a star, those offering particularly good value for the money with a dollar sign.

1 Best Bets

Best for Kids   Kids adore the meals with Disney characters offered at almost all Walt Disney World resorts. The Sci-Fi Dine-In Theater at Disney-MGM Studios is also fun.

Best Spot for a Romantic Dinner   The elegant candlelit Dux at The Peabody Orlando combines a warmly inviting ambience with great food.

Best Spot for a Business Lunch   Much of the restaurant clientele in this town consists of screaming kids. Generally, Hemingway's, an upscale Key West–style restaurant at the Hyatt Regency Grand Cypress, is kid-free, and its intimate dining areas are perfect for business lunches.

Best Spot for a Celebration   Victoria & Albert's at Disney's Grand Floridian Beach Resort, where a seven-course feast is flawlessly served in an exquisite setting by a maid and butler.

Best Decor   Victoria & Albert's once again, with its plush Louis XIII–style furnishings, brocaded walls, and central dome. Also notable: La Venezia Cafe in Winter Park, where the interior includes six Tiffany windows.

Best View   La Coquina at the Hyatt Regency Grand Cypress, with big windows overlooking swans and flamingos on Lake Windsong and verdant landscaping.

Best Wine List   Once again, it's Dux at the Peabody Orlando.

Best Value   Hearty all-you-can-eat family-style meals served up in iron skillets at the Whispering Canyon Cafe, at Disney's Wilderness Lodge.

Best American Cuisine   The Fireworks Factory—for American regional fare ranging from Cajun shrimp pasta to smoked baby back ribs.

Best Chinese Cuisine   Ming Court, featuring delicacies from all regions of China, can compete with New York's best Chinese restaurants.

Best Barbecue   Wild Jack's, an upscale Wild West–themed restaurant with an open-pit exhibition kitchen; try the smoked brisket here.

Best Italian Cuisine   Northern Italian fare at the sophisticated Capriccio, in The Peabody Orlando. Also the sedate and elegant Tuscany at Marriott's Orlando World Center.

Best Seafood   The 19th-century–style clambake buffet at the Cape May Cafe at Disney's Beach Club Resort—seafood stews, clams, mussels, lobster, and more cooked in a rockwood steamer pit.

Best Tapas   Cafe Tu Tu Tango takes the tapas (tasting portion) concept international with items ranging from Cajun egg rolls to Thai salad.

Best Steakhouse   The Yachtsman Steakhouse at Disney's Yacht Club Resort, where aged prime steaks, chops, and seafood are grilled over oak and hickory.

Best Desserts   La Venezia Cafe in Winter Park, which also has the best coffees to accompany its oven-fresh creations.

Best Late-night Dining   The trendy B-Line Diner at The Peabody Orlando, open round the clock for eclectic fare ranging from filet mignon to a falafel sandwich.

Best Character Breakfast   The Coral Reef, in Epcot's Living Seas Pavilion, where Mickey dives into a 5.6-million gallon aquarium inhabited by more than 4,000 sea creatures.

Best Outdoor Dining   The terrace at Artist Point, the premier restaurant at Disney's Wilderness Lodge, overlooks a lake, waterfall, and scenery evocative of America's national parks.

Best People Watching   It can only be Planet Hollywood!

Best Afternoon Tea   The Garden View Lounge at Disney's Grand Floridian Beach Resort—a plushly furnished venue amid potted palms with a wall of Palladian windows overlooking formal gardens; a pianist entertains while you dine on tea sandwiches and scones. The Peabody Orlando hosts afternoon tea in its gorgeous skylit atrium lobby. And frolicking in a nearby fountain while you sip your Earl Grey are the Peabody's five resident ducks.

Best Brunch   It's a tie: Capriccio at The Peabody Orlando and La Coquina at the Hyatt Regency Grand Cypress, both of which offer lavish buffets of first-rate fare with free-flowing champagne.

2 In Walt Disney World

The following listings encompass restaurants at the Magic Kingdom, Epcot, Disney-MGM Studios, and Walt Disney World Village.

How to Make Reservations at WDW Restaurants

You can make restaurant reservations up to 60 days in advance at almost all full-service Magic Kingdom, Epcot, Disney-MGM Studios, resort, and Disney Village Marketplace restaurants—as well as character meals and shows throughout the complex—by calling **407/ WDW-DINE.** Nighttime shows can actually be booked as far in advance as you wish. Exceptions to this reservations format are noted in the listings below.

Since this advance-reservation phone number was instituted in 1994, it has become much more difficult to obtain on-the-spot reservations. So I strongly advise you to avoid disappointment by planning ahead.

However, if you don't reserve in advance, you can take your chances reserving in the parks themselves:

At Epcot: Make reservations at the WorldKey interactive terminals at Guest Relations in Innoventions East, at Worldkey Information Service Satellites located on the main concourse to World Showcase and at Germany in World Showcase, or at the restaurants themselves.

At the Magic Kingdom: Reserve at the restaurants themselves; Diamond Horseshoe reservations can also be made at Disneyana Collectibles on the east side of Main Street.

At Disney-MGM Studios: Make reservations at the Hollywood Junction Station on Sunset Boulevard or at the restaurants themselves.

- All park restaurants have nonsmoking interiors; you can smoke on patios and terraces.
- Magic Kingdom restaurants serve no alcoholic beverages, but liquor is available at Epcot and Disney-MGM eateries and elsewhere in the WDW complex.
- All sit-down restaurants in Walt Disney World take American Express, MasterCard, Visa, and the Disney Card.
- Guests at Disney resorts and official properties can make restaurant reservations through guest services or concierge desks.
- All WDW restaurants offer low-priced children's menus.

AT EPCOT

An ethnic meal at one of the World Showcase pavilions is part of the Epcot experience. However, the major restaurants are expensive, so you might also want to consider the many lower-priced cafeterias throughout the park that require no reservations. Some are listed below; consult your **Epcot Guidemap** for additional suggestions. Almost all of the establishments listed below offer lunch and dinner daily (hours vary with park hours).

WORLD SHOWCASE

These restaurants are arranged geographically, beginning at the Canada pavilion and proceeding counterclockwise around the World Showcase Lagoon.

Canada   Located in the Victorian Hotel du Canada, with its French Gothic facade and steeply pitched copper roofs, **Le Cellier** has a castlelike ambience with seating in tapestried chairs under vaulted stone arches, and amber light emanating from black wrought-iron sconces. It's a self-service buffeteria, for which no reservations are required. Regional dishes include Cheddar cheese soup, poached fresh salmon, a pork- and potato-filled pie called tourtière, chicken and meatball stew, maple syrup pie, and Canadian beers. Appetizers cost $2.50 to $5.20; entrées $6.75 to $8.75 at lunch, $8.95 to $15.25 at dinner.

United Kingdom   The plank-floored **Rose & Crown,** entered via a cozy pub with a pungent aroma of ale, evokes Victorian England with beamed Tudor ceilings, and English and Scottish folk music. It additionally offers outdoor seating at umbrella tables overlooking the lagoon—a good place to watch IllumiNations. Servers in period costume enhance the village-inn ambience. The menu features traditional items like fish-and-chips, steak-and-kidney pie, and sherry trifle. Dinner might begin with an appetizer of Scotch egg (a hard-boiled egg encased in sausage meat, fried, and served cold with mustard sauce). Continue with an entrée of prime rib with Yorkshire pudding, conclude with raspberry fool (whipped cream and crushed raspberries atop a shortbread cookie), and wash it all down with a pint of Irish lager beer, Bass ale, or Guinness stout. Appetizers are $3.95 to $7.20; lunch entrées $9.25 to $11.50, dinner entrées $10.75 to $20.75. Traditional afternoon tea, with scones, pastries, and finger sandwiches, is served daily at 4pm; cost is $9.95.

Note: Rose & Crown reservations can be made up to seven days in advance (not 60) via WDW-DINE.

France   **Chefs de France** is under the auspices of a world-famous culinary triumvirate—Paul Bocuse, Roger Vergé, and Gaston LeNôtre. Its art nouveau/fin-de-siècle interior is agleam with mirrors and brass candelabra chandeliers. Etched-glass and brass dividers create intimate dining areas and tables are elegantly appointed. To start off, I recommend the seafood cream soup with crab dumplings (as featured by Vergé at Moulin de Mougins). Entrée selections at dinner include a superb broiled salmon in sorrel cream sauce à la façon de Bocuse (it's served with ratatouille and new potatoes) and Vergé's sautéed beef tenderloin with raisins and brandy sauce. Classic French desserts range from LeNôtre's soufflé Grand-Marnier to a pêche Melba crêpe filled with peaches and vanilla ice cream and topped with raspberry sauce. The distinguished chefs also composed the restaurant's wine list, any item of which can be purchased at Au Palais du Vin, a wine shop in the pavilion. Appetizers cost $3.75 to $7.75 at lunch, $3.75 to $8.50 at dinner; entrées $8.95 to $14.95 at lunch, $15.95 to $24.25 at dinner.

The ✪ **Bistro de Paris,** upstairs from Chefs de France and serving dinner only, offers similar fare in a more serene country-French setting. Also under the auspices of Bocuse, Vergé, and LeNôtre, it's rather elegant, with seating in burgundy tufted-leather banquettes, French windows, candlelit white-linened tables, and art nouveau lighting fixtures. Highlights here include Bocuse's duck foie gras salad appetizer with fresh greens and artichoke hearts, and Vergé's classic bouillabaisse served with garlic sauce and croutons. Another notable entrée: Bocuse's roast red snapper wrapped in thin-sliced potato crust and served on a bed of sautéed spinach with red wine lobster sauce. Stay with Bocuse for dessert; his crème brûlée is unbeatable. Appetizers cost $7.95 to $13.95, entrées $20.50 to $26.95.

Lighter fare is available throughout the day at **Au Petit Café,** a sidewalk bistro adjacent to Chefs de France on an awninged terrace overlooking the lagoon. It's a great venue for watching IllumiNations. Traditional café fare is featured—ham and cheese-filled croissants or crêpes, quiche Lorraine, salade niçoise, and a few heartier entrées such as chicken baked in puff pastry with port wine cream sauce and brochette of prawns with rice and basil butter. No reservations are required. Entrées range from $7.75 to $14.95.

And the **Patisserie/Boulangerie,** its interior redolent of baking croissants and pastries, offers tempting French treats—apple turnovers, eclairs, quiches, chocolate mousse, and French coffees and wines.

Morocco The palatial ✪ **Restaurant Marrakesh**—with its hand-set mosaic tilework, latticed teak shutters, and intricate cut-brass chandeliers suspended from a ceiling painted with elaborate Moorish motifs—represents 12 centuries of Arabic design. Exquisitely carved faux-ivory archways frame the central dining area, where belly dancers perform to *oud, kanoun,* and *darbuka* music. The Moroccan *diffa* (traditional feast) that lets you sample a variety of dishes is recommended. At dinner it includes a hearty saffron-seasoned harira soup flavored with onions, tomatoes, lentils, and lamb; beef *brewats* (minced beef seasoned with coriander, ginger, cinnamon, and saffron, rolled in thin pastry layers, and fried); roast lamb served with almond- and raisin-studded rice; braised tagine of chicken with green olives and preserved lemon; couscous with seasonal vegetables; Moroccan pastries; and mint tea. Combination appetizer plates are another way to experience culinary diversity. French and Moroccan wines are available to complement your meal. Appetizers cost $3.75 to $5.95, entrées $9.95 to $12.95 at lunch, $13.50 to $19.95 at dinner; Moroccan diffa is $29.95 for two at lunch, $49.95 for two at dinner.

Epcot Dining

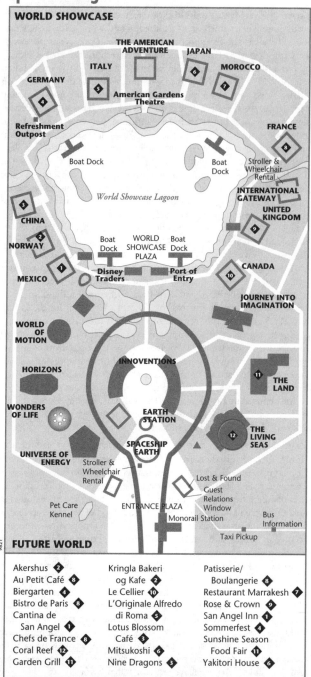

WORLD SHOWCASE

THE AMERICAN ADVENTURE

JAPAN

MOROCCO

ITALY

GERMANY

American Gardens Theatre

Refreshment Outpost

FRANCE

Boat Dock

Boat Dock

Stroller & Wheelchair Rental

World Showcase Lagoon

INTERNATIONAL GATEWAY

CHINA

UNITED KINGDOM

NORWAY

Boat Dock

WORLD SHOWCASE PLAZA

Boat Dock

MEXICO

Disney Traders

Port of Entry

CANADA

JOURNEY INTO IMAGINATION

WORLD OF MOTION

INNOVENTIONS

HORIZONS

THE LAND

WONDERS OF LIFE

EARTH STATION

THE LIVING SEAS

SPACESHIP EARTH

UNIVERSE OF ENERGY

Stroller & Wheelchair Rental

Lost & Found

Guest Relations Window

Pet Care Kennel

ENTRANCE PLAZA

Monorail Station

Bus Information

Taxi Pickup

FUTURE WORLD

Akershus ②
Au Petit Café ⑧
Biergarten ④
Bistro de Paris ⑧
Cantina de
 San Angel ①
Chefs de France ⑧
Coral Reef ⑫
Garden Grill ⑪

Kringla Bakeri
 og Kafe ②
Le Cellier ⑩
L'Originale Alfredo
 di Roma ⑤
Lotus Blossom
 Café ③
Mitsukoshi ⑥
Nine Dragons ③

Patisserie/
 Boulangerie ⑧
Restaurant Marrakesh ⑦
Rose & Crown ⑨
San Angel Inn ①
Sommerfest
Sunshine Season
 Food Fair ⑪
Yakitori House ⑥

Japan   The **Mitsukoshi Restaurant** centers on a teppanyaki steakhouse where diners sit at grill tables and white-hatted chefs rapidly dice, slice, stir-fry, and propel cooked food onto your plate with amazing dexterity. Kids especially love watching the chef wield his cleaver and utensils. Intimate dining areas are created by lacquered shoji screens, and walls are embellished with murals and paintings. Since you share a table with strangers, teppanyaki makes for a convivial dining experience. An elaborate dinner for two (of which an abbreviated version is available at lunch) includes a shrimp appetizer, green salad with ginger dressing, soup (ask for the *miroshiru*—soybean soup with tofu and mushrooms), grilled fresh vegetables with udon noodles, succulent morsels of grilled beef tenderloin and lobster, steamed rice, choice of dessert (perhaps chestnut cake), and green tea. And even à la carte entrées include plenty of extras. Kirin beer, plum wine, and sake are among your beverage options, along with specialty drinks (some of them nonalcoholic for kids) such as *tachibana* (light rum, orange curaçao, and mandarin orange juice). Appetizers cost $4.95 to $5.95; entrées $15.50 at lunch, $14.50 to $24.95 at dinner; complete dinner described above costs $39 for two at lunch, $59 for two at dinner.

Adjoining the teppanyaki rooms is a U-shaped **tempura counter** where you can eat shrimp, scallops, chicken, and fresh vegetables that have been lightly battered and deep-fried. Some sushi and sashimi items are served here as well. Entrées cost $9.50 to $11.75 at lunch, $14.50 to $21.95 at dinner. No reservations required for counter seating.

Another gem in this complex is a peaceful plant-filled **cocktail lounge** with large windows overlooking the lagoon and torii gate—a very pleasant setting for appetizers (perhaps shrimp tempura or sashimi) and warm sake. Japanese music plays softly in the background. Menu items are $4.75 to $7.95, and no reservations are required.

And housed in a replica of the 16th-century Katsura Imperial Villa in Kyoto is **Yakitori House,** a cafeteria serving tempura, teriyaki, yakitori, and other Japanese snack fare.

Italy   Patterned after Alfredo De Lelio's celebrated establishment in Rome, ✪ **L'Originale Alfredo di Roma Ristorante** evokes a seaside Roman palazzo with crystal candelabra chandeliers and beautiful *trompe l'oeil* frescoes of 16th-century patrician villas inspired by Veronese. In the entrance foyer, three arched windows look into an exhibition kitchen where pasta dough is kneaded and noodles are hung up to dry. Charming Italian waiters and exuberant strolling musicians—who play accordion, guitar, and tambourine—create a festive ambience. If you want a quieter setting, ask for a seat on the veranda. Noteworthy antipasto selections include sage-stuffed baked mushrooms, baked stuffed clams, and deep-fried calamari with spicy tomato sauce. De Lelio invented fettuccine Alfredo—and it remains an excellent entrée choice here. Also recommendable are ziti in a piquant vodka-spiked tomato cream sauce, garlicky linguine al pesto (made with fresh Italian basil and tossed with pignoli nuts and Parmesan), and veal scaloppine Seven hills of Rome (thinly sliced pan-fried veal topped with prosciutto, roasted green peppers, and mozzarella; it's served with roasted potatoes and vegetables). An extensive array of Italian wines is available. And there's a sublime tiramisu for dessert. On your way in or out, note the entrance room walls; they're covered with photographs of celebrity diners in Rome—everyone from Douglas Fairbanks and Mary Pickford (who discovered Alfredo's on their honeymoon and told *tout* Hollywood) to Dwight and Mamie Eisenhower. Appetizers cost $3.75 to $7; entrées $9.25 to $15.95 at lunch, $12.75 to $24.75 at dinner. For an extra $3.75 you can get an appetizer and a side order of pasta with meat, poultry, or fish dinner entrées.

Germany   Lit by streetlamps, **The Biergarten** simulates a Bavarian village courtyard at Oktoberfest with autumnal trees, a working water wheel, and geranium-filled flower boxes adorning Tudor-style houses. The setting was inspired by the town of Rothenburg. Waiters are in lederhosen, waitresses in peasant dresses, and entertainment is provided by oom-pah bands, singers, dancers, and a strolling accordionist. Musical shows, which take place five to seven times a day (depending on the season) incorporate performances on instruments such as a 15-foot Alpine horn and cowbells. Guests are encouraged to dance as the band strikes up polkas and waltzes and to sing along with yodelers and folksingers. At this writing, all-you-can-eat buffet meals featuring traditional fare (sauerbraten, herring salad, red cabbage, spaetzle with gravy, roasted potatoes, sauerkraut with ham and spicy sausage, pork with fruit, roast chicken, salads) are offered at lunch and dinner. Beverages and desserts are extra. There is, however, some talk of changing to an à la carte menu. Either way, wash it all down with a stein of Beck's or a glass of Liebfraumilch. Lunch buffets cost $9.95, dinner buffets $14.50. Children 3 to 9 pay $3.95 at either meal.

At **Sommerfest,** a cafeteria in this pavilion, you can purchase bratwurst sandwiches with sauerkraut and desserts such as apple strudel.

China   One of the most attractive of the World Showcase restaurants, ✪ **Nine Dragons,** with windows overlooking the lagoon, has intricately carved rosewood paneling and furnishings, lacquer screens, and a beautiful dragon-motif ceiling. Begin with a selection of dim sum (appetizers) such as honey-glazed spareribs, delicious shrimp toast, pan-fried dumplings (pot stickers) stuffed with pork and vegetables, and ginger-nuanced steamed dumplings stuffed with pork, shrimp, and water chestnuts. Entrées highlight dishes from four regions of China— Mandarin Great Wall duck shredded with green and red peppers and served with pancakes; from Shanghai a saucy stir-fried boneless chicken with onions, carrots, and green peas; Cantonese tender sliced sirloin and broccoli stir-fried in oyster sauce; and Szechuan deep-fried shrimp ambrosia in a Mao Tai liqueur-spiked fruit sauce. You can order Chinese or California wines with your meal, but I especially love fresh melon juice, either nonalcoholic or mixed with rum or vodka. And for dessert there's red-bean ice cream with fried banana or Chinese pastries. Appetizers costs $4.25 to $6.50, entrées $9.50 to $18.50 at lunch, $10.50 to $23.75 at dinner. A multicourse sampler lunch (soup, spring roll, entrée, pastries, and tea) is $11.50; $39.50 buys an elaborate meal for two at dinner.

Or you can opt for egg rolls, fried rice, and entrées such as stir-fried chicken and vegetables served over noodles at the open-air **Lotus Blossom Café,** a pleasant self-service eatery.

Norway   **Akershus** re-creates a 14th-century castle fortress that stands in Oslo's harbor. Its pristine white stone interior, with lofty pine and cherrywood-beamed ceilings and leaded-glass windows, features intimate dining niches divided by Gothic stone archways. Soft lighting emanates from gas lamps (on crisply white-linened tables), wrought-iron and brass candelabra chandeliers, and flickering sconces. The meal is an immense smörgåsbord of traditional *småvarmt* (hot) and *koldtbord* (cold) dishes—smoked pork with honey mustard, strips of venison in cream sauce, gravlax in mustard sauce, smoked mackerel, poached salmon, Norwegian tomato herring, an array of Norwegian breads and cheeses, stuffed pork loin, potato salad, red cabbage, boiled red potatoes, eggs Nordique, and much more. Norwegian beer and aquavit complement a list of French and California wines. And do consider the post-Olympic Lillehammer brandy for an after-dinner drink. For dessert order a "veiled maiden"—an applesauce and whipped cream concoction. Norwegian hosts and hostesses can answer all your questions. Lunch buffet costs $11.95 for adults, children 4 to 9 pay $4.50, 3 and under free. Dinner buffet costs $17.95 for adults, $7.50 for children 4 to 9, 3 and under free. Desserts and beverages are à la carte. A la carte children's entrées are $3.99.

Another facility in this pavilion, the **Kringla Bakeri og Kafe,** offers covered outdoor seating and inexpensive light fare—open-faced sandwiches like smoked salmon stuffed with hard-boiled egg, cheese and fruit platters, waffles sprinkled with powdered sugar, and fresh-baked Norwegian pastries. No reservations are required.

Mexico   The ✪ **San Angel Inn** evokes a hacienda courtyard in the shadow of a crumbling Yucátan pyramid and dense jungle foliage. It is nighttime: Tables are candlelit (even at lunch), and lighting is very low. The Popocatepetl volcano erupts in the distance, spewing molten lava, and you can hear the sounds of faraway birds. Thunder, lightning, and swiftly moving clouds add a dramatic note, but the overall ambience is soothing. The fare is authentic and prepared from scratch. Order an appetizer of *queso fundido* (melted cheese with Mexican pork sausage, served with homemade corn or flour tortillas). At dinner, filet of blackened mahi-mahi in spicy chili sauce, served with Mexican rice and vegetables, is a house specialty. Also very good are *mole poblano* (chicken simmered with more than 20 spices and a hint of chocolate), and *filete ranchero* (grilled tenderloin of beef served over corn tortillas with sauce ranchero, poblano pepper strips, Monterey jack cheese, onions, and refried beans). Dinner entrées are served with soup or salad and Mexican rice. Order a side dish of guacamole. Combination platters are available at both meals. There's chocolate Kahlúa mousse pie for dessert, and drink options include Dos Equis beer and margaritas. Appetizers cost $5.95 to $8.95 (they're large enough to share); entrées $8.50 to $15.75 at lunch, $13.25 to $23.25 at dinner.

Cantina de San Angel, a cafeteria with outdoor seating at umbrella tables overlooking the lagoon, offers inexpensive tacos, burritos, enchiladas, and combination plates, along with frozen margaritas.

FUTURE WORLD

As at World Showcase above, Future World restaurants are arranged geographically, beginning at the Living Seas pavilion and proceeding counterclockwise.

Living Seas Pavillon Dine "under the sea" at the enchanting **Coral Reef,** where tables ring a 5.6-million-gallon aquarium inhabited by more than 4,000 denizens of the deep. Tiered seating—much of it in semicircular booths—ensures everyone a good view, and diners are given "fish-identifier" sheets with labeled pictures so they can put names to the species swimming by. The menu features (what else?) fresh fish and seafood. A satisfying appetizer is the seas' sampler—a platter of mesquite-grilled jumbo shrimp, oysters Rockefeller, and garlicky baked clams. Seafood entrées range from Caribbean jerk tuna (served with fruit sauce, rice pilaf, and fresh vegetables) to pan-seared swordfish with Thai curry-lobster sauce with angel hair pasta. Non-seafood eaters can dine on beef tenderloin or broiled chicken, and low-priced hot dogs with french fries are an option for kids. Desserts include a white chocolate mousse topped with dark chocolate Mickey Mouse ears. Coral Reef features premium wines by the glass and also offers a nightly entrée matched with a selected label. Appetizers cost $4.25 to $9.75; entrées $12.25 to $19.95 at lunch, $20.50 to $26.95 at dinner—more for lobster at either meal.

Coral Reef also hosts a daily character breakfast; see details below in Section 6.

The Land As you dine at the revolving **Garden Grill,** on the upper level of this pavilion, you'll travel past desert, prairie, farmland, and rain forest environments. A planter of seedlings on each table further promotes The Land's ecology-awareness theme, and many menu selections feature produce grown in its on-premises greenhouses. Your meal here might begin with an appetizer of spicy chicken wings with celery stalks and tangy blue cheese dressing. Entrées range from a platter of barbecued chicken and pork served with grilled corn and baked beans to spicy Cajun jambalaya (rice tossed with andouille sausage, chicken, and shrimp). For dessert, there's a fruit crisp à la mode. Wine and beer are available. The same menu is offered all day. Appetizers cost $2.75 to $5.50, entrées $8.75 to $12.95. Three-course early-bird dinners served 4 to 7pm cost $13.50.

The Land also houses a lower-level food court called the **Sunshine Season Food Fair,** where vendors proffer an array of low-priced items—barbecued chicken and ribs, homemade soups and fresh salads, immense cinnamon rolls, fresh fruit and cheeses, pastas, stuffed baked potatoes, sandwiches, oven-fresh cakes and pastries, ice cream, and more. Colorful umbrella tables under a skylit dome ring a splashing fountain, and hot-air balloons add to the festive decor.

IN THE MAGIC KINGDOM

There are three major restaurants in the **Magic Kingdom** offering full-service dining—the **Liberty Tree Tavern, King Stefan's Banquet Hall,** and **Tony's Town Square.** And though there are plenty of fast-food eateries as well, I find a quiet sit-down meal an essential respite from theme park hullaballoo.

Also highly recommended is the **Diamond Horseshoe Jamboree** in Frontierland, combining a light, inexpensive meal with a 40-minute western-themed musical revue (details in Chapter 7).

Main Street Inspired by the Disney movie *Lady and the Tramp,* **Tony's Town Square Restaurant** is Victorian plush, with rich cherrywood beams and paneling, a central fountain, cut-glass mirrors, and globe lighting fixtures. Walls are hung with original cels from the movie. There's additional seating in a sunny plant-filled solarium. Tony's opens early for breakfast (you can eat here while waiting for the other lands to open); menu items include frittatas served with buttermilk biscuits, Lady and the Tramp–shaped waffles, and French toast tossed in cinnamon sugar and served with warm maple or fruit syrup. The rest of the day, the fare is Italian, featuring appetizers such as a five-cheese vegetable pizza and fried calamari with marinara sauce. The lunch menu lists a variety of pastas, calzones, meatball and sausage subs, and salads. At dinner your options range from garlicky sautéed shrimp and seasonal vegetables over linguine in a light cream sauce to a

---

🍴 Family-Friendly Restaurants

In a town where the major attractions are amusement parks, just about every restaurant is child-oriented. Do see the listings for **meals hosted by Disney characters** on p. 121. Some additional suggestions include:

Cape May Cafe Clambake Buffet *(see p. 114)* This old-fashioned nightly clambake at Disney's beach Club Resort is fun for the whole family.

Chef Mickey's *(see p. 104)* Great food pleases mom and dad, and kids love the nightly appearances by Mickey Mouse. If you want to linger over dinner, the kids can retreat to a lounge where cartoons are shown.

Mickey's Tropical Luau *(see p. 123)* Not just a meal but a Polynesian floor show featuring Minnie, Mickey, Pluto, and Goofy along with a cast of South Sea Islanders. At Disney's Polynesian Resort. Character breakfasts here, too.

Hoop-Dee-Doo Musical Revue *(see p. 193)* I've never met anyone who didn't have a great time at this country music dinner show in Fort Wilderness Pioneer Hall.

Sci-Fi Dine-In Theater Restaurant *(see p. 102)* A drive-in movie theater where you sit in actual convertible cars and the waitstaff is on roller skates. At Disney-MGM Studios.

Magic Kingdom Dining

Aunt Polly's Landing 1
Crystal Palace Buffeteria 6
Diamond Horseshoe
Jamboree 4
King Stefan's Banquet Hall 2
Liberty Tree Tavern 3
Pecos Bill Café 5
Plaza Restaurant 7
Tony's Town Square
Restaurant 8

12-ounce sirloin steak/sautéed lobster combination, also served with linguine in garlic cream sauce. Desserts include spumoni, gelatos, and Italian pastries. Open for breakfast, lunch, and dinner. Breakfast items cost $2.75 to $7.75; appetizers $4.50 to $7.50; entrées $8.95 to $15.25 at lunch, $16.25 to $22.75 at dinner.

Another appealing Main Street–area eatery is the **Crystal Palace Buffeteria,** housed in an exquisite Victorian structure—a replica of a glass edifice constructed for the Great London Exhibition of 1851 in Hyde Park. Baskets of flowers suspended from the rafters and a central octagonal planter add garden-conservatory ambience. Additional seating is offered on a covered veranda. Breakfast—served from a half-hour before park opening—offers items ranging from bacon and eggs with roasted potatoes to sausage biscuits with gravy. Lunch fare includes salads and sandwiches (from poor boys to grilled turkey), along with hot entrées—also offered at dinner—such as spit-roasted chicken seasoned with fresh rosemary and thyme, served with fresh vegetables and mashed potatoes. And for dessert there's fresh-baked apple pie, carrot cake, or cheesecake. Open for breakfast, lunch, and dinner. Breakfast items cost $2.50 to $5.50; entrées $8.25 to $11.75 at lunch, $8.75 to $16.25 at dinner.

Near the end of Main Street is the pretty **Plaza Restaurant,** with an art nouveau interior. It serves burgers and sandwiches (tuna and Swiss on whole wheat, a Reuben or pastrami on rye, hot roast beef double-deckers) which you can wash down with a vanilla, chocolate, or strawberry shake. Or skip the shake and leave room for a hot-fudge sundae topped with whipped cream and a maraschino cherry. There's waiter service, but you don't need reservations. Open from lunch to park closing. Sundaes are $3.50 to $5.75 (for an elaborate create-your-own concoction); sandwiches, burgers, and salads, $7.75 to $10.75.

Frontierland   Highly recommended is the **Diamond Horseshoe Jamboree,** combining a light meal with a 40-minute western-themed musical revue (details in Chapter 7).

The **Pecos Bill Café,** a vast Wild West-themed indoor/outdoor eatery serves burgers, hot dogs, chili, and barbecued chicken sandwiches.

I also like **Aunt Polly's Landing** on Tom Sawyer's Island, reached via a short raft trip across the Rivers of America. With its outdoor tables on a porch overlooking the water, it provides a tranquil respite from park hyperactivity. Inexpensive light fare includes sandwiches—peanut butter and jelly, fried chicken, ham and cheese—and soft drinks. And you can relax over refreshing lemonade while the kids explore the island's dark caves and abandoned mines. It's open for lunch only.

Liberty Square   The ✪ **Liberty Tree Tavern** replicates an 18th-century pub, with peg-plank oak floors, displays of pewterware in oak hutches, and a vast brick fireplace hung with copper pots in its entranceway. Diners sit at sturdy candlelit tables, waitstaff is in period garb, background music is appropriate to the period, and even the windows have panes of hand-pressed glass, a detail typical of Disney thoroughness. Entrées range from New England pot roast braised in burgundy and served with mashed potatoes and vegetables to a traditional roast turkey dinner with all the trimmings. Precede these with a bowl of creamy New England clam chowder. Meals are accompanied by baskets of three-grain bread and apple butter. At lunch there are sandwiches as well. And all-American desserts include strawberry shortcake or apple pie topped with cinnamon ice cream. Open for lunch and dinner. Appetizers cost $4.75; entrées are $9.75 to $14.25 at lunch, $13.75 to $19.25 at dinner.

By the way, I'm also partial to the **baked and sweet potato cart** in Liberty Square and the adjacent fruit stand.

Fantasyland   Housed in Cinderella Castle, the focal point of the park, **King Stefan's Banquet Hall** has a Gothic interior with leaded-glass windows and heraldic banners suspended from a vaulted ceiling. Suits of armor and shields are on display, and servers in 13th-century garb address guests as "Milord" and "Milady." Sturdy oak tables are candlelit. The only anachronistic note: Background music is from Disney movies. The menu features hearty cuts of beef such as prime rib and grilled sirloin served with fresh sautéed vegetables and soup (or salad at dinner). And while you're piling on cholesterol, might as well opt for the fried cheese appetizer—Havarti, smoked Gouda, and mozzarella served with marinara sauce. Less caloric entrées include pasta tossed with mixed seafood and fresh vegetables and a vegetarian plate. The crown-shaped kid's menu lists burgers, hot dogs, chicken tenders, and macaroni and cheese. And dessert choices include a hot fudge sundae, berry and apple cobbler topped with cinnamon ice cream, and a southern classic—red velvet cake. *Note:* Cinderella often greets guests in the downstairs entrance hall where the Disney family crest (three lions) is displayed over a fireplace. Open for lunch and dinner. Appetizers $5.95 to $6.95; entrées $9.75 to $16.75 at lunch, $21.95 to $25.95 at dinner.

King Stefan's also hosts a daily character breakfast; see details below in "Only in Orlando: Dining with Disney Characters."

AT DISNEY-MGM STUDIOS

There are over a dozen eateries in this Hollywood-themed park with movie-lot monikers like the Studio Commissary and Starring Rolls Bakery. The two below-listed are my favorites.

The **Hollywood Brown Derby,** modeled after the famed L.A. celebrity haunt where Louella Parsons and Hedda Hopper held court, evokes its one-time West Coast counterpart with interior palm trees, roomy semicircular leather booths, and derby-shaded sconces. Mahogany-wainscoted walls are hung with 1,600 caricatures of major stars who patronized the restaurant—everyone from Bette Davis to Sammy Davis. Brown Derby legend abounds: It was at this Hollywood shrine that Clark Gable proposed to Carole Lombard, Wallace Beery poured ketchup over his sponge cake, and Lucille Ball and Jack Haley chucked dinner rolls at each other across the tables! A pianist entertains while you dine. The Derby's signature dish is the Cobb salad, invented by owner Bob Cobb in the 1930s. It's a good appetizer choice, as are the pan-fried Maryland crabcakes (to which a hint of cayenne adds piquancy) served with spicy marinara sauce. Dinner entrées come with a choice of soup or salad (select the oyster Brie, available à la carte at lunch—a champagne-flavored soup garnished with a slice of lemon). Go on to an entrée of baked grouper meunière served atop pasta in a light lemony white wine cream sauce. Grapefruit cake with cream cheese frosting is the Derby's signature dessert, but I prefer the white chocolate cheesecake. There's a full bar, California wines are featured, and after-dinner drinks are a specialty. Appetizers cost $5.25 to $7.75

at lunch, $5.25 to $10.50 at dinner; entrées, $10.50 to $17.95 at lunch, $15.95 to $29.95 at dinner.

The **Sci-Fi Dine-In Theater Restaurant** replicates an archetypical 1950s Los Angeles drive-in movie emporium. Diners are ensconced in flashy chrome-trimmed convertible cars (complete with fins and whitewalls) under a twinkling starlit sky with the Hollywood hills as a backdrop. Friendly carhops bring your food order and complimentary popcorn. While you eat, you can watch the movie screen, where a mix of zany newsreels (e.g., *News of the Future*) is interspersed with cartoons, horror movie clips (*Frankenstein Meets the Space Monster*), and coming attractions. Menu items have names like Terror of the Tides (deep-fried shrimp, served with fries and coleslaw), 20,000 Leafs Under the Sea (a seafood salad in citrus vinaigrette dressing), and Monster Mash (oven-roasted turkey with all the trimmings). And though the restaurant basically appeals to kids (whose menu items are all under $5), beverages include wine and beer (there's a full bar) as well as milkshakes. Finish up with The Cheesecake that Ate New York. Your bill is presented as a speeding ticket. Entrées cost $6.50 to $12.95 at lunch, $7.75 to $18.50 at dinner.

WALT DISNEY WORLD VILLAGE/PLEASURE ISLAND

Located about 2¹/₂ miles from Epcot off Buena Vista Drive, Walt Disney World Village is a very pleasant complex of cedar-shingled shops and restaurants overlooking a scenic lagoon. Pleasure Island, a nighttime entertainment center, adjoins. *Note:* You don't have to pay the entrance fee to Pleasure Island to dine at the Fireworks Factory or Portobello Yacht Club.

VERY EXPENSIVE

✪ The Empress Room

Aboard the *Empress Lilly* in Walt Disney World Village. ☎ **407/WDW-DINE.** Reservations required (*note:* You can reserve up to 60 days in advance). Jackets required for men. Appetizers $5–$15; main courses $26–$34. AE, MC, V. Dinner seatings daily 6:30–9:30pm. Free self-parking and validated valet parking. CONTINENTAL.

The *Empress Lilly* (named for Walt Disney's wife) is a plush replica of a 19th-century Mississippi riverboat permanently moored on the shores of Lake Buena Vista. It houses several restaurants and lounges, among them this ornate dining room with gold satin-damask wall coverings and a crystal candelabra chandelier. Gilded etched-glass dividers create intimate dining alcoves where patrons are ensconced in apricot velvet Louis XV–style chairs at white-linened tables, each adorned with a rose in a silver vase.

The exquisitely presented fare (almost, but not quite, too beautiful to eat) is every bit as *haute* as its setting. Two hors d'oeuvres are especially wonderful: Sautéed oysters and jumbo lump crabmeat on a bed of fennel are glazed with champagne sauce and garnished with julienned vegetables. And escargots en croûte, deriving its garlicky flavor from Boursin cheese, is served on yellow tomato butter sauce marbleized with puréed watercress. Entrées—served in silver cloches—include roast breast of duck with mandarin honey-vinegar sauce served over a bed of tri-grain rice with crisp sautéed watercress and garnishes as thrilling as gifts—a morsel of honeycomb, fresh duck liver, and Peking kumquats. Sorbets served in frosted-glass flowers refresh your palate between courses. Dessert—perhaps a soufflé Grand Marnier topped with crème anglaise—is followed by complimentary chocolates infused with rum and amaretto and rolled in crushed pistachios. And coffee is accompanied by a silver tray laden with cinnamon sticks, rock and anisette sugar, shaved chocolate, and unsweetened whipped cream. Needless to say, an extensive wine list complements the menu.

Note: There has been talk of revamping the concept for the Empress Room, so you may find the menu changed when you visit. It will, however, remain a first-rate WDW gourmet room.

EXPENSIVE

Fisherman's Deck

Aboard the *Empress Lilly* in Walt Disney World Village. ☎ **407/WDW-DINE.** Reservations recommended (*note:* You can reserve up to 60 days in advance). Appetizers $4.95–$8.50, main courses $16.95–$23.95. AE, MC, V. Daily 5:30–10pm. Free self-parking, valet parking $5. SEAFOOD.

This very appealing restaurant aboard Disney's triple-decker white paddlewheeler is decorated in 18th-century style. Semicircular in shape, its seating—in plush tufted-velvet Louis XVI–style chairs—faces a curved window wall overlooking Lake Buena Vista. Early arrivals at dinner enjoy glorious sunsets.

Tempting appetizers include baked sea scallops served in the shell with buttery garlic-breadcrumb topping and a trio of baked cheeses (sharp cheddar, gorgonzola, and meunster) embellished with roasted pine nuts and sun-dried tomatoes. An entrée of hot and spicy sautéed catfish is served with green rice (mixed with finely chopped parsley and scallions) and Cajun mushroom sauce. Also accompanied by green rice is shrimp Imperial—baked crabmeat-stuffed shrimp with lobster cream sauce and fresh seasonal vegetables. Finish up with chocolate truffle cake. Children's entrées are $3.75 to $6.50.

✪ Steerman's Quarters

Aboard the *Empress Lilly* in Walt Disney World Village. ☎ **407/WDW-DINE.** Reservations recommended (*note:* You can reserve up to 60 days in advance). Appetizers $5.75–$8.50, main courses $18–$28. Daily 5:30–9pm. Free self-parking, valet parking $5. STEAK.

Plush and clublike, Steerman's Quarters seats diners in floral-tapestried booths and comfortable burgundy leather chairs at candlelit white-linened tables. A gaslight-style chandelier and sconces complement the glow of candlelight, and framed 19th-century prints line mahogany-paneled walls.

Begin with a classic Caesar salad or oysters Rockefeller generously topped with spinach and browned hollandaise. Continue with a mixed grill of filet mignon, broiled lamb chop with mint sauce, and roasted chicken, served with roasted red-skin potatoes. Or choose the nightly-changing fresh seafood entrée—on my last visit, baked red snapper in a boursin cheese/sun-dried tomato/butter sauce. A silver basket filled with warm French breads and rolls flavored with herbs and sun-dried tomatoes is a plus. And it's a good idea to order à la carte vegetables such as a cast-iron pot of creamed spinach or asparagus hollandaise. There's a full bar and an extensive wine list. Desserts include crème brûlée, key lime pie, and a hot fudge sundae—all of them most satisfying.

MODERATE

Chef Mickey's

In Walt Disney World Village. ☎ **407/WDW-DINE.** Reservations recommended (note: You can reserve up to 60 days in advance). Breakfast entrées $6.50–$7.95; main courses $6.50–$8.95 at lunch, mostly $12.50–$19.95 at dinner. AE, MC, V. Daily 9–11am, 11:30am–2pm, and 5–10pm. Free self-parking (use lot A). STEAK/SEAFOOD.

Rustically attractive, Chef Mickey's plant-filled interior has ficus trees growing towards a skylight ceiling. About half of the seats over-look Buena Vista Lagoon. One dining area is ski lodgey with redwood-paneled walls and a beamed pine cathedral ceiling; another offers a view of white-hatted chefs at work in an exhibition kitchen. And should you have to wait for a table, you can do so in a lounge where kids can watch cartoons on a large-screen TV, while adults view sporting events at the bar. Mickey turns out some pretty terrific food here (a cookbook of his recipes is available), and, at dinner, he table-hops, greeting patrons and signing autographs.

All entrées include a salad tossed in creamy garlic-honey dressing, choice of potato or rice, and a vegetable. You might select a 16-ounce flame-grilled T-bone steak seasoned with garlic and black pepper, a generous portion of smoky ribs in tangy barbecue sauce, or a 10-ounce cut of juicy prime rib. Leave room for dessert—peach cobbler in a hot butter/cinnamon/vanilla sauce topped with vanilla-bean ice cream. The breakfast menu features traditional items—waffles, omelets, steak and eggs, and so on. And at lunch there are salads, burgers, and sandwiches in addition to items like country-fried chicken.

Fireworks Factory

1630 Lake Buena Vista Dr., Pleasure Island. ☎ **407/934-8989.** Reservations recom-mended. Appetizers $4.95–$8.95; main courses $6.95–$12.95 at lunch, mostly $13.95–$17.95 at dinner. AE, MC, V. Daily 11:30am–11:30pm (dinner served from 4pm); light fare and drinks served to 2am. Free self-parking, valet parking $5. AMERICAN REGIONAL.

According to Disney legend, Captain Merriweather Adam Pleasure, the mythological 19th-century ship merchant and adventurer who devel-oped Pleasure Island, manufactured fireworks as a hobby and staged dazzling spectaculars every July 4th. Pleasure was lost at sea in 1839, but his former corrugated-tin warehouse survives in the form of this "explosively" exuberant casual restaurant. The Factory has big red pipes overhead and exposed-brick walls hung with neon signs and vintage advertisements for fireworks. Dozens of unopened boxes of beer are strewn around the floor, and missile fireworks are prominently displayed.

Lunch or dinner, you might start off with an appetizer sampler of spicy chicken wings tossed in Louisiana hot sauce, shrimp quesadillas,

More Walt Disney World Dining

Ariel's ⑤	Fireworks Factory ⑮	Ohana at Papeete Bay ③
Artist Point ④	Fisherman's Deck ⑭	Planet Hollywood ⑭
The Black Swan ⑫	Garden Grove Cafe ⑧	Portobello Yacht Club ⑮
Boatwrights Dining Hall ⑩	Garden View Lounge ②	Sci-Fi Dine-In
Bonfamille's Café ⑪	Harry's Safari Bar & Grille ⑥	Theater Restaurant ⑨
Cape May Café ⑤	Hemingway's ⑫	Soundstage Restaurant ⑨
Cascade Grill ⑫	Hollywood Brown Derby ⑦	Steerman's Quarters ⑭
Chef Mickey's ⑭	La Coquina ⑫	Tuscany ⑯
Contemporary Cafe ①	Luau Cove ③	Victoria & Albert's ②
Empress Room ⑭	Mikado Japanese Steak House ⑯	Watercress Cafe ⑬
Empress Lilly ⑬	1900 Park Fare ②	Yachtsman Steakhouse ⑥

roasted chilies, pepperjack and cheddar cheeses, and applewood-smoked baby back ribs. Dinner entrées here range from Cajun shrimp pasta to oak-roasted salmon served with roasted tomato/corn relish and angel hair sweet potatoes. And at lunch you might opt for mesquite-smoked barbecued beef sandwich on an onion roll or applewood-smoked breast of chicken tossed with fettuccine, bacon, red peppers, mushrooms, and onions in cream sauce. For dessert: a giant tollhouse cookie served warm in a cast-iron skillet topped with vanilla ice cream and hot fudge. In addition to "explosive" specialty drinks (try a 21 Rum Salute) and wines, the Fireworks Factory offers several dozen varieties of domestic and imported beer, ale, and stout, including microbrewery selections.

Planet Hollywood

1506 E. Buena Vista Dr., Pleasure Island. ☎ **407/827-7827.** Reservations not accepted. Appetizers $5.25–$9.25; main courses $6.75–$17.95 (most under $13). AE, DC, MC, V. Daily 11am–2am. Free self-parking, valet parking $5. AMERICAN/ INTERNATIONAL.

Planet Hollywood crashed cometlike into the Pleasure Island solar system in 1994, with a lavish opening-night party hosted by stockholders Arnold Schwarzenegger, Sylvester Stallone, Bruce Willis, and Demi Moore. A galaxy of stars made the scene, among them Roseanne, Luke Perry, Don Johnson and Melanie Griffith, Samuel Jackson, Charlie Sheen, Wesley Snipes, and Cindy Crawford. The Planet is indeed spherical, with a 120-foot-diameter and tri-level seating overlooking a lagoon. Its interior, under a fiber-optics planetarium ceiling, is a veritable show-business museum jam-packed with movie and TV memorabilia, costumes, and props—more than 300 items ranging from a *Mrs. Doubtfire* mannequin to Peter O'Toole's *Lawrence of Arabia* costume—not to mention the front end of the bus from the movie *Speed*, which is suspended from the ceiling! Outside, the landscaping includes *Edward Scissorhands* topiaries. While you're here, you'll catch previews of soon-to-be-released movies and video montages from films and TV.

You can opt to nosh on appetizers here such as hickory-smoked buffalo wings with chunky blue cheese dressing, pot stickers, or nachos. Entrée choices include burgers, fajitas, salads, pizzas, pastas (perhaps Thai shrimp tossed with linguine in spicy chili-peanut sauce) sandwiches, and big platters of grilled steak, ribs, chicken, or pork chops served with fries and black bean relish. Beverages run the gamut from chocolate malts to exotic specialty drinks with movie-inspired names like "Beetle Juice" and "Die Harder." Try Arnold's mother's apple strudel topped with nutmeg ice cream for dessert.

Portobello Yacht Club

1650 Lake Buena Vista Dr., Pleasure Island. ☎ **407/934-8888.** Reservations not accepted (arrive early to avoid a wait). Appetizers $5.95–$10.95; main courses $6.95– $9.95 at lunch, $12.95–$22.95 at dinner; pizzas $6.95–$8.95. AE, MC, V. Daily 11:30am–midnight (dinner served from 4pm). Free self-parking, valet parking $5. NORTHERN ITALIAN.

Occupying a gabled Bermuda-style house, the Yacht Club is nautically themed, its interior, though casual, evoking a luxury cruise ship. Inside, the walls are plastered with photographs of racing yachts, navigational charts, and yachting flags, and shelves are lined with racing trophies. From the lively mahogany-paneled bar, you can watch oak-fired pizzas being prepared in an exhibition kitchen. And, weather permitting, you can dine al fresco, on an awninged patio overlooking Lake Buena Vista.

Those oak-fired pizzas have crisply thin crusts and toppings such as *quattro formaggi* (mozzarella, Romano, Gorgonzola, and provolone with sun-dried tomatoes). And lunch or dinner, you might follow an antipasto of steamed clams and mussels served with garlic croutons in buttery white wine sauce with an entrée of charcoal-grilled half chicken marinated in olive oil, garlic, and fresh rosemary, served with roasted garlic mashed potatoes (grilled polenta at lunch) and seasonal vegetables. Or choose a pasta dish such as penne with plum tomatoes, Italian bacon, garlic, and fresh basil. Entrées are served with sourdough bread and roasted spreadable garlic cloves. There's an extensive award-winning list of Italian and California wines (many of them hard-to-find vintages), supplemented by a selection of grappas, single-malt scotches, and cognacs. A dessert of *crema bruccioto* (white-chocolate custard with a caramelized sugar glaze) served with fresh berries is recommended.

3   Lake Buena Vista Area

This section is largely composed of notable restaurants at Disney resorts and other area accommodations. Since most of these are gorgeous properties, they're fun to visit. Before or after your meal, take a stroll around the grounds and public areas.

VERY EXPENSIVE

The Black Swan

In the Grand Cypress Resort, 1 N. Jacaranda (off FL 535). ☎ **407/239-1999.** Reservations recommended. Appetizers $8–$12; main courses $25–$34. AE, CB, DC, DISC, ER, JCB, MC, V. Daily 6–10pm. Free self-parking, validated valet parking. AMERICAN/CONTINENTAL.

Overlooking the magnificent emerald fairways of this posh resort's golf course, the Black Swan has a lodgelike, split-level interior with a big working fireplace (don't worry if it's hot outside; there's air conditioning) and a cross-beamed knotty-pine cathedral ceiling. Large, pine-framed windows overlook the ninth hole, and that verdant view is echoed by lovely floral arrangements and planters of greenery. Golfers make up the majority of the clientele. It's not unusual here to see someone rise up excitedly from a table and demonstrate how he eagled the 17th and birdied the 18th hole to win a match. Barring that, dinner entertainment consists of a pianist at a white baby grand.

Hearty portions are presented on large white Villeroy & Boch platters—veritable canvases for the chef's aesthetically exquisite arrangements. Appetizers range from tempura-battered yellowfin tuna sashimi with soy and sake dipping sauce to a blackberry, brie, and smoked duck quesadilla with avocado Key lime crème fraîche. A consommé of duck is beautifully garnished with julienne of shiitake, vegetable confetti, and decorative gold leaf. And Caribbean jerk-seasoned sea scallops tossed with mixed baby field greens in rum and a tropical fruit vinaigrette makes an excellent salad course. The menu changes seasonally. On my last visit I selected an entrée of sautéed jumbo prawns served with a bouquetière of six fresh steamed vegetables and Key lime pasta in a citrusy cilantro-flavored vinaigrette garnished with diced avocado and tomato. A friend's roast rack of lamb (thick, juicy slices grilled in a coating of honey mustard and crushed pecans) was also noteworthy. Whatever you eat, save room for the Swan's superb desserts such as a warm, crisp apple tart on caramel sauce topped with honey-vanilla ice cream and whipped cream. There's an extensive wine list, and dessert libations (cognacs, ports, etc.) are featured. *Note:* Park your car at the main entrance to the adjacent Hyatt Regency Grand Cypress, 1 Grand Cypress Blvd., off FL 535; a complimentary van will take you from there to the restaurant.

✪ Victoria & Albert's

In Disney's Grand Floridian Beach Resort, 4401 Floridian Way. ☎ **407/824-2383.** Reservations required. Jackets required for men. Prix-fixe meal $80 per person, $25 additional for Royal Wine Pairing. AE, MC, V. Two dinner seatings daily, 6–6:45pm and 9–9:45pm. Free self-parking, validated valet parking. AMERICAN/INTERNATIONAL.

It's not often one describes a dining experience as flawless, but at Victoria & Albert's, the World's most elite restaurant (Walt Disney World, that is), I experienced nothing less than perfection. The intimate dining room is plushly furnished. Brocaded walls are hung with gilt-framed ink drawings, and an exquisite floral arrangement serves as an aesthetic centerpoint. Diners sit in leather-upholstered Louis XIII–style chairs at tables lit by silver-shaded Victorian lamps and exquisitely appointed with Royal Doulton china, Sambonet silver from Italy, and Schott-Zweisel crystal from Germany. A maid and butler provide deft and gracious service, and a harpist plays softly while you dine.

Dinner, a seven-course affair, is described in a personalized menu sealed with a gold wax insignia. The fare changes nightly. On a recent visit, I began with an hors d'oeuvre of Florida lobster tail with aïoli. It was supplanted by a more formal appetizer—vermouth-poached jumbo sea scallops served in a crisp rice-noodle basket on shallot-chive sauce with garnishes of caviar and Chinese tat soi leaves. A shot of peppered vodka added piquancy to a velvety plum tomato bisque sprinkled with smoked bacon and lightly topped with pesto cream sauce. For an entrée I selected a fan of pinkly juicy sautéed Peking duck breast with wild rice and crabapple chutney. A salad of esoteric greens in an orange sherry vinaigrette cleared the palate for the next course—English Stilton served with pine-nut bread, port wine, and a pear poached in burgundy, cognac, and cinnamon sugar. The conclusion: a sumptuous hazelnut and Frangelico soufflé, followed by coffee and chocolate truffles. This is a highly nuanced cuisine to be slowly savored. There is, of course, an extensive *recherché* wine list. I suggest you opt for the Royal Wine Pairing, which provides an appropriate wine with each course and lets you sample a variety of selections from the restaurant's distinguished cellars. Smoking is not permitted.

EXPENSIVE

✪ Ariel's

In Disney's Beach Club Resort, 1800 Epcot Resorts Blvd. ☎ **407/934-3357.** Reservations recommended. Appetizers $4.25–$8.95; main courses mostly $17.95–$24. AE, MC, V. Daily 6–10pm. Free self- and valet parking. SEAFOOD.

Named for the *Little Mermaid* character, this exquisite restaurant over-looking Stormalong Bay is awash in seafoam green, peach, and coral. White-linened tables are elegantly appointed with fish and seashell–motif china; a prismed 2,000-gallon coral-reef tank is filled with tropical fish; walls are hung with oil paintings of scenes from the movie; and whimsical fish mobiles and glass bubbles dangle from a vaulted ceiling. You'll feel like you're dining in an underwater kingdom.

Appetizers (which supplement a complimentary smoked clam dip) include scrumptious New England silver dollar crabcakes served with a spicy tartar sauce. And a Cajun-style shellfish gumbo is replete with chunks of shrimp, lobster, and smoky andouille sausage. For your entrée, a traditional Spanish paella—an array of fresh lobster, scallops, mussels, calamari, and shrimp inside a ring of saffroned rice—is highly recommended. Also excellent: Maine lobster sautéed with shiitake mushrooms, lemon, and garlic and served atop a nest of tricolor angelhair pasta with two sauces—a buttery lobster sauce (sauce américaine) and herbed cream sauce. A few non-seafood options are offered as well, among them USDA choice New York strip steak grilled over a hickory and oak fire and oven-roasted boneless game hen stuffed with wild rice and lentils served with a light pesto sauce. Desserts include a rich Chambord raspberry chocolate cake, and an extensive award-winning wine list indicates which selections best complement your entrée. A children's menu lists items like chicken nuggets and spaghetti with meat sauce in the $4 to $6 range.

Artist Point

In Disney's Wilderness Lodge, 901 Timberline Dr. ☎ **407/WDW-DINE.** Reservations recommended. Appetizers $5–$9; main courses $14–$21. AE, MC, V. Daily 5:30–10pm. Free self- and valet parking. STEAK AND SEAFOOD/GAME SPECIALTIES.

This resort restaurant centers on western-themed murals inspired by Rocky Mountain School artists Albert Bierstadt and Thomas Moran (they do deviate a bit, however—look for the hidden Mickeys). Beamed ceilings, Mission-style oak tables, tree-trunk pillars, and a mossy-green color scheme mirror the ambience of turn-of-the-century

---

Japanese Breakfast

Tired of the same old bacon and eggs? The Cascade Grill at the Hyatt Regency Grand Cypress, 1 Grand Cypress Boulevard (☎ 407/239-1234), offers a traditional Japanese breakfast of miso soup, grilled salmon, steamed rice, seaweed, fresh fruit, and green tea. The price is $15.75. American breakfasts here are great, too, with choices ranging from banana-nut French toast served with caramelized bananas and orange sauce to eggs scrambled with baby shrimp, chives, and Boursin cheese. And the gardenlike setting is gorgeous. The restaurant centers on an exquisite mermaid-motif fountain backed by a waterfall, and windows all around overlook Lake Windsong. The grill opens at 6:30am.

national park lodges, with lighting fixtures and window frames reflecting the Chinese influence in interior design that typified that era. The park illusion is further enhanced by large windows overlooking a lake and waterfall. Weather permitting, there's also terrace seating.

The menu changes seasonally. On a recent visit, appetizers included a Northwest salmon sampler (smoked pepperlachs, cured gravlax, and pan-seared salmon served with onion/pepper/caper relish). A Caesar salad, tossed with julienned smoked duck, was another noteworthy starter. Entrées ranged from a 16-ounce grilled porterhouse steak (served with red skin potatoes, fire-roasted onions, garlic, and mushrooms) to grilled maple-glazed king salmon served with roasted vegetables, roasted apples, and couscous studded with morsels of sun-dried cherries, pignoli nuts, and smoked onion. Game specials included sautéed elk sausage, venison chop, and roasted pheasant. Pacific Northwestern wines are featured, and desserts are immense (consider sharing) and delicious: perhaps chocolate silk bread pudding topped with vanilla ice cream and chocolate sauce.

✪ Hemingway's

In the Hyatt Regency Grand Cypress, 1 Grand Cypress Blvd. (off FL 535). ☎ **407/239-1234.** Reservations recommended. Appetizers $6–$7.50 at lunch, $6.50–$9 at dinner; main courses $7.50–$17 at lunch, $18–$24 at dinner. AE, CB, DC, DISC, ER, JCB, MC, V. Tues–Sat 11:30am–2:30pm; daily 6–10:30pm. Free self- and validated valet parking. FLORIDA SEAFOOD.

Fronted by a waterfall that cascades into stone-bedded streams, Hemingway's evokes Key West and honors its most famous denizen. Waiters are dressed as beachboys and walls are hung with sepia photographs of Papa in Key West and his fishing and hunting trophies. A warren of intimate dining areas under a high weathered-pine ceiling have oak-framed glass doors, making for an outdoorsy feeling. Elegantly appointed tables are adorned with orchids and lit by gleaming brass hurricane lamps; fans whirr lazily overhead. Weather permitting, you can sit on a screened wooden deck near the waterfall. Or, if you have a party of six to eight people, reserve a private open-air dining room.

Ask not for whom the bell tolls but rather for an appetizer of deep-fried baby squid and grilled eggplant in garlicky herb-seasoned tomato coulis. Or begin with angelhair pasta tossed with lime-seared shrimp and scallops in ancho-chili tomato sauce. Among the entrées, golden brown beer-battered coconut shrimp is served with roast potatoes, a colorful array of al dente vegetables, and orange marmalade–horseradish sauce. And crabcakes (made with jumbo lump crabmeat) are deliciously light, moist, and fluffy; ask for Cajun tartar sauce with them. For dessert Key lime pie appropriately reaches its apogee here, though the apple walnut pie topped with vanilla cream sauce and Häagen-Dazs—is equally ambrosial. Order both and share. The lunch menu offers similar fare, along with paella, sandwiches, and salads. In the adjoining Hurricane Lounge—a most congenial setting with a beautiful oak bar—specialties include a variety of island rums and the Papa Doble, a potent tropical rum and fruit libation invented by Hemingway himself (legend has it he once drank 16 of them at one sitting!).

Mikado Japanese Steak House

In Marriott's Orlando World Center, 8701 World Center Dr. (off FL 536). ☎ **407/238-8664**. Reservations recommended. Appetizers $4.50–$6.95; main courses $12.95–$28.95. Daily 6–10pm. Free self-parking and validated valet parking. JAPANESE.

This gorgeous 230-acre resort houses a beautiful teppanyaki restaurant traditionally constructed by Japanese craftsmen. Its serene interior, with intimate seating areas created by shoji screens, has beautifully paneled skylit pagoda areas and windows overlooking rock gardens. Japanese music helps set the tone. Plan to arrive early and enjoy a cocktail at sunset on the wooden deck overlooking the swimming pool.

Meals here are teppanyaki style—which means you're seated with other patrons at a grill-topped table. A highly trained chef wheels a cart full of raw food to the table and with samurailike dexterity trims, chops, sautés, and flips it onto your waiting plate. It's a dazzling display, and the chefs are not only nimble-fingered but entertaining. Appetizer selections include softshell crab, smoked salmon and cucumber sushi, and assorted tempura vegetables and shrimp. Entrées offer various combinations of steak (New York sirloin or filet mignon), shrimp, scallops, lobster, chicken, and fresh fish. They include a complimentary hors d'oeuvre of grilled shrimp or scallops, soup (select the tastier miso), a salad with sesame or ginger dressing, steamed rice (yummy fried rice is available for an additional $1.95), vegetables, and green tea. A decanter of warm sake is recommended. And green tea or ginger ice cream makes a refreshing dessert. Low-priced meals are available for children.

✪ Tuscany

In Marriott's Orlando World Center, 8701 World Center Dr. ☎ **407/239-4200**. Reservations recommended. Appetizers $6–$10, main courses $15–$27. AE, CB, DC, DISC, ER, JCB, MC, Optima, V. Daily 6–10pm. Free self-parking, valet parking available. TUSCAN.

The showplace restaurant of a luxury resort, Tuscany is a plush dining venue. Rich cherry- and mahogany-paneled walls are hung with gilt-framed Michelangelo prints, white-linened tables are set with fresh flowers, and diners are comfortably seated in roomy tapestried archairs, booths, and Regency chairs. Soft lighting and opera music complete the ambience.

A pasta appetizer is a good way to begin your meal here—most notably the gnocchi served with gorgonzola sauce and a garnish of diced plum tomatoes. Impressive entrées—aesthetically presented on large white platters—include rack of lamb in a light demiglace sauce with roasted eggplant puree, white beans, potato croquette, and haricots verts. I also recommend the sage-roasted rabbit served with julienned vegetables and porcini mushroom risotto in grappa sauce. Herbed foccacia bread served with light, garlicky goat cheese accompanies your meal. An extensive European/California wine list includes many by-the-glass selections; your waiter can suggest appropriate wines with each course. Desserts change nightly; I recently enjoyed an exquisite thin-sliced apple tart served atop crème anglaise and garnished with fresh berries.

✪ Yachtsman Steakhouse

In Disney's Yacht Club Resort, 1700 Epcot Resorts Blvd. ☎ **407/934-3415.** Reservations recommended. Appetizers $6.95–$10.95: main courses $16.95–$25.50. AE, MC, V. Daily 6–10pm. Free self- and valet parking. STEAK.

The Yacht Club, a gorgeous resort inspired by New England's grand turn-of-the-century summer mansions, houses a fittingly elegant signature restaurant. Lacquered knotty-pine beams, paneling, and plank flooring create a warm woody feel that is enhanced by burgundy leather-upholstered oak chairs. USDA grain-fed beef—hand selected to ensure top marbling for natural juices and tenderness—is aged, cured, cut, and ground on the premises. You can see these prime cuts on display in a glass-enclosed beef-aging room, and an exhibition kitchen provides a tantalizing glimpse of sizzling steaks, chops, and seafood being grilled over oak and hickory.

You might begin your meal here with an appetizer of smoked salmon with Grand Marnier caper dressing or garlicky escargots marinated in dry vermouth and served en crôute with rich burgundy sauce. A salad course (perhaps a classic Caesar tossed tableside) is recommended. Beef entrées—such as succulent filet mignon (available in 6- or 10-ounce servings), slow-roasted prime rib of beef au jus, an 18-ounce Kansas City strip steak served on the bone (it's a cattle drive tradition), or a filet mignon and crabmeat-stuffed lobster combination—are served with baked potato, a board of fresh-baked bread, and a choice of béarnaise or bordelaise sauces. Other dishes run the gamut from lamb chops with apple mint butter and rosemary gin sauce to crisp-grilled chicken in apricot brandy sauce, both accompanied by savory rice. Side dishes, such as a skillet of fresh mushrooms sautéed in cognac and creamed spinach, are noteworthy. And if you have room for dessert, selections include a chocolate mousse cake spiked with Jack Daniels and, for the truly intrepid, a brownie fudge sundae. An extensive wine list is available, and a children's menu offers full meals for $3.75 to $6.50.

MODERATE

Pebbles

12551 FL 535 in the Crossroads Shopping Center, in Lake Buena Vista. ☎ **407/827-1111.** Reservations not accepted. Appetizers mostly $3.95–$5.95; sandwiches and salads $4.95–$8.50; main courses $9.95–$19.95. AE, CB, DC, DISC, MC, V. Daily 11am–1am. Free self-parking. CALIFORNIA-STYLE AMERICAN.

Pebbles is one of Orlando's most popular restaurants. The multilevel dining room centers on a sunken bar under a cross-beamed skylight ceiling, and though it's a large space, white wooden shutters and windowed enclosures create a warren of intimate dining areas. Lush tropical greenery, fountains, and canvas tenting contribute to the garden-party ambience. During the day, sunshine streams in; at night flickering hurricane lamps provide romantic lighting. Weather permitting, you can dine at umbrella tables on an outdoor deck overlooking Lake Buena Vista. During busy seasons a guitar soloist entertains at dinner; otherwise, the background music is light jazz.

The same menu is offered throughout the day, supplemented by lunch and dinner specials. Start off with a "lite bite" of creamy baked chèvre served atop chunky tomato sauce with hot garlic bread. Pebbles offers the option of a casual meal—perhaps a Cheddar burger on toasted brioche, honey-roasted spareribs, or a Caesar salad tossed with grilled chicken. Or you can select a more serious entrée such as tender leg of smoked duck that has been rubbed with fennel, glazed with triple sec, and slow roasted to sear in flavorful juices. Also excellent is rack of lamb baked in a coating of chèvre, Dijon mustard, and rosemary-flavored breadcrumbs and served with roasted potatoes and an array of vegetables baked with asiago dill cheese. Dessert of choice: the gold brick sundae—a scoop of vanilla ice cream encased in a candylike chocolate/almond shell and served atop caramel sauce with fresh strawberries. There's a full bar, and many premium wines are offered by the glass.

INEXPENSIVE

Boatwright's Dining Hall

In Disney's Dixie Landings Resort, 1251 Dixie Dr. (off Bonnet Creek Pkwy.) ☎ **407/ 934-5422** or WDW-DINE. Reservations recommended at dinner. Breakfast items $4.25– $6.95; dinner appetizers $3.95–$7.95, main courses $8.25–$14.95, sandwiches $6.95. AE, MC, V. Daily 7–11:30am and 5–10pm. Free self-parking. AMERICAN/ CAJUN.

Boatwright's is themed to look like an 1800s boat-building factory, complete with the wooden hull of a Louisiana lugger (fishing boat) suspended from its lofty beamed ceiling. An untypically pretty factory, it has oak plank floors, stucco walls hung with antique boat-building tools, and two large working brick fireplaces. Wooden toolboxes on the bare oak tables contain a salt shaker that doubles as a level, a wood-clamp sugar dispenser, a pepper-grinder-cum-ruler, a jar of unmatched utensils, shop rags (to be used as napkins), and a little metal pail of crayons for the kids.

Cajun breakfasts offer intriguing possibilities. French toast here is made with sourdough-sweet potato baguette tossed in rich egg custard, deep-fried, and coated with cinnamon sugar. Another option: a pan of sautéed crawfish, mushrooms, green onions, and tomatoes in mustard cream sauce (served with home-style potatoes topped with two eggs, and an oven-fresh buttermilk biscuit). At dinner, appetizer selections include deep-fried bacon-wrapped oysters and scallops and roasted baby back ribs with stone-ground honey-mustard sauce, served on a mound of onion straws. Among your entrée choices are rich bouillabaisse redolent of oaken cognac and a blackened seafood dish (shrimp, scallops, and bayou catfish served over brown-buttered pasta in creamy garlic sauce), both served with salad and oven-fresh pumpernickel and sweet-potato bread. For dessert: homemade fruit cobblers topped with vanilla ice cream and smothered in whipped cream.

Bonfamille's Cafe

In Disney's Port Orleans Resort, 2201 Orleans Dr. (off Bonnet Creek Pkwy.) ☎ **407/ 934-5504** or WDW-DINE. Reservations recommended at dinner. Breakfast items $4.25– $6.95; dinner appetizers $3.95–$7.95, main courses mostly $8.25–$14.95, salads and po'boy sandwiches $6.95. AE, MC, V. Daily 7–11:30am and 5–10pm. Free self-parking. AMERICAN/CRÉOLE.

Named for a character in *The Aristocats,* the charming Bonfamille's is patterned after a fountained French Quarter courtyard. Exposed-brick walls are hung with paintings of New Orleans, big baskets of flowering plants are suspended from beams overhead, and Dixieland jazz plays softly in the background. During breakfast it's light and sunny, and evenings, candle lamps provide soft lighting.

Louisiana-style breakfasts range from fresh hot beignets and café au lait to a skillet of crawfish and andouille sausage in zesty Créole sauce and melted sharp Cheddar. The latter is served with home-style fried potatoes topped with eggs and a hot buttermilk biscuit. Pancakes stuffed with blueberries are another possibility. A typical dinner here: an appetizer of crawfish and andouille sausage tossed with linguine and parmesan (also available as an entrée), followed by grilled Atlantic salmon (served with a spicy pecan butter sauce, rice, and sautéed vegetables), and a dessert of Bourbon Street pudding topped with strawberry and caramel bourbon sauces. After dinner, families can head over to the hotel's Scat Cats Lounge where entertainment—sing-alongs and live music with lots of audience participation—is featured Thursday to Monday evenings through midnight.

❽ Cape May Café

In Disney's Beach Club Resort, 1800 Epcot Resorts Blvd. ☎ **407/934-3415.** Reservations not accepted. Adults $16.95, ages 6–11 $8.95, under 6 free. Lobster is additional. AE, MC, V. Daily 5:30–9:30pm. Free self- and valet parking. CLAMBAKE BUFFET.

A hearty 19th-century–style New England clambake is featured nightly at this charming peach and seafoam-green restaurant, where sand sculptures, paintings of turn-of-the-century beach scenes, croquet mallets, and furled striped beach umbrellas evoke an upscale seaside resort. Diners sit in oversized chairs at birchwood tables. Large towel napkins are provided. Aromatic stews and chowders, steamed clams and mussels, corn on the cob, chicken, lobster, and redskin potatoes are cooked up in a crackling rockweed steamer pit that serves as the restaurant's centerpiece. And these traditional clambake offerings are supplemented by dozens of salads (pasta, seafood, fruit, vegetables), hot entrées (barbecued baby back ribs, smoked sausage, fried chicken, pasta dishes), and a wide array of oven-fresh breads and desserts. There's a full bar.

4 International Drive Area

Some of the best area restaurants are along International Drive within about 10 minutes of Walt Disney World parks by car.

VERY EXPENSIVE

✪ Dux

In The Peabody Orlando, 9801 International Dr. ☎ **407/345-4550.** Reservations recommended. Appetizers $8.25–$10.95, main courses $25–$31.95. AE, CB, DC, DISC, ER, JCB, MC, Optima, V. Mon–Sat 6–11pm. Free self-parking, validated valet parking. INTERNATIONAL.

Named for the hotel's signature ducks that parade ceremoniously into the lobby each morning to Sousa's *King Cotton* march, this is one of central Florida's most highly acclaimed restaurants. And since The Peabody is the headquarters hotel for nearby Universal Studios, you're likely to see a celebrity or two among the diners. The textured gold walls are hung with ornately framed mirrors and watercolors representing 72 ducks! Upholstered bamboo chairs and cushioned banquettes provide seating at candlelit, white-linened tables set with flowers and beautiful ceramic show plates. A lavish dessert display table with a floral centerpiece serves as a visual focus.

The menu varies seasonally. At a recent dinner, appetizer selections included a unique version of potstickers—stuffed with portabello mushrooms, scallions, and creamed goat cheese and garnished with asiago twigs. Another choice was foie gras with semolina toast and blackberry/sweet-onion jam. An entrée of Sonoma lamb chops glazed with Hunan barbecue sauce was accompanied by roasted Chinese mushrooms and green onions, with a small "treasure packet" of Pacific rice concealed under the lamb. Also listed that night: grilled Florida black grouper marinated in fearless (read *hot*) West Indian spices and served with a plantain-yam mash and tropical chutney. Dessert was a sublime hazelnut meringue napoleon topped with homemade frangelico ice cream and a dusting of Brazilian cocoa. Dux has an extensive, award-winning wine list.

MODERATE

✪ Cafe Tu Tu Tango

8625 International Dr. (just west of the Mercado). ☎ **407/248-2222.** Reservations not accepted. AE, DISC, MC, V. Tapas (tasting portions) $3.75–$7.95. Daily 11:30am–2am. Free self- and valet parking. INTERNATIONAL/TAPAS.

This is a welcome respite from Orlando's predictable "chain gang." For one thing, there's an ongoing performance-art experience taking place while you dine: one evening, an elegantly dressed couple might tango past your table. Another time, it could be an exotically clad belly dancer. Then again, a magician might perform a few tricks tableside—or perhaps a fortune teller will stop by and predict your future. In addition, there are always artists in a studio area creating pottery, paintings, and jewelry. And if that's not enough activity, an exhibition kitchen adjoins the bar. The decor is an eclectic clutter, with a faux skylight, soiled windows, and a beamed ceiling meant to suggest an artist's loft. Bright yellow walls are hung with a changing art show (it's all for sale), and one dining area has food-motif ornamental lights (an ear of corn, a pizza slice, hot dogs) strung overhead. Your silverware is presented in a Windsor & Newton brush pot, complete with paint-brushes.

Tu Tu's colorful ambience is a lot of fun, but its food is the real draw. The larger your party, the more dishes you can sample; two full plates will sate most appetites. My favorites are: Cajun chicken egg rolls (filled with blackened chicken, corn, and cheddar and goat cheese) served with chunky tomato salsa and créole mustard; a skewer of grilled shrimp, wrapped in Italian bacon and served on rice with garbanzo bean sauce; pepper-crusted seared tuna sashimi with crispy rice noodles and cold spinach in a sesame-soy vinaigrette; a Thai salad studded with plump shrimp on a crunchy bed of julienned jicama, cucumber, carrot, and rice noodles; and yummy chicken potstickers garnished with julienned vegetables. A basket of warm mini-pitas glazed with rosemary butter accompanies these dishes, and international wines can be ordered by the glass or bottle. Great desserts here, too—such as creamy almond/amaretto flan and rich guava cheesecake with strawberry sauce.

✪ Capriccio

In The Peabody Orlando, 9801 International Dr. ☎ **407/352-4000.** Reservations recommended. Appetizers $4.75–$8.50, main courses mostly $12–$22 (with most pizza and pasta dishes priced below $14); Sun champagne brunch buffet $24.95 for adults, $12.95 for children 4–12, under 4 free. AE, CB, DC, DISC, ER, JCB, MC, Optima, V. Tues–Sun 6–10pm; brunch Sun 11am–2:30pm. Free self-parking, validated valet parking. NORTHERN ITALIAN.

Capriccio's striking Italian *moderne* interior features a gleaming black-and-white-checkerboard marble-tile floor and black Italian marble tables elegantly appointed with Tuscan-look Villeroy & Boch show plates. An exhibition kitchen occupying an entire wall showcases chefs tending mesquite-burning pizza ovens and grills, and a dessert display table is graced by a lavish floral centerpiece.

Chef Rafael Rabino's seasonal menus bring verve and imagination to traditional northern Italian cooking. On a recent visit I enjoyed an appetizer of fried calamari served with three *aïolis* (aïoli is a garlicky Basque mayonnaise) flavored, respectively, with sun-dried tomato, basil, and saffron. Also scrumptious: a pasta dish of *bucatini* (a long, fat, hollow pasta), tossed with chunks of mesquite-grilled chicken and mushrooms in a slightly garlicky herbed white wine/pesto sauce and finished with tomato concasse. Listed under pizzas was a thin-crusted *rustica* topped with slivers of *soppresata* (spicy Italian salami), prosciutto, veal sausage, and mozzarella and pecorino cheeses. And an entrée of pan-seared tuna with braised fennel and radicchio was served with lentil flan and a buttery citrus sauce. The kitchen turns out fabulous oven-fresh breads such as herbed focaccia and *bruschetta* (mesquite-grilled sourdough rubbed with pesto and roasted garlic and topped with mozzarella, pecorino cheese, and Roman tomatoes) accompanied by extra virgin olive oil that has been infused with rosemary, thyme, and garlic. Dip and exult. But do save room for Capriccio's desserts, which include the definitive *zuppa inglese* (sponge cake layered with fresh berries, kiwi, and Grand Marnier–spiked whipped cream on raspberry-marbleized crème anglaise with garnishes of chocolate shavings and sprigs of fresh mint). An extensive, award-winning wine list is available. Consult your server for suggestions to complement your meal. *Note:* Capriccio also serves a great champagne Sunday brunch.

✪ Ming Court

9188 International Dr. (between Sand Lake Rd. and Beeline Expy., just across from the Peabody Orlando Hotel). ☎ **407/351-9988.** Reservations recommended. Appetizers $4.50–$7.95; dim sum items mostly $1.95–$2.50; main courses $4.50–$7.95 at lunch, mostly $12.50–$18.95 at dinner (tasting portions $8.95–$12.95). AE, CB,

DC, DISC, JCB, MC, V. Daily 11am–2:30pm and 4:30pm–midnight. Free self-parking. CHINESE/ASIAN.

I was thrilled to find an Orlando restaurant whose culinary offerings are on a par with the finest Chinese haute cuisine of New York and California. Ming Court is fronted by a serpentine "cloud wall" crowned by engraved sea-green Chinese tiles (it's a celestial symbol; you dine above the clouds here, like the gods). Its candlelit interior is stunningly decorated in soft earth tones and unfinished oak wainscoting. Glass-walled terrace rooms overlook lotus ponds filled with colorful koi, a plant-filled area under a lofty skylight ceiling evokes a starlit Ming dynasty courtyard, and an interior green-roofed gazebo that seats 8 to 10 people is perfect for small private parties. Beautiful Chinese paintings and pottery are on display, and between 7 and 10pm nightly a musician plays classical Chinese music on a *zheng* (a long zither).

The menu offers specialties from diverse regions of China—all of them uniquely spiced and sauced and prepared with the finest ingredients (including fresh Florida fish and seafood). Begin by ordering a variety of appetizers such as wok-charred Mandarin pot stickers, crispy wontons stuffed with vegetables and cream cheese, and wok-smoked shiitake mushrooms topped with sautéed scallions. Entrées will open up new culinary vistas to even the most sophisticated diners. Lightly battered deep-fried chicken breast is served with a delicate lemon-tangerine sauce. Szechuan charcoal-grilled filet mignon, marinated in olive oil and crushed herbs, is topped with a toasted onion/garlic/chili sauce and served with stir-fried julienne vegetables. And crispy stir-fried jumbo Szechuan shrimp is enhanced by a light fresh tomato sauce nuanced with sake, ginger, chili oil, scallion, garlic, and cilantro. Ming Court augments its Chinese menu with other Asian specialties such as Thai Shrimp in red curry sauce and Japanese beef teriyaki. At lunch you can order dim sum items in addition to regular menu offerings. An extensive wine list includes everything from Pouilly-Fuissé to Chinese rice wines, plum wines, and sake. And as a concession to Western palates, Ming Court features sumptuous desserts such as a moist cake layered with mandarin oranges, Key lime, and fresh whipped cream in orange-vanilla sauce.

✪ Siam Orchid

7575 Republic Dr. (between Sand Lake Rd. and Carrier Dr.) ☎ **407/351-0821.** Reservations recommended. Appetizers $3.55–$5; main courses $10.25–$18.95. AE, DC, DISC, MC, V. Daily 5–11pm. Free self-parking. THAI.

Patterned after a palace in northern Thailand, Siam Orchid centers on a platform used to display wood carvings of angels and musicians representing figures from the *Ramayana*, an ancient Hindu epic poem. The split-level dining room, with lofty knotty-pine cathedral ceilings on either side, seats diners in cushioned booths and banquettes and bamboo chairs at white-linened tables, some of them overlooking a lake. For intimate dining request a *khun toke*—a private carved teak enclosure that is the Thai answer to Japanese tatami rooms. On your way out, browse in the adjoining shop stocked with lacquerware and wood carvings from Thailand.

Owners Tim and Krissnee Martsching grow many necessary ingredients—fresh chiles, mint, cilantro, lemongrass, and wild lime—in their own garden, and their fare is authentic and delicious. Begin with *tom kha gai* (a savory chicken and mushroom soup flavored with lemon juice, lemongrass, wild ginger, and coconut milk). Continue with shared appetizers such as *satay* (skewered pork or chicken, marinated in coconut cream and mild curry, grilled, and served with hot peanut sauce) or *tod man* (crispy fried chicken patties flavored with lemongrass, basil, and wild lime leaf). Both are served with cucumber salad in a sweet vinaigrette. Not to be missed (share an order) is *pad Thai* (soft rice noodles tossed with ground pork, fresh minced garlic, shrimp, crab claws, crabmeat, crushed peanuts, and bean sprouts in a tangy-sweet sauce). Curries are another specialty. Try the royal Thai replete with chunks of chicken, potato, and onion in a yellow curry sauce or *panang* (tender beef or chicken cooked in red curry sauce with mushrooms, basil leaves, and eggplant). There's a full bar, and beverage choices include sake, plum wine, and Thai beers along with French, German, and American wines. Homemade coconut ice cream topped with crushed peanuts makes a refreshing dessert.

INEXPENSIVE

B-Line Diner

The Peabody Orlando, 9801 International Dr. ☎ **407/345-4460.** Reservations not accepted. Appetizers $5.95–$7.25; main courses $3.25–$8.25 at breakfast, $6.95–$10.95 at lunch, $6.95–$17.95 at dinner. AE, CB, DC, DISC, ER, JCB, MC, Optima, V. Daily 24 hours. Free self-parking, validated valet parking. INTERNATIONALLY NUANCED AMERICAN.

This popular local eatery is of the nouvelle art deco diner genre, an idealized version of America's ubiquitous roadside establishments. A high-gloss peach and gray interior, with black-and-white tile floor, gleams with chrome edging that adorns everything from a cove ceiling to peach Formica tables. Seating is in comfortable leatherette booths or Breuer chairs, and a jukebox is stocked with oldies tunes. You can also sit on stools along the sleek black marble-topped counter facing an open kitchen. It's lined with glass-domed cake trays, here filled with duck-shaped cookies. Gorgeous flower arrangements add further upscale panache. It's not your average greasy spoon.

The menu offers sophisticated versions of diner food such as honey-ginger buffalo wings, a grilled pork chop with hazelnut wild rice and sun-dried cherry sauce, or a ham and cheese sandwich (on baguette). Even a steak here is no plain, homespun affair—it's filet mignon served with multibean ragout and shiitake mashed potatoes. Other items—such as a falafel sandwich on pita bread with mint yogurt sauce, fresh Florida seafood cakes with jicama lime slaw and a fruity chili marmalade, and Oriental chicken salad tossed in a zesty peanut vinaigrette, bear no relation to traditional diner fare. Portions are hearty. You may notice a glass display case filled with scrumptious fresh-baked desserts when you come in—everything from banana cream pie to white chocolate/Grand Marnier mousse cake. If you can guess how many ducks are behind a glass wall by the dessert display, you'll win a free piece of cake or pie. The dessert area adjoins **B-Line Express,** a 24-hour take-out counter. There's a full bar. And kids get their own low-priced menu, a duck-themed coloring/activities book, and crayons.

Enzo's

7600 Dr. Phillips Blvd., in the Marketplace Shopping Center, off Sand Lake Rd. just west of I-4. ☎ **407/351-1187.** Reservations not accepted. Appetizers $3.95–$5.95 at lunch, $4.50–$6.50 at dinner; panini (sandwiches) $4.75–$5.95; main courses $4.50–$6.95 at lunch, $8.50–$12.75 at dinner. AE, CB, DC, DISC, MC, V. Mon–Thurs 11:30am–10pm, Fri–Sat 11:30am–11pm. Free self-parking. ITALIAN.

Upon entering this charming little restaurant and Italian charcuterie, you'll walk past display cases filled with olives, antipasti, deli meats, pâtés, and cheeses and shelves stocked with homemade pastas, virgin olive oils, jars of sun-dried tomatoes, and other fancy foodstuffs. And if that's not enough to whet your appetite, you'll also glimpse chefs tending a pizza oven in an exhibition kitchen. The dining area is cheerful and inviting, with glossy pine-plank floors, peach walls hung with fine art prints, and tables covered with red-and-white-striped oilcloth. There's also counter seating; Enzo's is a casual kind of place. Italian music (most of it operatic arias) and exuberant Italian waiters enhance the atmosphere.

Pretty much the same menu is available throughout the day, offering a variety of dining experiences. Families troop in for pizzas—either the traditional American kind or Napoli pies with more sophisticated toppings and crisp, delicate crusts. Until 4:30pm, you can also opt for *panini* (sandwiches on crusty Italian bread) with fillings such as Italian sausage, grilled onions, and peppers; they're served with potato salad. A more serious dinner might begin with an appetizer of paper-thin slices of Norwegian salmon and onion served with extra virgin olive oil, capers, lemon, and red peppers. Homemade pastas include *bucatini* (thick, hollow pasta) tossed with mushrooms, fresh-grated Parmesan, prosciutto, bacon, and peas in a robust sauce. And Enzo's most fabulous entrée is *pollo alla cecco* (roasted breast of free-range chicken with rosemary potatoes roasted with the skins and a ratatouillelike mixture of crushed tomatoes, diced zucchini and eggplant, onions, and peppers in herbed olive oil). Beer and wine are available. For dessert try *zuccotto* (Italian sponge cake soaked in Grand Marnier, layered with fresh fruit and crème anglaise, and topped with chocolate shavings). In busy seasons, arrive off-hours to avoid a wait.

Wild Jacks

7364 International Dr. (between Sand Lake Rd. and Carrier Dr.). ☎ **407/352-4407.** Reservations not accepted. AE, CB, DC, DISC, ER, JCB, MC, V. Appetizers $4.95–$6.95; main courses $9.45–$17.95. Daily 4:30–11pm. Free self-parking. STEAKS AND BARBECUE.

This upscale steak and barbecue restaurant whimsically combines honky-tonk and haute elements in its decor. Pine and cement-block walls display neon beer signs, mounted buffalo and steer heads, western murals depicting the legend of Wild Jack, and drawings of movie-star cowboys. Soft lighting emanates from massive wrought-iron

wagon-wheel chandeliers as well as antlered and steer-head-motif fixtures. There's an exhibition kitchen with an open-pit grill. And a long-
horn steer is poised to jump from a giant horseshoe above the copper
bar. Diners are seated in big comfortable chairs or roomy cowhide-
upholstered booths at tables covered with checkered plastic cloths.

Appetizers here are first rate: skewers of tangy barbecued shrimp
served over Texas rice (it's studded with corn kernels and red and green
peppers), miniature tacos filled with smoked chicken and cheeses, and
spicy potato skins topped with melted cheese, chunks of chicken, pico
de gallo, sour cream, and guacamole. Best entrée choice is the smoked
brisket barbecue, served with salad, warm molasses bread and honey,
and your choice of two side dishes—take the jalapeño mashed potatoes
and grilled corn on the cob. Steaks and prime rib are other options. For
dessert, there's peach cobbler topped with vanilla ice cream sprinkled
with cinnamon. The bar has an iced beer well.

5 Casselberry/Orlando

Generally, visitors don't drive 40 minutes to downtown Orlando or
Casselberry to eat. Buckets, however, is close to major sightseeing
attractions in Orlando. Rolando, in Casselberry, is for those of you who
want to experience authentic Cuban cuisine while you're in Florida.

For further Orlando eateries, check out the Church Street Station
listing in Chapter 9.

MODERATE

Buckets

1825 N. Mills Ave. (just across the street from Loch Haven Park museums). ☎ **407/
894-5197.** Reservations recommended (required Fri/Sat nights). Appetizers
$4.95–$6.95; main courses $4.95–$10.95 at lunch, $8.95–$17.95 at dinner. AE,
CB, DC, DISC, MC, V. Mon–Fri 11am–4pm, Sat–Sun 11:30am–4pm; Sun–Thurs
4–10pm, Fri–Sat 4–11pm; late-night menu Sun–Thurs till midnight, Fri–Sat till 1am.
AMERICAN.

This is a great choice when you're visiting Orlando sights such as Leu
Gardens and Loch Haven Park museums. Its attractive interior has big
teak-framed windows overlooking Lake Rowena. There's additional
lake-view seating on an open-air deck under a canvas awning. At
dinner, there's live entertainment—light jazz or acoustical guitar.

Lunch items include salads (such as chicken Caesar topped with
asiago cheese and almonds), sandwiches (such as smoked turkey breast
with mozzarella cheese and tomato salsa), and hot entrées ranging from
blackened catch of the day to stir-fried chicken with fresh vegetables
and yellow rice tossed with walnuts. At dinner you might follow up an
appetizer of baked seafood-stuffed mushrooms or fried calamari with
baked tortellini in homemade marinara sauce, shrimp scampi served
over pasta, jumbo lump crabcakes, barbecued ribs, or grilled filet
mignon. And dessert options range from tiramisu to Key lime pie.
There's a full bar and an extensive wine list, the latter including many
by-the-glass selections.

INEXPENSIVE

⑤ Rolando's

870 E. FL 436 (Semoran Blvd., between Red Bug Rd. and U.S. 17-92), in Casselberry.
☎ **407/767-9677.** Appetizers 85¢–$1.75; main courses $3.05–$4.75 at lunch,
mostly $5.75–$11.50 at dinner. AE, DISC, MC, V. Tues–Thurs 11am–9pm, Fri–Sat
11am–10pm. Sun 1–8:15pm. Reservations not accepted. Free self-parking. Directions:
Take I-4 east to the East-West Expy., head east, and make a left on FL 436. CUBAN.

About 40 minutes from Walt Disney World, this inexpensive
mom-and-pop eatery—run by Rolando and Maria Vieitez with daugh-
ters Mirtha and Maritza—serves up huge portions of authentic Cuban
fare. Its two dining rooms are pleasant but plain, with Formica tables,
stucco walls hung with photographs of Cuba, and pots of philodendrons suspended from the ceiling. Soft lighting adds a bit of ambience.

I recommend ordering up a bunch of appetizers to share: deep-fried
ripe plantains, *papas rellenas*—breaded deep-fried balls of mashed
potato stuffed with spicy *picadillos* (garlicky ground beef cooked with
onions, olives, raisins, and green peppers in a tomato sauce)—
flavorful Cuban tamales topped with picadillos, and slightly sweet
batter-fried corn fritters that are light as air. An entrée of roast chicken
is brushed with crushed garlic, white wine vinegar, cumin, and oregano
and briefly deep-fried just before serving. Tender shredded beef is simmered in a richly seasoned tomato-based sauce with potatoes, olives,
peas, pimentos, onions, green peppers, and sweet red peppers. And
paella is an option if you call a few hours in advance to order it. Entrées
are served with fresh-baked hot rolls, house salad, rice, and plantains
or *yuca* (a chewy root plant). Take the plantains. For dessert try the
dulce de tres leche (a meringue-topped yellow cake mixed with condensed milk, evaporated milk, and cream). At lunch a hearty sandwich
of hot Cuban bread stuffed with slices of ham, roast pork, Swiss cheese,
and pickles is served with black bean soup. Beer and wine are available.

6 Only in Orlando: Dining with Disney Characters

Especially for the 10-and-under set, it's a thrill to dine in a restaurant
where costumed Disney characters show up to greet the customers, sign
autographs, pose in family photos, and interact with little kids. And for
adults, it's lots of fun to watch the kids going nuts over Mickey or
Donald. The following restaurants throughout the Walt Disney World
complex offer character breakfasts and dinners. All accept American
Express, MasterCard, and Visa. Reserve as far in advance as possible;
many of the below-listed take reservations as long as 60 days in advance.

Many of the restaurants listed below are fully described earlier in this
chapter.

Artist Point, at Disney's Wilderness Lodge, 901 Timberline Dr.
(☎ **407/WDW-DINE**), offers daily character breakfasts between 7:30
and 11:30am. The rustic setting—with western murals, a beamed
ceiling supported by tree-trunk columns, and large windows providing
scenic lake views—was inspired by the grandeur of Rocky Mountain national park country. Goofy, Pluto, and Chip 'n' Dale make the

scene. The meal is an all-you-can-eat buffet consisting of fresh fruit, stuffed French toast, waffles, and pancakes with a variety of syrups; bacon and sausage; scrambled eggs; potatoes; juices and other beverages. Price is $12.95 for adults, $7.95 for children 3 to 11.

Baskerville's, an elegant Sherlock Holmes–themed restaurant at the Grosvenor Resort, 1850 Hotel Plaza Blvd. (☎ 407/828-4444), hosts character breakfasts Tuesday, Thursday, and Saturday mornings from 8 to 10am and character dinners Wednesday evenings from 7:30 to 9:30pm. At either meal you can order à la carte. Breakfast buffets cost $8.95 for adults, $4.95 for children ages 3 to 11, under 3 free. Dinner buffets, always centering on prime rib and themed around a different cuisine (Italian, Créole, etc.) nightly, also include seafood, chicken, and other meat dishes, along with a full salad bar, side dishes, and an extensive choice of desserts; price is $14.95 for adults, $5.95 for children 3 to 11, under 3 free. A la carte, you might order anything from a cheddar burger or Philadelphia cheese steak sandwich to a char-broiled porterhouse steak. Reservations are not accepted; arrive early to avoid a wait.

The delightful New England–themed **Cape May Café,** at Disney's Beach Club Resort, 1800 Epcot Resorts Blvd. (☎ 407/WDW-DINE), serves lavish buffet character breakfasts daily from 7:30 to 11am. Food tables are laden with quiches, waffles, roast beef hash, bread pudding, fruit fritters, cheese blintzes, biscuits with sausage gravy, fresh-baked pastries and muffins, and many other goodies. Admiral Goofy and his crew—Chip 'n' Dale and Pluto—(characters may vary) are hosts. Adults pay $12.95, children 3 to 11 pay $7.95, under 3 free. Reservations are suggested.

At the very attractive **Chef Mickey's** in Walt Disney World Village (☎ 407/WDW-DINE), Mickey is on hand to greet dinner patrons each night from 5 to 10pm. Reservations are suggested; however, only 10% of tables are alloted via reservations, with the rest reserved for walk-ins. On the other hand, you can reserve up to 60 days in advance. Walk-ins should arrive early to avoid a wait. This is an especially appealing choice, since there's first-rate food for adults, and the menu also offers burgers, chicken bits, and other low-priced kid pleasers. See full listing above.

The garden-themed **Contemporary Cafe,** at Disney's Contemporary Resort, 4600 N. World Dr. (☎ 407/WDW-DINE), is the setting for buffet character breakfasts from 7:30 to 11:30am daily. On hand to meet, greet, and mingle with guests are Goofy and the gang. The prix-fixe buffet ($12.95 for adults, $7.95 for children 3 to 11, under 3 free) features a wide array of breakfast foods. Reservations are suggested.

Over at **The Coral Reef,** in the Living Seas Pavilion at Epcot (☎ 407/WDW-DINE), tables ring a 5.6-million-gallon aquarium inhabited by more than 4,000 sea creatures. Goofy, Pluto, Chip 'n' Dale, and Minnie host daily character breakfasts—from 8:30 to 10:30am (from 7:30am Tuesdays and Fridays for Disney resort guests only)—along with Mickey, who dives into the tank! There's talk of bringing in the Little Mermaid in the future. Bubble machines and balloons add to the fun. The meal is a buffet, including eggy breakfast "pizza," bacon and sausage, fresh fruit, sticky buns, and beverages. Price is $14.95 for adults, $7.95 for children under 9. Reservations are essential; they can be made up to seven days in advance only.

Five opulently Victorian dining rooms aboard the *Empress Lilly* (☎ **407/WDW-DINE**)—a plushly furnished triple-decker paddlewheeler docked on Lake Buena Vista in Walt Disney World Village—are used for morning character breakfasts. There are three seatings daily at 7:30, 9, and 10:30am (arrive at least 20 minutes ahead of time). A prix-fixe menu ($12.95 for adults, $7.95 for children 3 to 11, under 3 free), features sausage and eggs, a Mickey-shaped waffle, fresh fruit, and blueberry muffins. Donald, Mickey, Minnie, and Pluto are on hand to greet the guests, and Disney movie music and friendly waiters enhance the party atmosphere. The restaurant is amenable to menu substitutions for fussy kids, and adults who want a lighter meal can also ask for a fruit and yogurt plate. Reservations are essential, and can be made anytime in advance; do so as soon as you decide the dates of your trip.

The plant-filled **Garden Grove Café,** at the Walt Disney World Swan, 1200 Epcot Resorts Blvd. (☎ **407/934-3000**), is an airy three-story domed greenhouse with festive striped canvas awnings, colorful wooden birds perched overhead, and a central terra-cotta fountain. It is the setting for character breakfasts Wednesday and Saturday from 8 to 11am and dinners Monday and Thursday from 6 to 10pm. Breakfast offers a choice of à la carte or buffet meals (the latter is $10.95 for adults, $6.95 for children 3 to 11, under 3 free). Dinner is à la carte, featuring steak and seafood. Character meals here are hosted by Goofy, Pluto, Pooh, and Tigger. Reservations suggested.

Harry's Safari Bar & Grille, at the Walt Disney World Dolphin, 1500 Epcot Resorts Blvd. (☎ **407/934-4025**), is jungle themed with stuffed tigers, elephants, and giraffes in residence. Goofy, Pluto, and Chip 'n' Dale host buffet brunches here every Sunday from 8:30am to noon. Adults pay $14.95, it's $8.95 for children 3 to 12, under 3 free. Reservations suggested.

King Stefan's Banquet Hall, in Cinderella Castle in the Magic Kingdom (☎ **407/WDW-DINE**), serves up character breakfast buffets daily from 8:30 to 10am (from 7:30am Saturday, Monday, and Thursday for Disney resort guests only). Hosts vary, but Cinderella always puts in an appearance. Fare includes eggs, blintzes, Mickey waffles, fresh fruit, cinnamon rolls, juice, and more. Adults pay $14.95, children 3 to 9 pay $7.95, under 3 free. It's a great way to start your day in the Magic Kingdom. Reservations are essential; they can be made up to seven days in advance only.

Luau Cove, at Disney's Polynesian Resort, 1600 Seven Seas Dr. (☎ **407/WDW-DINE**), is the setting for an island-themed character show called **Mickey's Tropical Luau** daily at 4:30pm. It's an abbreviated version of the Polynesian Luau Dinner Show described in Chapter 9, "Walt Disney World & Orlando After Dark," featuring Polynesian dancers along with Mickey, Minnie, Pluto, and Goofy. Your prix-fixe meal ($29 for adults, $22 for ages 12 to 20, $13 for ages 3 to 11, under 3 free) includes tropical fruit salad, a trio of entrées (seafood stir-fry, barbecued ribs, and teriyaki chicken), rice, coconut-almond bread with mandarin- orange butter, and a Disney character ice-cream bar. Guests are presented with shell leis on entering. Reserve far in advance.

The Polynesian also hosts **Minnie's Menehune Character Breakfast** buffets (☎ 407/WDW-DINE) daily from 7:30 to 10:30am in the Polynesian-themed **O'Hana at Papeete Bay.** A wide selection of hot and cold breakfast foods is featured. Adults pay $12.95, children 3 to 11 pay $7.95, under 3 free. Minnie, Goofy, and Chip 'n' Dale appear. Reservations are essential.

Disney's elegant Grand Floridian Beach Resort, 4001 Grand Floridian Way (☎ 407/WDW-DINE), hosts character meals in its festive exposition-themed restaurant, **1900 Park Fare.** The room is decorated with old-fashioned carved wooden merry-go-round animals, antique toys, and circus-themed paintings. Big Bertha—a French band organ that plays pipes, drums, bells, cymbals, castenets, and xylophone—provides music. Mary Poppins, Winnie the Pooh, Goofy, Pluto, Chip 'n' Dale, and Minnie Mouse appear at elaborate buffet breakfasts served daily between 7:30am and noon. Adults pay $14.95, children 3 to 11 pay $9.75, under 3 free. Mickey and Minnie appear at nightly buffets (featuring prime rib, stuffed pork loin, fresh fish, and more) from 5 to 9pm. Adults pay $17.95, children 3 to 11 pay $9.75, under 3 free. Reservations are essential for both meals.

One of the most popular WDW character breakfasts takes place at the **Soundstage Restaurant** at Disney-MGM Studios, adjacent to the Magic of Disney Animation (☎ 407/WDW-DINE). Characters from the movie *Aladdin*—the genie, Jafar, and Aladdin or Jasmin—plus Mickey in Moroccan garb, visit tables and sign autographs in this exotic Middle Eastern–motif restaurant adorned with shelves of brass coffee urns and murals of onion-domed mosques. A vast buffet—fresh and dried fruits, breakfast meats, eggs, pastries, muffins and bagels, cereals, waffles, and blintzes—evokes an Arab marketplace, and there's a magic lamp on every table. It takes place daily from 8:30 to 10:30am. Cost is $14.95 for adults, $7.95 for kids 3 to 11, free for kids under 3. Reservations are essential.

The tropically festive and plant-filled **Watercress Café,** at the Buena Vista Palace, 1900 Buena Vista Dr. (☎ 407/827-2727), has paintings of parrots and flamingos adorning peach stucco walls and large windows overlooking Lake Buena Vista. It's the setting for Sunday morning character breakfasts (8 to 10:30am) featuring Minnie, Goofy, and Pluto. You can order à la carte or buffet meals. The buffet costs $11.95 for adults, $6.95 for kids 4 to 12, under 4 free. Reservations are not accepted; arrive early to avoid a wait.

What to See & Do in the Walt Disney World Area

We all know what the big attraction is here—the one that put Orlando on the map. With the exception of conventioneers (and I'm sure many of them sneak off to the parks as well), most people who come to Orlando have come to meet the Mouse.

Walt Disney World, attracting more than 13 million annual visitors, is one of the world's most popular travel destinations. And why not? It provides a welcome retreat from personal and global problems to a star-spangled all-American fantasyland where wonderment, human progress, and old-fashioned family fun are the major themes. And these themes are presented in a dazzling format of spectacular parades and fireworks displays, 3-D and 360-degree movies, and adventure-filled journeys through time and space. Though it's not inexpensive, you'll seldom hear people complain about not getting their money's worth. Disney delivers!

The Magic Kingdom opened in 1971. Later additions include Epcot, where guests take exhilarating voyages around the world and into the future; Disney-MGM Studios, centered on "Hollywood Boulevard" and providing a thrilling behind-the-scenes look at motion-picture and TV studios; Pleasure Island, an ongoing street festival in a six-acre complex of nightclubs and shops, featuring live concerts nightly; Walt Disney World Village, a charming lakeside enclave of shops and restaurants; Typhoon Lagoon, a 56-acre water park where you can catch the world's largest manmade waves or plummet down steep water flumes; River Country, another fabulous water park; and Discovery Island, an utterly delightful nature preserve and aviary. Blizzard Beach, a new water park with the zany theme of "a ski resort in the tropics," opened shortly after press time.

Outside the Disney complex, visitors are lured to two other major theme parks. Universal Studios, a working production facility, is filled with thrilling high-tech rides and attractions and gives visitors a behind-the-scenes look at motion-picture and television development and technology. New to Universal this year will be A Day in the Park with Barney featuring the purple superstar in a musical show (a must-see for young children). Nearby, Sea World, whose most famous denizen is Shamu, offers 200 acres of marine-oriented shows, rides, and entertainments. Wild Arctic, using flight-simulator technology to re-create the experience of a polar expedition, and the Mermaids, Myths & Monsters nighttime multimedia spectacular are Sea World's newest highlights. And theme parks aside, many other museums, gardens, and attractions in the area beckon visitors.

You won't see all the attractions at any of the parks in a single day. Read through the upcoming descriptions, decide which are musts for you, and try to get to them. My favorite rides and attractions are starred.

SUGGESTED ITINERARIES

A Day in the Magic Kingdom

Get to the park well before opening time, tickets in hand. When the gates open, head for the kiosk just outside Disneyana Collectibles, and make a reservation for a lunchtime show at the Diamond Horseshoe Jamboree. Then hightail it to Frontierland and ride Splash Mountain before long lines form. When you come off, it will still be early enough to beat the lines at another major attraction. Double back to Adventureland and do Pirates of the Caribbean. Then relax and take it slow. Complete whatever else interests you in Adventureland, and enjoy Frontierland attractions until it's time for your lunch show. After lunch, continue visiting Frontierland attractions as desired or proceed to the Hall of Presidents and the Haunted Mansion in Liberty Square. By 2:30pm (earlier in peak seasons), you should snag a seat on the curb in Liberty Square along the parade route. After the parade, continue around the park taking in Fantasyland and Tomorrowland attractions. If SpectroMagic is on during your stay, don't miss it.

If you have little kids (8 and under) in your party, after making the above-mentioned lunch reservations for Diamond Horseshoe Jamboree, take the WDW Railroad from Main Street to Mickey's Starland to see the show. Work your way through Fantasyland until lunch. After lunch visit the Country Bear Jamboree in Frontierland and proceed to Adventureland for the Jungle Cruise, Swiss Family Treehouse, and Tropical Serenade. Once again, stop in good time to get parade seats (in Frontierland). Little kids need to sit right up front to see everything. That's a long enough day for most young children, and your best plan is to go back to your hotel for a nap or swim. If, however, you wish to continue, return to Frontierland and/or Fantasyland for the rides you didn't complete earlier.

If You Can Spend Only One Day at Epcot

Epcot really requires at least two days, so this is a highlight tour. As above, arrive early, tickets in hand. If you haven't already made lunch reservations via (407) WDW-DINE (see Chapter 6, "Orlando Dining"), make your first stop at the WorldKey terminals in Innoventions East. I suggest a 1pm lunch at the San Angel Inn Restaurant in Mexico. If you don't like Mexican food, move up one pavilion to Norway and reserve for the buffet at Akershus. You can make dinner reservations at the same time. Plan dinner for about 7pm, which will allow you time

Walt Disney World Parks & Attractions

Blizzard Beach **10**   Fort Wilderness   Typhoon Lagoon **7**
Discovery Island **2**   Campground **4**   Walt Disney World
Disney-MGM Studios   The Magic Kingdom **1**   Village **9**
   Theme Park **6**   Pleasure Island **8**
Epcot **5**   River Country **3**

to eat and find a good viewing spot for IllumiNations (usually at 9pm, but check your schedule). Spend no more than an hour exploring Innoventions East. Then move on to the Universe of Energy show. Continue to the Wonders of Life Pavilion where must-sees include Body Wars, Cranium Command, and The Making of Me. And if time allows—it will depend on line waits at attractions—take in the show at Horizons before heading into World Showcase for lunch. Over lunch, check your show schedule and decide which shows to

---

A Word About Epcot Dining

Sit-down meals at World Showcase Pavilions and the Living Seas are a pleasant—but pricey—part of the Epcot experience. There are plenty of less-expensive eateries throughout the park, including ethnic ones with café seating in many World Showcase Pavilions. And since these don't require reservations, you're not tied down to specific mealtimes. See your Guidemap for details.

---

incorporate into your day. Then walk around the lagoon, visiting highlight attractions: *Wonders of China, The American Adventure, Impressions de France,* and *O' Canada,* allowing yourself some time for browsing and shopping. After dinner, stay on for IllumiNations.

If You Can Spend Two Days at Epcot

Ignore the one-day itinerary above, but do begin your day by making all necessary restaurant reservations—once again for lunch in Mexico or Norway at about 1pm. Make reservations for Day 2 at the same time. Skip Innoventions East for the nonce, and work your way thoroughly through the Universe of Energy, Wonders of Life, Horizons, and World of Motion pavilions, keeping your lunch reservation time in mind. After lunch, walk clockwise around the lagoon, visiting each pavilion and taking in as many shows as you like (consult your show schedule and try to keep pace as well as possible). Leave IllumiNations for your second day's visit.

Begin your second day exploring Innoventions East, and proceed counterclockwise, taking in Spaceship Earth, Innoventions West, The Living Seas (a good choice for lunch), and all the other pavilions on the west side of the park. Cap your Epcot visit with IllumiNations.

A DAY AT DISNEY-MGM STUDIOS THEME PARK

Since show times change frequently here, it's impossible to really give you a workable itinerary. Upon entering the park, if you haven't already made dining arrangements, stop at the Hollywood Brown Derby (details in Chapter 6) and make reservations for lunch. Or you might want to conserve park-touring time by having a light lunch at a casual eatery and saving the Derby for a relaxing dinner. Nutritional needs accounted for, make a beeline for the Twilight Zone Tower of Terror. While you're waiting in line, plan the rest of your schedule, being sure to include these not-to-be-missed attractions: The Magic of Disney Animation, the Great Movie Ride, Jim Henson's Muppet

In the Words of Walt Disney

"Family fun is as necessary to modern living as a kitchen refrigerator."

"Part of the Disney success is our ability to create a believable world of dreams that appeals to all age groups."

Vision 3D, and the Monster Sound Show. If you have girls under 11 in your party, the Voyage of the Little Mermaid and *Beauty and the Beast* are probably priorities; for the latter, get in line 45 minutes prior to showtime at the Theater of the Stars. And all kids love the parade; snag a good seat on the parade route 45 minutes ahead of time as well. Time for more? Do Superstar Television, the Indiana Jones Epic Stunt Spectacular, Star Tours, Inside the Magic, and the Backstage Studio Tour. In peak seasons stay on for fireworks.

IF YOU HAVE EXTRA DAYS IN TOWN

If you're staying longer than the four days accounted for above, you'll probably want to spend at least one them in the Magic Kingdom and/ or Epcot seeing whatever you've missed. If you have an additional day:

Adults and families with kids over 10 should head for **Universal Studios** which is choc-a-bloc with thrilling hi-tech rides and attractions. Families with younger kids will do better at **Sea World.**

Consider also an excursion to **Cypress Gardens** or the **John F. Kennedy Space Center.**

Still more time? By now you need rest and refreshment. You'll find it at any of the Disney water theme parks. Spend the morning splashing around, and in the afternoon tour Discovery Island.

1 Tips on Visiting Walt Disney World

PLANNING YOUR VISIT

How you plan your time at Walt Disney World will depend on a number of factors, including the ages of children in your party, what you've seen on previous visits, your specific interests, and whether you're traveling at a peak time or off-season (when lines are shorter and you can cram more in). Planning, however, is essential. Unless you're staying for considerably more than a week, you can't possibly experience all the rides, shows, and attractions here—not to mention the vast array of recreational facilities. And you'll only wear yourself to a frazzle trying. It's far better to follow a relaxed itinerary, including leisurely meals and recreational activities, than to make a demanding job out of trying to see everything. *Note:* Many of these suggestions are also applicable at non-Disney theme parks.

INFORMATION

Before leaving home, call or write the **Walt Disney World Co.,** Box 10,000, Lake Buena Vista, FL 32830-1000 (☎ 407/934-7639) for a copy of the very informative *Walt Disney World Vacations*—an invaluable planning aid. When you call, also ask about special events that will be on during your stay (see also "When to Go," in Chapter 2 of this book). Once you've arrived in town, **guest services** and **concierge desks** in all area hotels—especially Disney properties and official hotels—have up-to-the-minute information about happenings in the parks. Stop by to ask questions and pick up literature, including a schedule of park hours and special events. If you have questions your hotel can't answer, call 407/824-4321. There are also **information**

locations in each park—at City Hall in the Magic Kingdom, at Innoventions East near the World Key terminals in Epcot, and the Guest Services Building in Disney-MGM Studios.

BEST DAYS TO VISIT

The busiest days at the Magic Kingdom and Epcot are Monday to Wednesday, at Disney-MGM Studios Wednesday to Friday. Surprisingly, weekends are the least busy at all parks. In peak seasons, especially, arrange your visits accordingly.

CREATE AN ITINERARY FOR EACH DAY

Read the above-mentioned *Walt Disney World Vacations* and the detailed descriptions in this book and plan your visit to include all shows and attractions that pique your interest and excitement. It's a good idea to make a daily itinerary, putting these in some kind of sensible geographical sequence, so you're not zigzagging all over the place. Familiarize yourself in advance with the layout of each park. I repeat this advice—do schedule in sit-down shows, recreational activities (a boat ride or swim late in the afternoon can be wonderfully refreshing), and at least some unhurried meals. My suggested itineraries are above.

BUY TICKETS IN ADVANCE

You can purchase four- or five-day passes (see details below) prior to your trip by calling **Ticket Mail Order** (☎ 407/824-6750). There's a $2 postage and handling charge, and you must allow 21 days for processing your request. Of course, you can always purchase tickets at any of the parks, but why stand on an avoidable line? *Note:* One-day tickets can be purchased only at park entrances.

OPERATING HOURS & TICKETS

OPERATING HOURS

Hours of operation vary somewhat throughout the year.

The **Magic Kingdom** and **Disney-MGM Studios** are generally open 9am to 7pm, with extended hours—sometimes as late as midnight—during major holidays and the summer months.

Epcot hours are generally 9am to 9pm, with Future World open 9am to 7pm, World Showcase 11am to 9pm—once again with extended holiday hours.

Typhoon Lagoon and **Blizzard Beach** are open 10am to 5pm most of the year (with extended hours during some holidays), 9am to 8pm in summer.

River Country and **Discovery Island** are open 10am to 5pm most of the year (with extended hours during some holidays), 10am to 7pm in summer.

Note: Epcot and Disney-MGM sometimes open a half-hour or more before posted time. Keep in mind, too, that Disney resort guests enjoy early admission to all three major parks on designated days.

TICKETS

There are several ticket options. Most people get the best value from four- and five-day passes. All passes offer unlimited use of the WDW

🔵 Did You Know?

- It's not a small world after all! Covering 43 square miles, Walt Disney World is about the size of San Francisco.
- In a recent year, guests at Universal Studios consumed 1,101,245 burgers and 131 miles of hot dogs.
- The manatees at Sea World each eat about 10% of their body weight daily. Their daily diet consists of about 100 pounds of romaine lettuce along with assorted fruits and vegetables, especially apples.
- The pesticide DDT was developed solely in Orlando by a group of government entomologists who were exploring its military uses. Though later abandoned as dangerously toxic, DDT was widely used during World War II.
- The famous Florida sinkhole, appearing in Winter Park in May of 1981, consumed several Porsche cars, part of a city street, a home, and a large corner of a public swimming pool. It became a central Florida tourist attraction, with vendors lining up nearby to hawk T-shirts and sinkhole-related merchandise.

---

transportation system. Prices quoted below do not include sales tax, and they are, of course, subject to change.

Adult prices are paid by anyone over 10 years of age.

Children's rates are for ages 3 to 9.

Children under 3 are admitted free.

The **Four-Day Value Pass** provides admission for: one day at the Magic Kingdom, one day at Epcot, one day at Disney-MGM Studios, and one day at your choice of any of those three parks; you can use it on any four days following purchase, but you cannot visit more than one park on any given day. Adults pay $124, children $97.

The **Four-Day Park-Hopper Pass** provides unlimited admission to the three major parks on any four days; in other words, you can hop from park to park on any given day. Adults pay $134, children $107.

The **Five-Day World-Hopper Pass** provides unlimited admission to the Magic Kingdom, Epcot, and Disney-MGM Studios on any five days; you can visit any combination of parks on any given day. It also includes admission to Typhoon Lagoon, River Country, Blizzard Beach, Discovery Island, and Pleasure Island for a period of seven days beginning the first date stamped. Adults pay $179, children $143.

A **one-day, one-park ticket for the Magic Kingdom, Epcot, or Disney-MGM Studios** is $36 for adults, $29 for children.

A **one-day ticket to Typhoon Lagoon or Blizzard Beach** is $22.50 for adults, $17 for children.

A **one-day ticket to River Country** is $14.75 for adults, $11.50 for children.

A **one-day ticket to Discovery Island** is $10 for adults, $5.50 for children.

A **one-day ticket to Pleasure Island** is $14.95.

A **combined one-day ticket for River Country and Discovery Island** is $18.50 for adults, $13.25 for children.

If you are staying at any Walt Disney World Resort or official hotel you are also eligible for a money-saving **Be Our Guest Pass** priced according to length of stay. It also offers special perks.

If you plan on visiting Walt Disney World more than one time during the year, inquire about a money-saving **annual pass.**

IN THE PARKS
PARKING

Parking—free to guests at WDW resorts—otherwise costs $5 per day no matter how many parks you visit. Be sure to note down your parking location before leaving your car. There is a spot for this information on your parking ticket. There are special handicapped lots at each park (call 407/824-4321 for details). Don't worry about parking far from the entrance gates; trams constantly ply the route.

ARRIVE EARLY

Unless you're an incorrigible night person, always arrive at the parks a good 30 to 45 minutes before opening time, thus avoiding a traffic jam entering the park and a long line at the gate. Early arrival also lets you experience one or two major attractions before big lines form. In high season parking lots sometimes fill up and you may even have to wait to get in.

Upon entering any of the three major Disney parks, you'll be given an **entertainment schedule** and a comprehensive **park guidebook** that contains a map of the park and lists all attractions, shops, shows, and restaurants. If by some fluke you haven't obtained these, they are available at the above-mentioned information locations in each park. If, as suggested above, you've formulated an itinerary prior to arrival, you already know the major shows (check show schedules for additional ideas) you want to see during the day and what arrangements you need to make. If you haven't done this, use your early arrival time, while waiting for the park to open, to figure out which shows to attend, and, where necessary, make reservations for them as soon as the gates swing open.

LOST CHILDREN

All parks have a place for separated adults and children to meet up. Find out where it is when you come into the park (it's in your park guidebook), and tell your kids to ask a park attendant to take them there if you get separated. Children under 7 should have name tags.

PETS

Don't leave your pet in a parked car, even with a window cracked. The interior of a car becomes incredibly hot baking in the Florida sun. A dead pet will not enhance your trip. Pets are not permitted in the parks, but there are four kennels in the WDW complex. Those at the Transportation and Ticket Center in the Magic Kingdom and near the entrance to Fort Wilderness board animals overnight. Day accommodations are offered at kennels just outside the Entrance Plaza at Epcot and at the entrance to Disney MGM-Studios.

DINING

Try to eat lunch before noon or after 2pm. That way you can hit popular rides when most people are eating (and lines are a bit shorter), and eat when restaurants are less crowded. Make restaurant reservations far in advance of your trip by calling 407/WDW-DINE.

SHOPPING

All of the Disney parks have dozens of shops filled with kid-pleasing items. To avoid a lot of whining and pleading, agree in advance on the amount a child can spend on souvenirs. Leave shopping for the last activity of the day, so that you don't have to lug your purchases around.

LEAVING THE PARKS

If you leave any of the parks and plan to return later in the day, be sure to get your hand stamped on exiting.

REMEMBER TO HAVE FUN

A theme park provides a unique opportunity to spend some quality time with the kids, but your attitude can make or break the experience. For instance, it's more fun to chat, play games, and tell stories on long lines than to grouse about them. Parents set the tone. So get your priorities in order, and go with the flow.

Staying at Disney properties simplifies many of the above tasks and procedures. See the full list of perks for Disney and "official" hotel guests in Chapter 5.

2 The Magic Kingdom

Centered around Cinderella Castle—its medieval spires Walt Disney World's most recognizable symbol after Mickey Mouse—the Magic Kingdom occupies about 100 acres, with 45 major attractions and numerous restaurants and shops in seven themed sections or "lands." From the parking lot, you have to take a short monorail or ferry ride to the Magic Kingdom entrance. During peak attendance times, arrive at the Magic Kingdom no later than an hour prior to opening time to avoid long lines at these conveyances. Sections of the parking lot are named for Disney characters (Goofy, Pluto, Minnie, and so on), and aisles are numbered.

Upon entering the park, consult your *Magic Kingdom Guidemap* to get your bearings. It details every shop, restaurant, and attraction in every land. Also consult your **entertainment schedule** to see what's on for the day. There are parades, musical extravaganzas featuring Disney characters, fireworks, band concerts, barbershop quartets, Disney character appearances, and more. If you have questions, all park employees are very knowledgeable, and City Hall, on your left as you enter, is both an information center, and, along with Mickey's Starland (details below) a likely place to meet up with costumed characters. There's a stroller rental shop just after the turnstiles to your right, and the Kodak Camera Center, near Town Square, supplies all conceivable photographic needs, including camera and camcorder rentals and two-hour film developing.

MAIN STREET, U.S.A.

Designed to replicate an archetypical turn-of-the-century American street—albeit one that culminates in a 13th-century castle—this is the gateway to the Kingdom. Don't dawdle on Main Street when you enter the park; leave it for the end of the day when you're heading back to your hotel.

WALT DISNEY WORLD RAILROAD & OTHER MAIN STREET VEHICLES   You can board an authentic 1928 steam-powered railroad here for a 15-minute journey clockwise around the perimeter of the park. There are stations in Frontierland, Mickey's Starland, and Tomorrowland. There are also horse-drawn trolleys, horseless carriages, jitneys, omnibuses, and fire engines plying the short route along Main Street from Town Square to Cinderella Castle.

MAIN STREET CINEMA   A mannequin is in charge of the ticket booth here, so you can sneak right in without paying. Just kidding—there's no charge for admission. Main Street Cinema is an air-conditioned hexagonal theater where vintage black-and-white Disney cartoons (including the 1928 *Steamboat Willie* in which Mickey and Minnie debuted) are aired continually on six screens. Viewers have to watch these standing; there are no seats.

PENNY ARCADE   At this old-fashioned penny arcade, even the prices evoke nostalgia. Its 1¢ hand-cranked Cail-o-scopes (one of them featuring Charlie Chaplin), test-your-grip machines, old pinball games, kiss-o-meter, Gypsy fortune-teller, and shooting gallery evoke pleasant childhood memories to those of a certain age and are a novelty to the Nintendo generation.

🔵 Did You Know?

- The movie portion of Universal Studio's *Back to the Future* attraction took two years to make and was the most expensive film per minute ever made.
- Mickey Mouse has more than 80 different outfits, ranging from a scuba suit to a tuxedo. Minnie has only 50.
- There are enough Mickey Mouse ear hats sold each year to cover the head of every man, woman, and child in Pittsburgh.
- In a typical week in Orlando, 396 new jobs are created, 1,117 new residents move in, 243 marriages and 325 births are recorded, retail sales total $188 million, and more than 230,000 visitors arrive in town.
- You could fit New York's Empire State Building into the Vehicle Assembly Building at the Kennedy Space Center $3^{3}/_{4}$ times.
- Shamu, the killer whale at Sea World, eats more than 65,000 pounds of fish a year.
- Every day an average of 100 pairs of sunglasses are turned into the Lost and Found at the Magic Kingdom.

ADVENTURELAND

Cross a bridge to your left, and stroll into an exotic jungle of lush tropical foliage, thatch-roofed huts, and carved totems. Amid dense vines and stands of palm and bamboo, drums are beating, and swashbuckling adventures are taking place. *Note:* If you're heading toward Adventureland or Frontierland first thing in the morning, wait for the gates to open at the bridge in front of the Crystal Palace, to your left as you enter.

SWISS FAMILY TREEHOUSE   This attraction is based on the 1960 Disney movie version of Johann Wyss's *Swiss Family Robinson,* about a shipwrecked family of five who created an ingenious dwelling for themselves in the branches of a sprawling banyan tree. Using materials and furnishings salvaged from their downed ship, the Robinsons created bedrooms, a kitchen, a library, and a living room. Visitors traverse a rope-suspended bridge and ascend the 50-foot tree for a close-up look into these rooms. Do note the Rube Goldberg rope-and-bucket device with bamboo chutes that dips water from a stream and carries it to treetop chambers. The "tree" itself, designed by Disney "Imagineers," has 330,000 polyethylene "leaves" sprouting from a 90-foot span of branches; although it isn't real, it is draped with actual Spanish moss.

JUNGLE CRUISE   What a cruise! In the course of about 10 minutes, your boat sails through an African veldt in the Congo, an Amazon rain forest, the Mekong River in Southeast Asia, and along the Nile. Lavish scenery, with ropes of hanging vines, cascading waterfalls, and lush tropical and subtropical foliage (most of it real), includes dozens of Audio-Animatronic™ birds and animals—elephants, zebras, lions, giraffes, crocodiles, tigers, even fluttering butterflies. On the shore you'll pass a *Raiders*-like Cambodian temple cave fronted by a Buddha and guarded by snakes; a rhino and jackal chasing terrified African beaters up a tree; and a jungle camp taken over by apes. But the adventures aren't all on shore. Passengers are menaced by everything from water-spouting elephants to fierce warriors who attack with spears. The guide keeps up an amusing patter.

✪ PIRATES OF THE CARIBBEAN   This is Disney magic at its best. You'll proceed through a long grottolike passageway to board a boat into a pitch-black cave. Therein, elaborate scenery and hundreds of Audio-Animatronic™ figures (including lifelike dogs, cats, chickens, pigs, and donkeys) depict a rambunctious pirate raid on a Caribbean

In the Words of Walt Disney

"Sheer animated fantasy is still my first and deepest production impulse. The fable is the best storytelling device ever conceived. . . . And, of course, animal characters have always been the personnel of fable—animals through which the foibles as well as the virtues of humans can best and most hilariously be reflected."

"Never get bored or cynical. Yesterday is a thing of the past."

The Magic Kingdom

MAIN STREET, U.S.A.:

Walt Disney
World Railroad ❶
Main Street Cinema ❷
Penny Arcade ❸
Magic Kingdom
Baby Care Center ❹
First Aid Center ❺
City Hall ❻

ADVENTURELAND:

Pirates of the Caribbean ❼
Jungle Cruise ❽
Swiss Family Treehouse ❾
Tropical Serenade ❿

FRONTIERLAND:

Splash Mountain ⓫
Tom Sawyer Island ⓬
Diamond Horseshoe
Jamboree ⓭

Frontierland Shootin' Arcade ⓮
Country Bear Jamboree ⓯
Frontierland Railroad Station ⓰
Big Thunder
Mountain Railroad ⓱

LIBERTY SQUARE:

Haunted Mansion ⓲
Mike Fink Keel Boats ⓳
Liberty Square Riverboat ⓴
Hall of Presidents ㉑

town. To a background of cheerful "yo-ho-yo-ho" music, the sound of rushing waterfalls, squawking sea gulls, and screams of terror, passengers pass through the line of fire in a raging pirate battle and view tableaux of fierce-looking pirates swigging rum, looting, and plundering. This might be scary for kids under 5.

TROPICAL SERENADE   In a large hexagonal Polynesian-style dwelling, with a thatched roof, bamboo beams, and tapa-bark murals,

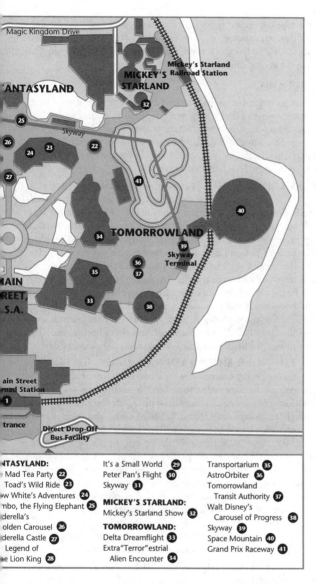

Magic Kingdom Drive

Mickey's Starland
Railroad Station

MICKEY'S
STARLAND

ANTASYLAND

32

25

Skyway

26

24 **23** **22**

27

41

40

34 TOMORROWLAND

39
Skyway
Terminal

MAIN

36

35

37

REET,

.S.A.

33

38

ain Street
oad Station

1

trance

**Direct Drop-Off
Bus Facility**

NTASYLAND:
Mad Tea Party **22**
Toad's Wild Ride **23**
w White's Adventures **24**
mbo, the Flying Elephant **25**
derella's
olden Carousel **26**
derella Castle **27**
Legend of
e Lion King **28**

It's a Small World **29**
Peter Pan's Flight **30**
Skyway **31**

MICKEY'S STARLAND:
Mickey's Starland Show **32**

TOMORROWLAND:
Delta Dreamflight **33**
Extra"Terror"estrial
Alien Encounter **34**

Transportarium **35**
AstroOrbiter **36**
Tomorrowland
Transit Authority **37**
Walt Disney's
Carousel of Progress **38**
Skyway **39**
Space Mountain **40**
Grand Prix Raceway **41**

250 tropical birds, chanting totem poles, and singing flowers whistle, tweet, and warble songs such as "Let's All Sing Like the Birdies Sing." The audience is encouraged to sing along. The show is hosted by four feathered friends named José, Michael, Pierre, and Fritz, all with appropriate national accents—who perch atop an "enchanted" fountain. Highlights include a thunderstorm in the dark (the gods are angry!), a light show over the fountain, and, of course, the famous "in the tiki,

tiki, tiki, tiki, tiki room" song. Like it or not, you'll find yourself singing it all day. An amusing preshow, in which two wisecracking parrots
relate their jungle adventures, takes place out front while you wait. This
is a must for young children.

FRONTIERLAND

From Adventureland, step into the wild and woolly past of the American frontier, where Disney employees are clad in denim and calico,
sidewalks are wooden, rough-and-tumble architecture runs to log cabins and rustic saloons, and the landscape is southwestern scrubby with
mesquite, saguaro cactus, yucca, and prickly pear. Across the river is
Tom Sawyer Island, reachable via log rafts.

✪ **SPLASH MOUNTAIN**   Themed after Walt Disney's 1946 film,
Song of the South, Splash Mountain takes you on an enchanting journey in a hollowed-out log craft along the canals of a flooded mountain,
past 26 brilliantly colored tableaux of backwoods swamps, bayous,
spooky caves, and waterfalls. Riders are caught up in the bumbling
schemes of Brer Fox and Brer Bear as they pursue the ever-wily Brer
Rabbit, who, against the advice of Mr. Bluebird, has left his briar-patch
home in search of adventure and the "laughing place." The music from
the film forms a delightful audio backdrop. Your log craft twists, turns,
and splashes—sometimes plummeting in total darkness—all leading up
to a thrilling five-story, 45-degree angle splashdown from mountaintop
to briar-filled pond at 40 miles per hour! And that's not the end. The
ride continues, and finally it's a Zip-A-Dee-Doo-Dah kind of day.

✪ **BIG THUNDER MOUNTAIN RAILROAD**   This mining-
disaster- themed roller coaster—its thrills deriving from hairpin turns
and descents in the dark rather than sudden steep drops—is situated
in a 200-foot-high redstone mountain with 2,780 feet of track winding through windswept canyons and bat-filled caves. You enter the ride
via the ramshackle headquarters of the Big Thunder Mining Company
and board a runaway train that careens through the ribs of a dinosaur,
under a thundering waterfall, past spewing geysers and bubbling
mudpots, and over a bottomless volcanic pool. Riders are threatened
by flash floods, earthquakes, rickety bridges, and avalanches.
Audio-Animatronic™ characters (such as the longjohn-clad fellow
navigating the floodwaters in a bathtub) and animals (goats, chickens,
donkeys, possums), enhance the scenic backdrop, and several-
hundred-thousand dollars worth of authentic antique mining equipment, amassed from many auctions, adds verisimilitude.

✪ **DIAMOND HORSESHOE JAMBOREE**   This 40-minute show
provides an opportunity to sit down in air-conditioned comfort and
enjoy a rousing western revue. The "theater" is a re-creation of a turn-
of-the-century saloon. Owner/bartender Sam plays the washboard, tells
silly jokes, and shoots at the audience (with a water gun). Lily (a Mae
West type) and her troupe of dance-hall girls do a cancan (Sam, in
drag, joins in). And the cowboys perform feats of fast fiddling and
foot-stomping acrobatic dances. There's a vague story line behind the
action, which includes lots of good-natured audience participation.
There are five shows daily; plan on going around lunchtime so you can

eat during the show. The menu features deli or peanut butter and jelly sandwiches served with chips, and there are chocolate chip cookies and fruit for dessert. Make reservations when you enter the park just outside Disneyana Collectibles on the east side of Main Street in Town Square. Seating is reserved, so you can arrive shortly before show time.

✪ **COUNTRY BEAR JAMBOREE**   Call me corny. I've always loved the Country Bear Jamboree, a 15-minute show featuring a troupe of fiddlin', banjo strummin', harmonica playin' Audio-Animatronic™ bears belting out rollicking country tunes and crooning plaintive love songs. The chubby Trixie, decked out in a satiny skirt, laments lost love, as she sings "Tears Will Be the Chaser for Your Wine." Teddi Barra descends from the ceiling in a swing to perform "Heart We Did All That We Could." Other star performers include a country-western group called the Five Bear Rugs, Liver Lips McGrowl, and the seven-foot-tall master of ceremonies, Henry. In the rousing show finale the entire cast joins in a foot-stompin' singalong. Wisecracking commentary comes from a mounted buffalo, moose, and deer on the wall. A special holiday show plays throughout the Christmas season each year.

TOM SAWYER ISLAND   Board Huck Finn's raft for a one-minute float across the river to the densely forested Tom Sawyer Island, where kids can explore the narrow passages of Injun Joe's cave (complete with scary sound effects like whistling wind), a walk-through windmill, a serpentine abandoned mine, or Fort Sam Clemens, where an Audio-Animatronic™ drunk is snoring off a bender. Maintaining one's balance while crossing rickety swing and barrel bridges is also fun. Narrow winding dirt paths lined with oaks, pines, and sycamores create an authentic backwoods island feel. It's easy to get briefly lost and stumble upon some unexpected adventure. You might combine this attraction with lunch at Aunt Polly's restaurant, which serves light fare (fried chicken, sandwiches, and the like) and has outdoor tables on a porch overlooking the river. Adults can rest weary feet over coffee, while the kids explore the island.

FRONTIERLAND SHOOTIN' ARCADE   Combining state-of-the-art electronics with a traditional shooting-gallery format, this vast arcade presents an array of 97 targets (slow-moving ore cars, buzzards, gravediggers) in a three-dimensional 1850s gold-mining town scenario. Fog creeps across the graveyard, and the setting changes as a calm starlit night turns stormy with flashes of lightning and claps of thunder. Coyotes howl, bridges creak, and skeletal arms reach out from the grave. If you hit a tombstone, it might spin around and mysteriously change its epitaph. To keep the western ambience authentic, newfangled electronic firing mechanisms loaded with infrared bullets are concealed in genuine Hawkins 54-caliber buffalo rifles. When you hit a target, elaborate sound and motion gags are set off. Fifty cents buys you 25 shots.

LIBERTY SQUARE

Serving as a transitional area between Frontierland and Fantasyland, Liberty Square evokes 18th-century America with Federal and Georgian architecture, Colonial Williamsburg–type shops, and neat flower beds bordering manicured lawns. Thirteen lanterns, symbolizing the colonies, are suspended from the Liberty Tree, an immense live oak. You might encounter a fife and drum corps marching along Liberty Square's cobblestone streets. The Liberty Tree Tavern here (details in Chapter 6) is my favorite Magic Kingdom restaurant.

THE HALL OF PRESIDENTS   In this red-brick colonial hall, a giant bell suspended in its tower, all American presidents—from George Washington to Bill Clinton (whose actual voice was recorded for this attraction)—are represented by Audio-Animatronic™ figures who act out important events in the nation's history, from the signing of the Declaration of Independence through the space age. The show begins with a film, projected on a 180-degree, 70mm screen, about the importance of the Constitution. The curtain then rises on the 42 assembled American leaders, and, as each is spotlighted, he nods or waves with presidential dignity, Lincoln then rises and speaks, occasionally even referring to his notes. In a stunning example of Disney thoroughness, painstaking research was done in creating the figures and scenery, with each president's costume reflecting not only period fashion but period fabrics and tailoring techniques! Poet and author Maya Angelou narrates.

✪ **THE HAUNTED MANSION**   What better way to exhibit Disney special-effects wizardry than a haunted mansion? Macabre attendants harry groups of visitors past a graveyard, turning them over to a ghost host who encloses them in a windowless, doorless portrait gallery (are those eyes following you around?), lit by gargoyle torchiers, where the floor seems to be descending. Its ambience enhanced by inky darkness, spooky music, eerie howling, and mysterious screams and rappings, this mansion is replete with bizarre scenes and objects: a ghostly banquet and ball, a graveyard band, a suit of armor that comes alive, cobweb-covered chandeliers, luminous spiders, a talking head in a crystal ball, weird flying objects, and much more. At the end of the ride, a ghost joins you in your car. The experience is more amusing than terrifying, so you can take small children inside.

BOAT RIDES   A steam-powered sternwheeler called the *Richard F. Irvine* and two Mike Fink Keel Boats (the *Bertha Mae* and the *Gullywhumper*) depart from Liberty Square for scenic cruises along the Rivers of America. The passing landscape evokes the wild west. Both ply the identical route and make a restful interlude for foot-weary parkgoers.

FANTASYLAND

The attractions in this happy "land"—themed after Disney film classics such as *Snow White, Peter Pan,* and *Dumbo*—are especially popular, with young visitors. If your kids are 8 or under, you might want to make it your first stop in the Magic Kingdom. *Note:* Mr. Toad's Wild Ride is a bit scary. If your under-5 frightens easily, skip it.

✪ **LEGEND OF THE LION KING**   This stage spectacular based on Disney's blockbuster motion-picture musical combines animation, movie footage, sophisticated puppetry, and high-tech special effects.

The show is enhanced by the Academy Award–winning music of Elton John and Tim Rice. Other voices are provided by Whoopi Goldberg and Cheech Marin as laughing hyenas.

SNOW WHITE'S ADVENTURES   This attraction used to focus only on the more sinister elements of Grimm's fairy tale—most notably the evil queen and the cackling toothless witch—leaving small children screaming in terror. It's been toned down now, with Snow White appearing in a number of pleasant scenes—at the castle court-yard wishing well, in the dwarfs' cottage, receiving the prince's kiss that breaks the witch's spell, and riding off with the prince to live "happily ever after." There are new Audio-Animatronic™ dwarfs and new transportation vehicles (wooden carts named for the dwarfs). The interior colors have also been brightened up and made less menacing.

MAD TEA PARTY   This is a traditional amusement park ride à la Disney with an *Alice in Wonderland* theme. Riders sit in oversized pastel-hued teacups on saucers that careen around a circular platform, tilt, and spin. In the center of the platform is a big teapot, out from which pops a mouse. Believe it or not, this can be a pretty wild ride—or a tame one. It depends on how much you spin, a factor under your control via a wheel in the cup.

MR. TOAD'S WILD RIDE   This ride is based on the 1949 Disney film, *The Adventures of Ichabod and Mr. Toad,* which was itself based on one of my favorite children's classics, the divine *Wind in the Willows.* In colorful cars named for characters (Weasel, Toady, Moley), riders navigate a series of dark rooms, hurtling into solid objects—a fireplace, a bookcase, a haystack—and through barn doors into a coop of squawking chickens. They're menaced by falling suits of armor, snorting bulls, and an oncoming locomotive in a pitch-black tunnel, and are sent to jail (for car theft), to hell (complete with pitchfork-wielding demons), and through a fiery volcano. The ride's interior space is illuminated by invisible ultraviolet light, which makes whites and neons in the scenery glow.

CINDERELLA CASTLE   At the end of Main Street, in the center of the park, you'll come to a fairyland castle, 180 feet high and hous-ing a restaurant (King Stefan's Banquet Hall) and shops. Mosaic mu-rals inside depict the Cinderella story, and Disney family coats of arms are displayed over a fireplace. Cinderella herself, dressed for the ball, often makes appearances in the lobby area.

In the Words of Walt Disney

"Fantasy, if it's really convincing, can't become dated, for the simple reason that it represents a flight into a dimension that lies beyond the reach of time . . . nothing corrodes or gets run down . . . And nobody gets any older."

"We have never lost our faith in family entertainment—stories that make people laugh, stories about warm and human things, stories about historic characters and events, and stories about animals."

CINDERELLA'S GOLDEN CAROUSEL   It's a beauty, built by Italian wood-carvers in the Victorian tradition in 1917 and refurbished by Disney artists who added 18 hand-painted scenes from the Cinderella story on the wooden canopy above the horses. The carousel organ plays Disney classics such as "When You Wish upon a Star."

DUMBO, THE FLYING ELEPHANT   This is a very tame kiddie ride in which the cars—large-eared baby elephants (Dumbos)—go around and around in a circle gently rising and dipping. But it's very exciting for wee ones.

IT'S A SMALL WORLD   You know the song—and if you don't you will. It plays continually as you sail "around the world" through vast rooms designed to represent different countries. They're inhabited by appropriately costumed Audio-Animatronic™ dolls and animals—all singing "It's a small world after all . . ." in tiny doll-like voices. This cast of thousands includes Chinese acrobats, Russian kazatski dancers, Indian snake charmers in front of the Taj Mahal, French cancan dancers, Irish leprechauns, singing geese and windmills in Holland, Arabs on magic carpets, mountain goats in the Swiss Alps, African drummers and lunging hyenas in the jungle, a Venetian gondolier, and Australian koala bears. Cute. Very cute.

PETER PAN'S FLIGHT   Riding in airborne versions of Captain Hook's ship, passengers career through dark passages while experiencing the story of *Peter Pan.* The adventure begins in the Darlings's nursery, and includes a flight over nighttime London to Never-Never Land, where riders encounter mermaids, Indians, a ticking crocodile, the lost boys, Princess Tiger Lilly, Tinkerbell, Hook, Smee, and the rest—all to the movie music "You Can Fly, You Can Fly, You Can Fly." It's fun.

SKYWAY   Its entrance close to Peter Pan's Flight, the Skyway is an aerial tramway to Tomorrowland that makes continuous trips throughout the day.

MICKEY'S STARLAND

This small land adjacent to Fantasyland, with a topiary maze of Disney characters and a block of Duckburg architecture, is accessible from Main Street via the Walt Disney World Railroad. It includes a Walk of Fame à la Hollywood, with Disney character "voiceprints" activated when you step on a star; a hands-on fire station; storefronts that come alive at the push of a button; Grandma Duck's Farm (a petting zoo); funhouse mirrors; a treehouse; and an interactive video area. And Mickey's house is here, too, complete with living room TV tuned to the Disney channel, a shopping list of six kinds of cheese tacked to the refrigerator, and his familiar outfits hanging on a clothesline in the yard. Pluto's doghouse is out front.

The main attraction is **Mickey's Starland Show,** which is presented on a stage behind his house. While waiting to enter the theater, you can watch Disney cartoon videos on monitors in the preshow room. The show—a lively musical—features the Goof Troop, Chip 'n' Dale, a perky hostess named CJ, and a vocal computer-control system called

---

Did You Know?

- Since Walt Disney World opened in 1971, the total miles logged by monorail trains would be equal to more than 24 trips to the moon.
- During launch, it takes just eight minutes for the space shuttle to reach its orbiting speed of 17,500 m.p.h.
- Both Disneyland and Walt Disney World were built on former citrus groves in counties named Orange.

Dude. The story line: The show is about to start, but Mickey is missing! While CJ frantically searches for him, Goofy and his son, Max, get accidentally locked in the house. But it all works out in the end. The cheerful cartoon-inspired scenery, audience participation, and dramatic special effects are all designed to appeal to young viewers. After the show there's an opportunity to meet Mickey backstage in his dressing room.

TOMORROWLAND

This futuristic land focuses on space travel and exploration, but much like the Contemporary Hotel (built to complement it), its early 1970s architecture and vision of the future have become as retro-looking today as an old *Star Trek* episode. Don't think the folks at Disney haven't noticed. At this writing, they're revamping the exhibit to reflect the future as a galactic, science fiction–inspired community inhabited by humans, aliens, and robots.

ASTRO ORBITER   This is a tame, typical amusement park ride. The "jets" are on arms attached to a "missile" and they move up and down while traveling in a circle. It's a good choice for little kids; older kids can add a bit of a thrill by working a lever to ascend or descend.

DELTA DREAMFLIGHT   The history and wonder of aviation—from barnstorming to space shuttles—is captured in this whimsical fly-through adventure presented by the official airline of Walt Disney World. High-tech special effects and 70mm live-action film footage add dramatic 3-D-style verisimilitude. Guests travel from a futuristic airport up a hillside to witness a flying circus, parachutists, stunt flyers, wing walkers, crop dusters, and aerial acrobats. The action moves on to the ocean-hopping age of commercial flight, as passengers are transported to a Japanese tea garden, Mt. Fuji, and Paris at sunset. Finally, your vehicle is pulled into a giant jet engine and sent into hypersonic flight through psychedelic tunnels of light for a journey to outer space at a simulated speed of 300 m.p.h.

✪ EXTRA "TERROR" ESTRIAL ALIEN ENCOUNTER   Director George Lucas contributed his space-age vision to this major new Tomorrowland attraction. The action begins as a mysterious corporation called X-S Tech—a company from a distant planet—is marketing a "teletransporter" to earthlings. The device is capable of beaming living beings between planets light years apart. After a slick corporate presentation, T.O.M. 2000, a bumbling robot, demonstrates the product on Skippy, a cute and fuzzy alien, though not with total success; Skippy ends up discombobulated and with singed fur! Despite this dubious beginning, X-S technicians try to teleport their sinister corporation head, Chairman Clench, to Earth. But the machine malfunctions again, sending Clench to a distant planet, teleporting a fearsome extraterrestrial to earth instead. Lots of high-tech special effects here—from the Alien's breath on your neck to a mist of Alien slime.

GRAND PRIX RACEWAY   This is a great thrill for kids—including pre-drivers-license teens—who get to put the pedal to the metal, steer, and *vroom* down a speedway in an actual gas-powered sports car. Maximum speed on the four-minute drive around the track is about 7 m.p.h., and kids have to be at least 4 feet, 4 inches tall to drive alone.

TOMORROWLAND TRANSIT AUTHORITY   A futuristic means of transportation, the PeopleMover has no engine. It works by electromagnets, emits no pollution, and uses little power (don't ask me to explain it; I didn't do so well in physics). Narrated by a computer guide named Horack I, it offers an overhead look at Tomorrowland, including a pretty good preview of Space Mountain. If you're only in the Magic Kingdom for one day, this can be skipped.

TRANSPORTARIUM   Nearing completion at presstime, this Jules Verne/H. G. Wells–inspired multimedia presentation combines Circle-Vision™ with Audio-Animatronics™. It's hosted by Timekeeper, a mad scientist robot and his assistant, 9-EYE, a flying female camera-headed droid and time machine test pilot who will fly through history and send back photographs. In an unpredictable jet-speed escapade, the audience hears Mozart as a young prodigy playing his music to French royalty, visits medieval battlefields in Scotland, watches Leonardo at work, careens down an Austrian mountain in a bobsled, and explores underwater in the Bahamas. Timekeeper also throttles his calendar forward—to the 300th anniversary of the French Revolution in 2089.

SKYWAY   Its Tomorrowland entrance just west of Space Mountain, this aerial tramway to Fantasyland makes continuous round-trips throughout the day.

✪ SPACE MOUNTAIN   In a precursor to the concept of preshows, Space Mountain entertains visitors on its long, long lines with space-age music, exhibits, and meteorites, shooting stars, and space debris whizzing about overhead. These "illusioneering" effects, enhanced by appropriate audio, continue during the ride itself, which is something like a cosmic roller coaster in the inky starlit blackness of outer space. Your rocket climbs high into the universe, before racing—at what feels like breakneck speed—through a serpentine complex of aerial galaxies, making thrilling hairpin turns and rapid plunges. The exit from Space Mountain is a moving sidewalk, past scenes of Audio-Animatronic™ figures who demonstrate the future uses of electronic media in displays such as Astrodate 2250—farm communications on a once-barren planet. *Note:* Though the line may seem long, take heart; Space Mountain accommodates 3,000 people an hour.

WALT DISNEY'S CAROUSEL OF PROGRESS   Originally seen at New York's 1964–65 World's Fair, this 22-minute show was recently revamped to reflect later technological advances. Shown in a revolving theater, it features an Audio-Animatronic™ family (including grandparents, a freeloading cousin, and a dog) in humorous tableaux demonstrating a century of development in electric gadgetry. The action begins on Valentine's Day in a turn-of-the-century home, where telephones, Victrolas, indoor running water, and gaslight are the marvels of the age; train travel and horseless trolleys are coming into vogue; and there's even talk of "flying contraptions." We travel through time, tracking advances and their detriments (e.g., car travel leads to the commuter rat race), culminating circa the year 2000 on Christmas Eve. Gifts include virtual-reality headgear and a voice-activation system. A pre-show featuring Walt Disney traces the history of this production.

PARADES, FIREWORKS & MORE

You'll get an *Entertainment Show Schedule* when you enter the park, which lists all goings-on for the day. These include concerts (from steel drums to barbershop quartets), encounters with Disney characters, holiday events, and the three major happenings listed below.

❁ **THE 3 O'CLOCK PARADE**   You haven't really seen a parade until you've seen one at Walt Disney World. The spectacular daily Mickey Mania parade—celebrating 6½ decades of Mickey Mouse—kicks off at 3pm year-round on Main Street and meanders through Liberty Square and Frontierland. The route is outlined on your *Entertainment Show Schedule.* The only problem: In slow seasons you have to snag a seat along the curb a good half hour before it begins—even earlier during peak travel times. That's a long time to sit on a hard curb. Consider packing inflatable pillows. But the parade is worth a little discomfort. Twenty-eight Disney characters include all Mickey's pals—everyone from Minnie to Winnie (the Pooh). There are elaborate floats, stunning costumes, dazzling special effects, and a captivating cavalcade of rollerbladers, bikers, skateboarders, stilt-walkers, dancers, and storybook characters (Snow White, Alice in Wonderland, Pinnochio). Great music, too.

❁ **SPECTROMAGIC**   Along a darkened parade route (the same one as above), 72,000 watts of dazzling high-tech lighting effects (including holography) create a glowing array of pixies and peacocks, sea horses and winged horses, flower gardens and fountains. Roger Rabbit is the eccentric conductor of an orchestra producing a rainbow of musical notes that waft magically into the night air. There are dancing ostriches from *Fantasia,* whirling electric butterflies, flowers that evoke Tiffany glass, bejeweled coaches, luminescent ElectroMen atop spinning whirlyballs, and, of course, Mickey, surrounded by a sparkling confetti of light. And the music and choreography are on par with the technology. It's like nothing you've ever seen before. Once again, very early arrival is essential to get a seat on the curb. SpectroMagic takes place nightly in summer, on selected nights during Christmas and Easter vacation times, and during other special celebrations. Consult your *Entertainment Show Schedule* for details.

10 Best Orlando Area Attractions For Adults

1. **Innoventions** Epcot, generally, is more geared to adults than the other Disney parks, but this display of future technologies is especially intriguing, providing a cogent preview of life in the 21st century.

2. **The Disney Institute** This new Disney concept, which allows guests to custom-design non-theme-park vacations, features exciting programs in diverse areas ranging from gourmet cooking to landscape design.

3. **World Showcase Pavilions** Experience a round-the-world journey visiting 11 nations in microcosm—with authentically reproduced architectural highlights, restaurants, shops, and cultural performances.

4. **Universal Studios** Okay, I'm an adult, but sometimes "All I wanna do, is have some fun" and "I get the feeling, I'm not the only one." This is a good place to do it.

5. **Swimming with the Manatees** Sign up for a five-day program with a manatee biologist for an ecotour on the Crystal River that also includes birdwatching, snorkeling, and informative lectures.

6. **Cypress Gardens** Stroll 200 acres of gorgeous botanical gardens—roses, bougainvillea, crape myrtles, and magnolias, amid ponds, lagoons, waterfalls, Italian fountains, and manicured lawns.

7. **Kennedy Space Center** Acquaint yourself with the history, present state, and future of America's space program.

8. **A Day in Winter Park** This charming town has a museum filled with masterpieces by Louis Comfort Tiffany and other noted 19th-century artists, great upscale shopping, and fine restaurants. Stay overnight at the Langford and arrange a day of beauty at its multifacility spa.

9. **A Resort Vacation** Top-of-the-line accommodations, fine restaurants, magnificent grounds, golf, tennis, swimming, first-rate health clubs, and other elements of a plush resort vacation are available at: the Hyatt Regency Grand Cypress, Marriott's Orlando World Center, The Peabody Orlando, and Disney's Grand Floridian.

10. **Japanese Breakfast** The Cascade Grill of the Hyatt Regency Grand Cypress serves up a traditional Japanese breakfast of miso soup, grilled salmon, steamed rice, seaweed, fresh fruit, and green tea. (If only one of you finds this exciting, the other *can* opt for bacon and eggs here as well).

✪ **FIREWORKS** Like SpectroMagic, Fantasy in the Sky Fireworks, immediately preceded by Tinker Bell's magical flight from Cinderella

Castle, take place nightly in summer, on selected nights during Christmas and Easter vacation times, and during other special celebrations. Consult your *Entertainment Show Schedule* for details. Suggested viewing areas are Liberty Square, Frontierland, and Mickey's Starland.

3   Epcot

In 1982, Walt Disney World opened its second major attractions park, the world's fair–like Epcot (Experimental Prototype Community of Tomorrow). Its aims are described in a dedication plaque: "May Epcot entertain, inform and inspire. And, above all . . . instill a new sense of belief and pride in man's ability to shape a world that offers hope to people everywhere." Ever growing and changing, Epcot today occupies 260 acres so stunningly landscaped as to be worth visiting for botanical beauty alone. Do stop and smell the roses. There are two major sections, Future World and World Showcase.

Epcot is huge, and walking around it can be exhausting (some people say its acronym stands for "Every Person Comes Out Tired"). Don't try to do it all in one day. And conserve your energy by taking launches across the lagoon from the edge of Future World to Germany or Morocco. There are also double-decker buses circling the World Showcase Promenade and making stops at Norway, Italy, France, and Canada. Unlike the Magic Kingdom, Epcot's parking lot is right at the gate. Sections of the parking lot are named for Epcot themes (Harvest, Energy, etc.), and aisles are numbered. Stop by the **Guest Relations lobby** to the left of Spaceship Earth to pick up an **Epcot Guidemap** and **entertainment schedule,** and, if you so desire, make reservations for lunch or dinner at WorldKey terminals just outside the lobby. Many Epcot restaurants are described in Chapter 6. Then check out your show schedule and incorporate shows you want to see into your itinerary. Strollers can be rented to your left at the Future World entrance plaza and in World Showcase at the International Gateway between the United Kingdom and France.

FUTURE WORLD

The northern section of Epcot (where you enter the park) comprises Future World, centered on a giant geosphere known as Spaceship Earth. Future World's 10 themed areas, sponsored by major American corporations, focus on discovery, scientific achievements, and tomorrow's technologies in areas running the gamut from energy to undersea exploration.

SPACESHIP EARTH   Spaceship Earth, housed in a massive silvery geosphere 180 feet high and 165 feet in diameter, is Epcot's most cogent symbol. Inside, a show created by sci-fi writer Ray Bradbury, presented by AT&T, and narrated by Jeremy Irons takes visitors on a 14-minute journey through the history of communications beginning 40,000 years ago. We board time-machine vehicles and are drawn into a whirling space-warp vortex to the distant past where an Audio-Animatronic™ Cro-Magnon shaman recounts the story of a hunt while others record it on cave walls. We advance thousands of years to ancient Egypt, where hieroglyphics adorn the temple walls and writing is recorded on papyrus scrolls (with typical Disney thoroughness, the hieroglyphics are authentic, and words being recorded by a scribe are taken from an actual letter sent by a pharaoh to one of his agents). As our time machine moves ahead, the Greeks have added vowels to the Phoenician alphabet and refined its use. Roman roads expand the network of communications, and the vast Islamic empire furthers the dispersion of manuscripts that enhance knowledge of science, astronomy, and art. In the Middle Ages, we see Benedictine monks painstakingly reproducing classical and religious wisdom by hand, prior to the development of the Gutenberg press in 1456. Man's increasing ability to disseminate ideas becomes a catalyst for the Renaissance. Technologies develop at a rapid pace, enlarging our communications spectrum via steam power, electricity, the telegraph, telephone, radio, movies, and TV. It is but a short step to the age of computers and electronic communications. We are catapulted into outer space to see spaceship earth from a new perspective, returning via a kaleidoscopic passageway in a dazzling special-effects finale.

At the end of this journey through time, AT&T invites guests to sample its "global neighborhood" in an interactive computer-video wonderland that includes a motion-simulator ride through the company's electronic network. This exhibit complements Innoventions, detailed below.

INNOVENTIONS The pair of crescent-shaped buildings to your right and left just beyond Spaceship Earth house a constantly evolving 100,000-square-foot exhibit that showcases cutting-edge technologies and future products for home, work, and play. Leading manufacturers—IBM, General Electric, AT&T, Apple, Honeywell, Hammacher Schlemmer, LEGO, General Motors, Sega, and others—sponsor exhibit areas here, and their representatives are on hand to answer questions. Visitors get a chance to preview electric cars, experience interactive television, and try out more than 200 new computer programs and games. On display are dozens of new high-tech products: video phones, the latest advances in TV remote-control, voice-activated appliances, solar-powered lawn mowers, self-cleaning toilets, automatic plant-watering and pet-feeding devices, and many more. At the IBM exhibit, you can access entire libraries via CD Rom, experience Olympic events as they're happening, travel the world, and examine rare manuscripts that were hitherto too fragile for public perusal. Kids will be thrilled to preview new Sega and other interactive computer and video games (including Virtual Formula racing) designed for fun and learning. They can also build with LEGOS via computer.

There are several **show areas:** Be sure to see Dr. Digital's recording studio of tomorrow (volunteers with no musical training are chosen from the audience to lay down four tracks of an original song). You can be interviewed by Jay Leno on TV. Alec Tronic, a robotic comedian, imitates everyone from Johnny Carson to John Wayne. Bill Nye The Science Guy presents an entertaining multimedia show about how new ideas move from the laboratory to the marketplace. The Great Carrotini, in GE's Magic House Show, demonstrates new home

Epcot

WORLD SHOWCASE

THE AMERICAN ADVENTURE

JAPAN

MOROCCO

ITALY

GERMANY

American Gardens Theatre

Refreshment Outpost

FRANCE

Boat Dock

Boat Dock

Stroller & Wheelchair Rental

World Showcase Lagoon

INTERNATIONAL GATEWAY

CHINA

UNITED KINGDOM

NORWAY

Boat Dock

WORLD SHOWCASE PLAZA

Boat Dock

MEXICO

Disney Traders

Port of Entry

CANADA

JOURNEY INTO IMAGINATION

WORLD OF MOTION

INNOVENTIONS

HORIZONS

THE LAND

WONDERS OF LIFE

EARTH STATION

THE LIVING SEAS

SPACESHIP EARTH

UNIVERSE OF ENERGY

Stroller & Wheelchair Rental

Lost & Found

Guest Relations Window

Pet Care Kennel

ENTRANCE PLAZA

Monorail Station

Bus Information

Taxi Pickup

FUTURE WORLD

9826

products. And Disney's Imagineering Laboratory offers an Aladdin-themed virtual-reality experience. You can easily spend several hours browsing in the future here.

The two-story **Discovery Center,** located on the right side of Innoventions, includes an information resource area where guests can get answers to all their questions about Epcot attractions in particular and Walt Disney World in general. For instance, if after visiting The

Land, you would like to learn more about hydroponics, they can print out an information sheet on it. The Discovery Center also houses a shop called Field Trips featuring educational products and software.

✪ THE LIVING SEAS   This United Technologies–sponsored pavilion contains the world's sixth "ocean," a 5.6 million-gallon saltwater aquarium (including a complete coral reef), inhabited by more than 4,000 sea creatures—sharks, barracudas, parrot fish, rays, and dolphins among them. While waiting on line, visitors pass exhibits tracing the history of undersea exploration, including a glass diving barrel used by Alexander the Great in 332 B.C., and Sir Edmund Halley's first diving bell (1697). A $2^{1}/_{2}$-minute multimedia preshow highlighting today's undersea technology (sophisticated robotics and computers) is followed by a seven-minute film demonstrating the formation of the earth and seas as a means to support life.

After the films, visitors enter hydrolators for a rapid descent to the sunlit ocean floor. Upon arrival, they board Seacabs that wind around a 400-foot-long tunnel to enjoy stunning close-up views (through acrylic windows) of ocean denizens in a natural coral-reef habitat. The ride concludes in the Seabase Concourse, which is the visitors center of Seabase Alpha, a prototype ocean-research facility of the future. Here exhibits include a $22^{1}/_{2}$-foot scuba tube used by Seabase Alpha scientists to enter and leave the waters. And seven informational modules contain numerous exhibits focusing on ocean ecosystems, harvestable resources grown in controlled undersea environments, marine mammals (dolphins, sea lions, manatees), earth systems (the relationship between the planet's seas and its landmasses), the study of oceanography from space, undersea exploration (featuring an Audio-Animatronic™ deep-sea submersible robot), and life in a coral-reef community. Many of these exhibits are hands-on. You can expand your knowledge of oceanography via interactive computers or step into a diver's JIM Suit and use controls to complete diving tasks.

THE LAND   Sponsored by Nestlé, this largest of the Future World pavilions highlights man's relation to food and nature in a variety of intriguing attractions.

A 13-minute excursion in a canopied boat, **✪ Living with the Land** takes us through three ecological environments, each populated by Audio-Animatronic™ denizens. In the rain forest—with its dense foliage and tangle of vines, tree ferns, cascading waterfalls, and serene lagoon—we meet up with chattering birds and insects, whooping howler monkeys, and crocodiles. Its humidity is replaced by the dry, oppressive heat of an African desert, where we experience a sandstorm. It subsides as we approach a fog-filled tunnel en route to America's midwestern windswept plains—scene of a thunder and lightning storm that precipitates a grass fire, rousing a swarm of locusts. We sail on, into pastoral American autumn scenery, where a film in a barn theater examines 100 years of American farming from early plows to modern machinery. And from here on, new farming methods and experiments—such as hydroponics, aeroponics, aquaculture, desert farming, even plants growing in simulated Martian and lunar soil!—are showcased in real gardens. The food grown here is utilized in Walt Disney World restaurants. If you'd like a more serious overview, take a one-hour **guided walking tour** of the growing areas. They're given every half hour between 9:30am and 4:30pm. Adults pay $5, children ages 3 to 9 pay $3. You have to sign up at the Green Thumb Emporium near the entrance to Food Rocks, and the boat tour is a recommended prerequisite. I found it fascinating.

✪ **Circle of Life:** Combining spectacular live-action footage with animation, this 15-minute, 70mm motion picture based on the Disney feature, *The Lion King,* stars Simba (now king of the Pridelands), Timon (the meerkat), and Pumbaa (the warthog) in a cautionary environmental tale. The message: Everything is connected in the great circle of life.

In **Food Rocks,** Audio-Animatronic™ mock rock performers deliver an entertaining message about nutrition. Neil Moussaka sings "Don't Take My Squash Away From Me," the Refrigerator Police perform "Every Bite You Take," and the Peach Boys harmonize a rendition of "Good Vibrations" ("Good, good, good, good nutrition . . ."), while Excess, a trio of disheveled, obnoxious hard rockers, counters by extolling the virtues of junk food. Rapper Tone Loc (as Füd Wrapper, the show's host), Chubby Checker, Neil Sedaka, Little Richard, and the Pointer Sisters perform the actual voiceover parodies of their music.

JOURNEY INTO IMAGINATION   In this wondrous pavilion, presented by Kodak and housed in glass pyramids, even the fountains are magical, with arching streams of water that leap into the air like glass rods.

✪ **Honey I Shrunk the Audience** is a 15-minute 3-D "misadventure" based on the Disney hit films *Honey I Shrunk the Kids* and *Honey I Blew Up the Kid,* with Rick Moranis and Marcia Strassman. The action begins at an Imagination Institute awards ceremony where zany scientist Dr. Wayne Szalinski is being honored as "Inventor of the Year." The audience, after being menaced by hundreds of mice and a 3-D cat, is shrunk and given a good shaking by a giant five-year-old. Finally, everyone returns to proper size—everyone but the family dog, who creates the final (not altogether pleasant) special effect. A photo-montage preshow extols the virtues of imagination.

Journey Into Imagination Ride: Visitors board moving cars for a 14-minute ride, hosted by a red-bearded adventurer named Dreamfinder and his sidekick, Figment—a mischievous baby dragon with a childlike ability to dream. After a simulated flight across the nighttime sky, we enter the "Imaginarium," where a dream-catching machine is vacuuming up "sparks of imagination, ideas, and natural elements" into a giant storage bag. We then ride past whimsical tableaux in which Audio-Animatronic™ characters explore the creative worlds of the fine arts, literature, the performing arts (complete with laser-light dancers), science (Dreamfinder's lab is filled with magical gadgetry), and image technology (aka movies). The ride culminates at:

Image Works, housing dozens of hands-on electronic devices and interactive computers. Here you can activate different musical instruments by stepping on hexagons of colored light (remember Tom Hanks in *Big?*), participate in a TV drama, paint on a magic palette, draw patterns with laser beams, operate a giant kaleidoscope, wend your way through the Rainbow Corridor of a sensor maze, and conduct an electronic philharmonic orchestra.

WORLD OF MOTION　Everything you always wanted to know about transportation—past, present, and future—is explored in this General Motors–sponsored, vast wheel-shaped, gleaming stainless-steel pavilion.

Its highlight is the **World of Motion Show,** a whimsical 15-minute ride-through attraction—utilizing animated scenery, 70mm film, and a cast of 140 Audio-Animatronic™ characters—that documents civilization's eternal quest for movement. It begins with sore-footed cavemen, early attempts at riding animals (test-driving a zebra), and the invention of the wheel. Leonardo is shown experimenting with ideas for flight, the era of railroads is represented by a train being held up by masked desperadoes, and an astonished horse looks on as a man cranks up a car. Just about every mode of transport is covered—from paddlewheelers to ocean liners, from wagon trains to barnstorming planes. We proceed—always to a cheerful background score called "It's Fun to Be Free"—to the widening travel opportunities presented by auto and air travel. And, this being Walt Disney World, the ride climaxes with a dizzying journey through computer-graphics space for a look at the future—spaceship transportation.

Transcenter, the other major attraction here, offers a behind-the-scenes look at General Motors' advanced engineering and manufacturing facilities, its prototype vehicles of the future, and its concerns in creating nonpolluting engines and fuel economy. Here you can test your knowledge of automotive signals, learn how robotics are used in automobile manufacturing (via a humorous show starring a wisecracking toucan and an assembly-line robot named Tiger), find out about the use of computer diagramming in car design, and, of course, sit down in the prototype models and examine the controls.

HORIZONS　The theme of this pavilion is the future, which presents an unending series of new horizons. We board sideways-facing gondolas for a 15-minute journey into the next millennium. The first tableau honors visionaries of past centuries (like Jules Verne) and looks at outdated visions of the future and classic sci-fi movies. We ascend to an area where an IMAX film projected on two 80-foot-high screens presents a kaleidoscope of brilliant micro and macro images—growing crystals, colonies in space, solar power, a space shuttle launching, DNA molecules, and a computer chip. We then travel to 21st-century cityscapes, desert farms, floating cities under the ocean's surface, and outer space colonies populated by Audio-Animatronic™ denizens who use holographic telephones, magnetic levitation trains, and voice-controlled robotic field hands. For the return to earth from a space colony, riders have a choice of three futuristic transportation systems—a personal spacecraft, desert Hovercraft, or mini-submarine.

WONDERS OF LIFE　Housed in a vast geodesic dome fronted by a 75-foot replica of a DNA molecule, this pavilion, presented by

Metropolitan Life, offers some of Future World's most engaging shows and attractions.

Starring zany comedian Martin Short, ✪ **The Making of Me** is the sweetest introduction imaginable to the facts of life. In a captivating 15-minute film combining live action with animation, Short travels back in time to witness his parents as children, their meeting at a college dance, their wedding, and their decision to have a baby. Along with him, we view his development inside his mother's womb (via spectacular in-utero photography) and witness his birth. If you've not yet told your kids about sex, you couldn't find a better springboard to that important conversation.

In ✪ **Body Wars,** audience members join ex-fighter pilot Jack Braddock on a medical rescue mission inside the immune system of a human body. Our objective: to save Dr. Cynthia Lair, a miniaturized immunologist who has been accidentally swept into the bloodstream (while studying the body's response to a splinter) and come under attack from white blood cells! After passing through dermatopic purification stations and undergoing miniaturization (to the size of a single cell), visitors board moving theaters for this motion-simulator ride that utilizes special computer-graphics and 70mm motion-picture footage to evoke a wild journey through gale-force winds (in the lungs) and pounding heart chambers. Leonard Nimoy directed.

In ✪ **Cranium Command,** a totally delightful multidimensional theater attraction, Buzzy, an Audio-Animatronic™ brain-pilot-in-training, is charged with the seemingly impossible mission of controlling the brain of Bobby, a typical 12-year-old boy. A five-minute animated film introduces the story line and characters. Cranium Command is a training center for brain pilots, in which Buzzy has to prove his ability at the helm. The boy's left brain (logic) is played by Charles Grodin, his right brain (emotion/creativity) by Jon Lovitz, his out-of-control adrenal gland by Bob Goldthwait, his "pumped-up" heart by Kevin Nealon and Dana Carvey (as Hans and Franz of "Saturday Night Live"), and his oft-upset stomach by George Wendt (Norm from "Cheers"). The audience is seated inside Bobby's head as Buzzy guides him through a day of typical preadolescent traumas—running for the school bus, meeting a girl, fighting bullies, and a run-in with the school principal.

Finally, there's **Fitness Fairgrounds,** a large area filled with fitness-related shows, exhibits, and participatory activities. These include an eight-minute multimedia presentation called Goofy About Health (stressed-out Goofy has the *Unhealthy Livin' Blues* until he reforms and extols the joys of healthy living), the Anacomical Players (a live improvisational theater troupe who perform 15-minute health-related comic skits), and Coach's Corner (your tennis, golf, or

In the Words of Walt Disney

"In my view, wholesome pleasure, sport, and recreation are as vital to this nation as productive work and should have a large share in the national budget."

baseball swing is videotaped and replayed in slow-motion, with specific video tips for improvement provided by Chris Evert, Nancy Lopez, and Gary Carter, respectively). You can also do a light workout on a video-enhanced exercise bike here, receive a personalized computer-generated evaluation of your health habits, play sensory games, and take a video voyage to investigate the effects of drugs, tobacco, and alcohol on your heart. There's much, much more. You could easily spend hours here.

UNIVERSE OF ENERGY   Sponsored by Exxon, this pavilion—its roof glistening with solar panels—aims to better our understanding of America's energy problems and potential solutions via a 35-minute ride-through attraction with visitors seated in solar-powered "traveling theater" cars (hard to explain, you'll see what I mean).

The experience begins with an introductory preshow tracing our use of energy from primitive to modern times. On a massive screen in Theatre I, an animated motion picture depicts the earth's molten beginnings and the first stirrings of life—microscopic ocean plants. As they die, their organic matter accumulates on the ocean floor and begins a slow transformation (over eons) into oil and gas. Meanwhile, life is evolving in the primeval forest, and a similar process ensues as dying leaves form peat that will emerge after many millennia as coal.

We move from Theatre I to travel back 275 million years into an eerie storm-wracked landscape of the Mesozoic era. Here, we're menaced by giant Audio-Animatronic™ dragonflies, pterodactyls, dinosaurs, earthquakes, and streams of molten lava before entering a steam-filled tunnel and traveling through the bowels of a volcano to emerge back in the 20th century in Theatre II. In this new setting, which looks like a NASA mission control room, a 70mm film, projected on a massive 210-foot wraparound screen, depicts the challenges of the world's increasing energy demands and the emerging technologies that will help meet them.

Our moving seats now return to Theatre I where swirling special effects herald a film about how energy impacts our lives in areas such as mobility, communications, agriculture, health, education, and recreation. It ends on a dramatically upbeat note complete with a light show and musical crescendo—a vision of an energy-abundant future.

WORLD SHOWCASE

Surrounding a 40-acre lagoon at the park's southern end is World Showcase—a permanent community of 11 miniaturized nations, all with authentically indigenous landmark architecture, landscaping, background music, restaurants, and shops. The cultural facets of each nation are explored in art exhibits, dance performances, and innovative rides, films, and attractions. And all of the employees in each pavilion are natives of the country represented.

✪ **CANADA**   Our neighbors to the north are represented by diverse architecture ranging from a mansard-roofed replica of Ottawa's 19th-century French-style Château Laurier (here called the Hôtel du Canada) to a British-influenced rustic stone building modeled after a famous landmark near Niagara Falls. An Indian village—complete with rough-hewn log trading post and 30-foot replicas of Ojibwa totem poles—signifies the culture of the northwest, while the Canadian wilderness is reflected by a steep mountain (a Canadian Rocky), a waterfall cascading into a whitewater stream, and a "forest" of evergreens, stately cedars, maples, and birch trees. Don't miss the stunning floral displays of azaleas, roses, zinnias, chrysanthemums, petunias, and patches of wildflowers inspired by the Butchart Gardens in Victoria, B.C. The pavilion's highlight attraction is *O Canada!*—a dazzling 360-degree Circle-Vision™ film that reveals Canada's scenic splendor from sophisticated Montréal to the thundering flight of thousands of snow geese departing an autumn stopover near the St. Lawrence River. The film is 18 minutes in length. Canada pavilion shops carry sandstone and soapstone carvings, fringed leather vests, snowshoes, duck decoys, fur-lined parkas, moccasins, a vast array of Eskimo stuffed animals and Native American dolls, turquoise jewelry, and, of course, maple syrup.

UNITED KINGDOM   Centered on Brittania Square—a formal London-style park, complete with copper-roofed gazebo bandstand and a statue of the Bard—the U.K. pavilion evokes Merry Olde England. Four centuries of architecture are represented along quaint cobblestoned streets; troubadours and minstrels entertain in front of a traditional British pub; and a formal garden with low box hedges in geometric patterns, flagstone paths, and a stone fountain replicates the landscaping of 16th- and 17th-century palaces. High Street and Tudor Lane shops display a broad sampling of British merchandise— toy soldiers, Paddington bears, personalized coats of arms, tobaccos and pipes, Scottish clothing (cashmere and Shetland sweaters, golf wear, tams, knits, and tartans), Royal Doulton china, and Waterford crystal. A tea shop occupies a replica of Anne Hathaway's thatch-roofed 16th-century cottage in Stratford-upon-Avon. Background music ranges from "Greensleeves" to the Beatles.

✪ FRANCE   Focusing on La Belle Epoque (1870–1910)—a flourishing period for French art, literature, and architecture—this pavilion is entered via a replica of the beautiful cast-iron Pont des Arts footbridge over the "Seine." It leads to a park with pleached sycamores, Bradford pear trees, flowering crape myrtles, and sculptured parterre flower gardens that was inspired by Seurat's painting *A Sunday Afternoon on the Island of La Grande Jatte*. A one-tenth replica of the Eiffel Tower constructed from Gustave Eiffel's original blueprints looms above *les grands boulevards,* and period buildings feature copper mansard roofs and casement windows. The highlight attraction is *Impressions de France.* Shown in a palatial (mercifully sit-down) theater à la Fontainebleau, this 18-minute film is a breathtakingly scenic journey through diverse French landscapes projected on a vast 200-degree-view wraparound screen and enhanced by music of French composers. Emporia in the covered shopping arcade, with art nouveau Métro facades at either end, have interiors ranging from a turn-of-the-century bibliothèque to a French château. Merchandise includes French art prints and original art, cookbooks, cookware, fashions, wines (there's a tasting counter) and foods, Madeline and Babar books and dolls, and perfumes. Another marketplace/tourism center revives the defunct Les Halles, where Parisians used to sip onion soup in the wee hours. The heavenly aroma of a *boulangerie* penetrates the atmosphere, and mimes, jugglers, and strolling chanteurs entertain.

MOROCCO   This exotic pavilion—its architecture embellished with intricate geometrically patterned tilework, minarets, hand-painted wood ceilings, and brass lighting fixtures—is heralded by a replica of the Koutoubia Minaret, the prayer tower of a 12th-century mosque in Marrakesh. The Medina (old city), entered via a replica of an arched gateway in Fez, leads to Fez House (a traditional Moroccan home) and the narrow winding streets of the *souk,* a bustling marketplace where all manner of authentic hand-crafted merchandise is on display. Here you can peruse or purchase pottery, brassware, hand-knotted Berber carpets, colorful Rabat carpets, ornate silver and camel-bone boxes, and prayer rugs. There are weaving demonstrations in the *souk* throughout the day. The Medina's rectangular courtyard centers on a replica of the ornately tiled Najjarine Fountain in Fez, the setting for musical entertainment. The pavilion's Royal Gallery contains an ever-changing exhibit of Moroccan art, and the Center of Tourism offers a continuous three-screen slide show. Morocco's landscaping includes a formal garden, citrus and olive trees, date palms, and banana plants.

JAPAN   Heralded by a flaming red *torii* (gate of honor) on the banks of the lagoon and the graceful blue-roofed Goju No To pagoda (inspired by a shrine built at Nara in 700 A.D.) this pavilion focuses on Japan's ancient culture. In a traditional Japanese garden, cedars, yew trees, bamboo, "cloud-pruned" evergreens, willows, and flowering shrubs frame a contemplative setting of pebbled footpaths, rustic bridges, waterfalls, exquisite rock landscaping, and a pond of golden koi. The Yakitori House is based on the renowned 16th-century Katsura Imperial Villa in Kyoto, designed as a royal summer residence and considered by many to be the crowning achievement of Japanese architecture. Exhibits ranging from 18th-century Bunraki puppets to samurai armor take place in the moated White Heron Castle, a replica of the Shirasagi-Jo, a 17th-century fortress overlooking the city of Himeji. And the Mitsukoshi Department Store (Japan's answer to Macy's) is housed in a replica of the Shishinden (Hall of Ceremonies) of the Gosho Imperial Palace built in Kyoto in 794 A.D. It sells lacquer screens, kimonos, kites, fans, dolls in traditional costumes, origami books, samurai swords, Japanese Disneyana, bonsai plants, Japanese foods, pearl necklaces, china, and pottery, even modern electronics. In the courtyard, artisans demonstrate the ancient arts of *anesaiku* (shaping brown rice candy into dragons, unicorns, and dolphins), *sumi-e* (calligraphy), and *origami* (paper folding). Be sure to include a show of traditional Japanese music and dance at this pavilion in your schedule. It's one of the best in the World Showcase.

✪ THE AMERICAN ADVENTURE   Housed in a vast Georgian-style structure, *The American Adventure* is a 29-minute dramatization of U.S. history utilizing a 72-foot rear-projection screen, rousing music, and a large cast of lifelike Audio-Animatronic™ figures, including narrators Mark Twain and Ben Franklin. The "adventure" begins with the voyage of the *Mayflower* and encompasses major historic events. We view Jefferson writing the Declaration of Independence, the expansion of the frontier, Mathew Brady photographing a family about to be divided by the Civil War, the stock market crash of 1929, Pearl Harbor, and the *Eagle* heading toward the moon. John Muir and Teddy Roosevelt discuss the need for national parks, Susan B. Anthony speaks out on women's rights, Frederick Douglass on slavery, Chief Joseph on the situation of Native Americans. While waiting for the show to begin, you'll be entertained by the wonderful Voices of Liberty Singers performing American folk songs in the Main Hall. Note the quotes from famous Americans on the walls here. Formally symmetrical gardens shaded by live oaks, sycamores, elms, and holly complement the pavilion's 18th-century architecture. A shop called Heritage Manor Gifts sells signed presidential photographs, needle-point samplers, Coca-Cola memorabilia, books on American history, historically costumed dolls, classic political campaign buttons, and vintage newspapers with banner headlines like "Nixon Resigns!" An artisan at the shop makes jewelry out of coins.

Note: The Barbie show (details below) is presented in an outdoor theater in this pavilion.

ITALY   One of the prettiest World Showcase pavilions, Italy lures visitors over an arched stone footbridge to a replica of Venice's intricately ornamented pink and white Doge's Palace. Other architectural highlights include the 83-foot Campanile (bell tower) of St. Mark's Square, Venetian bridges, and a central piazza enclosing a version of Bernini's Neptune Fountain. A garden wall suggests a backdrop of provincial countryside, and Mediterranean citrus, olive trees, cypress, and pine frame a formal garden. Gondolas are moored on the lagoon. Shops sell Benetton clothing, Perugina chocolates, biscotti, cameo and filigree jewelry, Murano and Venetian glass, alabaster figurines, and inlaid wooden music boxes. A troupe of street actors perform a contemporary version of 16th-century commedia dell'arte in the piazza.

GERMANY   Enclosed by towered castle walls, this festive pavilion is centered on a cobblestoned *Platz* with pots of colorful flowers girding a fountain statue of St. George and the Dragon. An adjacent clock tower is embellished with whimsical glockenspiel figures that herald each hour with quaint melodies. The pavilion's outdoor Biergarten— where it's Oktoberfest all year long—was inspired by medieval Rothenberg. And 16th-century building facades replicate a merchant's hall in the Black Forest and the town hall in Frankfurt's Römerberg Square. Shops here carry Hummel figurines, glassware, cookware, cuckoo clocks, cowbells, music boxes, pewterware, German wines (there's a tasting counter) and specialty foods, toys (German Disneyana, teddy bears, dolls, and puppets), Christmas ornaments, and books. An artisan demonstrates the molding and painting of Hummel figures, another paints exquisitely detailed scenes on eggs. Background music runs the gamut from oom-pah bands to Mozart symphonies.

✪ CHINA Bounded by a serpentine wall that snakes around its outer perimeter, the China pavilion is entered via a vast triple-arched ceremonial gate inspired by the Temple of Heaven in Beijing, a summer retreat for Chinese emperors. Passing through the gate, you'll see a half-size replica of this ornately embellished red and gold circular temple, built in 1420 during the Ming dynasty. Gardens simulate those in Suzhou, with miniature waterfalls, fragrant lotus ponds, groves of bamboo, corkscrew willows, and weeping mulberry trees. The highlight attraction here is **Wonders of China,** a 20-minute, 360-degree Circle-Vision™ film that explores 6,000 years of dynastic and Communist rule and the breathtaking diversity of the Chinese landscape. Narrated by 8th-century Tang dynasty poet Li Bai, it includes scenes of the Great Wall (begun 24 centuries ago!), a performance by the Beijing Opera, the Forbidden City in Beijing, rice terraces of Hunan Province, the Gobi Desert, and tropical rain forests of Hainan Island. Adjacent to the theater, an art gallery houses changing exhibits of Chinese art. A bustling marketplace—the Yong Feng Shangdian Shopping Gallery—offers an array of merchandise including silk robes, lacquer and mother-of-pearl-inlay furniture, jade figures, cloisonné vases, tea sets, silk rugs and embroideries, stuffed pandas, kites, dolls, fans, wind chimes, and Chinese clothing. Note the towering stone elephant nearby: Legend has it that if you throw a stone on its back and it remains there, luck will follow you the rest of your days. Artisans here paint wooden ducks and demonstrate calligraphy.

NORWAY Centered on a picturesque cobblestone courtyard, this pavilion evokes ancient Norway. A *stavekirke* (stave church), styled after the 13th-century Gol Church of Hallingdal, its eaves embellished with wooden dragon heads, houses changing exhibits. A replica of Oslo's 14th-century Akershus Castle, next to a cascading woodland waterfall, is the setting for the pavilion's featured restaurant. Other buildings simulate the red-roofed cottages of Bergen and the timber-sided farm buildings of the Nordic woodlands. There's a two-part attraction here. **Maelstrom,** a boat ride in a dragon-headed Viking vessel, traverses Norway's fjords and mythical forests to the music of *Peer Gynt*—an exciting journey during which you'll be menaced by polar bears prowling the shore and trolls who cast a spell on the boat. The watercraft crashes through a narrow gorge and spins into the North Sea where a violent storm is in progress. But the storm abates, and passengers disembark safely in a 10th-century Viking village to view the 70mm film *Norway,* which documents a thousand years of history. Featured images include *Oseberg bat* (a 1,000-year-old Viking ship), a small fishing village, festive national holiday celebrations in Oslo, and soaring jumps at the Holmenkollen ski resort. Shops feature hand-knit wool hats and sweaters, toys (Legos—there's a table where kids can play with them while you shop—trolls, dolls, children's books), china, wood carvings, pewterware, and jewelry made from Norwegian gemstones.

MEXICO You'll hear the music of marimba and mariachi bands as you approach the festive showcase of Mexico, fronted by a towering Mayan pyramid modeled on the Aztec temple of Quetzalcoatl (God of Life) and surrounded by dense Yucatán jungle landscaping. Upon entering the pavilion, you'll find yourself in a museum of pre-Columbian artifacts. Down a ramp is a small lagoon, the setting for **El Rio del Tiempo** (River of Time), where visitors board boats for eight-minute cruises through Mexico's past and present. Passengers get a close-up look at the above-mentioned pyramid and the erupting Popocatepetl volcano. Dance performances focusing on the cultures of Mayan, Toltec, Aztec, and colonial Mexico are presented in film segments and by an Audio-Animatronic™ cast in vignettes ranging from a Day of the Dead skeleton band to children breaking a piñata. Additional film footage focuses on Mexican tourist spots. The show culminates in a Mexico City fiesta with exploding fiber-optics fireworks. Shops in and around the Plaza de Los Amigos (a "moonlit" Mexican *mercado* with a tiered fountain and streetlamps) display an array of leather goods, baskets, sombreros, piñatas, pottery, embroided dresses and blouses, worry dolls, turquoise jewelry, carved onyx, cut-tin candle lamps, weavings, and blown-glass objects (an artisan gives demonstrations). La Casa de Vacaciones, sponsored by the Mexican Tourist Office, provides travel information.

ILLUMINATIONS & SHOWS

✪ **IllumiNations,** a $16^1/_2$-minute spectacular using high-tech lighting effects, darting laser beams, fireworks, strobes, and rainbow-lit dancing fountains, takes place nightly. A backdrop of classical music by international composers (representing World Showcase nations) enhances the drama. Each nation is highlighted in turn. Colorful kites fly over Japan, the giant Rockies loom over Canada, a gingerbread house rises in Germany, and so on. Find a seat around the lagoon about a half hour before show time.

Live shows, especially those in World Showcase, make up an important part of the Epcot experience. Among others, these might include lion dancers in China, oom-pah bands playing lively polkas in Germany, Caledonian bagpipers in Canada, jesters and stilt-dancing puppeteers in the United Kingdom, and Moroccan belly dancers. Two especially good shows are the Voices of Liberty singers at The American Adventure Pavilion and the traditional music and dance displays in Japan. Check your show schedule when you come in, and plan your day to include some of them.

In **The Magical World of Barbie,** presented at the outdoor America Gardens Theater (just across from the American Adventure Pavilion in World Showcase), Barbie, Ken, Skipper, Stacy, and the rest of the ever-exuberant doll family and friends come to life in a perky 30-minute around-the-world stage show. Amid lively music and dance numbers, Barbie and pals travel to the Australian outback with "Wombat Dundee," frolic with giraffes and gorillas in the African jungle, and take a hot-air balloon to Paris for a fashion show—always, of course, in appropriate outfits from their vast wardrobes. Barbie's 40-foot fuschia stretch limo is often parked in front of the theater. By the way, I picked up this bit of trivia from Mattell reps at the premiere show: Barbie's full name is Barbara Millicent Roberts, and her birthday is March 9, 1959.

4   Disney-MGM Studios

In 1989, Walt Disney World premiered its third "magical kingdom," Disney-MGM Studios, offering exciting movie- and TV-themed shows and behind-the-scenes "reel-life" adventures. Heralded by the 130-foot-high Mouseketeer-hatted "Earffel Tower," its main streets include Hollywood and Sunset boulevards, where you'll encounter starlets, casting directors, and gossip columnists amid art deco movie sets evocative of Hollywood's glamorous golden age. There's also a New York Street lined with Gotham landmarks (the Empire State, Flatiron, and Chrysler buildings) and typical New York characters including wise-cracking workmen, peddlers hawking knockoff watches, and cops. More importantly, this is a working movie and TV studio, where shows are in production even as you tour the premises.

Arrive at the park early, tickets in hand. Unlike the Magic Kingdom and Epcot, Disney-MGM's 110 acres of attractions can pretty much be seen in one day. The parking lot is right at the gate. If you don't get a **Disney-MGM Studios Guidemap** and/or **entertainment schedule** when you enter the park, you can pick them up at **Guest Services.** First thing to do is check show times and work out an entertainment schedule based on highlight attractions and geographical proximity. Then, if you haven't done so by calling 407/WDW-DINE, make restaurant reservations for lunch or dinner (my favorite restaurants here are described in Chapter 6). Strollers can be rented at Oscar's Super Service inside the main entrance. Major attractions include:

✪ **THE TWILIGHT ZONE TOWER OF TERROR**   Legend has it that during a violent storm on Halloween night of 1939, lightning struck the Hollywood Tower Hotel, causing an entire wing—along with an elevator full of people—to disappear. And you're about to meet them as you become the star in a special episode of . . . *The Twilight Zone.* After various spooky adventures, the ride ends in a dramatic climax: a terrifying 13-story free-fall plunge into *The Twilight Zone!* Rod Serling is your host.

✪ **THE MAGIC OF DISNEY ANIMATION**   You'll see Disney characters come alive at the stroke of a brush or pencil as you tour actual glass-walled animation studios and watch artists at work. Walter Cronkite and Robin Williams (guess who plays straight man?) explain what's going on via video monitors, and they also star in a very funny eight-minute Peter Pan–themed film about the basics of animation. It's painstaking work: To produce an 80-minute film, the animation team must complete more than a million individual cels (drawings/paintings on clear celluloid sheets) of characters and scenery! Original cels from famous Disney movies, and some of the many Oscars won by Disney artists, are on display here. The tour also includes very entertaining video talks by animators and a grand finale of magical moments from Disney classics such as *Pinocchio, Snow White, Bambi, Beauty and the Beast,* and *Aladdin.* This very popular attraction should be visited first thing in the morning; long lines form later in the day.

Disney-MGM Studios Theme Park

Catastrophe Canyon

Residential Street

Backlot Theater

The Backlot

Backlot

New York Street

Water Effects Tank

Backstage Plaza

Special Effects Workshop and Shooting Stage

Sci-Fi Drive-In Theater Restaurant

Soundstages

Scenic Shop

Backlot Annex

Lakeside Circle

Costuming

Earffel Tower

Mann's Chinese Theater

Post Production Editing and Audio

Echo Lake

The Walt Disney Theater

Backstage Shuttle Station

Hollywood Blvd.

Hollywood Brown Derby

Sunset Blvd.

Entrance Plaza

The Magic of Disney Animation

Twilight Zone Tower of Terror

BACKSTAGE STUDIO TOUR   This 25-minute tram tour takes you behind the scenes for a close-up look at the vehicles, props, costumes, sets, and special effects used in your favorite movies and TV shows. You'll see costumers at work in the wardrobe department (Disney has the world's largest costume collection—more than two million garments), house facades of "The Golden Girls" and "Empty

Nest" on Residential Street, and carpenters building sets in the scenic shop. All very interesting until the tram ventures into Catastrophe Canyon where an earthquake in the heart of desert oil country causes canyon walls to rumble and riders are threatened by a raging oil fire, massive explosions, torrents of rain, and flash floods! Then you're taken behind the scenes to see how filmmakers use special effects to create such disasters. Almost as interesting as the ride is the preshow. While waiting on line, you can watch entertaining videos hosted by Tom Selleck and Carol Burnett of well-known actors and directors on overhead monitors: Penny Marshall talking about the piano scene in *Big*, Leonard Nimoy on the challenge of directing babies in *Three Men and a Baby*, Richard Dreyfuss sharing how he landed the role in *Jaws* that launched his movie career, Mel Brooks on why he was "forced" to become a director/producer, and many more. After the tram tour, visit Studio Showcase, a changing walk-through display of sets and props from popular and classic movies.

INSIDE THE MAGIC   Movie and TV special effects and production facets are the focus of this behind-the-scenes walking tour of studio facilities. You'll see how a naval battle—complete with burning ships, torpedos, and undersea explosions—is created, then view the results on videotape. Two young volunteers from the audience help demonstrate how miniaturization was achieved in *Honey, I Shrunk the Kids*. You'll visit three studio soundstages, including the home of the Disney channel's *Mickey Mouse Club* (on some tours you'll get to see movies or TV shows being filmed from a soundproof catwalk); view a short comedy called *The Lottery* starring Bette Midler and learn how its special effects were achieved; a video postproduction area to see a scene from *Star Wars* before and after editing (C-3PO, R2-D2, and George Lucas explain how it's done on video monitors); and head to the Walt Disney Theater for a behind-the-scenes look at the company's latest animation feature. A very entertaining video preshow features Jane Fonda, Oliver Stone, Leonard Nimoy, Paul Newman, Eddie Murphy, and other actors and directors discussing their films. To find the entrance to this attraction follow the big pink footsteps of Roger Rabbit.

✪ VOYAGE OF THE LITTLE MERMAID   Hazy light, creating an underwater effect in a reef-walled theater, helps set the mood for this charming musical spectacular based on the Disney feature film. The show combines live performers with more than 100 puppets, movie clips, and innovative special effects. Sebastian sings the movie's Academy Award–winning song, "Under the Sea"; the ethereal Ariel shares her dream of becoming human in a live performance of "Part of Your World"; and the evil, tentacled Ursula, 12 feet tall and 10 feet wide, belts out "Poor Unfortunate Soul." It all has a happy ending, as most of the young audience knows it will; they've seen the movie.

✪ THEATER OF THE STARS   This 1,500-seat covered amphiteater is currently presenting a 25-minute live Broadway-style production of ***Beauty and the Beast*** based on the Disney movie version. Musical highlights from the show range from the rousing "Be Our Guest" opening number to the poignant title song featured in a romantic waltz-scene finale complete with the release of white doves. A highlight is "The Mob Song" scene in a dark forest, in which villagers led by Gaston (the beast's rival for Belle) and armed with axes, hoes, and pitchforks set out on a rampage to "kill the beast." Sets and costumes are lavish, production numbers spectacular. Consider going to the last show; it makes for a feel-good (and sit-down) ending to your day. Arrive early to get a good seat. One feminist comment: When is someone going to do a version of this tale in which the beast is a woman and a man loves her for her inner qualities? *Note: Beauty and the Beast* has been enjoying a long run here; a new show, based on a more recent Disney hit, may be in progress by the time you visit.

✪ **JIM HENSON'S MUPPET VISION 3D**   This utterly delightful film starring Kermit and Miss Piggy combines Jim Henson's puppets with Disney Audio-Animatronics™ and special-effects wizardry, 70mm film, and cutting-edge 3-D technology. Wow! The coming-at-you action includes flying Muppets, cream pies, cannonballs, high winds, fiber-optics fireworks, bubble showers, even an actual spray of water. Kermit is the host, Miss Piggy sings "Dream a Little Dream of Me," Statler and Waldorf critique the action (which includes numerous mishaps and disasters) from a mezzanine balcony, and Nicki Napoleon and his Emperor Penguins (a full Muppet orchestra) provide music from the pit. Kids in the first row get to interact with the characters. In the preshow area, guests view a hilarious Muppet video on overhead monitors and see movie props belonging to Muppet superstars. Note the cute fountain out front.

STAR TOURS   A wild galactic journey based on the *Star Wars* trilogy (George Lucas collaborated on its conception), this action-packed adventure uses dramatic film footage and flight-simulator technology to transform the theater into a vehicle careening through space. We enter a preshow area—where R2-D2 and C-3PO are running an intergalactic travel agency—and board 40-passenger "spacecraft" for a voyage to the Moon of Endor. En route, we encounter robots, aliens, and droids, among them our inexperienced pilot, RX-24. No sooner has he extricated our spaceship from an asteroidlike tunnel of frozen ice fragments than he's drawn into combat with a massive Imperial Star Destroyer. The ship lurches out of control, and passengers experience sudden drops, violent crashes, and oncoming laser blasts. The harrowing ride ends safely, and we exit into a *Star Wars* merchandise shop.

✪ **THE GREAT MOVIE RIDE**   Film footage and Audio-Animatronic™ replicas of movie stars are used to re-create some of the most famous scenes in filmdom on this thrilling ride through movie history. You'll relive magic moments from the 1930s through the present—Bergman and Bogart's classic airport farewell in *Casablanca,* Rhett carrying Scarlett up the stairs of Tara for a night of passion, Brando bellowing "Stelllllaaaa," Sigourney Weaver fending off slimy *Alien* foes, Gene Kelly singin' in the rain, Johnny Weissmuller's trademark Tarzan yell and vine swing across the jungle, and many more. Action is enhanced by dramatic special effects as you experience everything from the highjacking of your ride vehicle by an outlaw to thieves blowing up a safe and setting the bank on fire in a western town. "Fasten your seat belts. It's going to be a bumpy night." The setting for this attraction is a full-scale reproduction of Hollywood's famous Mann's Chinese Theatre, complete with hand, foot, and paw prints (Mickey and Kermit) of the stars out front.

✪ **MONSTER SOUND SHOW** Four "Foley artists" (Foley is the Hollywood sound-effects system named for its creator, Jack Foley) are chosen from the audience to create sound effects for a two-minute comic Gothic thriller starring Chevy Chase and Martin Short. We see the film three times, first with professional sound, then without sound as volunteers frantically try to create an appropriate track, and finally with the sound effects they've provided. Errors in timing and volume make it all quite funny, as a knock at the door or crashing glass comes just a few seconds too late. The show features some of the 20,000-plus ingenious gadgets created by sound master Jimmy Macdonald during his 45 years with Disney Studios. David Letterman narrates a terrific video preshow, including one of his famous "top-ten" lists, in this case "most entertaining sounds" (number 10: "A sweaty fat guy getting up out of a vinyl beanbag chair"). In a postshow area called Soundworks, guests can attempt to reproduce flying saucer sounds from the film *Forbidden Planet,* dub the voice of Roger Rabbit, and create the gallop of the Headless Horseman in *Legend of Sleepy Hollow.*

SUPERSTAR TELEVISION This 30-minute show takes guests through a broadcast day that spans television history. During the preshow, "casting directors" choose a few dozen volunteers from the audience to reenact 15 famous television scenes (arrive early and station yourself near the stage if you want to snag a role). The broadcast day begins with a 1955 black-and-white "Today" show featuring Dave Garroway (the date is July 18, the morning after Disneyland opened) and continues with a classic "I Love Lucy" episode (the candy factory), a scene from "General Hospital," the Ed Sullivan show, "Bonanza," "Gilligan's Island," Walter Cronkite doing the news (Neil Armstrong's moon landing), a Three Stooges sequence (a volunteer gets a pie in the face), "Cheers," "The Golden Girls," "Home Improvement," "Howard Cosell's Sportsbreak" the "Tonight" show, and "Late Night With David Letterman." Real footage is mixed with live action, and though occasionally a star is born, it's more often fun watching amateur actors freeze up, flub lines, and otherwise deviate from the script.

✪ **INDIANA JONES EPIC STUNT SPECTACULAR** Visitors get a glimpse into the world of movie stunts in this dramatic 30-minute show that re-creates major scenes from the Indiana Jones series. It takes place in a vast 2,000-seat covered amphitheater. The show opens on an elaborate Mayan temple backdrop. Indiana Jones crashes dramatically onto the set in a free fall, and, as he searches with a torch for the golden idol, he encounters booby traps and spears popping up from the ground before being chased by a rolling boulder. The set is then dismantled to reveal a colorful Cairo marketplace where a swordfight ensues and the action includes virtuoso bullwhip maneuvers, lots of

In the Words of Walt Disney

"A family picture is one the kids can take their parents to see and not be embarrassed."

"I don't like downbeat pictures, and I cannot believe that the average family does either . . . when I go to the theater, I don't want to come out depressed."

gunfire, and a truck bursting into flame. An explosive finale takes place in a desert scenario. The action is enhanced by movie theme music and entertaining narrative, and throughout, guests get to see how elaborate stunts are pulled off. During the preshow, volunteers are chosen to participate as extras.

PARADES, SHOWS, FIREWORKS & MORE

✪ **Aladdin's Royal Caravan,** a dazzling Disney parade based on the movie, takes place once or twice daily (check your entertainment schedule for route and times). Its exotic cast includes a 26-foot genie on a bejeweled float, brass bands, amazing acrobats, scimitar dancers, a fire-eater, a snake charmer, magicians, a harem, and the grand entrance of Prince Ali and Princess Jasmin on Abu (transformed from a monkey into an elephant), followed by Aladdin's old nemesis, the villainous Jafar, now reduced to pushing the honey bucket behind them. Don't miss it. Find a curbside seat (or grab a bench near the Monster Sound Show) along the parade route a half hour before it begins.

The **Sorcery in the Sky** fireworks show is presented nightly during summer and peak seasons. Check your entertainment schedule to see if it's on.

The **Star Today** program features frequent appearances by major stars such as Betty White, Burt Reynolds, Howie Mandel, Sally Struthers, Alice Ghostley, and Marlee Matlin. They appear at attractions, record their handprints in front of the Chinese Theater, and appear at question-and-answer sessions with park guests. Check your entertainment schedule to see if it's on.

The *Honey, I Shrunk the Kids* **Movie Set,** an 11,000-square-foot playground based on the film, is located near New York Street. Everything in it is larger than life. A thicket of grass is 30 feet tall, mushroom caps are three stories high, and a friendly "ant" makes a suitable seat. Play areas—enhanced by sounds such as the buzzing of giant crickets and bees—include a massive cream cookie, a 52-foot garden hose (with leaks), cereal loops nine feet in diameter (cushioned for jumping), a waterfall cascading from a leaf to a dell of fern sprouts (the sprouts form a musical stairway, activated when guests step from sprout to sprout), a root maze with a flower petal slide, a "film strip" slide in a giant Kodak film can, and a huge spider web with 11 levels to climb.

Centering on a gleaming 14^1/$_2$-foot bronze Emmy, the **Academy of Television Arts & Sciences Hall of Fame Plaza,** adjacent to SuperStar Television, honors TV legends. Bronze statues of television luminaries Carol Burnett, Sid Caesar, James Garner, Andy Griffith, Barbara

Walters, Rod Serling, Bill Cosby, Mary Tyler Moore, Red Skelton, Danny Thomas, and Milton Berle are displayed, along with one of Walt Disney. Additional statues will be added each year. ATAS holds its annual Hall of Fame induction ceremonies at the Disney-MGM Studios.

5   Other WDW Attractions

TYPHOON LAGOON

Ahoy swimmers, floaters, run-aground boaters!
A furious storm once roared 'cross the sea
Catching ships in its path, helpless to flee . . .
Instead of a certain and watery doom
The winds swept them here to TYPHOON LAGOON

✪ Such is the Disney legend relating to Typhoon Lagoon, which you'll see posted on consecutive signs as you enter the park. Located off Lake Buena Vista Drive halfway between Walt Disney World Village and Disney-MGM Studios, this is the ultimate in water theme parks. Its fantasy setting is a palm-fringed tropical island village of ramshackle, tin-roofed structures, strewn with cargo, surfboards, and other marine wreckage left by the "great typhoon." A storm-stranded fishing boat dangles precariously atop the 95-foot-high Mt. Mayday, the steep setting for several major park attractions. Every half hour the boat's smokestack erupts, shooting a 50-foot geyser of water into the air.

In summer, arrive no later than 9am to avoid long lines. The park is often filled to capacity by 10am and closed to later arrivals. Beach towels and lockers can be obtained for a minimal fee, and all beach accessories can be purchased at Singapore Sal's. Light fare is available at two eateries—Leaning Palms and Typhoon Tillie's Galley and Grog, a beach bar called Let's Go Slurpin' sells beer and soft drinks, and there are also picnic tables (consider bringing picnic fare; you can keep it in your locker until lunchtime). Guests are not permitted to bring their own flotation devices into the park. A full day's worth of water attractions and activities includes:

TYPHOON LAGOON   This large and lovely lagoon, the size of two football fields and surrounded by white sandy beach (complete with volleyball set-up), is the park's main swimming area. The chlorinated water's turquoise hue evokes the Caribbean. Large waves for surfing and bobbing crash against the shore every 90 seconds. A foghorn sounds to warn you when a wave is coming. Young children can wade in the lagoon's more peaceful tidal pools—Blustery Bay or Whitecap Cove.

CASTAWAY CREEK   Hop onto a raft or inner tube and meander along this 2,100-foot lazy river. Circling the lagoon, Castaway Creek tumbles through a misty rain forest, past caves and secluded grottoes. It has a themed area called Water Works where jets of water spew from shipwrecked boats and a Rube Goldberg assemblage of broken bamboo pipes and buckets spray and dump water on passersby. There are exits along the route where you can leave the creek; if you do the whole thing, it takes about a half hour. Tubes are complimentary.

WATER SLIDES   Humunga Kowabunga consists of two 214-foot Mt. Mayday water slides that drop you down the mountain before rushing into a cave and out again at 30 m.p.h. Three longer (about 300 feet each), but less steep slides—Jib Jammer, Rudder Buster, and Stern Burner—take you on a serpentine route through waterfalls and bat caves, past nautical wreckage at about 20 m.p.h. before depositing you in a bubbling catch pool; each offers slightly different views and thrills. There's seating for nonparticipatory parents whose kids have commissioned them to "watch me."

WHITEWATER RIDES   Mt. Mayday is the setting for three whitewater rafting adventures—Keelhaul Falls, Mayday Falls, and Gangplank Falls—all of them offering steep drops, coursing through caves, and passing lush scenery. Keelhaul Falls has the most winding spiral route, Mayday Falls the steepest drops and fastest water, while the slightly tamer Gangplank Falls uses large tubes so the whole family can ride together.

SHARK REEF   Guests are given free snorkel equipment (and instruction) for a 15-minute swim through this 362,000-gallon simulated coral-reef tank populated by about 4,000 rainbow parrotfish, queen angelfish, yellowtail damselfish, rock beauties, blue tang, puddingwife fish, and other colorful denizens of the deep. Underwater scenery includes shipwrecked boats, and there's a rock waterfall at one end. If you don't want to get in the water, you can observe the fish via portholes in a walk-through area. Shark Reef is housed in a sunken upside-down tanker.

KETCHAKIDDIE CREEK   Many of the above-mentioned attractions require guests to be at least four feet tall. This section of the park is a kiddie area exclusively for those *under* four feet. An innovative water playground, it has bubbling fountains to frolic in, mini–water slides, a pint-sized whitewater tubing adventure, spouting whales and squirting seals, rubbery crocodiles to climb on, grottoes to explore, and waterfalls to loll under.

BLIZZARD BEACH

Opening soon after we go to press is Blizzard Beach, Disney's newest, and zaniest, water park—one designed to evoke a ski resort in the midst of a tropical lagoon! Disney legend has it that Blizzard Beach came about as the result of a freak winter storm; when the ice and snow melted, it was turned into a ski-themed water park. Hence chair lifts carry swimmers up water slides here, the park centers on a 90-foot snow-capped mountain (Mt. Gushmore), and an on-premises restaurant evokes a ski lodge—why not?

Blizzard Beach is on World Drive just north of the All-Star Sports and Music Resorts. Arrive at—or before—park opening to avoid long lines and be sure you get in; if the park is filled to capacity, you'll be turned away. Beach towels and lockers are available for a small charge, and you can buy beach accessories at the Beach Haus.

MT. GUSHMORE ATTRACTIONS

SUMMIT PLUMMET   Starting 120 feet up, 30 feet above Mt. Gushmore, this is a speed slide/thrill ride that makes a 55 m.p.h. plunge straight down to a splash landing at the base of the mountain.

SLUSH GUSHER   Another Mt. Gushmore speed slide (a bit tamer than the above) that travels through a snow-banked mountain gully.

TEAMBOAT SPRINGS   The world's longest white-water raft ride, with six-passenger rafts twisting down a 1,200-foot series of rushing waterfalls.

TOBOGGAN RACER   An eight-lane water slide that sends guests racing head first over exhilarating dips as they descend a snowy slope.

SNOW STORMERS   Three flumes descending from the top of Mt. Gushmore and following a switchback course through ski-type slalom gates.

RUNOFF RAPIDS   An inner-tube run, where guests can careen down three different twisting, turning flumes—sometimes in total darkness.

CHAIR LIFT   Converted ski lifts, complete with snow skis on their underside, that carry guests to the top of the mountain.

OTHER ATTRACTIONS

A sandy beach below Mt. Gushmore offers the following.

TIKE'S PEAK   A scaled-down kiddie version of Mt. Gushmore attractions, including a snow-castle fountain play area.

MELT-AWAY-BAY   A one-acre free-form wave pool fed by melting-snow waterfalls.

CROSS COUNTRY CREEK   Inner tubers can float lazily along this meandering 2,900-foot creek, which circles the entire park, but beware: it will take you inside a mysterious cave.

BLIZZARD BEACH SKI PATROL TRAINING CAMP   Designed for preteens, it features bungi cord slides, a T-bar drop over water, slides, and a challenging ice-floe walk along slippery floating icebergs.

RIVER COUNTRY

One of the many recreational facilities at the Fort Wilderness Resort campground, this mini–water park is themed after Tom Sawyer's swimming hole. Kids can scramble over manmade boulders that double as diving platforms for a 330,000-gallon clearwater pool. Two 16-foot water slides also provide access to the pool. Attractions on the adjacent Bay Lake, which is equipped with ropes and ships' booms for climbing, include a pair of flumes—one 260 feet long, the other 100 feet—that corkscrew through Whoop-N-Holler Hollow; White Water Rapids, which carries inner-tubers along a winding 230-foot creek with a series of chutes and pools; and the Ol' Wading Pool, a smaller version of the swimming hole designed for young children. There are pool and beachside areas for sunning and picnicking, plus a 350-yard board-walk nature trail through a cypress swamp. Beach towels and lockers can be obtained for a minimal fee. Light fare is available at Pop's Place. To get here without a car take a launch from the dock near the entrance to the Magic Kingdom or a bus from its Transportation and Ticket Center.

DISCOVERY ISLAND

This lushly tropical 11$^{1}/_{2}$-acre zoological sanctuary—just a short boat ride away from the Magic Kingdom entrance, the Contemporary Resort, or Fort Wilderness Resort—provides a tranquil counterpoint to Disney World dazzle. Plan to spend a leisurely afternoon strolling its scenic mile-long nature trail, which, shaded by a canopy of trees, winds past gurgling streams, groves of palm and bamboo, ponds and lagoons filled with ducks and trumpeter swans, a bay that is a breeding ground for brown pelicans, and colonies of rose-hued flamingos. Peacocks roam free, and aviaries house close to 100 species of colorful exotic birds, including macaws, cockatoos, roseate spoonbills, scarlet ibis, kookaburras, bald eagles, toucans, parrots, partridges, king vultures, East African crowned cranes, and white-crested hornbills. Discovery Island denizens also include Patagonian cavies (they're a kind of guinea pig), alligators and caimans, Galápagos tortoises, small primates, and muntjac miniature deer from Southeast Asia. Two different bird shows and a reptile show are scheduled several times throughout the day; they take place outdoors with seating on log benches. Guests can also look through a viewing area to see the nursery complex of the island's animal hospital, where baby birds and mammals are often hand-raised.

6   Universal Studios

Universal Studios Florida, 1000 Universal Studios Plaza (☎ 407/363-8000), is a working motion-picture and television-production studio that invites the public in for a glimpse behind the scenes. As you stroll along "Hollywood Boulevard" and "Rodeo Drive," you'll pass more than 40 full-scale sets and large props from famous movies (from the hedges used in *Edward Scissorhands* to New York's Central Park). On hand to greet visitors are Hanna-Barbera characters (Yogi Bear, Scooby Doo, Fred Flintstone, and others). While waiting on line, you'll be entertained by excellent preshows. Work out a show schedule when you arrive.

MAJOR ATTRACTIONS

After 75 years of moviemaking, Universal knows how to create a supercolossal theme park experience. Steven Spielberg is the park's creative consultant, and thrilling rides and attractions utilize cutting-edge technology—such as OMNIMAX™ 70mm film projected on seven-story screens—to create unprecedented special effects. Top attractions include:

A Day in the Park with Barney   Nearing completion at presstime, this new attraction will feature the popular purple one, Baby Bop, and BJ in a musical show that uses song, dance, and interactive play to deliver an environmental message. It will take place in a park-like theater-in-the-round setting with brilliantly colored plants, trees, clouds, and stars.

E.T. Adventure   This is the movie sequel Spielberg said he'd never make. Visitors are given a passport to E.T.'s planet, which needs his healing powers to rejuvenate it. You'll soar with E.T. on a mission to save his ailing planet, through the forest and into space, aboard a star-bound bicycle—all to the accompaniment of that familiar movie theme music.

✪ **Back to the Future**   The year is 2015. The incompetent but evil Biff has penetrated Doc Brown's Laboratory of Future Technology, imprisoned Doc, and taken off in the DeLorean. On a mission to save the time machine from Biff, visitors blast through the space-time continuum, plummeting into volcanic tunnels ablaze with molten lava, colliding with Ice Age glaciers, thundering through caves and canyons, and are briefly swallowed by a dinosaur, in a spectacular multisensory adventure. Actors Christopher Lloyd (Doc) and Tom Wilson (Biff) appear on video.

✪ **Kongfrontation**   It's the last thing the Big Apple needed. King Kong is back! As you stand in line—in a replica of a grungy, graffiti-scarred New York subway station—CBS newsman Roland Smith reports on Kong's terrifying rampage. Everyone must evacuate to Roosevelt Island. So it's all aboard the Roosevelt Island tram. Cars collide and hydrants explode below, police helicopters hover overhead putting us directly in the line of fire, the tram malfunctions, and, of course, we encounter Kong, 32 feet tall, 13,000 pounds, with over 100 facial expressions. He emits banana breath in our faces, and menaces passengers, dangling the tram over the East River. A great thrill—or just another day in New York.

✪ **Earthquake, The Big One**   You board a BART train in San Francisco for a peaceful subway ride, but just as you pull into the Embarcadero station there's an earthquake—the big one—8.3 on the Richter scale! As you sit helplessly trapped, vast slabs of concrete collapse around you, a propane truck bursts into flames, a runaway train comes hurtling at you, and the station floods (60,000 gallons of water cascade down the steps). Your feet will get wet. Earthquake is preceded by several interesting preshows narrated by Charlton Heston, during which the audience is briefed for roles as extras and taken behind the scenes to see how special effects were achieved.

Ghostbusters   There are so many ghosts these days, Ghostbusters just has to sell franchises. Lewis Tully delivers a zany high-pressure sales pitch to the audience, and volunteers come up on stage and get slimed. Tully demonstrates flushing ghosts into the Ectoplasmic Container Chamber and discusses starter kits in three price ranges. But the ghosts, of course, break loose from Gozer's Temple, and demons lunge at the audience.

Jaws   You're in the charming New England town of Amity. Did you really think it was safe to go back into the water? Guests are assured the waters are shark-free, but as your boat heads out to the open seas, an ominous dorsal fin appears on the horizon. What follows is a series of terrifying face-to-glistening-jaw attacks from a three-ton, 32-foot-long great white shark who tries to sink its teeth into passengers. Just as you begin to feel safe in the confines of a deserted boat house, "Jaws" breaks through the walls sending oars, lobster traps, and buoys hurtling through the air. And there's more trouble ahead. The boat is surrounded by a 30-foot wall of flame from burning fuel. I won't tell you how it ends, but here's a hint: The pungent stench of charred shark flesh comes into it.

Nickelodeon Studios Tour   Kids get a bang out of touring the studios of their own cable network, the premises of which are fronted by a slime geyser. Along the tour route guests get a look at the soundstages where shows such as "Clarissa Explains It All" are produced; view concept pilots for Nick shows; visit the kitchen where Gak and Green Slime are produced (you can touch and taste, if you like); play games typical of Nickelodeon shows; and try out new Sega video games. There's lots of audience participation, and a volunteer will get slimed.

Wild, Wild, Wild West Show   Stunt people demonstrate falls from balconies, gun and whip fights, dynamic explosions, and other oater staples.

The Beetlejuice Graveyard Revue   Dracula, Wolfman, the Phantom of the Opera, Frankenstein and his bride, and Beetlejuice put on a funky—and very funny—rock music show with pyrotechnic special effects and MTV-style choreography.

The FUNtastic World of Hanna-Barbera   This motion-simulator ride takes guests careening through the universe in a spaceship piloted by Yogi Bear to rescue Elroy Jetson. Prior to this wild ride, you'll learn about how cartoons are created. After it, in an interactive area, you can experiment with animation sound effects—boing! plop! splash!

ADDITIONAL ATTRACTIONS

Other attractions here include:

Casper—a behind-the-scenes look at the movie.

A **Rocky and Bullwinkle** character show with those scheming no-goodnik spies, Boris and Natasha.

The **Gory, Gruesome & Grotesque Horror Make-up Show,** all about makeup and special effects in movies such as the transformation scenes from *An American Werewolf in London, The Fly,* and *The Exorcist.* The lobby of the theater houses **Jurassic Park Behind the Scenes,** an exhibit comprising props, costumes, and videos from the movie, most notably the 26-foot-long ailing triceratops.

Lucy: A Tribute, honoring America's queen of comedy, consists of a vast collection of Lucy-Desi memorabilia, home movies, costumes, props, awards, fan letters, a scale model of the "I Love Lucy" soundstage, and a Lucy computer trivia game.

Fievel's Playland, based on the Spielberg movie, is a very innovative western-themed playground with giant props and sets (in which kids experience being mouse-size), including a 200-foot-long water ride, a 30-foot spider web to climb, and a Gulliver-sized harmonica that makes music as kids glide down the keys.

At **Murder She Wrote,** you're on the set with Angela Lansbury trying to solve a crime involving a rare black pearl. Via computer, the audience gets to make postproduction executive decisions—choose the murder weapon, the murderer, and Jessica's dinner companion. Robert Wagner narrates the preshow.

At **Alfred Hitchcock's 3-D Theatre** a volunteer is chosen from the audience to play Norman Bates. The attraction is a tribute to the "master of suspense" who directed 53 films, eight of them for Universal. The late Tony Perkins narrates a reenactment of the famous shower scene from *Psycho,* and *The Birds,* as if it weren't scary enough, becomes an in-your-face 3-D movie.

Across from the Hitchcock Theater is **T-Rex Attack!,** a photo-op with the jeep and a T-Rex from *Jurassic Park.*

Lassie, Benji, Mr. Ed (descendants of, actually), and other animal superstars perform their famous pet tricks in the **Animal Actors Show.**

During **Screen Test Home Video Adventure,** a director, crew, and team of "cinemagicians" put visitors on the screen in an exciting video production.

And **Dynamite Nights Stuntacular,** a nightly show, combines death-defying stunts with a breathtaking display of fireworks.

Over 25 **shops** in the park sell everything from Lucy collectibles to Bates Motel towels, and **restaurants** run the gamut from Mel's Drive-In (of *American Graffiti* fame), to the Hard Rock Café, to Schwab's.

ADMISSION   A one-day ticket costs $36 for ages 10 and over, $29 for children 3 to 9. A two-day ticket is $55 for ages 10 and over, $44 for children 3 to 9. An annual pass (admission for a full year) is $87.50 for ages 10 and over, $70 for children 3 to 9. Ages 2 and under free. Parking costs $5 per vehicle, $6 for RVs and trailers.

OPEN   Universal Studios is open 365 days a year from 9am; closing hours vary seasonally. Call before you go.

DIRECTIONS   Take I-4 east, making a left on Sand Lake Road, then a right onto Turkey Lake Road, and follow the signs.

7 Sea World

This popular 200-acre marine-life park, at 7007 Sea World Drive (☎ 407/351-3600), explores the mysteries of the deep in a format that combines entertainment with wildlife-conservation awareness. Its beautifully landscaped grounds, centering on a 17-acre lagoon, include flamingo and pelican ponds (more than 1,500 birds, primarily waterfowl, make their home in the park), and a lush tropical rain forest. Sea World's involvement in marine-life research, education, animal rescue and release programs, and preserving and breeding endangered species is impressive. Shamu, a killer whale, is the star of the park. Do work out a show schedule upon entering the premises.

MAJOR ATTRACTIONS

There are a dozen major shows and attractions:

✪ **Wild Arctic**   Enveloping guests in the beauty, exhilaration, and danger of a polar expedition, Wild Arctic combines a high-definition adventure film with high-tech flight-simulator technology to evoke a flight over the frozen north. After a hazardous jet helicopter journey—albeit one affording breathtaking Arctic panoramas—guests emerge at a remote research base built around the skeleton of a British ship that once searched the Northwest Passage and has been frozen in the ice for 150 years. In this frigid Arctic environment of ice floes, snow-covered rocky outcroppings, surge pools, and boulders, seals and polar bears romp, lumbering walruses haul themselves up from the sea to sprawl on icy perches, white beluga whales surface, and salmon sparkle in clear, cold water. In 28 stations designed to provide tableaux vivants of life in the Arctic, guests participate in record-gathering aboard the shipwreck, explore polar bear dens, log on to ArcticNET, and pop their heads through openings in a simulated ice floe.

✪ **Mermaids, Myths & Monsters**   This nighttime multimedia spectacular is a must-see, featuring fireworks and hologram-like imagery against a towering 60-foot screen of illuminated water. King Neptune rises majestically from the deep, as do terrifying sea serpents, storm-tossed ships, and frolicking mermaids. It's thrilling!

Big Splash Bash   The show begins as an old-fashioned seaside themed musical but goes high-tech with fire-optic fireworks and lightning (in a sequence about the destruction of Atlantis) and later includes a Bermuda Triangle–themed laser light show. Bright neon fish, seahorses, and other denizens of the deep do a jazzy "dance" to Fats Waller's "This Joint Is Jumpin'." The finale is a rousing rock gospel sequence with a fabulous dancing-waters display.

Mission: Bermuda Triangle   Combining a high-definition underwater adventure film with state-of-the-art flight-simulator technology, this attraction takes visitors aboard a scientific research submarine. Your "mission": to explore the 444,000-square-mile expanse of the Atlantic Ocean known as the Bermuda Triangle, in which thousands of people and hundreds of ships and planes have vanished without a trace. Computer-controlled movements authentically replicate a real deep-sea expedition. Your "cabin" pitches, lunges, and sways with the waves as you plunge into the ocean to study the magnetic anomalies of this enigmatic area. Hugh Downs narrates a preshow video and briefs mission participants. It's all very rational and scientific . . . until an underwater earthquake threatens the expedition!

Terrors of the Deep   This exhibit houses 220 specimens of venomous and otherwise scary sea creatures in a tropical reef habitat. Immense acrylic tunnels provide close encounters with slithery eels and three dozen sharks. Barracudas, lionfish, and poisonous pufferfish are also on display. A theatrical presentation focusing on sharks puts across the message that pollution and uncontrolled commercial fishing make humankind the ultimate "terror of the deep."

Manatees: The Last Generation?   For centuries seagoing cultures have been fascinated by the gentle manatee, which some believe is the basis for mermaid myths (though you'd have to be at sea a long, long time for a manatee to suggest a woman). Today the Florida manatee is in danger of extinction, with as few as 2,000 remaining. Underwater viewing stations, innovative cinema techniques, and interactive displays combine to create an exciting format for teaching visitors about the manatee and its fragile ecosystem. In a winding tropical $3^1/_2$-acre lagoonlike setting, visitors view the world from a manatee's perspective, perceiving what the creatures hear, see, and feel. Also on display here are hundreds of other native fish as well as alligators, turtles, and shorebirds, and there's a nursing pool for manatee mothers and their babies.

Sea World Theatre: Window to the Sea   A multimedia presentation—which begins with a ballet of dancing waters shimmering in a rainbow of colored lights—takes visitors behind the scenes at Sea World and explores a variety of marine subjects. These include an ocean dive in search of the rare six-gilled shark, a killer whale giving birth, babies born at Sea World (dolphins, sea horses, penguins, walruses), dolphin anatomy, and underwater geology.

Shamu: World Focus   Sea World trainers develop close relationships with killer whales, and in this partly covered open-air stadium, they direct performances that are extensions of natural cetacean behaviors—twirling, waving tails and fins, rotating while swimming, and splashing the audience (sit pretty far back if you don't want to get soaked). Trainers also ride the whales. An informative video, narrated by Jane Seymour and projected on a vast 16- by 20-foot monitor, adds an underwater perspective to the show. The stadium includes a research and breeding area where you might see killer whale calves. The evening show here, called *Shamu: Night Magic,* utilizes rock music and special lighting effects; I suggest attending it instead of the daytime show. It's a fun way to wind up your day at Sea World.

   Shamu: Close Up!, an adjoining exhibit, lets you get close to the killer whales and talk to trainers; don't miss the underwater viewing area here.

The Whale and Dolphin Discovery Show   At Discovery Cove—a big partially covered open-air stadium—whales and Atlantic bottlenose dolphins perform flips and high jumps, swim at rapid speeds, twirl, swim on their backs, and give rides to trainers, all to the accompaniment of calypso music. Once again, these are extensions of natural behaviors that showcase the abilities of these creatures. A child volunteer gets to work as an apprentice trainer. While you're being seated, a guitarist leads a sing-along. Those sitting up front get wet.

The Gold Rush Ski Show   This wacky waterski exhibition features a cantankerous prospector and a talented team of cowboy waterskiers performing long-distance jumps, water ballet (performed by the miners' mail-order brides), flips, and backward and barefoot skiing. Their antics are accompanied by rollicking hoedown music and dance.

Penguin Encounter   This display of hundreds of penguins and alcids (including adorable babies) native to the Antarctic and Arctic regions also serves as a living laboratory for protecting and preserving polar life. On a moving walkway, you'll view six different penguin species congregating on rocks, nesting, and swimming underwater. If you want to observe their antics for a longer period, there is a viewing area for that purpose. The attraction is augmented by video displays about penguins and an additional area for puffins and murres—flying Arctic cousins of penguins.

Hotel Clyde and Seamore   Two sea lions, along with a cast of otters and walruses, appear in this fishy *Fawlty Towers* comedy with a conservation theme.

Shamu's Happy Harbor   This innovative three-acre play area provides facilities for kids to climb a four-story net tower with a 35-foot crow's nest lookout, fire water cannons, play steel drums, swing on tires, operate remote-controlled vehicles, navigate a water maze, do a ball crawl, and propel themselves upward on an air bounce. One section is especially for children under 42 inches tall.

ADDITIONAL ATTRACTIONS

The park's other attractions include:

Pacific Point Preserve is a 2½-acre naturalistic setting with beaches and ocean waves that duplicates the rocky northern Pacific coast. It is home to California sea lions and harbor and fur seals.

A **Tropical Reef** aquarium, fronted by a tide pool of touchables—sea anemones, starfish, sea cucumbers, and sea urchins. Inside, the 160,000-gallon manmade coral reef is home to 1,000 brightly hued tropical fish—including blue surgeon fish, sergeant majors, porkfish, French angelfish, guitarfish, and conch—displayed in 17 vignettes of undersea life.

Stingray Lagoon, where visitors enjoy hands-on encounters with harmless southern diamond and cownose rays. You can buy them treats and feed them as well; their diet consists of clams, shrimp, smelt, and squid.

A **Dolphin Community Pool,** where guests can feed and touch Atlantic bottlenose dolphins.

Ocean-themed **musical spectaculars** take place in the park's Nautilus Theatre.

A **Hawaiian dance troupe** that entertains with island songs and dances in an outdoor facility at Hawaiian Village; if you care to join in, grass skirts and leis are available.

You can ascend 400 feet to the top of the **Sea World Sky Tower** for a revolving 360-degree panorama of the park and beyond (there's an extra charge of $3 per person for this activity).

And at the 5½-acre **Anheuser-Busch Hospitality Center**—set amid tropical lagoons, waterfalls, and lush landscaping—you can view turn-of-the-century brewery equipment and a restored beer wagon, try free samples of Anheuser-Busch beers (there are soft drinks for kids) and snacks, and stroll through the stables to watch the famous Budweiser Clydesdale horses being groomed. There's indoor and terrace seating overlooking a lake. Anheuser-Busch is the owner of Sea World.

The **Aloha! Polynesian Luau Dinner and Show**—a musical revue featuring South Seas food, song, and fire dancing—takes place nightly at 6:30pm. Park admission is not required. Cost is $29.63 for adults, $20.09 for children 8 to 12, $10.55 for children 3 to 7, under 3 free. Reservations are required (☎ 407/363-2559, or 800/227-8048).

There are, of course, numerous restaurants, snack bars, and food kiosks throughout the park. My favorites are the Bimini Bay Café—a very pleasant full-service restaurant featuring seafood and basic American fare—and Mango Joe's, specializing in fajitas and offering a fresco seating at umbrella tables overlooking the lagoon. Dozens of shops carry marine-related gifts, toys, clothing, diving gear, and souvenirs, as well as wilderness/conservation-oriented items.

Visitors can take a 90-minute **behind-the-scenes tour** of the park's breeding, research, and training facilities and/or attend a **45-minute presentation** about Sea World's animal behavior and training techniques. Cost for either tour is $5.95 for ages 10 and over, $4.95 for children 3 to 9, 2 and under free.

ADMISSION   A one-day ticket costs $35.95 for ages 10 and over, $30.95 for children 3 to 9. A two-day ticket is $40.95 for ages 10 and over, $35.95 for children 3 to 9. A one-year pass is $64.95 for ages 10 and over, $54.95 for children 3 to 9. Ages 2 and under free. There are discounts for seniors, military, AAA members, and the handicapped. Discounted admissions in conjunction with Cypress Gardens (see Chapter 10) and Busch Gardens in Tampa are also available; call for details or inquire at the gate. Parking costs $5 per vehicle, $7 for RVs and trailers.

OPEN   The park is open 365 days a year, 9am to 7pm, later during summer and holidays when there are additional shows at night.

DIRECTIONS   Take I-4 to the Beeline Expressway (Hwy. 528) and follow the signs.

8 Additional Area Attractions

KISSIMMEE

Kissimmee sights are close to the Walt Disney World area—about a 10- to 15-minute drive.

✪ Cypress Island

1541 Scotty's Road, Kissimmee. ☎ **407/935-9202.** Admission $24 adult for an all-day pass, including boatride; $17 children 3–12, under 3 free. Call for rates for additional activities. Daily 9am to 5pm. Directions: Take U.S. 192 east, make a right at Shady Lane, and follow the signs.

About 12 miles from Walt Disney World, you can get a feel for old-time Florida at Cypress Island, located on Lake Tohopekaliga, the second-largest lake in Central Florida. Throughout the 1800s the 200-acre island was a Seminole fort site, and it was the childhood home of Cacoochee, one of the last great chiefs of that tribe. Visitors reach the island via an excursion boat which offers an ecotour narrative en route (there are frequent departures throughout the day). On arrival, you can explore (on foot or in a golf cart) two miles of pristine sign-posted nature trail lined with ancient live oaks and cypress. Another island attraction is abundant wildlife. Emus, peacocks, Sicilian donkeys, Barbados mountain sheep, African pygmy goats, and llamas freely roam grassy savannahs; snakes, panthers, and alligators are in a fenced-in preserve; and avian residents include American bald eagles, osprey, blue herons, white egrets, hummingbirds, cranes, cardinals, ibis, hawks, and owls. Bring your camera and binoculars. By prior reservation, you can also arrange airboat and sea plane rides, waterskiing, fishing, jet skiing, tubing, and horseback riding here. And there are nighttime gator safaris (led by experienced guides) through marshy areas of the lake. On-premises facilities include volleyball, horseshoes, picnic tables, a country store, and a concession that sells home-cooked barbecued-chicken dinners.

Flying Tigers Warbird Air Museum

231 Hoagland Blvd., off U.S. 192, one traffic light west of Armstrong Blvd. and Yates Rd. ☎ **407/933-1942.** Admission $6 adults, $5 seniors over 60 and children under 12. Daily 9am–6pm.

Flying Tigers is actually a World War II aircraft restoration facility where vintage planes are rebuilt and test-flown. Seventy-five percent of the displays—which run the gamut from 1920s antiques to 1970s fighter jets—are permanent, the rest are in shop on a temporary basis. On free guided tours, which depart every 30 minutes throughout the day, you'll visit the rebuilding facility where planes in various stages of assemblage are being restored. Exhibits include a U.S. Navy pilot trainer, many World War II bombers (including B-17s), Navy helicopters, torpedo bombers, cargo planes, and a rare World War II Paisacki Hup 1, as well as actual bombs, military jeeps and command cars from World War II and the Korean War, a large display of World War II memorabilia, and much, much more. Visitors can sit in the cockpit of a jet fighter simulator, or—for a more realistic Red Baron fantasy experience—arrange to go up in a 1935 three-seat open biplane (call ahead for information on the latter, as well as other flight and piloting opportunities, some for families). An on-premises shop sells everything from airplane model kits and air force patches to grenades (not live ones). There are picnic tables on the grounds.

Gatorland

14501 South Orange Blossom Trail (U.S. 441), between Osceola Pkwy. and Hunter's Creek Blvd. ☎ **407/855-5496,** 800/393-JAWS. Admission $10.95 adults, $8.75 seniors over 65, $7.95 for children 3–11, under 3 free. Daily 8am–dusk. Parking is free.

Founded in 1949 with a handful of alligators living in huts and pens, Gatorland today features thousands of alligators and crocodiles on a 70-acre spread. Breeding pens, nurseries, and rearing ponds are situated throughout the park, which also displays monkeys, snakes, deer, goats, birds, sheep, Florida lake turtles, a Galapagos tortoise, and a bear. A 2,000-foot boardwalk winds through a cypress swamp and a 10-acre breeding marsh with an observation tower. Or you can take the free Gatorland Express Train around the park. There are three educational shows scheduled throughout the day—Gator Wrestlin', the Gator Jumparoo, and Snakes of Florida. Facilities include an open-air restaurant (where you can sample smoked gator ribs and nuggets), a shop (Gatorland also functions as an alligator-breeding farm for meat and hides; you'll find a wide array of alligator leather products here, not to mention canned gator chowder), and a picnic area.

✪ Green Meadows Farm

1368 S. Poinciana Blvd., off U.S. 192 between Polynesian Blvd. and S.R. 535. ☎ **407/846-0770.** Admission $12 adults, children under 3 free. Daily 9:30am–5:30pm, with tours departing throughout the day until 4pm.

Though kids of any age will enjoy it, if your children are 8 or younger, a visit to this delightful 40-acre farm—home to over 200 animals—will give you better value for your money than any major theme park. On guided two-hour farm tours, visitors view, learn about, and in some cases feed or pet, sheep, goats, exotic chickens, turkeys, ducks, pigs, donkeys, ostriches, peacocks, and bison. Kids especially love to see the baby animals, and for parents, it's really fun to watch the kids in this setting. Everyone also gets a turn to milk a cow, and a hayride and pony ride are included in the entrance fee. Call before you go to find out about special events such as shows, pumpkin harvesting, and barn dances. There's a large shaded picnic area, so pack your lunch and make a day of it.

Splendid China

Formosa Gardens Blvd. off W. Irlo Bronson Memorial Hwy. (U.S. 192), between Entry Point Blvd./Sherbeth Rd. and Black Lake Rd. ☎ **407/396-7111.** Admission $23.55 for adults, $13.90 for children 5–12, under 5 free. Daily from 9:30am. Parking is free. Closing hours vary seasonally; call ahead.

This 76-acre outdoor attraction features more than 60 miniaturized replicas of China's most noted manmade and natural wonders, spanning 5,000 years of history and culture. Visitors enter via a bustling commercial street in the "water city" of Suzhou (the Venice of the East) circa A.D. 1300 to view a short orientation film about China. Park highlights include: a half-mile-long copy of the 4,200-mile Great Wall; the Forbidden City's 9,999-room Imperial Palace, built in 1420; Tibet's sacred Potala Palace, former mountain home of the Dalai Lama; carved Buddhist grottoes with statuary dating from A.D. 477 to A.D. 898; the massive Leshan Buddha, carved out of a mountainside between A.D. 713 and A.D. 803; the Stone Forest of Yunan, a natural formation of towering limestone peaks; and the Mongolian mausoleum of Genghis Khan. Live shows (acrobats, martial-arts demonstrations, storytelling, dance, puppetry, and more) take place throughout the day on stages around the park and in a 900-seat open-air amphitheater; check your entertainment schedule. Over a dozen shops sell Chinese merchandise. Food concessions, a gourmet restaurant, and a Chinese cafeteria are on the premises. Two-hour guided walking tours, departing several times a day, cost $5 per person (children under 12 free), and one-hour golf-cart tours ($45 per six-person cart) depart every half hour. There is also recorded commentary at each attraction.

Water Mania

6073 W. Irlo Bronson Memorial Hwy. (U.S. 192), just east of I-4. ☎ **407/396-2626.** Admission $20.95 adults, $12.95 children 3–12, under 3 free. Open daily. Hours vary seasonally (call before you go). Parking is $3.

This conveniently located 36-acre water park offers a variety of aquatic thrill rides and attractions. You can boogie-board or body-surf in continuous wave pools, float lazily along an 850-foot river, enjoy a whitewater tubing adventure, and plummet down spiraling water slides and steep flumes. Or dare to ride the Abyss—an enclosed tube slide that corkscrews through 300 feet of darkness, exiting into a splash pool. There's a rain forest–themed water playground for children. A miniature golf course and wooded picnic area—with arcade games, a beach, and volleyball—adjoin.

A World of Orchids

2501 Old Lake Wilson Rd. (C.R. 545), off U.S. 192. ☎ **407/396-1887.** Admission $8.95 adults, 15 and under free. Daily 10am–6pm. Closed New Year's Day, Memorial Day, July 4th, Thanksgiving, and Christmas.

Lovers of horticulture will enjoy touring this 30,000-square-foot conservatory filled with tropical trees (including 64 varieties of palms and 21 of bamboo), ferns, lush tropical foliage, and, most notably, thousands of orchids—many of them rare—magnificently abloom at all times. Streams, waterfalls, koi ponds, and birds enhance this little enchanted garden. Free guided tours are given by resident horticulturalists at 11am and 3pm weekdays, 11am and 2 and 4pm on weekends. *Note:* If this is the kind of attraction you enjoy, be sure to also visit Harry P. Leu Gardens in Orlando (details below).

INTERNATIONAL DRIVE

Like Kissimmee attractions, these are about a 10- to 15-minute drive from the Disney area.

Ripley's Believe It or Not!™ Museum

8201 International Dr., 1¹/₂ blocks south of Sand Lake Rd. ☎ **407/345-0501.** Admission $8.95 adults, $5.95 children 4–11, under 4 free. Daily 10am–11pm.

It's always fun to peruse a Ripley collection of oddities, curiosities, and fascinating artifacts from faraway places. Among the hundreds of items and mannequins on display here are a 1,069-pound man, a two-headed kitten, a five-legged cow, a ³/₄-scale model of a 1907 Rolls-Royce made from a million matchsticks, a mosaic of the *Mona Lisa* created from 1,426 pieces of toast, torture devices from the Spanish Inquisition, a Tibetan flute made from human bones, an Ecuadorean shrunken head, a painting on a grain of rice, a "disappearing" nude bather (they do it with mirrors), Ubangi women with wooden plates in their lips, Burmese Padaung women who stretch their necks up to 15 inches long by wearing heavy brass rings around them, and the Lighthouse Man from China (a tour guide, he has a 7-inch candle inserted into his head). There are exhibits on Houdini and Florida sinkholes, and a film documents daredevil stunts at Niagara Falls. Guests are greeted by a hologram of Robert Ripley.

Wet 'N Wild

6200 International Dr., at Republic Dr. ☎ **407/351-WILD** or 800/992-WILD. Admission $20.95 adults, $17.95 children 3–9, under 3 free. Open 365 days a year. Hours vary seasonally (call before you go). Parking is $3. Directions: Take I-4 east to Exit 30A and follow the signs.

When temperatures soar, head for this 25-acre water park and cool off by jumping waves, careening down steep flumes, and running rapids. Among the highlights: The Surge, the longest, fastest multipassenger tube ride anywhere in the southeast, with 580 feet of exciting banked curves; Surf Lagoon, a vast pool with four-foot ocean waves; Bomb Bay (enter a bomblike casing 76 feet in the air for a speedy vertical flight straight down to a target pool); Black Hole (step into a spaceship and board a two-person raft for a 30-second, 500-foot, twisting, turning, space-themed reentry through total darkness propelled by a 1,000-gallon-a-minute blast of water!); Raging Rapids, a simulated whitewater tubing adventure with a waterfall plunge; and Lazy River, a leisurely float trip. There are additional flumes, a children's water playground, a miniature golf, a sunbathing area, and a picnic area. Food concessions are located throughout the park, lockers and towels can be rented, and you can purchase beach accessories at the gift shop.

ORLANDO

All of the below-listed Orlando attractions are close to one another, making for a pleasant day's excursion. Loch Haven Park is about 35 minutes by car from the Disney area. You can probably also incorporate Winter Park sights in the same day (see Chapter 10 for details).

✪ Harry P. Leu Gardens

1730 N. Forest Ave., between Nebraska St. and Corrine Dr. ☎ **407/246-2620.** Admission $3 for adults, $1 for children 6–16, under 6 free. Daily 9am–5pm. Leu House tours Tues–Sat 10am–3:30pm, Sun–Mon 1–3:30pm. Closed Christmas. Directions: Take I-4 east to Exit 43 (Princeton Street), follow Princeton Street east, make a right on Mills Avenue and a left on Virginia Drive; look for the gardens on your left.

This delightful 56-acre botanical garden on the shores of Lake Rowena offers a serene respite from theme park razzle-dazzle. Meandering paths lead through forests of giant camphors, moss-draped oaks, palms, cycads, and camellias (one of the world's largest collections, comprising some 2,000 plants in 50 species; they bloom October through March). Exquisite formal rose gardens (the largest in Florida, displaying 75 varieties) are enhanced by Italian fountains, a gazebo, and statuary. Other highlights include orchids, azaleas, desert plants, beds of colorful annuals and perennials, a flowering tree garden (mimosa, cherry, plum, and others), and a 50-foot floral clock. The gardens were created by Orlando businessman Harry P. Leu, who donated his 49-acre estate to the city in the 1960s. Free 20-minute tours of the Leu House, built in 1888 and restored to reflect the period between 1910 and 1930, take place on the hour and half hour. The house is a veritable decorative-arts museum filled with beautiful Victorian, Chippendale, and Empire pieces and other furnishings and objets d'art. It takes about two hours to see the house and gardens. Inquire about lectures and workshops, including some for children.

Orange County Historical Museum

812 E. Rollins St., between Orange and Mills aves., in Loch Haven Park. ☎ **407/ 897-6350.** Admission $2 for adults, $1.50 for seniors 65 and over, $1 for children 6–12, under 6 free. Mondays admission is by donation. Mon–Sat 9am–5pm, Sun noon–5pm. Closed Martin Luther King Day, Memorial Day, July 4th, Labor Day, Thanksgiving, Christmas, and New Year's Day. Directions: Take I-4 east to Exit 43 (Princeton Street) and follow the signs to Loch Haven Park.

Sharing a building with the Orlando Science Center (details below), this museum focuses on Central Florida history, beginning with prehistoric projectile points, a Timucuan canoe, and tooled animal bones from hunting cultures that existed here 12,000 years ago. Other exhibits include: displays of Seminole pottery and clothing; items from a pioneer kitchen; artifacts from an 1892 courthouse; a chronicle of the citrus industry and the role it played in the development of central Florida; and re-creations of a turn-of-the-century country store, a Victorian parlor, and the old **Orlando Sentinel** composing room. Also on the premises is Fire Station No. 3, a restored 1926 firehouse containing historic fire trucks, equipment, and memorabilia. The permanent collection is supplemented by changing exhibits of local, national, and international significance.

Orlando Museum of Art

2416 N. Mills Ave., in Loch Haven Park off Hwy. 17-92. ☎ **407/896-4231.** Admission $4 for adults, $2 for children 4–11, under 4 free. Tues–Sat 9am–5pm, Sun noon–5pm. Art Encounter hours are Tues–Fri and Sun noon–5pm, Sat 10am–5pm. Parking is free. Closed Mon, New Year's Day, Memorial Day, July 4th, Labor Day, Thanksgiving, and Christmas. Directions: Take I-4 east to Exit 43 (Princeton Street) and follow the signs to Loch Haven Park.

Founded in 1924, the Orlando Museum of Art displays its permanent collection of 19th- and 20th-century American art, pre-Columbian art dating from 1200 B.C. to A.D. 1500, and African art on a rotating basis. These holdings are augmented by long-term loans focusing on Mayan archaeology (recently discovered ceramics, sculptured stucco, and jade pieces from Belize) and art of the African sub-Saharan region (cast bronze works, intricate beaded objects, and wood figures from the ancient kingdoms of Yoruba and Benin). Art Encounter is an interactive hands-on area for young children, where they might weave on a giant loom, piece together a pre-Columbian pot, or play African instruments. And recent temporary exhibits have ranged from Hudson River School landscapes to works of Andy Warhol. Inquire about guided tours, workshops for adults and children, gallery talks, and other activities. The museum shop carries many appealing gift items.

Orlando Science Center

810 E. Rollins St., between Orange and Mills aves., in Loch Haven Park. ☎ **407/ 896-7151.** Admission $6.50 for adults, $5.50 for children 3–11, under 3 free. Mon–Thurs and Sat 9am–5pm, Fri 9am–9pm, Sun noon–5pm. Closed Thanksgiving and Christmas. Directions: Take I-4 east to Exit 43 (Princeton Street) and follow the signs to Loch Haven Park.

The Orlando Science Center specializes in hands-on interactive exhibits. In its Tunnel of Discovery you can play with an echo tube, encase yourself in a giant soap bubble, create a tornado, or learn about anatomy from an immense soft-sculpture doll named Stuffee. Nature Works focuses on the flora and fauna of four Florida habitats—cypress swamp, sand pine scrub, sinkhole lake, and pine flatwood. In Water Works, an area for pre-kindergarten through fourth grade, children can learn how water moves objects by building dams and canals, crawl under a glass-bottom turtle tank, touch starfish and sponges, and examine discovery drawers filled with fossils, plants, insects, and bones. In addition, you can search for cardinals in a bird-watching area, find out what the weather is back home, take in a free planetarium show, or touch live frogs and turtles during daily reptile and amphibian demonstrations. About 50% of the museum is given over to changing exhibits on subjects ranging from dinosaurs to exotic insects. A café serves light fare at outdoor umbrella tables, and a gift shop carries many interesting science projects for children. Inquire about workshops for children and nighttime planetarium shows and laser-show rock concerts.

9 Outdoor Activities

Recreational facilities of every description abound in Walt Disney World and the surrounding area. These are especially accessible to guests at Disney-owned resorts, official hotels, and Fort Wilderness Resort and Campground, though many other large resort hotels also offer comprehensive facilities (see details in Chapter 5). The Disney facilities listed below are all open to the public, no matter where you're staying. For further information about WDW recreational facilities call 407/824-4321. Guests at Disney properties can inquire when making hotel reservations or at guest services/concierge desks.

BICYCLING Bike rentals (single and multispeed bikes for adults, tandems, and children's bikes—though none with training wheels) are available from the **Bike Barn** (☎ 407/824-2742) at Fort Wilderness Resort and Campground. Rates are $3 per hour, $8 per day ($1 additional for tandems); overnight rentals are $15 ($18 for tandems). Both Fort Wilderness and Disney's Village Resort offer good bike trails.

BOATING Walt Disney World, with its many manmade lakes and lagoons, owns the nation's largest fleet of pleasure boats. At the **Walt Disney World Village Marina** you can rent Water Sprites, canopy boats, Sun Kats, and 20-foot pontoon boats. For information call 407/828-2204. The **Bike Barn** at Fort Wilderness (☎ 407/824-2742) rents canoes ($4 per hour, $10 per day) and paddleboats ($5 per half hour, $8 per hour). See hotel facilities listings in Chapter 5 for additional boating options.

FISHING Fishing excursions on Lake Buena Vista—mainly for largemouth bass—may be arranged from 2 to 14 days in advance by calling the **Walt Disney World Village Marina** (☎ 407/828-2204). Equipment can be rented. No license is required. The fee is $70 for one person for two hours, $90 for two people, $110 for three to six people, $25 for each additional hour; those rates include gear, guide, and refreshments. If you'd like to take your catch home, Walt Disney World has an arrangement with a local taxidermist.

You can also rent fishing poles at the **Bike Barn** (☎ 407/824-2742) to fish in Fort Wilderness canals. No license is required.

FLYING   The **Flying Tigers Warbird Air Museum** offers a variety of flight and piloting experiences including scenic seaplane flights over central Florida's lake region, a ride in a 1935 open-cockpit barnstormer, night flights to see theme-park fireworks and laser shows from the air, and hands-on dual-instruction adventures in an historic World War II fighter trainer. Call 407/933-1942 for details.

A slightly more offbeat experience is offered by **Fighter Pilots USA.** Ever dreamed of suiting up, jumping into a fighter plane, and engaging in high-speed one-on-one dogfighting? This is your chance to experience the excitement of aerial combat. Actual F-16 pilots are your instructors. To schedule a "mission" call 407/931-4333, or 800/ 56-TOPGUN. No license is required. Cost is $750 per person.

GOLF   Walt Disney World operates five championship 18-hole, par-72 golf courses and one nine-hole, par-36 walking course. All are open to the general public and offer pro shops, equipment rentals, and instruction. For tee times and information call 407/824-2270 up to seven days in advance (up to 30 days for Disney resort and official property guests). Call 407/W-DISNEY for information about golf packages.

HAYRIDES   The hay wagon departs from Pioneer Hall at **Fort Wilderness** nightly at 7pm and 9:30pm for hour-long, old-fashioned hayrides with singing, jokes, and games. Cost is $5 for adults, $4 for children 3 to 11, under 3 free. Children under 12 must be accompanied by an adult. No reservations; it's first-come, first-served.

HORSEBACK RIDING   Disney's Fort Wilderness Resort and Campground offers 50-minute scenic **trail rides** daily, with four to six rides per day. Cost is $17 per person. Children must be at least 9 years old. For information and reservations up to five days in advance, call 407/824-2832.

ICE SKATING   **Rock on Ice! Skating Arena,** in the Dowdy Pavilion, 7500 Canada Ave., between Sand Lake Road and Carrier Drive (☎ 407/352-9878), is a gorgeous Olympic-size indoor rink with high-tech lighting and sound systems. A DJ spins Top 40 tunes. There are ice-skating games with prizes throughout the day. Facilities include video games, a snack bar, and a complete skate shop offering a large selection of figure skating and hockey equipment. Rental skates are $1.50. Admission is $4.50 to $6, depending on the season. Hours vary seasonally; call ahead. To get here from the Disney World area take International Drive north, turn right at Sand Lake Road and left on Canada Avenue. It's about a 10-minute drive.

JOGGING   Many of the Disney resorts have scenic jogging trails. For instance, the **Yacht and Beach Club** resorts share a 2-mile trail, **Disney's Village Resort** has a 3.5-mile course with 32 exercise stations,

---

Swimming with the Manatees

An organization called **Oceanic Society Expeditions** (☎ 415/441-1106 or 800/326-7491), offers a "Swim with the Manatees" program in the Crystal River area, two hours east of Orlando. A manatee biologist leads five-day Monday-to-Friday trips aboard a 12-person skiff, which include swimming with manatees, bird-watching, snorkeling, slide presentations, and an excursion to a facility for the care of injured and orphaned wildlife. Cost is $985, including accommodations, excursions, and most meals. Reserve as far in advance as possible.

---

the **Caribbean Beach Resort's** 1.4-mile promenade circles a lake, **Dixie Landings** has a 1.7-mile riverfront trail, and **Fort Wilderness's** tree-shaded 2.3-mile jogging path has exercise stations about every quarter mile. After your run, you can cool off in a hotel pool. Pick up a jogging trail map at any Disney property's guest services desk.

TENNIS   Seventeen lighted tennis courts are located throughout the Disney properties. Most are free and available on a first-come, first-served basis. If you're willing to pay for court time, courts can be reserved at two Disney resorts: the Contemporary (fee is $10 per hour) and the Grand Floridian (fee is $12 per hour). The Contemporary offers a large pro shop, a ball machine, rebound walls, and equipment rentals. To reserve a court or lesson time with resident pros call 407-824-3578 at the Contemporary, 407/824-2433 at the Grand Floridian.

WATER PARKS/SWIMMING   See "Other WDW Attractions" for information on River Country and Typhoon Lagoon as well as parks listed in "Additional Area Attractions," above.

WATERSKIING   Waterski trips (including boats, drivers, equipment, and instruction) can be arranged at Walt Disney World by calling 407/824-2621. Make reservations up to seven days in advance. Cost is $75 per hour.

10 Spectator Sports

As we go to press, construction is under way on the multimillion-dollar **Walt Disney World International Sports Center,** a 100-acre facility for amateur sports. It will include a 5,000-seat main-event stadium, as well as a 2,000-seat professional-level tennis arena, baseball diamonds, and much more. The center is scheduled to open in 1996.

The **Orlando Centroplex** administers six public sports and entertainment facilities in the downtown area. These include three major sporting arenas: the Florida Citrus Bowl, the Orlando Arena, and Tinker Field.

BASEBALL   From April to September, the Orlando Cubs—the Chicago Cubs' Class AA Southern League affiliate—play at Tinker Field,

287 S. Tampa Ave., between Colonial Dr. (Hwy. 50) and Gore St. (☎ 407/872-7593 for information and to charge tickets). Tickets are $3 to $6. Directions: Take I-4 east to the East-West Expwy. and head west to Hwy. 441; make a left on Church St. and follow signs. Tinker Field adjoins the Citrus Bowl. Parking is $2.

BASKETBALL   The 17,500-seat Orlando Arena, 600 W. Amelia St. between I-4 and Parramore Ave. (☎ 407/849-2020 for information, 839-3900 to charge tickets) is home to the NBA Orlando Magic during their October-to-April season. Tickets to games (about $12 to $32) have to be acquired far in advance; they usually sell out by September before the season starts. Directions: Take I-4 east to Amelia Ave., turn left at the traffic light at the bottom of the off-ramp, and follow signs. For up-to-the-minute parking information turn your car radio to 1620 AM.

FOOTBALL   The Florida Citrus Bowl, 1610 W. Church St., at Tampa St. (☎ 407/849-2020 for information, 839-3900 to charge tickets), hosts the annual New Year's Day Citrus Bowl classic, college football games, and NFL pre-season games. Tickets to all football events are hard to come by, but you may have some luck if you try far enough in advance. Directions: Take I-4 east to the East-West Expwy. and head west to Hwy. 441, make a left on Church St. and follow the signs. Parking is $5.

GREYHOUND RACING   The **Sanford-Orlando Kennel Club,** 301 Dog Track Rd. between FL 427 and U.S. 17/92, in Longwood (☎ 407/831-1600) offers a pleasant way to spend a day or evening, especially if you opt to watch the races over lunch or dinner in the glassed-in clubhouse restaurant. The restaurant is moderately priced and has a full bar; reservations are suggested. There are a variety of ways to bet on the greyhounds; if you've never done it before, pick up a free brochure that explains trifectas, quinelas, boxing, and wheeling and also shows you how to read your ticket. You can also buy tip sheets here recommending computer and expert picks. Each meet includes 14 races. You must be at least 18 years old to enter the track.

Admission is $1, plus $1 admission to the clubhouse restaurant. Parking is free, preferred parking (closer to the entrance) is $1, and valet parking is $2.

Open Nov–early May. Nighttime races Mon–Sat at 7:30pm; matinees Mon, Wed, and Sat at 12:30pm. Directions: From Walt Disney World area, take I-4 east, make a right at Maitland Blvd., go north on 17/92, and make a left into Dog Track Rd. It's about a 40-minute drive.

Seminole Greyhound Park, 2000 Seminola Blvd., just east of U.S. 17/92, in Casselberry (☎ 407/699-4510), offers a very similar set-up to the above. Its attractive third-floor restaurant, Osceola Terrace, has tiered seating with big picture windows overlooking the track and TV monitors enhancing the view at higher tables. Prices are moderate, and there's a full bar; reservations are suggested. Each meet here includes 14 or 15 races. Children are welcome but must be at least 18 years old to enter the betting area.

Admission is $1, free for seniors 55 and over at matinees, $2 for clubhouse seating, $3 for restaurant seating. Children under 18 pay half price throughout. Parking is free, preferred parking (closer to the entrance) is $1, and valet parking is $2.

Open May–Oct. Nighttime races Mon–Sat at 7:30pm; matinees Mon, Wed, and Sat at 1pm. Directions: From the Walt Disney World area, take I-4 east, make a right at Exit 48 (FL 436), a left at U.S. 17/92, and right on Seminola Blvd., which dead-ends at the track. It's about a 40-minute drive.

JAI ALAI   Orlando Jai-Alai, 6405 S. U.S. 17/92, at S.R. 436 in Fern Park. (☎ 407/339-6221) offers the action-packed Basque sport of jai-alai (it's the world's fastest game). It's played on a 180-foot court with three walls. The ball is hurled at speeds of up to 150 miles an hour from baskets strapped to the players' wrists, and the object of the game is to throw the ball with such force, spin, and/or placement that the opponent is unable to return it before it bounces twice. A score of seven points wins. There are two opposing singles or doubles teams on the court at all times. Your program offers extensive information about how the game is played and how to wager, and the public-address announcer elucidates what is happening on the court. Best bet is to watch the action from the moderately priced, and very attractive, open-air Terrace Restaurant, with some tables as close as 20 feet from the court. There's a color TV monitor at every table. Fare is American/continental; there's a full bar; reservations are suggested. Children 39 inches and taller are admitted into the fronton with parents, but not allowed in the betting area. *Note:* The fronton also features inter-track wagering; you can place bets here on thoroughbred and harness races as well as Miami jai-alai.

Admission is $1, reserved seats are $2, restaurant seating is $3, box seats are $5 to $6. Seniors 55 get free admission to matinees. Parking is free, valet parking is $1.50.

Open year-round Wed–Sun. Evening games at 7:30pm Wed–Sat, matinees at noon Thurs and Sat and 1pm Sun. Directions: From the Walt Disney World area, take I-4 east, make a right at Exit 47A (Maitland Exchange), a right at U.S. 17/92, and look for the fronton two miles along on your right. It's about a 40-minute drive.

8

Shopping

You probably didn't come down here to shop, but I doubt you'll leave without a purchase or two. All Orlando area theme parks abound with emporia, in addition to which Walt Disney World has its own shopping complex. Shops in all WDW parks will deliver purchases to Disney resorts and official hotels.

1 Shopping in Walt Disney World

Just about every shop throughout the parks carries Disneyana—plush Mickey Mice, *Little Mermaid* T-shirts, etc. But you may be surprised at some of the other merchandise on display here. Among the many dozens of shops, the following are especially notable:

IN THE MAGIC KINGDOM

MAIN STREET AREA The vast **Disneyana Collectibles** carries limited-edition movie cels, antique Disney clocks and porcelain figures, collectible dolls, and items such as a 1947 Donald Duck cookie jar that is today worth $2,000! Why did you ever let Mom throw out your old toys?

The Emporium, in Town Square, houses the park's largest selection of Disneyana—everything from Mickey logo golf balls to Dumbo cookie jars. Note the Audio-Animatronics™ window displays.

The **Market House**—basically an old-fashioned candy store—also carries an interesting line of pipes and tobaccos. Disney-themed kitchenware, too, including Mickey and Minnie corn picks, cupcake papers, ice-cube molds, and cookie cutters.

Over at the **Harmony Barber Shop,** where nostalgic men's grooming items are sold (moustache wax, spice colognes, shaving mugs), a barbershop quartet performs on the hour, except at 3pm, throughout the day.

The **House of Magic** is the place to acquire double-headed nickels, folding quarters, squirting calculators, invisible ink, and other items with which to amaze and impress your friends.

The **Main Street Book Store** carries Disney books and books about Disney as well as cassettes and CDs.

The best selection of Mickey Mouse watches is at **Uptown Jewelers.**

Stop by the **Main Street Confectionary** for chocolate Mickey heads, fudge, almond pecan clusters, and other candy treats.

At **Crystal Arts** you can watch craftspeople create intricate animals, cut-glass vases and bowls, and other glittering items.

And at the adjoining **Shadow Box,** silhouette artists create cut-out portraits of customers on black paper.

ADVENTURELAND **Traders of Timbuktu** carries carved wooden and soapstone animals, masks, and cowhide drums from Kenya, among other exotic wares.

Plaza del Sol Caribe, a colorful Mexican *mercado* complete with courtyard fountain, sells baskets, piñatas, stuffed toucans and parrots, and other Mexican handicrafts.

Adventure (Raiders-look) clothing and accessories for men and women are available from **Elephant Tales.**

The **Zanzibar Shell Shop** is the place for shell mobiles and hangings, plus a wide selection of straw hats.

Island Supply carries nature/ecology-themed books, toys, clothing, posters, and T-shirts.

The **House of Treasures** retails pirate merchandise—hats, Captain Hook T-shirts, ships in bottles, skull-and-crossbone flags, and toy muskets and daggers.

And rather fun is **Laffite's Portrait Deck,** where you can have a costumed photo taken in any of six elaborate Disney sets.

FRONTIERLAND Mosey into the **Frontier Trading Post** for western-look leather items, cowboy boots and hats, turquoise jewelry, belts, and toy rifles.

And look for country bears at the **Prairie Outpost & Supply.**

LIBERTY SQUARE **Olde World Antiques** is an actual antiques emporium selling items which might range from an 18th-century pine hutch to 19th-century Staffordshire china.

The adjoining **Silversmith** carries Revere-style silver and pewter butter dishes, candlesticks, bowls, trays, and picture frames.

Over at **Heritage House** you can purchase parchment copies of famous American documents as well as actual historic framed letters (on a recent visit, one signed by Andrew Johnson in 1864 was priced at $2,350). Old campaign buttons, Civil War hats, and presidential signatures are here, too. A craftsperson on the premises makes jewelry from cut coins.

FANTASYLAND It's always the holiday season at **Mickey's Christmas Carol**—supply central for Disney-motif ornaments, caroller dolls, Christmas stockings, and charming Christmas-themed music boxes.

The **King's Gallery,** inside Cinderella Castle, is cluttered with family crests, tapestries, suits of armor, and other medieval wares. An artisan demonstrates damascening—a form of metal engraving that originated in Damascus circa A.D. 600.

TOMORROWLAND Kids love browsing over **Merchant of Venus's** space-themed merchandise and games, sonic blaster guns, robots, alien masks, and astronaut-costumed Mickeys.

There's more Disneyana—some of it space-themed—at **Mickey's Star Traders.**

EPCOT

The most fascinating shops are found in **World Showcase** pavilions, which comprise an international bazaar selling everything from Berber rugs to Japanese kimonos. You'll find descriptions of merchandise available at each of these pavilions in World Showcase descriptions in Chapter 7.

DISNEY-MGM STUDIOS

There's some really interesting shopping here. **Sid Cahuenga's One-Of-A-Kind** sells autographed photos of the stars, original movie posters, and star-touched items. Obviously, the inventory of the latter is ever changing. On my last visit it included a bracelet that once belonged to Joan Rivers, Richard Dreyfuss's director's chair from *Lost in Yonkers,* Cher's black spiked wig, and an original letter written by Tyrone Power.

Once Upon a Time is a good place to shop for current movie merchandise and unique Disney figurines.

The **Animation Gallery** carries one-of-a-kind and limited-edition production cels (some of them valuable collector's items), books about animation and the making of Disney classics, and Paint-a-Cel kits for future animators.

Over at **Cover Story** you can have your photograph put on the cover of your favorite magazine—anything from *Forbes* to *Psychology Today* to *Golf Digest.* Costumes are available.

Celebrity 5 & 10, modeled after a 1940s Woolworth's, has movie-related merchandise—*Gone With the Wind* memorabilia, MGM Studio T-shirts, movie posters, Elvis mugs, James Dean clocks, and more.

And major park attractions all have complementary merchandise outlets selling Indiana Jones adventure clothing, *Little Mermaid* stuffed characters and logo wear, *Star Wars* souvenirs, and so on.

DISNEY VILLAGE MARKETPLACE

Just 2¹/₂ miles from Epcot, this complex of restaurants and shops on the shores of Buena Vista Lagoon makes for a very pleasant browse. Designed to evoke a quaint seaside town, the Marketplace (☎ 407/828-3058) has about 20 weathered-wood and shingled shops offering a wide variety of giftware, Disneyana (the Character Shop here has the largest selection of Walt Disney merchandise in WDW, while Art of Disney carries cels and other Disney art), toys, resort wear (including many logo items), designer clothing for men and women, Christmas-year-round merchandise, books, jewelry, crystal, housewares, country/folk crafts, shells, surfboarding gear, wines and spirits, and sports shoes. Artisans demonstrate crafts such as glass-blowing, pottery-making, silhouette-cutting, and caricaturing at various locations throughout the complex, and many special events—ranging from boat shows to Easter-egg hunts—take place here. There's plenty of free parking. See Chapter 6 for restaurant suggestions here. You can also rent mini-speedboats and pontoons at the marina here. The Marketplace is open daily from 9:30am to 10pm.

CROSSROADS OF LAKE BUENA VISTA

Also under Walt Disney World auspices, this retail center at Exit 27 off I-4 (☎ 407/827-7300) is anchored by a 24-hour Goodings super-market with a full-service pharmacy. Other shops sell sportswear, electronics, books, cards, gifts, shoes, and Disney merchandise. There's also a post office, and restaurants/fast-food outlets include, among others, T.G.I. Friday's, Johnny Rockets, Pebbles (see Chapter 6), Pizzeria Uno, and Red Lobster. Shops are open daily 10am to 10pm. It's just like a shopping center in the real world.

2 Orlando Area Malls

FACTORY OUTLETS

Belz Factory Outlet World, 5401 W. Oak Ridge Rd., at the north end of International Drive (☎ 407/354-0126 or 352-9600), is the largest of these, with 180 stores in two huge enclosed malls and four shopping annexes. It offers an immense range of merchandise at savings up to 75% off retail prices. There's even a carousel for the kids. Among its emporia: 18 shoestores (including Bass, Bally, and Capezio); 14 housewares shops (including Fieldcrest/Cannon, Corning, Oneida, and Mikasa); and more than 60 clothing shops for men, women, and children (including London Fog, Van Heusen, Jonathan Logan, Guess Jeans, Aileen, Danskin, Jordache, Leslie Fay, Carole Little, Harvé Benard, Calvin Klein, and Anne Klein). You can also shop for books and records, electronics, sporting goods, health and beauty aids, jewelry, toys, gifts, accessories, lingerie, and hosiery here. Open Monday through Saturday from 10am to 9pm, Sunday from 10am to 6pm.

Close to the above is the **Quality Outlet Center,** on International Drive a block east of Kirkman Road (☎ 407/423-5885). It has about 20 outlets, including Arrow, American Tourister, a vast book warehouse, Corning-Revere (glassware and cookware), Florsheim shoes, Magnavox, Laura Ashley, Adidas, Great Western Boots, Petals (silk flowers), Totes, Le Creuset (cookware), Linens 'N Things, Mikasa, Royal Doulton, and Villeroy & Boch. Once again, big savings. Open Monday through Saturday from 9:30am to 9pm, Sunday from 11am to 6pm.

Manufacturer's Outlet Mall, U.S. 192, a mile east of FL 535 in Kissimmee (☎ 407/396-8900), houses about 35 stores, including Van Heusen, Nike, London Fog, Fieldcrest/Cannon, Bass Apparel, Geoffrey Beene, American Tourister, Westport (women's fashions), Acme Boot, and Levis. Open Monday through Saturday from 10am to 9pm, Sunday from 11am to 5pm.

INTERNATIONAL DRIVE AREA MALLS

The Mercado, 8445 International Dr., just south of Sand Lake Road (☎ 407/345-9337)—a Mediterranean-style shopping center with brick and cobblestone streets, terra-cotta-roofed buildings, brightly colored awnings, and splashing fountains—is home to the Orlando/ Orange County Visitor Information Center. There's a carousel and family fun center (video and brand arcade games) to keep kids amused, and evenings a one-man band entertains with rock, jazz, pop, and big band music in the central courtyard. More than 60 specialty shops here include Once Upon A Star (movie-motif gifts and clothing), Kandlestix (handcrafted candles), American Cola Company (Coca-Cola and Anheuser-Busch memorabilia), House of Ireland (china, crystal, claddagh jewelry), Historic Families (find your family's coat of arms), Earth Matters (conservation/ecology-themed merchandise), Lady Bug (needlecrafts), The Magic Shop (novelties, tricks, and pranks), and The Looking Glass (blown glass). It makes good browsing, and there are over a dozen restaurants and bars on the premises. Open daily from 10am to 10pm, till 11pm late spring through the end of August.

The **Florida Mall,** 8001 S. Orange Blossom Trail, at Sand Lake Road (☎ 407/851-6255), is your basic massive shopping mall with more than 200 shops, restaurants, and services. Centered on a 500-room Sheraton Hotel, it is anchored by six department stores—Belk Lindsey, two Dillard's stores, J. C. Penney, Gayfers, and Sears. In addition there are more than 10 jewelry shops, about 50 clothing and accessory shops (including mall regulars such as Benetton, Warner Bros. Studio Store, The Gap/Gap Kids, The Limited, and Victoria's Secret), over a dozen shoestores, bookstores, electronics stores, eateries, and much, much more. Open Monday through Saturday from 10am to 9:30pm, Sunday from 11am to 6pm.

9

Walt Disney World & Orlando After Dark

My hat's off to those of you who after a long day traipsing around amusement parks still have the energy to venture out at night in search of entertainment. You'll find plenty to do. And this being a kid's world, many evening shows are geared to families.

In addition to the below-listed suggestions check the "Calendar" section of Friday's *Orlando Sentinel* for up-to-the-minute details on local clubs, visiting performers, concerts, and events—and many are world-class.

Tickets to many performances are handled by Ticketmaster. Call 407/839-3900 to charge tickets.

1 Major Concert Halls & Auditoriums

Three large entertainment facilities, administered by the Orlando Centroplex, host the majority of big-name performers playing the Orlando area. The **Florida Citrus Bowl,** 1610 W. Church St. at Tampa St. (☎ 407/849-2020 for information, 839-3900 to charge tickets), with 70,000 seats, is the largest. This is the setting for major rock concerts and headliners like Billy Joel, Elton John, The Eagles, Guns N' Roses, Metallica, and the Rolling Stones. To reach the Citrus Bowl, take I-4 east to the East-West Expwy. and head west to Hwy. 441; make a left on Church St. and follow the signs. Parking is $5.

The 17,500-seat **Orlando Arena** at 600 W. Amelia St., between I-4 and Parramore Ave. (☎ 407/849-2020 for information, 839-3900 to charge tickets) also hosts major performers in addition to an array of family-oriented entertainment: Ringling Bros. Barnum & Bailey Circus in January, Discover Card Stars on Ice in February, Tour of World Figure-Skating Champions in April or May, and *Walt Disney's World on Ice* in September. To reach the arena take I-4 east to Amelia Ave., turn left at the traffic light at the bottom of the off-ramp and follow signs. For up-to-the minute parking information turn your car radio to 1620 AM. Parking is $5.

The area's major culture venue is the **Bob Carr Performing Arts Centre,** 401 W. Livingston St., between I-4 and Parramore Ave. (☎ 407/849-2020 for information, 839-3900 to charge tickets). The center is home to the **Orlando Opera Company and the Southern Ballet Theater** (both have October-to-May seasons), and also to the **Orlando Broadway Series** (September to May) featuring original-cast Broadway shows such as *Phantom of the Opera, Jesus Christ Superstar,* and *Grease.* To get to the Bob Carr center take I-4 east to Amelia Ave., turn left at the traffic light at the bottom of the off-ramp and follow signs. For up-to-the-minute parking information, turn your car radio to 1620 AM. Parking is $5.

2 Walt Disney World Dinner Shows

Two distinctly different dinner shows are hosted by Walt Disney World. Other nighttime park options include SpectroMagic, fireworks, and IllumiNations (details in Chapter 7).

Hoop-Dee-Doo Musical Revue

Disney's Fort Wilderness Resort and Campground, 3520 N. Fort Wilderness Trail. ☎ **407/W-DISNEY.** $35 adults 21 and over, $25 ages 12–20, $17 children 3–11. Taxes and gratuities are extra. Show times 5, 7:15, and 9:30pm nightly. Free self-parking.

Fort Wilderness's rustic log-beamed Pioneer Hall is the setting for this two-hour foot-stompin', hand-clappin' down-home musical revue. It's a high-energy show, with 1890s costumes, corny vaudeville jokes, rousing songs, and lots of good-natured audience participation. During the show, the audience chows down on an all-you-can-eat barbecue dinner including chips and salsa, salad, smoked ribs, country-fried chicken, corn on the cob, baked beans, loaves of fresh-baked bread with honey butter, and a big slab of strawberry shortcake for dessert. Beverages (coffee, tea, beer, sangría, and soda) are included. Reservations required. If you catch an early show stick around for the Electrical Water Pageant at 9:45pm, which can be viewed from the Fort Wilderness Beach.

Polynesian Luau Dinner Show

Disney's Polynesian Resort, 1600 Seven Seas Dr. ☎ **407/W-DISNEY.** $33 adults 21 and over, $25 ages 12–20, $17 children 3–11. Taxes and gratuities are extra. Show times 6:45 and 9:30pm nightly. Free self- and valet parking.

This delightful two-hour dinner show features a colorfully costumed cast of exotic South Pacific entertainers (from New Zealand, Tahiti, Hawaii, and Samoa) performing authentic hula, warrior, ceremonial, love, and fire dances on a flower-bedecked stage. The show also includes a Hawaiian/Polynesian fashion show. It all takes place in an open-air theater (dress for the weather) with candlelit tables, red-flame lanterns suggesting torchiers, and tapa-bark paintings adorning the walls. The all-you-can-eat meal includes a marvelous tropical fruit and greens salad, coconut-almond bread, fried rice with vegetables, seafood stir-fry, barbecued ribs, chicken teriyaki, fresh fruit with chocolate dipping sauce and coconut haupia (pudding) for dessert, and beverages (mai-tais, melon coladas, beer, soft drinks, and tea or coffee; nonalcoholic specialty cocktails are available for kids). Everyone is presented with a shell lei on entering, and if the weather's chilly, hot cocoa is served while you're waiting for the show to begin. Reservations required. There is also a 4:30pm version daily (see character meal listings in Chapter 6).

3 Entertainment Complexes

Pleasure Island

In Walt Disney World, adjacent to Walt Disney World Village. ☎ **407/934-7781.** Admission $14.95. Admission is included in the Five-Day World-Hopper Pass. There's no admission prior to 7pm, but you have to pay after that. Clubs 8pm–2am, shops 10am–1am. Free self-parking, valet parking $5.

Opened in 1989, this Walt Disney World theme park is a rollicking six-acre complex of nightclubs, restaurants (a branch of Planet Hollywood just opened), shops, and movie theaters (details below) where, for a single admission price, you can enjoy a night of club-hopping till the wee hours. The park is designed to evoke an abandoned waterfront industrial district with clubs in "converted" ramshackle lofts, factories, and warehouses, but the streets are festive with brightly colored lights and balloons. Dozens of searchlights play overhead, and rock music emanates from the bushes. You'll be given a map and show schedule when you enter the park; take a look at it, and plan your evening around shows that interest you. The mood here is always festive. For one thing, every night at Pleasure Island is New Year's Eve, celebrated on the stroke of midnight with a high-energy street party, live entertainment, a barrage of fireworks, and showers of confetti. You can feel perfectly secure sending your teenage kids here for the evening, though they must be 18 to get in unless accompanied by a parent or legal guardian. The on-premises clubs do come and go. At this writing they include:

Mannequins Dance Palace: Housed in a vast dance hall with a small-town movie-house facade, Mannequins is supposed to be a converted theatrical mannequin warehouse (remember, you're still in Disney World). It's a high-energy club with a large rotating dance floor. Three levels of bars and hangout space are festooned with elaborately costumed mannequins and moving scenery suspended from overhead rigging. A DJ plays contemporary tunes at ear-splitting decibel level, and there are high-tech lighting effects. You must be 21 to get in, and they're very serious about it. They even carded me, and I learned to dance to the Platters.

Neon Armadillo Music Saloon: You guessed. This trilevel club is country—with neon beer signs, rustic tables mounted on beer barrels, walls hung with spurs and saddles, and a spur-shaped neon chandelier. Live country bands play nightly, and dancers whirl around the floor doing the Texas two-step or cotton-eyed Joe (lessons are given Sundays from 7 to 8pm). Sometimes name stars come in and take the stage. The staff is in cowboy/cowgirl garb. A specialty at the bar is jello shooters—jello cubes laced with rum, vodka, and other alcoholic beverages. You can also order southwestern fare here such as chili and fajitas.

The **Pleasure Island Jazz Company:** This big barnlike club—purported to be an abandoned waterfront carousel factory—features contemporary and traditional live jazz. Performers are mostly locals, but about once a month there are big names such as Kenny Rankin, Lionel Hampton, Maynard Ferguson, the Rippingtons, and Billy Taylor. Light fare, international coffees, and a variety of foreign and domestic wines are available.

Adventurers Club: The most unique—and my personal favorite—of Pleasure Island's clubs occupies a multistory building that, according to Disney legend, was designed to house the vast library and archeological trophy collection of island founder and compulsive explorer Merriweather Adam Pleasure. It's also headquarters for the Adventures Club, which Pleasure headed up until he vanished at sea in 1941. The plushly furnished club is chock-full of artifacts—early aviation photos, hunting trophies, shrunken heads, Buddhas, Indian goddesses, spears, and a mounted "yakoose" (half yak, half moose) who occasionally speaks. He's not the only one. In the eerie Mask Room, strange sounds are often heard, and more than 100 masks move their eyes, jeer, and make odd pronouncements. Also on hand are Pleasure's zany band of globe-trotting friends and club servants, played by skilled actors who interact with guests and always stay in character. Improvisational comedy shows take place throughout the evening in the main salon, diverse 20-minute cabaret shows/events in the library (during which "volunteers" are dragooned from the audience). You could easily hang out here all night imbibing potent tropical drinks in the library and at the bar—where elephant-foot barstools rise and sink mysteriously.

Blazing Pianos: A Perfect Hell for the Shy

A wildly rambunctious crowd hangs out at the popular Blazing Pianos Singalong club, where a zany, talented cast of singers and musicians—on fire-engine-red grand pianos—perform classic rock tunes, do a bit of comedy, and try to embarrass audience members. Most of the songs they select are on the lively side—"Great Balls of Fire," "The Twist," "Jailhouse Rock," and the like.

Audience members occasionally get up on the stage—or are dragooned there—to dance. And probably once a night everyone stands up to perform "Hand Jive." Blazing Pianos promotes audience participation to the max; it's an exhibitionist's paradise, and perhaps unbearable for the sensitive (you might be spotlighted if they see you're not singing!). The ambience is slick and upscale; special effects include smoke, mirror balls, and strobe lights. A fairly extensive bar menu lists items such as fried calamari and buffalo wings, plus gourmet desserts.

Blazing Pianos is located in the Mercado at 8445 International Blvd., just south of Sand Lake Rd. (☎ 407/363-5104).

Admission is $5 Monday to Thursday, $7 Friday to Saturday, and free on Sunday. Though it opens earlier, the action begins about 9:30pm and continues through 2am nightly. No one under 21 is admitted.

Comedy Warehouse: Housed in the island's former power plant, the Comedy Warehouse—another favorite of mine—has a rustic interior with tiered seating. A very talented troupe performs 45-minute improvisational comedy shows based on audience suggestions. There are five shows a night, and bar drinks are available. Arrive early.

Rock & Roll Beach Club: Once the laboratory in which Pleasure developed a unique flying machine, this three-story structure today houses a dance club where live bands play "classic rock from the '60s through the '90s." There are bars on all three floors, including one serving international beers. The first level contains the dance floor. The second and third levels offers air hockey, pool tables, basketball machines, pinball, video games, darts, and a pizza and beer stand.

8 Trax: This 1970s-style club, with about 50 TV monitors airing diverse shows and videos over the dance floor, occupies three levels, all with bars. Period movie posters (*Bananas, Star Wars*) adorn the walls, and the top-floor lounge is vaguely psychedelic in decor. A DJ plays disco music, and guests engage in games of Twister.

In addition, live bands—including occasional big-name groups—play the **West End Plaza** outdoor stage and the **Hub Stage;** check your schedule for show times. You can star in your own music video at **SuperStar Studios.** And there are carnival games, a video-game arcade, Virtual Reality games, a Velcro wall (don a jumpsuit over your clothes, bounce on a trampoline, and stick yourself on), and an Orbitron (a "21st-century workout machine," originally developed for NASA, that lets you experience weightlessness). Shops and eateries (with outdoor umbrella tables) are found throughout the park. A jazz club is in the works.

Church Street Station

129 W. Church St., off 1-4, between Garland and Orange aves. in downtown Orlando. ☎ **407/422-2434.** Admission $16.90; free prior to 5pm, after which you have to pay. Clubs are open nightly until 2am, shops until 11pm. Valet parking, at Church St. and Garland Ave., is $6. Directions: Take 1-4 east to Exit 38 (Anderson St.), stay in the left lane, and follow the blue signs. Most hotels offer transportation to and from Church Street, and, since you'll probably be drinking, I advise it. There are several lots nearby (call for specifics).

Though not part of Walt Disney World, Church Street Station in downtown Orlando operates on a similar principle to Pleasure Island (in fact, it innovated the concept). Occupying a cobblestoned city block lined with turn-of-the-century buildings (real ones), it, too, is a shopping/dining/nightclub complex offering a diverse evening of entertainment for a single admission price. There are 20 live shows nightly; consult your show schedule on entering. Stunning interiors are the rule here. It's worth coming by just to check out the magnificent woodwork, stained glass, and thousands of authentic antiques. And capitalizing on the traffic Church Street generates, many other clubs have opened in the immediate area, further enlarging your bar-hopping potential. Entry to restaurants, the Exchange Shopping Emporium, and the Midway game area is free. Highlights include:

Rosie O'Grady's Good Time Emporium: This 1890s-style gambling hall–cum-saloon, with beveled- and leaded-glass panels, etched mirrors, and vast globe chandeliers suspended from a high pressed-tin ceiling, is filled with interesting antiques. The train benches came from an old Florida rail station, backbar mirrors from a Glasgow pub, and bank teller's cages from a 19th-century Pittsburgh bank. Dixieland bands, banjo players, singing waiters, and cancan dancers entertain nightly. Light fare (deli sandwiches, chili dogs) is available. The house specialty drink is a rum and fruit concoction called the Flaming Hurricane (served in a souvenir glass).

Apple Annie's Courtyard: Adjoining Rosie's, this brick-floored establishment, domed by arched trusses from an early 19th-century New Orleans church, evokes a Victorian tropical garden. The room is further embellished by 12-foot hand-carved filigree mirrors created in Vienna circa 1740 and magnificent 1,000-pound chandeliers. An 18th-century French communion rail serves as the front bar. Seating is in wicker peacock chairs at English pub tables. Patrons sip potent tropical fresh fruit and ice-cream drinks while listening to folk and bluegrass music.

Lili Marlene's Aviator's Pub & Restaurant: Its plush oak-paneled interior is embellished with World War I memorabilia, stained-glass transoms, and accoutrements from an 1850 Rothschild town house in Paris, the latter including a walnut fireplace and wine cabinets. Eclectic seating ranges from hand-carved oak pews that came from a French church to a place at a large drop-leaf mahogany table where Al Capone once dined. Model airplanes and marvelous Victorian chandeliers are suspended from a beamed pine ceiling with a stained-glass skylight. The menu features premium aged steaks, prime rib, and fresh seafood.

Phineas Phogg's Balloon Works: This whimsical bar, with hot-air balloons and airplanes over the dance floor, is a high-energy club playing loud, pulsating music. It doubles as a virtual ballooning museum housing photographs and artifacts from historic flights, including Orlando native Joe Kittinger—first man to cross the Atlantic in a gas balloon. Every Wednesday from 6:30 to 7:30pm, beers cost just 5¢ here. No one under 21 is admitted.

Cheyenne Saloon and Opera House: This stunning trilevel balconied saloon, crowned by a lofty stained-glass skylight, is constructed of golden oak lumber from a century-old Ohio barn. Quality western art is displayed throughout, including many oil paintings and 11 Remington sculptures. Balcony seating, in restored church pews, overlooks the stage—setting for entertainment ranging from country bands (some big names) to clogging exhibitions—and the dance floor. The menu features steaks, barbecued chicken and ribs, and hickory-smoked brisket.

The Orchid Garden Ballroom: This stunning space, with ornate white wrought-iron arches and Victorian lighting fixtures suspended from an elaborate oak-paneled ceiling, is the setting for an oldies dance club. A DJ plays rock 'n' roll classics like "Great Balls of Fire" and "Let's Go to the Hop" interspersed with live bands. As the evening progresses, so do the musical decades.

Crackers Oyster Bar: Brick columns, oak paneling, and a gorgeous antique oak and mahogany bar characterize this cozy late 1800s-style dining room. Fresh Florida seafood is featured, along with more than 50 imported beers. You can nibble on appetizers such as oysters Rockefeller, smoked fish dip, and steamed mussels. Or opt for more serious entrées ranging from crabcakes rémoulade to paella.

In addition, the 87,000-square-foot Exchange houses the carnival-like **Commander Ragtime's Midway of Fun, Food and Games** (including an enormous video-game arcade), a food court, and more than 50 specialty shops. You can rent a horse-drawn carriage out front for a drive around the downtown area and Lake Eola. And hot-air balloon flights can be arranged (☎ 407/841-8787).

4 More Entertainment

LITTLE HOUSE OF HORRORS
Terror on Church Street

135 S. Orange Ave., at Church St. in downtown Orlando, a block from Church Street Station. ☎ **407/649-FEAR** or 407/649-1912. Admission $12 adults, $10 children under 17. Tues–Thurs and Sun 7pm–midnight, Fri–Sat 7pm–1am. Closed Mon. Most hotels offer transportation to the area. There are several lots nearby (call for specifics). You can use Church Street Station's valet parking ($6) at Church St. and Garland Ave. Directions: Take I-4 east to Exit 38 (Anderson St.), stay in the left lane, and follow the blue signs to Church Street Station parking.

Terror on Church Street is a multimedia, high-tech house of horrors incorporating innovative special effects and 23 highly theatrical sets on two floors. On a labyrinthine 25-minute tour of the darkened premises, guests are menaced by cleaver- and chain-saw-wielding maniacs, ghoulish monks, assorted cadavers, vicious dogs, Freddie Kreuger, and Dracula, among others—all convincingly portrayed by actors. Children under 10 are not admitted without an adult. A gift shop on the premises sells stick-on warts and burn scars, coffin banks, and the like.

A SPORTS BAR
Champions

Marriott's Orlando World Center, 8701 World Center Dr. ☎ **407/239-4200.** Admission free. Open nightly until 2am. Free self-parking, valet parking $5.

Champions is a sports-bar chain—one so appealing it's easy to see why the concept has succeeded. Its interior is chockablock with $25,000 worth of signed sports photos, posters, and artifacts such as Lou Gehrig's baseball bat, a golf bag autographed by Dallas Cowboys coach Jimmy Johnson, and (of local interest) a wet suit belonging to Cypress Gardens' famed barefoot waterski star, Banana George. Some nights a DJ plays music (mostly Motown and oldies) for dancing. Otherwise, entertainments include three pool tables, video games, foosball, air hockey, darts, coin-op football and basketball, an indoor putting green, and blackjack tables. In addition, sporting events are aired on a large-screen TV and on smaller monitors around the room (a calendar at the entrance lists all game times). Champions offers a fairly extensive bar-food menu. *Note to single women:* Men outnumber women about five to one, so this is a good place to meet guys—if you can distract them from the sports action on the screen.

A DINNER SHOW

Wild Bill's Wild West Dinner Extravaganza,

5260 U.S. 192, just east of 1-4. ☎ **407/351-5151,** or 800/883-8282. Admission $31.95 adults, $19.95 children 3–11, under 3 free. Shows take place nightly at 7pm, with 9:30pm shows on selected nights.

Located at Fort Liberty, a 22-acre western-themed shopping/dining/ entertainment complex, this rambunctious dinner show takes place in a big barnlike wooden building. You'll be given a cardboard cowboy hat and vest when you sit down, which identifies you as a shepherd or cowherd for audience-participation activities (there are a lot of these). The show includes rousing song-and-dance numbers ("Annie Get Your Gun," "Oklahoma," "Back in the Saddle Again"); rodeo roping, knife-throwing, and archery demonstrations; singalongs; a cancan; and Comanche ceremonial and war dances. All the children in the audience get to go up on the stage. Dinner—served on pewterware—is a hearty four-course meal consisting of salad, soup, beef stew, fried chicken, barbecued pork ribs, biscuits with honey butter, corn on the cob, beans, a baked potato, hot apple pie, and ice cream. Beer, wine, or Coca-Cola are included.

MOVIES

Pleasure Island AMC Theater

In Walt Disney World adjacent to the Pleasure Island nightclub complex. ☎ **407/827-1300.** Matinees $4.50 adults, $3.75 seniors and children 2–13, under 2 free; twilight shows (4:30–6pm) $3.25 for all seats; evening shows $6.50 adults, $4.50 students, $3.75 seniors (over 55) and children 2–13, under 2 free.

This 10-screen AMC theater complex—equipped with state-of-the-art Dolby-digital sound systems and 70mm-projection capability—extends the variety of nighttime entertainment available to Disney World guests. A bridge connects the theater complex with Pleasure Island clubs. New Disney films premiere here, and first-run films are shown; check the *Orlando Sentinel* for show times.

10

Easy Excursions from Walt Disney World & Orlando

Get away from the thrill-a-minute glitter and glitz that characterizes most Orlando attractions to Cypress Gardens—a serene botanical paradise that was central Florida's first major tourist draw; to find out what NASA is up to over at the Kennedy Space Center; to Winter Park, a charming upscale town with some uniquely exquisite attractions; or to the self-proclaimed "World's Most Famous Beach" and "World Center of Racing"—Daytona Beach.

1 Cypress Gardens

40 miles SW of Walt Disney World, 45 miles SW of Orlando

Founded in 1936 when Dick and Julie Pope hired a crew of laborers to dig canals and drain swamps, Cypress Gardens, located on FL 540 at Cypress Gardens Boulevard in Winter Haven (☎ 813/324-2111, or 800/237-4826, 800/282-2123 in Florida), came into being as a 16-acre public garden along the banks of Lake Eloise with cypress-wood-block pathways and thousands of tropical and subtropical plants. Today it has grown to over 200 acres, with ponds and lagoons, waterfalls, classic Italian fountains, topiary, bronze sculptures, manicured lawns, and—most notably—ancient cypress trees shrouded in Spanish moss forming a backdrop to ever-changing floral displays of 8,000 varieties of plants from more than 90 countries. Southern belles in Scarlett O'Hara costumes stroll the grounds or sit on benches under parasols in idyllic tree-shaded nooks. They symbolize Florida's old-fashioned southern hospitality. In the late winter and early spring, more than 20 varieties of bougainvillea, 40 of azalea, and 100 of roses burst into bloom. Crape myrtles, magnolias, and gardenias perfume the late-spring air, while brilliant birds of paradise, hibiscus, and jasmine brighten the summer landscape. And in winter, the golden rain trees, floss silk trees, and camellias of autumn give way to millions of colorful chrysanthemums and red, white, and pink poinsettias.

GETTING THERE

BY CAR Take I-4 west to U.S. 27 south, and proceed west on to FL 540. (If you don't have a car, inquire about public transportation at your hotel.)

WHAT TO SEE & DO

Strolling the grounds is, of course, the main attraction (there are over two miles of winding botanical paths, and half of the park's acreage is devoted to floral displays), but this being central Florida it's not the only one. Four shows are scheduled several times each day. The world-famous **Greatest American Ski Team** performs daring freestyle jumps, swivel skiing, barefooting, ski ballet, and slalom exhibitions on Lake Eloise in a show augmented by an awesome hang-gliding display. **Feathered Follies,** a bird show, features trained cockatoos, macaws, and other exotic members of the parrot family roller-skating, playing basketball, and otherwise mimicking humans. **Variété Internationale** features specialty acts from all over the world, at this writing Russian acrobats. And since visitors can't be here to observe all seasonal changes, a slide show called **Seasons of Cypress Gardens** provides an overview of the year's blooms; it also takes visitors behind the scenes to learn how floral exhibits are created and maintained.

And there's still more. An enchanting exhibit called ○ **Wings of Wonder** surrounds visitors with more than 1,000 brightly colored free-flying butterflies (representing more than 50 species) in a 5,500-square-foot Victorian-style glass conservatory filled with tropical plantings, orchids, and waterfalls. **Electric boats** navigate a maze of lushly landscaped canals in the original botanical gardens area. You can ascend 153 feet to **Kodak's™ Island in the Sky** for a panoramic vista of the gardens and a beautiful chain of central Florida lakes. **Carousel Cove,** with eight kiddie rides and arcade games, centers on an ornate turn-of-the-century-style carousel. It adjoins another kid pleaser, **Cypress Junction™,** an elaborately landscaped model railroad (scenery includes everything from a burning house to Mount Rushmore) that travels 1,100 feet of track with up to 20 trains moving at one time. **Cypress Roots,** a museum of park memorabilia, displays photographs of famous visitors (Elvis on waterskis, Tiny Tim tiptoeing through the roses) and airs ongoing showings of *Easy to Love* starring Esther Williams (it was filmed here). Another museum commemorates the **age of radio** with a display of hundreds of vintage radios, radio memorabilia, and recordings of radio shows and music from the 1920s to the 1950s. Wind up your visit with a relaxing 30-minute narrated **pontoon cruise** on scenic Lake Eloise, past virgin forest, bulrushes, and beautiful shoreline homes. En route, you're likely to observe cormorants, osprey, ducks—maybe even an alligator or two. There's a $4 per-person charge.

Admission to Cypress Gardens is $26.95 for ages 10 and over, $16.45 for children 3 to 9; ages 2 and under, free. There are discounts for seniors. Discounted admissions in conjunction with Sea World (see Chapter 7) and Busch Gardens in Tampa are also available; call for details or inquire at the gate. Cypress Gardens is open 365 days a year, from 9:30am to 5:30pm, with extended hours during peak seasons. Parking is free.

WHERE TO DINE

Your options range from a food court to the Crossroads Restaurant, a cheerful full-service facility serving American fare; the latter also offers al fresco seating at umbrella tables on a terrace. I also like the more casual Lakeview Terrace, a cafeteria with covered outdoor seating overlooking Lake Eloise; it offers great views of the ski show. Fresh strawberries are sold throughout the park in season. And if you care to pack a basket, there are picnic tables. Over a dozen shops sell everything from quaint country-store merchandise (bayberry candles, herb wreaths) to gardening books and paraphernalia.

2 Kennedy Space Center

60 miles E of Walt Disney World, 45 miles E of Orlando

Operated by NASA, the John F. Kennedy Space Center (☎ 407/452-2121) has been the launch site for all United States manned space missions since 1968. Astronauts departed earth at this site en route to the most famous "small step" in history—man's first voyage to the moon. All space shuttle launches have also been staged from this site.

Nonoperational areas of the Kennedy Space Center are part of the 140,000-acre ❂ **Merritt Island National Wildlife Refuge** (☎ 407/861-0667). This pristine wilderness of dense woods, unspoiled beaches, fish-filled waterways, marshlands, and mud flats provides refuge for numerous bird species, deer, bobcats, otters, sea turtles, manatees, alligators, and other native Florida wildlife—more than 500 species in total. There are more threatened and endangered species here than at any other national wildlife refuge. To find out about guided nature walks and interpretive programs (November through March only), sea turtle watches in June and July, and year-round wildlife drives and self-guided hikes (trails range from a quarter of a mile to five miles) call or visit the Visitor Information Center, which is four miles east of Titusville on FL 402. It is open Monday to Friday from 8am to 4:30pm, Saturday from 9am to 5pm, and Sunday (April to November only) 9am to 5pm; closed all major holidays. (*Note:* You won't have time to tour nature trails and see the Space Center in the same day.)

GETTING THERE

BY CAR   Take the Beeline Expressway (Hwy. 528) east, where the road divides go left on FL 407, make a right on FL 405 and follow signs. (If you don't have a car, inquire about public transportation at your hotel.)

WHAT TO SEE & DO

At Spaceport USA, the visitor facility of the Kennedy Space Center, the past, present, and future of space exploration are explored on bus tours of the facility and in movie presentations and numerous exhibits. It takes at least a full day to see and do everything. Arrive early and make your first stop at **Information Central** (it opens at 9am) to pick up a schedule of events/map and for help in planning your day. Nearby, space-related exhibits and interactive computers allow visitors to "meet the astronauts," access current mission information, and look into the history of spaceflight.

On the two-hour **Red Tour** you'll board a double-decker bus to explore the complex. En route, your driver will point out significant buildings such as the laboratories where instruments are calibrated and maintained; the headquarters building, administrative hub for all Space Center activities; astronauts' living quarters during training; and the building where hardware bound for the launch pad is inspected and tested prior to use. You'll view a film about the *Apollo 11* mission in a simulated launch control firing room. The countdown, launch, and planting of a flag on the moon are thrilling even at second hand. In an adjoining room related exhibits include an *Apollo 11* command service module (home for the three crew members during their round-trip) and a lunar module (their home on the lunar surface). The tour continues to Complex 39 Space Shuttle launch pads (where a stop is made for exploration) and the massive Vehicle Assembly Building where space shuttles are assembled. In volume, the VAB is the world's second-largest building, with doors 456 feet high. Visitors get a close-up look at an actual *Apollo/Saturn V* moon rocket—America's largest and most powerful launch vehicle. Also on view are massive six-million pound Crawler Transporters that carry space shuttles to their launch pads. There are many photo opportunities, both on the tour and throughout the Spaceport complex. Tours depart at regular intervals beginning at 9:45am, with the last tour leaving in the late afternoon (call for details). Purchase tickets at the Ticket Pavilion as soon as you arrive. *Note:* Itinerary variations may occur subject to launch schedules.

Though most visitors are sated by the Red Tour, a second two-hour **Blue Bus Tour** (call for departure schedule) visits Cape Canaveral Air Force Station. On this tour, you'll see where America's first satellites and astronauts were launched in the Mercury and Gemini programs, view launch pads currently being used for unmanned launches, visit the original site of Mission Control, and stop at the Air Force Space Museum, which houses a unique collection of missiles and space memorabilia.

Satellites and You is a 45-minute voyage through a simulated future space station. In Disneyesque fashion, the attraction combines Audio-Animatronic™ characters with innovative audiovisual techniques to explain satellites and their uses. Passing through futuristic airlock spacecraft doors à la *Star Trek,* visitors enter work chambers with names like Central Module Alpha 1 and 2. In each chamber you'll learn something new about today's satellite technology and its uses in diverse areas. Farther along, the role of satellites in creating a global village focuses on the rapid dissemination of information worldwide. The final program explains how the space program is involved in improving the quality of life on earth.

In the ♻ **Galaxy Center building,** three spectacular IMAX films projected on $5^1/_2$-story screens are shown continually throughout the day in twin theaters. *Destiny in Space,* narrated by Leonard Nimoy, features unique exterior views of the Space Shuttle in flight around Earth, footage from the Hubble Space Telescope servicing mission, and thrilling flyovers of Mars and Venus. In *The Dream Is Alive*—featuring in-flight footage from three space shuttle missions—viewers join astronauts in preflight training, aboard the space shuttle in orbit, and on a breathtaking launch and landing. And *Blue Planet* is an environmentally themed look at Spaceship Earth from the vantage point of outer space.

The Galaxy Center also houses: a NASA Art Exhibit; a walk-through replica of a future space station, a manned research laboratory that will be orbiting the earth by 1999; and an exhibit called "Spinoffs From Space." The latter—which is hosted by hologram characters—displays some of the 30,000 spin-offs that have resulted from space-program research, including improved consumer products ranging from football helmets to cordless tools, and advances in medicine, computer sciences, energy, public safety, transportation, agriculture, and the environment.

The **Gallery of Manned Spaceflight,** a large museum, houses hardware and models relating to significant space projects such as the *Mercury* missions (1958–63), *Gemini 9* (a two-man mission in 1966), the *Apollo-Soyuz* Test Project (the world's first international space venture), Skylab, and the *Saturn V* moon rocket. It also contains interesting exhibits on lunar exploration and geology. You can view a moon rock and have a photograph taken of yourself in a lunar rover.

Spaceport Theater presents films and live demonstrations on topics ranging from how space shuttles are prepared for launch to activities of astronauts in space.

The **Astronauts Memorial**—a 42.5-by-50-foot black granite "Space Mirror" dedicated May 9, 1991—honors the 16 American astronauts who have lost their lives in the line of duty.

Aboard *Explorer,* a full-size replica of a space shuttle orbiter, visitors can experience the working environment of NASA astronauts. Adjoining it are two refurbished solid rocket boosters and an external tank.

A **playground** housed in a large geodesic dome features educational astronaut/space-related play equipment, along with a ball crawl, a maze, and a super slide.

And the **Rocket Garden** displays eight actual U.S. rockets.

There are two **cafeterias**—the Orbit and the Lunch Pad—on the premises. Try "Space Dots"—freeze-dried astronaut ice cream. The gift shop carries a wide array of innovative space-related books, toys, games, videotapes, astronaut flight suits, NASA and space logo clothing, and more.

Admission to the Kennedy Space Center is free. Tickets for either bus tour cost $7 for adults, $4 for children 3 to 11 and free to children under 3. IMAX film tickets are $4 for adults, $2 for children 3 to 11, and free to children under 3. The Kennedy Space Center is open daily from 9am to dusk; it's closed on Christmas. Parking is free.

Seeing a Launch   Today a rocket soaring skyward is not an uncommon sight, but it's still one that fills most observers with awe. If you'd like to see a launch, call **Spaceport USA** (☎ 407/452-2121 for current launch information, 407/452-2121, ext. 260 to make reservations). Tickets for viewing cost $7 for adults, $4 for children 3 to 11; under 3 free. You can reserve tickets up to seven days before a launch, but they must be picked up at least two days before the launch. A special bus takes observers to a site just six miles from the launch pad.

3   Winter Park

20 miles N of Walt Disney World, 5 miles N of Orlando

The beautiful lakefront community of Winter Park was created in the early 1880s as "a first class place" for "men and women of intelligence, culture, character, taste and means." Developers Loring A. Chase and Oliver E. Chapman priced their lots accordingly. The town was incorporated in 1887. To this day it remains an affluent haven—Florida's answer to Greenwich, Connecticut. You can visit on a day-trip, or spend a relaxing night or two here away from theme park hubbub. Its attractions include a lovely Beverly Hills–like shopping strip (Park Avenue) lined with posh boutiques and art galleries; golf courses; fine old homes along winding, tree-shaded streets; shimmering lakes and canals (Winter Park has been called the "Venice of America"); Central Park, a large village green with lush lawns, stately moss-draped live oaks, and rose gardens; and a museum housing a treasure trove of Tiffany windows, lamps, and objets d'art. And though (actually because) refined Winter Park takes no official notice of the fact, the town attracts numerous celebrities looking for a quaint and quiet retreat. Don't be surprised if you run into former president Gerald Ford or Paul Newman in a local shop.

For further information about Winter Park contact the **Chamber of Commerce,** 150 N. New York Ave., just north of Morse Boulevard (P.O. Box 280), Winter Park, FL 32790 (☎ 407/644-8281). Hours are 9am to 4pm Monday through Friday. *Note:* Street parking is sometimes difficult. There are convenient and free municipal lots on South New York Avenue on either side of Morse Boulevard.

GETTING THERE

BY CAR   Take I-4 east to Fairbanks Avenue (Exit 45), exit right and proceed east for about a mile, turn left on Park Avenue and follow signs to public parking.

BY BUS   Take LYNX bus no. 4 from the Osceola Square Mall at Columbia Street and Hoagland Avenue in Kissimmee. It will take you to the Orlando downtown terminal where you can transfer to bus no. 1 or 9, either of which makes several stops along Park Avenue in Winter Park. Call 407/841-8240 for schedule.

BY TRAIN   Amtrak service (☎ 800/USA-RAIL) is available from Orlando and Kissimmee (see Chapter 2 for locations). The Winter Park station is located right in the center of town at 150 W. Morse Blvd. (☎ 407/645-5055).

WHAT TO SEE & DO

Stroll Winter Park's main street, browse its boutiques, visit its museums, play a few rounds of golf, and take a leisurely lake cruise. Do note that most of the town's museums are closed on Monday.

The Charles Hosmer Morse Museum of American Art

445 Park Ave., at Canton St. ☎ **407/644-3686.** Admission $2.50 adults, $1 students of any age. Tues–Sat 9:30am–4pm, Sun 1–4pm. Closed Memorial Day, July 4th, Labor Day, Thanksgiving, Christmas, and New Year's Day.

Anyone who loves the sinuous, nature-inspired art nouveau genre (and who doesn't) will be amazed and thrilled by this gem of a gallery. It was founded by Hugh and Jeannette McKean in 1942 to display their peerless collection (more than 4,000 pieces), including 40 magnificent windows and 21 paintings created by Louis Comfort Tiffany! In addition, there are non-Tiffany windows by William Morris, Frank Lloyd Wright, Frederick Stymetz Lamb, and 15th- and 16th-century German masters; leaded lamps by Tiffany and Emile Gallé; a display of carnival glass; paintings by John Singer Sargent, Samuel F. B. Morse, Maxfield Parrish, Thomas Hart Benton, and Arthur B. Davies; jewelry designed by Tiffany, Lalique, and Fabergé; sculptures by Hiram Powers and Daniel Chester French (of Lincoln Memorial fame); prints by Cézanne, Childe Hassam, Rembrandt, Whistler, Winslow Homer, Mary Cassatt, and Grant Wood; photographic works by Tiffany and other 19th-century artists; and art nouveau furnishings by Tiffany, Gallé, and others. The collection also includes Tiffany memorabilia—letters, furnishings, personal effects, and photographs used by his studio as source materials. And furniture and accessories by Gustav Stickley and his contemporaries—plus a major collection of American art pottery—make the Morse's arts and crafts collection one of the most important in the Southeast. Be sure to peek into the gift shop, where unique items include art nouveau gift wraps, Tiffany coloring books, beautiful reproduction vases and goblets, Maxfield Parrish stationery, and much more.

The Cornell Fine Arts Museum

At the eastern end of Holt Ave., on the campus of Rollins College at Lake Virginia. ☎ **407/646-2526.** Free admission. Tues–Fri 10am–5pm, Sat–Sun 1–5pm. Free parking in adjacent lot "H." Closed July 4th, Thanksgiving, the Friday after Thanksgiving, Christmas Eve, Christmas Day, New Year's Eve, and New Year's Day.

Rollins College began its art collection in 1935 with several Italian Renaissance paintings. It was also the first home of Hugh and Jeanette McKean's (see listing above) Tiffany glass. Today, with close to 4,000 square feet of exhibition space, it houses an impressive century-spanning collection that includes works by Hiram Powers, Childe Hassam, Tiffany, Thomas Sully, William Glackens, Reginald Marsh, Leonard Baskin, and the studio of Peter Paul Rubens. Also displayed here: 19th-century silver,17th-century Dutch Delftware, French rococo decorative panels, and Chippendale furniture. Traveling exhibits supplement the collection.

Scenic Boat Tour

At the eastern end of Morse Blvd. on the lake. ☎ **407/644-4056.** Admission $5.50 adults, $2.75 children 2–11, under 2 free. Weather permitting, tours depart daily between 10am and 4pm, every hour on the hour. Closed Christmas.

Since 1938, tourists have been boarding pontoons at this location for leisurely hour-long cruises on Winter Park's beautiful chain of natural lakes. The ride traverses Lake Osceola (which flows north into the St. John's River), Lake Virginia, and Lake Maitland, winding through canals built by loggers at the turn of the century and tree-shaded fern gullies lined with bamboo and lush tropical foliage. You'll view magnificent lakeside mansions and villas (Margaret Mitchell used to winter on Lake Maitland), pristine beaches, cypress swamps, ancient trees draped with Spanish moss, and dozens of marsh birds—white herons, grackle, cormorants, osprey, and gallinule, possibly even an American bald eagle. The captain regales passengers with local lore. It's an utterly delightful trip. You can also rent canoes and small fishing boats here.

WHERE TO STAY

Though you could visit Winter Park on a day excursion from Orlando, do consider an overnight stay at one of the following properties.

The Langford Resort Hotel

300 E. New England Ave., at Interlachen Ave., Winter Park, FL 32789. ☎ **407/ 644-3400.** Fax 407/628-1952. 209 rms. 9 suites. A/C TV TEL. $65–$75 single; $75–$85 double; from $180 suite. Extra person $10. Children 17 and under stay free. Rooms with kitchenettes $10 additional. AE, DC, MC, V. Free self-parking.

In pre-Disney days, Winter Park was one of central Florida's most-visited resorts, and the Langford was the place to stay. Vaughn Monroe entertained in the lounge, and the guest roster listed people like Eleanor Roosevelt, Mamie Eisenhower, Lillian Gish, Vincent Price, and Dina Merrill. Ronald and Nancy Reagan celebrated their 25th wedding anniversary here. This friendly resort, run by the Langford family for four decades, still draws the occasional celebrity guest, but, more importantly, it offers extensive resort facilities at very reasonable rates. And its location, on a lovely street shaded by tall oaks draped with Spanish moss, is just a block from Park Avenue, Winter Park's ritzy shopping street. Rooms in the main building, all with balconies and large walk-in closets, are each uniquely decorated. Those in the seven-story East Wing are done up in soft resort colors and rattan and bamboo furnishings. All accommodations offer free HBO; many have balconies and/or fully equipped kitchenettes with two-burner stoves and small refrigerators.

Dining/Entertainment: The nautical/tropical Bamboo Room, with large windows overlooking the pool, offers a reasonably priced American menu at all meals; steak and seafood are featured at dinner. The adjoining pool view Del Prado bar/lounge provides piano bar entertainment and complimentary hors d'oeuvres from 5 to 8pm nightly and dancing to live band music Tuesday through Saturday from 8pm to midnight. The elegant Empire Room offers a lavish buffet champagne Sunday brunch and Saturday-night mystery dinner theater.

Services: Concierge (sells tickets, many of them discounted, to Walt Disney World and other Orlando attractions), room service from 7am to 10pm, *Orlando Sentinel* delivered to your room daily, babysitters.

Facilities: Olympic-size swimming pool, kiddie pool, car-rental desk, small video-game arcade, unisex hair salon. A full on-premises spa, heralded by a waterfall that cascades into a stream, offers sauna, steam, massage (shiatsu, Swedish, and deep athletic), body wraps, sea-weed wraps, salt glows, facials, manicures, and pedicures. A full day of beauty is $125, including lunch. Golf and tennis are close by.

Park Plaza Hotel

S. 307 Park Ave., at New England Ave., Winter Park, FL 32789. ☎ **407/647-1072**, or 800/228-7220. Fax 407/647-4081. 16 rms, 11 suites. A/C TV TEL. $80–$125 single; $90–$135 double; $150–$185 suite. During special events rates may be higher. (Rates include continental breakfast.) AE, DC, MC, V. Free self- and valet parking.

Centrally located in the heart of the Park Avenue shopping and restaurant district, this small elegant hotel dates to 1921. In 1975, John and Sandra Spang bought the property and did an exquisite renovation, fitting out rooms bed-and-breakfast style with antique furnishings, Persian rugs, patchwork quilts, and beautiful floral-print bedspreads. Wide wooden Bermuda shutters on the windows and wood-bladed ceiling fans overhead add tropical ambience, and homey touches include live plants in white wicker baskets and magazines in the rooms. Exposed-brick walls are hung with fine art posters. Most rooms open onto a wicker-furnished, plant-filled balcony, and many have cozy parlor areas. Especially lovely is the Balcony Suite, which has Victorian-reproduction wallpaper and a brass bed made up with a Ralph Lauren spread, throw pillows, and white dust ruffle. There are also four luxurious honeymoon suites with oversized oak beds and private balconies. In-room amenities include remote-control cable TVs with free HBO and complimentary fruit baskets at check-in.

The hotel's Park Plaza Gardens restaurant (see "Where to Dine," below) adjoins. The front desk offers conciergelike service. Other amenities here include room service during restaurant hours, the newspaper of your choice delivered to your door each morning, and nightly bed turndown; transport to/from Disney parks and Orlando airport can be arranged. A beauty shop is just behind the property, and, for a fee, guests can use the nearby Winter Park Wellness Center, a health club offering a full line of Nautilus equipment, steam, sauna, indoor track, and an Olympic-size lap pool. A complimentary continental breakfast of fresh-squeezed orange juice, fresh-baked muffins, and coffee or tea is served daily in the European-style lobby (or in your room). Golf and tennis are close by.

WHERE TO DINE

There are so many fine restaurants in Winter Park that Orlandoans often drive over just to dine and stroll the tree-lined streets. My first listing is in Altamonte Springs, a few minutes' drive from Winter Park.

Very Expensive

Maison & Jardin

430 S. Wymore Rd., off I-4 Exit 48 between FL 436 and Maitland Blvd., in nearby Altamonte Springs. ☎ **407/862-4410.** Reservations recommended. Brunch $18.50 prix-fixe; dinner appetizers $6.75–$8.75 (more for caviar-filled blinis); dinner main courses $17.95–$28.50. AE, CB, DC, ER, MC, V. Brunch Sun (Oct to mid-June only) 11am–2pm; dinner Mon–Sat 6–10pm, Sun (Oct to mid-June only) 6–9pm. Free self-parking. CONTINENTAL.

One of Florida's most highly acclaimed restaurants, Maison & Jardin was architecturally inspired by a mansion in southern France that dates to Roman times. Hence the pedimented neoclassic exterior, manicured formal gardens, and imposing doors with brass-lion knockers. The exquisite interior is furnished with museum-quality pieces and objets d'art—Austrian crystal chandeliers, Venetian and French chinoiserie cabinets, and mirrors in gilt frames from a 17th-century Venetian palazzo. I especially like the Gazebo Room, evocative of a 17th-century Mediterranean château, with hand-painted blue and white tile walls and balloon-curtained windows looking out on a tiered *putti* fountain, waterfall, and goldfish pond. Equally delightful is the airy canvas-roofed and brick-floored Patio Room. Elegantly appointed tables are candlelit throughout.

A featured appetizer is blinis à la Russe with your choice of caviars (Icelandic, Spanish, or Russian beluga), flamed tableside in brandy and served with chopped egg and onion, radishes, and frosted vodka. Also very recommendable: baked escargots en croûte topped with spinach, Boursin cheese, and garlic cream sauce. The chef does a beautiful job with frequent game specials, such as elk sautéed with morel mushrooms in a brandy cream sauce and served over pasta. I also recommend seafood entrées here—perhaps poached Norwegian salmon in a basil beurre blanc sauce served with an array of fresh vegetables, boiled red potato, and a red, green, and yellow pepper compote. The menu changes seasonally, so your options may vary from the above. The extensive, award-winning wine list is international in scope, with many selections available by the glass or half bottle. Desserts range from fresh raspberries with whipped cream to elaborate flaming finales such as bananas Foster and crêpes Suzette; there are also more than 40 post-prandial cognacs and brandies. The prix-fixe Sunday brunch, including free-flowing complimentary champagne, is composed of an appetizer (perhaps chilled smoked Norwegian salmon), a choice of entrées ranging from eggs Benedict to New Zealand rack of lamb, salad, and dessert. A Dixieland band entertains the first Sunday of every month.

Park Plaza Gardens

319 S. Park Ave., between Lyman and New England aves., in Winter Park. ☎ **407/ 645-2475.** Reservations recommended. Brunch $20.95 prix-fixe; appetizers $6.95– $7.95 at lunch $8.95–$10.95 at dinner; main courses $7.95–$12.95 at lunch (sandwiches and salads $5.95—$8.95), $19.95–$26.95 at dinner. AE, CB, DC, DISC, MC, Optima, V. Brunch Sun 11am–3pm; lunch Mon–Sat 11:30am–3pm; dinner Mon–Thurs 6–10pm, Fri–Sat 6–11pm. Sun 6–9pm. Free parking at city lot at New England and S. New York aves. CONTINENTAL/SEAFOOD.

This charming patio garden restaurant—with tables shaded by a striped canvas awning and seating amid a small forest of ficus trees—offers the feeling of outdoor dining in air-conditioned comfort. During the day sunlight streams in through a skylit ceiling; at night tables are romantically candlelit. Big planters of greenery enhance the airy al fresco ambience, and exposed-brick walls hung with changing exhibits serve as gallery space for local artists. Service is deft and gracious.

Chef Luis Colon's culinary creations—served on large white platters—are as exquisitely presented as they are delicious. There are many good beginnings here, among them an herbed escargot strudel layered with blue cheese and finely chopped shiitake mushrooms, served over tomato coulis; smoked duck pâté drizzled with goat cheese cream; and velvety lobster bisque beautifully marbleized with crème fraîche. Do opt for a salad course—the warm Montrachet goat cheese—tossed with frisé, toasted pine nuts, cracked black peppercorns, and pernod in lemon/olive oil dressing. Entrées include broiled sea bass wrapped in banana leaves, served with bulgur wheat pilaf and wild berry preserves. Also excellent are the rack of lamb dijonnaise with rosemary-thyme sauce and crisp cherrywood-smoked Muscovy duck served with sweet-potato haystack. For dessert ebony and ivory is a sweet dream—espresso chocolate mousse and thin semisweet chocolate leaves on a mirror of marbleized white chocolate sauce with blackberry garnish. And page after page of after-dinner cordials, cognacs, ports, sherries, and brandies. The well-chosen wine list offers many by-the-glass selections. The lunch menu adds pasta, sandwich, and salad options. And the $20.95 prix-fixe brunch—including complimentary champagne, mimosa, or Kir royale—offers the above-mentioned appetizers, a soup or salad course, and entrées ranging from an omelet Key West (a seafood frittata topped with creamy velouté and caviar) to sesame-seared Maui snapper glazed with Hawaiian fruit chutney and served on a bed of rice.

Moderate

La Venezia Cafe

142 Park Ave. S. between Morse Blvd. and Welbourne Ave. ☎ **407/647-7557.** Reservations not accepted. Breakfast pastries $1.75; main courses $5.50–$8.95 at lunch, $7.95–$17.95 at dinner; prix-fixe afternoon teas $7, $10, and $15. AE, DISC, MC, V. Mon–Thurs 7am–10pm, Fri–Sat 7am–11pm, Sun 8am–10pm. Parking on street only. ITALIAN/CAFE.

La Venezia Cafe is a highlight of a Winter Park visit, be it for continental breakfast, British-style afternoon tea, or a full meal. It's a charming place enhanced by classical music, flower-bedecked tables (white linened and candlelit at night), and photographs of Italy. A lovely bar, where several dozen premium wines are available by the glass, nestles in one corner, and a display case is filled with gorgeous desserts. There's an open-air patio overlooking Central Park here, but the pièce de résistance is inside: A collection of six authentic Tiffany windows.

La Venezia fresh-brews 52 different kinds of coffee and offers an extensive choice of gourmet teas. Come by in the morning for a steaming pot of fragrant Ethiopian Yrgacheffe or spicy mocha java with a fresh-baked croissant, jalapeño corn bread, or brown-sugar topped streusel coffee cake. Later in the day, menu options range from a Cajun eggplant and oyster stew to an international cheese platter. Dinner entrées include such exotica as lobster Martinque—chunks of lobster and sea scallops in an island sauce with sweet potato, banana, red peppers, and tomatillo. Other enticements here are flavored coffees, coffee/ice cream drinks and frappes, and a wide selection of liqueurs, apéritifs, and international beers. And do save some room for oven-fresh desserts like buttered rum apple pie and amaretto-praline buttercream torte. A $15 afternoon tea includes finger sandwiches (such as smoked trout with horseradish cream), fresh-baked scones and pastries, berries, tea, and champagne.

Inexpensive

The Briarpatch

252 Park Ave. N., at Garfield Ave. ☎ **407/628-8651.** Reservations not accepted. Breakfast $2.95–$6.95, lunch and dinner main courses and sandwiches $4.95–$8.95. AE, MC, V. Mon–Thurs 7am–9pm, Fri–Sat 7am–10pm, Sun 8am–5pm. Street parking only. AMERICAN.

A delightful way to start your day in Winter Park is with breakfast on the Briarpatch's open-air patio overlooking Central Park. If it's raining or chilly, the rustic garden-like interior is also alluring. Breakfast fare includes great coffee and fresh-baked biscuits, muffins, and cinnamon buns. Other options are buttermilk pancakes, waffles, French toast, a brie and parsley omelet, a bagel with Nova and cream cheese, or hot oatmeal with berries and bananas. Later in the day, come by for sandwiches, salads, stuffed baked potatoes, burgers, or pasta dishes— or for cappuccino with fresh-baked desserts such as Kahlua praline cream squares and mile-high chocolate layer or carrot cake.

4 Daytona Beach

73 miles NE of Walt Disney World, 50 miles NE of Orlando

The self-proclaimed "World's Most Famous Beach" is even more celebrated as "The Birthplace of Speed" and "World Center of Racing." It has been a mecca for car-racing enthusiasts since the days when automobiles were called horseless carriages. Early automobile magnates Ransom E. Olds, Henry Ford, the Stanley brothers (of steamer fame), and Louis Chevrolet—along with motor-mad millionaires like the Vanderbilts, Astors, and Rockefellers—wintered in Florida and raced their vehicles on the hard-packed sand beach. Most of these early beach events, by the way, were individual speed trials rather than actual races. The final speed trials were held in 1935.

Nineteen-thirty-six ushered in the era of stock-car racing with a new beach racecourse, a host of daredevil drivers, and thousands of cheering fans. In 1947, driver and race promoter Bill France founded the National Association for Stock Car Auto Racing (NASCAR), headquartered at Daytona Beach. Today it is the world's largest motorsports authority, sanctioning the Daytona 500 and other major races at the International Speedway and tracks throughout the United States. The final stock-car race on the beach took place in 1958. A year later, France's dream of a multimotorsports facility, the Daytona International Speedway, was realized.

Of course you don't have to be a racing aficionado to enjoy Daytona. It has 23 miles of sandy beach 500 feet wide at low tide (you can still drive and park—but not race—on the sand; maximum speed allowed is 10 m.p.h.). The town is mobbed with college students during spring break—the annual beach blanket Babylon—and during Bike Week in February thousands of leather-clad motorcycle buffs make the scene. But barring spring break and major speedway events, Daytona is a laidback beach resort, offering boating, tennis, golf, water sports, and the opportunity to stroll the sands, swim, and soak up some sunshine.

ESSENTIALS
GETTING THERE

BY PLANE American, Continental, Delta, and USAir fly into **Daytona Beach International Airport** (☎ 904/248-8030). A taxi from the airport to most beach hotels runs between $8 and $12.

BY TRAIN   Closest **Amtrak** station (☎ 800/USA-RAIL) is in De Land, 23 miles southwest of Daytona.

BY BUS   Greyhound buses connect Daytona with most of the United States. They pull into a very centrally located terminal at 138 S. Ridgewood Ave. (U.S. 1) between International Speedway Boulevard and Magnolia Avenue (☎ 904/255-7076 or 800/231-2222).

From Orlando, **Daytona-Orlando Transit Service (DOTS)** (☎ 904/257-5411, or 800/231-1965) provides van transport between the two cities. They offer 12 round-trips daily. One-way fare is $26 for adults, round-trip $46; children under 12 pay half price. The service brings passengers to the company's terminal at 1598 N. Nova Rd., at 11th Street (LPGA Blvd), or, for an additional fee, to beach hotels. In Orlando the vans depart from the airport.

BY CAR   If you're coming from north or south, take I-95 and head east on International Speedway Boulevard (U.S. Hwy. 92). From Tampa or Orlando take I-4 east and follow Daytona Beach signs to I-95 north to U.S. Hwy. 92. From northwest Florida take I-10 east to I-95 south to U.S. Hwy. 92.

TOURIST INFORMATION

The Daytona Beach Area Convention & Visitors Bureau, 126 E. Orange Ave., just west of the Silver Beach Bridge (P.O. Box 910 if you're writing), Daytona Beach, FL 32115 (☎ 904/255-0415, or 800/854-1234), can help you with information on attractions, accommodations, dining, and events. Call in advance for maps and brochures. Or visit their office when in town. They also maintain a branch at the speedway.

CITY LAYOUT

Daytona Beach is surrounded by water. The Atlantic Ocean borders its east coast, and the Halifax River flows north to south through the middle of the city. There are actually four little towns along its beach—**Ormond Beach** to the north, the centrally located **Daytona Beach** and **Daytona Beach Shores,** and **Ponce Inlet** at the southern tip just above New Smyrna Beach. A1A (Atlantic Avenue) runs along the beach north to south. U.S. 1 runs inland paralleling the west side of the Halifax River, and I-95 vaguely parallels it still farther west. International Speedway Boulevard is the main east-west artery.

Daytona Beach

ATTRACTIONS:
Daytona Beach
    Kennel Club 6
Daytona International
    Speedway 7
Halifax River
    Nature Cruises 16
Klassix Auto Museum 5
Museum of Arts
    and Sciences 8

ACCOMMODATIONS:
Captain's Quarters
    Inn 17
Coquina Inn 9
Days Inn 13
Econo Lodge 4
Live Oak Inn 11
Marriott 3
Perry's Ocean
    Edge Resort 14

DINING:
Alexander's 1
Anna's Italian
    Trattoria 2
Aunt Catfish's 15
The Chart House 10
Columbia Restaurant 12
Marko's
    Heritage Inn 18

GETTING AROUND

BY CAR   You can drive and park directly on the beach here. There is a $5 access fee between February 1 and Labor Day, the rest of the year it's free.

BY TROLLEY & BUS   VOTRAN, Volusia County's public transit system, runs buses throughout major areas of town between 6am and

7pm, Monday through Saturday. Adults pay 75¢, children under 17 and seniors pay 35¢, and children under 6 accompanied by an adult ride free.

SPECIAL EVENTS

The below-listed are Daytona's *major* annual events. Also check with The Daytona Beach Area Convention & Visitors Bureau (see above) to find out what else is happening in town during your stay.

FEBRUARY   Sixteen days of **Speedweeks** events (taking place the first three weeks of February) get under way with the **Rolex 24** (a 24-hour endurance road race for sports cars), which draws international entries. Following that, top names in NASCAR stock-car racing compete in the **Busch Clash, Arca 200, Gatorade Twin 125-mile Qualifying Races, International Race of Champions (IROC), Florida 200,** and **Goody's 300,** culminating in the **Daytona 500,** which is always held on the Sunday prior to the third Monday in February. All events take place at the Daytona International Speedway. Call 904/253-7223 for ticket information. For the Daytona 500, especially, tickets must be purchased far—even as much as a year—in advance. They go on sale January 1 of the prior year.

MARCH   Bike Week/Camel Motorcycle Week is the rallying point for an international gathering of motorcycle enthusiasts for 10 days early in the month. Major races (featuring the world's best road racers, motocrossers, and dirt trackers) at the speedway include the **Daytona 200 by Arai Motorcycle Classic,** the **Daytona Supercross by Honda,** and the **Camel Pro Grand National Kickoff.** There are many other races as well as motorcycle shows, beach parties, and festivities. The last day of Bike Week, after the early morning Blessing of the Bikes at St. Paul's Church, the Annual Motorcycle Parade with thousands of riders leaves Bellair Plaza and continues to the Speedway. Call 904/253-7223 for details.

Spring Break. For three weeks in March college students from all over the United States and Canada flock to Daytona Beach for fun in the sun—endless partying, wet T-shirt and bikini contests, free concerts, volleyball tournaments and other games on the beach, hotel pool deck parties, etc. Call 904/255-0981 for details.

Late in the month (sometimes early April), the **Spring Speedway Spectacular,** a car show and swap meet at the Daytona International Speedway, features a wide variety of collector vehicles. In addition, displays include automotive toys and memorabilia, auto-themed art, and a crafts sale. Admission is charged. Call 904/255-7355 for details.

MAY   During the **Greater Daytona Beach Striking Fish Tournament** on Memorial Day weekend, some 250 boats from all over the southeast compete for more than $75,000 in cash and prizes in seven fishing categories. Call 904/255-0415 for details.

JULY   The **Pepsi 400** race, marking the halfway point in the NASCAR Winston Cup Series for stock cars, is held the first Saturday in July at 11am at the Daytona International Speedway. Call 904/253-7223 for details.

The **Florida International Festival,** a week-long musical event taking place every other year (in odd-numbered years), features concerts by major classical and pop musicians from all over the world—everything from the London Symphony Orchestra to Skitch Henderson, as well as preconcert lectures, jazz bands, ballet, and special concerts for children. Events are scheduled at the Peabody Auditorium, Ocean Center, and other local performance places in late July, possibly early August. Call 904/257-7790 for details and ticket information.

SEPTEMBER   The **King of the Beach Volleyball Tournament** takes place in front of the Marriott Hotel in late September or early October. The top eight male players in the world compete, and a 3,000-seat stadium is erected on the beach. Admission is charged. Call 904/255-0981 for details.

OCTOBER   **AMA/CCS Motorcycle Championship.** During three days in mid-October, road-racing stars of tomorrow compete at the Daytona International Speedway. Events include a program of AMA/CCS "Races of Champions" National Championship Sprints for a variety of road-racing classes, as well as the season-ending U.S. Endurance Championship event and the season finales for the Honda CBR 900RR Series and the Harley-Davidson Twin Sports Series. Other activities for motorcycle enthusiasts take place in the area. Call 904/253-7223 for ticket information.

NOVEMBER   The **Daytona Beach Fall Speedway Spectacular,** featuring the Annual Turkey Rod Run, is the southeast's largest combined car show and swap meet, with thousands of street rods and classic vehicles on display and for sale. It takes place at the International Speedway Thanksgiving weekend. Events include an auto-parts swap meet, a collector vehicle auction, and a nonautomotive crafts show. Admission is charged. Call 904/255-7355 for details.

DECEMBER   **World Karting Association Enduro World Championships,** the biggest karting event in the country, takes place between Christmas and New Year's at the Daytona International Speedway. Call 904/253-7223 for details.

WHAT TO SEE & DO

The speedway and the beach are, of course, Daytona's major attractions. In addition, if you're interested in deep-sea fishing and/or whale watching, contact **Critter Fleet,** 4950 S. Peninsula Dr., Ponce Inlet (☎ 904/767-7676). **Sea Love Marina,** 4884 Front St., Ponce Inlet (☎ 904/767-3406), also offers deep-sea fishing. There are a dozen golf courses within 25 minutes of the beach, and most hotels can arrange starting times for you. The **Daytona Beach Golf Club,** 600 Wilder Blvd. (☎ 904/258-3119), is the city's largest, with 36 holes. **Shenandoah Stables,** 1759 Tomoka Farms Rd., off U.S. Hwy. 92 (☎ 904/257-1444), offers daily trail rides and horseback-riding lessons between 10am and 5pm. For jet ski rentals contact **Daytona High Performance—MBI,** 925 Sickler Dr., at the Seabreeze Bridge (☎ 904/257-5276). Additional water-sports equipment, as well as bicycles, beach buggies, and mopeds, can be rented along the beach in front of major hotels. A good place to look is in front of the Marriott at 100 N. Atlantic Ave. The **Daytona Flea Market** is one of the world's largest with 1,000 covered outdoor booths plus 100 vendors in an air-conditioned building. Located on Tomoka Farms Road, a mile west of the speedway at the junction of I-95 and U.S. Hwy. 92 (☎ 904/252-1999), it is open year-round, Friday to Sunday from 8am to 5pm (parking is free).

Daytona Beach Kennel Club

2201 W. International Speedway Blvd., just west of Fentress Blvd. ☎ **904/ 252-6484.** Admission $1 adults (seniors 55 and over free at matinees); grandstand seating, 50¢–$1.75; restaurant, $2. Night races usually Mon–Sat at 7:45pm (call before you go); matinees Mon, Wed, and Sat at 1pm. Doors and restaurant open an hour before post time. Parking is free on the premises; preferred parking (closer to entrance) is $1, and valet parking, $2.

This is a pleasant way to spend a day or evening, especially if you opt to watch the races over lunch or dinner in the upstairs restaurant. There are a variety of ways to bet on the greyhounds; if you've never done it before, pick up a free brochure that explains them all. You can also buy tip sheets recommending computer and expert picks. Each meet includes 14 races. You must be at least 18 years old to enter the betting area.

✪ Daytona International Speedway

1801 W. International Speedway Blvd. (U.S. 92), at Bill France Blvd. ☎ **904/ 253-RACE** for tickets, 254-2700 for information. Admission auto events, $30–$150; motorcycle events, $10–$35; go-kart events, under $10. Big events sell out months in advance (the Daytona 500 at least a year in advance), so plan far ahead and also reserve accommodations well before your trip. Open daily. Parking is free for grandstand seating; infield parking charges vary with the event. Closed Thanksgiving and Christmas Day.

Opened in 1959 with the first Daytona 500, this 450-acre "World Center of Racing" is practically the raison d'être for Daytona Beach—certainly the keynote of the city's fame. It presents about eight weekends of major racing events annually, featuring stock cars, sports cars, motorcycles, and go-karts, and is also used for automobile testing. Its grandstand, a mile long, seats over 100,000.

Major annual races here include Speedweeks (February), Bike Week (March), Pepsi 400 (July), and the AMA/CCS Motorcycle Championship (October). For further information, write to Daytona International Speedway, P.O. Box 2801, Daytona Beach, FL 32120-2801.

To learn more about racing, head for the **World Center of Racing** at the west end of the Speedway and NASCAR office complex. Open daily from 9am to 5pm, the center is also the departure site for entertainingly narrated 25-minute guided tram tours of the facility that provide a close look at the high-banked 2.5-mile trioval and 3.56-mile road courses, the Winston Tower, pit road, and the garage area. Admission is $5 for adults, free for children 6 and under. Tours depart daily every 30 minutes between 9:15am and 4:15pm, except during races and special events. Also at the Center are a large gift shop; a snack bar;

the Gallery of Legends, where the history of motorsports in the Daytona Beach area is documented through photographs and memorabilia; and the Budweiser Video Wall, presenting a continuous showing of racing in the Daytona Beach area, tracing its history from the "Birthplace of Speed" to the "World Center of Racing." You can "feel the thunder" while listening to a 20-minute Surround-Sound audio presentation called *The Daytona 500: From Dawn to Determination*. The center also stocks information on area accommodations, restaurants, attractions, and nightlife.

Note: As we go to press, the Speedway is undergoing an $18-million expansion to include **Daytona USA**—a state-of-the-art motorsports entertainment attraction that will vividly present the history of stock car, go-kart, and motorcycle racing in Daytona.

Eco-Tours at Hontoon Landing Resort & Marina

2317 River Ridge Rd., in DeLand. ☎ **904/734-2474**, or 800/248-2474. Eco-Tours, $12 adults, $10 children 5–16 and seniors 55 and over, free for kids under 5. Eco-Tours cruises depart daily October through April at 10am and 1pm, 10am only May through September (call for reservations). Directions: Follow International Speedway Boulevard west until it ends; then turn left on Spring Garden Avenue (Fla. 15A), right on Fla. 44, left on Old New York Avenue, left on Hontoon Road, and left again on River Ridge Road.

Just a 35-minute drive from Daytona, this rustic resort on the St. Johns River offers two-hour nature cruises in open-air pontoon boats. Knowledgeable guides point out local flora and fauna—the latter including abundant bird life, otters, manatees, turtles, alligators, and other endemic species. You'll pass an ancient Timucuan shell mound and the remains of stills that once flourished in the dense riverside marshlands. And there's a 15-minute stop at Blue Springs State Park to visit manatee- and alligator-viewing stations. Binoculars, which greatly, enhance the experience, can be rented at the resort store. Pack a picnic lunch (or request a deli luncheon when you call) and make a day—or overnight stay—of it. In addition to moderately priced accommodations (call for details), Hontoon Landing offers a swimming pool, volleyball, boat rentals (jet skis, fishing boats, pontoons, ski/cruise boats, and houseboats), freshwater fishing (licenses, bait, gear, and tackle can be obtained on the premises), and many other resort activities. In addition, there are camping cabins, nature trails, and a riverside picnic area at the adjacent 1,650-acre Hontoon Island State Park (☎ 904/736-5309).

Halifax River Nature Cruises

Departing from the west bank of the Halifax River at the Port Orange Bridge (at Aunt Catfish's restaurant). ☎ **904/767-4768**. Luncheon cruise $13.95; dinner cruise $15.95. Cruise only, $10 adults, $6 children 12 and under. Luncheon cruise departs daily at 9:45am, dinner cruise departs daily at 2:45pm.

Board the *Native III*, a comfortable canvas-covered 34-foot pontoon, for a delightful 1 1/2-hour eco-cruise on the Halifax River (part of the Intracoastal Waterway). En route, you'll learn Timucuan and Seminole lore and view dolphins, oyster beds, and abundant birdlife. Buy your ticket at Aunt Catfish's (see details in "Where to Dine" below); the price includes lunch or dinner the day of the cruise.

✪ Klassix Auto Museum

2909 W. International Speedway Blvd., at Tomoka Farms Rd., just west of I-95.
☎ **904/252-3800.** Admission $8.50 adults, $4.25 children 7–12, free for kids under 7. Open daily 9am–6pm, with extended hours during special events. Closed Christmas Day.

Opened with appropriate fanfare during 1994 Speedweeks, this exciting museum showcases Corvettes—a model from every year since 1953. Also on display are collector cars (including cars from the movie *Days of Thunder*), special-interest Corvettes (such as the Mako Shark, and mid-'60s prototype), historic Daytona race cars from all motorsports, motorcycles, and racing memorabilia, along with exhibits on the same. A 1950s-style soda shop and gift shop are on the premises.

✪ Museum of Arts and Sciences

1040 Museum Blvd., off Nova Rd. ☎ **904/255-0285.** Admission $4 adults, $1 children and students with ID, free for kids under 6; planetarium shows, $1. Tues–Fri 9am–4pm, Sat–Sun noon–5pm. Closed New Year's Day, Thanksgiving, and Christmas Day. Directions: Take International Speedway Boulevard west, make a left on Nova Road, and look for a sign on your right.

Housing both art and natural science exhibits, this eclectic museum dates to 1956, when Cuban dictator Fulgencio Batista donated his vacation home and art collection to the city. In 1971 the museum relocated to its present building. The Cuban collection—mostly paintings—spans two centuries from 1759 to 1959. "Masterworks of American Art" includes art and furnishings from the Pilgrim period, Abolitionist paintings, works by Gilbert Stuart and Samuel Morse, Federalist furnishings, and Tiffany silver. In the Karshan Center of Graphic Arts you'll view 18th- and 19th-century European prints, turn-of-the-century art nouveau posters, and lithographs by artists ranging from William Blake to Degas. A lobby gallery highlights fine and decorative arts from the Age of Napoleon. There's a prehistory of Florida section. And "Africa: Life and Ritual" documents African peoples from over 30 cultures in 15 countries. A contemporary sculpture garden and a one-mile nature trail are on the grounds. Planetarium shows take place at 1 and 3pm daily.

WHERE TO STAY

Daytona Beach hotels fill to the bursting point during major races at the speedway, whenever college students are on break, and during other special events. At these times room rates skyrocket, if you can find a room at all, and there's often a minimum-stay requirement. If you're planning to be in town at one of these busy times (see "Special Events," above, in this section), reserve far in advance. All of the accommodations listed below are on or near the beach and close to the speedway.

AT THE BEACH

Expensive

✪ Marriott

100 N. Atlantic Ave., between Earl St. and Auditorium Blvd., Daytona Beach, FL 32118. ☎ **904/254-8200,** or 800/228-9290. Fax 904/253-8841. 377 rms. 25 suites. A/C MINIBAR TV TEL. $149 single or double ($235–$275 during special

events, when there's also a seven-night minimum stay); $198 single or double on the Executive Level ($250–$265 during special events); $250–$1,000 suite. Additional person $20 extra. Children under 18 stay free in parents' room. AE, CB, DC, DISC, MC, V. Free parking in lot across the street; valet parking $8 per night.

This is Daytona's most luxurious—and most central—beachfront hotel, designed so that every room offers a gorgeous ocean view. It's right at the clock tower and bandshell (where Marriott hosts several admission-free rock concerts each year) and, in season, its beach and boardwalk are the site of concessions offering parasailing, bicycle rentals, motorized four-wheelers, pedal carts, surfboards, boogie boards, cabañas, and umbrellas. Accommodations are decorated in pleasing resort colors. In-room amenities include alarm-clock radios and remote-control cable TVs with Spectravision movie stations.

Dining/Entertainment: Coquinas, the hotel's premier dining room, features steak and seafood dinners. The pretty plant-filled Parkside Oceanfront Café, with picture windows overlooking the beach, serves moderately priced breakfasts, lunches, and dinners daily. Weather permitting, you can sit outside at umbrella tables. Splash, a tropically themed poolside bar, serves light fare and specialty drinks; it has indoor and outdoor seating. Also on the beach is a complex of small restaurants with outdoor café seating, serving varied international fare. There's a lively on-premises bar called Waves, and the sophisticated Clocktower Lounge offers live music (see "Evening Entertainment," below).

Services: Concierge, room service (7am to 11pm), free newspapers at bell desk.

Facilities: Indoor/outdoor swimming pool, two whirlpools, steam and sauna, kiddie pool, sand volleyball court, playground, video-game arcade, unisex hair and beauty salon (also offers massage), coin-op washer/dryers, complete health club, florist, an arcade shops.

Moderate

Perry's Ocean Edge Resort

2209 S. Atlantic Ave., between Moore and Bonner aves., Daytona Beach, FL 32118. ☎ **904/255-0581** or 800/447-0002. Fax 904/258-7315. 204 rms. A/C TV TEL. $50–$130 single or double. $108–$242 suite (formed by combining rooms). Two children under 12 stay free. Additional person $10. Rate range reflects view and season; rates may be even higher during major events when there's also a four- to five-night minimum stay. Inquire about packages/weekly rates. (Rates include continental breakfast.) AE, CB, DC, DISC, MC, V. Free parking on the premises.

Some people say the secret of this family-run property's popularity is the fresh-baked doughnuts served with your coffee, fresh fruit, and juice each morning. They certainly are a treat, but Perry's has more going for it than free frosted bear claws. Entered via an attractive knotty pine-paneled lobby, it has a grassy palm-fringed garden beachfront—the prettiest in Daytona. The staff is extremely friendly and helpful. And spacious rooms (75% of them with ocean views and private balconies or patios) are equipped with remote-control cable TVs, microwave ovens, coffee makers, and small refrigerators. Many units have full kitchens, living rooms, and dining areas, and most have hair dryers in the bath. A supermarket and 7-11 store are directly across the street.

Dining/Entertainment: A homey coffee shop is open for full American breakfasts and lunches daily. The above-mentioned doughnuts are served in two comfortable on-premises lounges equipped with pianos and large TVs. Guests gather for Monday night football in the lodgelike South Tower lounge.

Services: Year-round activities (Bingo, movies, tournaments, Monte Carlo nights, and more) for adults and children.

Facilities: A large free-form indoor pool with retractable roof, surrounded by a lushly planted garden sun deck; 2 large outdoor swimming pools; kiddie pool; whirlpool; shuffleboard; 9-hole putting green; horseshoes; bocci ball court; beach volleyball; coin-op washers/dryers; video-game arcade; car-rental desk; gift shop.

Inexpensive
Days Inn

1909 S. Atlantic Ave. (at Flamingo Ave.), Daytona Beach, FL 32118. ☎ **904/255-4492,** or 800/224-5056. Fax 904/238-0632. 184 rms, 7 efficiencies. A/C TV TEL. $25–$50 single; $45–$60 double; $55–$75 efficiency for one or two. During special events, $100–$125 single or double; $120–$145 efficiency for one or two. Additional person $6 extra. Children under 12 stay free in parents' room. AE, CB, DC, DISC, MC, V. Free parking.

At this recently renovated nine-story beachfront hotel, every room provides an ocean view. Pretty peach-and-teal rooms with oak furnishings offer remote-control cable TVs with Showtime channels and in-room sales. All have balconies, and some contain small refrigerators and microwave ovens. Large oceanfront efficiencies have fully equipped kitchens.

Facilities include a swimming pool/kiddie pool/sun deck overlooking the beach, an on-premises restaurant serving breakfast only, and a video-game arcade. During summer, light fare and drinks are offered at a pool bar.

Days Inns nationwide offer a Super Saver rate of just $29 to $49 single or double if you reserve 30 days in advance via the toll-free phone number. This deal is, of course, subject to availability, but it's worth a try. If you can't get in here, there are five other Days Inns intown, all conveniently located beachfront properties. Call 800/329-7466 for details.

BED & BREAKFAST
✪ Captain's Quarters Inn

3711 S. Atlantic Ave. (about a quarter mile south of Dunlawton Ave.), Daytona Beach, FL 32127. ☎ **904/767-0883,** or 800/332-3119. Fax 904/760-7712. 26 suites. A/C TV TEL. $75–$95 suite for one or two, $125–$185 oceanfront penthouse suite. During special events $90–$140 suite for one or two, $165–$225 oceanfront penthouse suite. Additional adult $5, free for children under 17. Lower rates available for weekly and monthly stays. (Rates include full breakfast.) AE, DISC, MC, V. Free parking.

This five-story beachfront inn offers large and lovely suites, most with ocean or river views. They have living/dining room areas, fully equipped kitchens, and country-look bedrooms furnished in oak antique reproductions. Residential decorator schemes utilize charming floral-print wall coverings and fabrics, balloon curtains, dried-flower wreaths, and framed botanical prints. French doors open onto balconies or patios furnished with wooden rockers.

Accommodations are equipped with remote-control cable TVs (two per unit) offering HBO and another free movie station, and VCRs (movies can be rented). Penthouse suites have fireplaces, spa tubs, and big picture windows overlooking the ocean. On-premises facilities include a country crafts/gift shop off the lobby, a heated swimming pool, coin-op washer/dryers, and the Galley Restaurant, which has an outdoor deck overlooking the ocean. Open for breakfast and lunch daily, it serves scrumptious fresh-baked cakes, cinnamon buns, and danish, as well as homemade soups, salads, and sandwiches on homemade breads. It's worth stopping by even if you're staying elsewhere. Transport is available to and from the airport. Other pluses: complimentary daily newspapers, chocolate mints on your night table, and a full breakfast of eggs, bacon, grits or home-fries, juice, and coffee served each morning in your room or the Galley. Owner Todd Morgan provides warm hospitality.

✪ Coquina Inn

544 S. Palmetto Ace. (at Cedar St.), Daytona Beach, FL 32114. ☎ **904/254-4969,** or 800/727-0678. 4 rms (all with bath). A/C. Fri–Sun $90, Mon–Thurs $60; special events rate $150. Additional person $10 extra, $30 during special events. No children under 12 accepted. (Rates include full breakfast.) AE, MC, V. Free parking.

This charming terra-cotta-roofed coquina and cream stucco house sits on a tranquil tree-shaded street half a block west of the Halifax River and Harbor Marina. Guests can relax before a working fireplace in a lovely parlor, and baskets of magazines, books, games, and a TV are in the adjoining sunroom. Breakfast—elegantly served on Lenox and Rosenthal china—includes a main course such as eggs Benedict or French toast stuffed with cream cheese, bananas, and pecans; fresh fruit; fresh-ground coffee; and homemade breads and muffins. Classical music is played in public areas.

Each room is exquisitely decorated, most with area rugs strewn on oak floors and ceiling fans overhead. The Jasmine Room, painted adobe peach, features a working coquina fireplace and a canopied mahogany bed. In the Hibiscus Room, decorated in soft greens and pinks, a black iron bed embellished with gold leaf is made up with a pretty floral chintz spread; French doors lead to a private plant-filled balcony. Painted in raspberry with a floral frieze, the sunny Azalea Room has light streaming in from corner windows. Overlooking the patio garden, it's furnished with a mahogany waterfall bed, white wicker chairs, and an antique Governor Winthrop desk. All rooms are provided with bubble bath and candles. Portable phones and TVs are available on request. Complimentary tea and sherry are served in the parlor throughout the day. Beach cruiser bikes are available at no cost, there's a whirlpool spa in the garden, and several restaurants are within easy walking distance.

✪ Live Oak Inn

448 S. Beach St. (at Loomis Ave.), Daytona Beach, FL 32114. ☎ **904/252-4667.** 4 rms (all with bath). A/C TV TEL. $90 single or double. Additional person $10

extra. Rates may be higher during peak events. (Rates include extended continental breakfast.) AE, MC, V. Free parking.

Occupying a restored 19th-century house, this charming B&B hostelry is surrounded by centuries-old live oaks. An inviting front porch with white wicker rocking chairs faces the street. The guest rooms—three with private sun porches or balconies—are exquisitely decorated, with area rugs strewn on highly polished oak floors and wood-bladed fans whirring slowly overhead. Live plants, old family photographs, and baskets of potpourri and dried flowers add to the residential ambience. Rooms look out on the Halifax Harbor Marina or a garden. All are stocked with books and magazines and equipped with VCRs; baths have Victorian soaking tubs or Jacuzzis.

Breakfast—fresh fruit, cold cuts and cheeses, fresh-squeezed juice, homemade breads and muffins, hard-boiled eggs, dry cereal, and coffee—is served on an enclosed porch overlooking a yacht basin. Public areas also include a comfortable living room. And a lobby restaurant and bar are in the works. Other amenities here: a washer/dryer and copy machine for guest use, a complimentary drink and flowers at check in, terry robes, and afternoon tea and cocktails. No smoking is permitted in the house. No children under 10 accepted.

WHERE TO DINE
EXPENSIVE

✪ Alexander's

123 W. Granada Blvd., between N. Ridgewood Ave. and U.S. 1. ☎ **904/673-5312.** Reservations recommended. Appetizers $3.75–$5.50 at lunch, $6.25–$7.75 at dinner; main courses $5.20–$6.95 at lunch, $18.95–$23.95 at dinner. AE, MC, V. Lunch Mon–Sat 11:30am–3pm, dinner Mon–Sat 6–10pm; bar open for lunch in the interim. FRENCH/CONTINENTAL.

This charming innlike restaurant has a beamed ceiling, lace-curtained windows, and white-linened tables lit (at night) by brass candle lamps. A pianist plays standards (Cole Porter et al) on a baby grand during dinner.

Though the menu changes frequently, you can always count on French chef Christian Drouin for a superb meal. If it's available, do order his tangy cheddar soup spiked with sherry. Other appetizers might include puff pastry filled with poached salmon and scallops, or garlicky escargots. Thick oven-baked pork chops in cranberry-orange-Dijon sauce make a memorable entrée. Also excellent are Drouin's large grilled sea scallops in a beurre blanc citrus cream sauce and his classic steak au poivre. All entrées are accompanied by a delicious salad, fresh vegetables, potatoes or rice du jour, and sorbets between courses; appropriate wines are recommended. Desserts might include a very rich black velvet chocolate cake or cherries jubilee, flamed tableside. The lunch menu lists sandwiches, salads, pastas, and a few entrées such as pan-blackened filet mignon. Alexander's offers an extensive international wine list (with many by-the-glass selections) and a good choice of single-malt scotches and draft beers.

MODERATE

✪ Anna's Italian Trattoria

304 Seabreeze Blvd., at Peninsula Dr. ☎ **904/239-9624.** Reservations recommended. Appetizers $4.25–$8; main courses mostly $8.50–$14; early-bird dinners (served 5–6:30pm) $5–$8. AE, MC, V. Free parking in a lot on Seabreeze Blvd. across Peninsula Dr. Dinner only, daily 5–10pm. ITALIAN.

At this charming little trattoria, the Triani family, from Sicily, have created a homelike atmosphere enhanced by cheerful Italian music and soft lighting. Everything here is homemade—from the creamy Italian dressing on your house salad to the basket of bread that accompanies all entrées. Two irresistible pasta dishes are the *fettuccine alla campagniola* (pasta tossed with strips of sautéed eggplant and chunks of sausage in tomato cream sauce) and rigatoni Siciliana (tubular pasta with sautéed broccoli, garlic, and pine nuts in a fresh tomato sauce). Non-pasta recommendables include salmon scampi and risotto alla Anna (rice cooked with chunks of chicken, shrimp, green peas, and onions in a light tomato sauce).

Portions are hearty. If you like a heavy hand with garlic, as I do, tell your waiter. Entrées come with soup or salad and a side dish of angelhair pasta or a vegetable. Take the pasta and order a vegetable side dish as well, perhaps asparagus, escarole, or broccoli rabe sautéed in oil and garlic. There's a nice selection of Italian wines.

⑤ Aunt Catfish's

4009 Halifax Dr., at the west end of the Port Orange Bridge. ☎ **904/767-4768.** Call ahead for priority seating (that means you get the first table available when you arrive). Appetizers $2.90–$4.95; main courses $3.99–$8 at lunch, mostly $8–$13.50 at dinner; early-bird dinners $7–$10.50. Reduced prices for children and seniors. Sun brunch $9 for adults, $5.50 for children 4–12, free for kids under 4. AE, DC, DISC, MC, V. Mon–Sat 11:30am–9:30pm, Sun 9am–9:30pm (brunch Sun 9am–2pm; early-bird dinners daily noon–6:30pm). Closed Christmas. SOUTHERN/SEAFOOD.

Aunt Catfish was the nickname of a gruff-voiced local character whom owner Jim Galbreath knew as a kid. She fished all day, drove around in a black Cadillac, and ate dinner every night in a restaurant owned by Jim's parents. Her namesake restaurant abounds in cozy southern-cracker ambience. During the day, ask for a window seat overlooking the Halifax River.

The food is great, and there's plenty of it. For one thing, all entrées include hush puppies, a chunk of watermelon, unbelievable yummy hot cinnamon rolls, a side dish (perhaps baked Mexican potato skins with melted Cheddar, salsa, and sour cream), and unlimited helpings from an extensive salad bar, which in addition to salads is laden with such down-home fare as cheese grits, cinnamon apples, fresh-baked cornbread, and hominy. A great entrée choice is the Florida cracker sampler platter—a spit-roasted quarter chicken with cranberry-orange relish, crabcakes, fried shrimp, and fried catfish fingerlings. Lightly breaded fried oysters here are also highly recommendable.

Sunday brunch provides an unparalleled opportunity for overindulgence. A buffet meal, it includes all the above-mentioned salad bar items, plus an omelet station, pancakes, French toast, hot entrées, a carving station, fresh-baked muffins and pastries (even bananas Foster), and more—all for under $10! Lunch choices include burgers, sandwiches, and a soup and salad buffet in addition to ribs, chicken, and seafood entrées.

The Chart House

1100 Marina Point Dr., off Beach St. ☎ **904/255-9022.** Reservations suggested. Appetizers $4.50–$8.95; main courses mostly $14.95–$21.95. AE, CB, DC, DISC, MC, V. Sun–Thurs 5–10pm, Fri–Sat 5–11pm. STEAK/SEAFOOD.

The plant-filled Chart House is of octagonal design, with palm trees growing towards a lofty skylit bamboo ceiling. Ship models, palm-frond-motif carpeting, and a waitstaff in Hawaiian shirts enhance the restaurant's tropical/marine ambience. And windowed walls overlooking the Halifax River and a marina insure every diner a water view. Consider having dessert or after-dinner drinks in the plush bar/lounge downstairs or on an open-air riverside deck with umbrella tables.

You might want to bypass appetizers here, since your entrée includes a very extensive salad bar (including items such as caviar, artichoke hearts, and an array of fresh fruits), a basket of hot sourdough and seven-grain squaw bread, and a baked potato or Chart House wild rice. For your main course select shrimp or chicken Santa Fe dusted with cumin, paprika, and cayenne, grilled in butter, and served with bleu cheese dip. Steak and surf-and-turf combinations are also options.

Columbia Restaurant

125 Basin St. at the Halifax Harbor Marina. ☎ **904/248-1200.** Reservations recommended. Appetizers (tapas) $3.95–$4.95 at lunch, $3.95–$5.95 at dinner; main courses mostly $5.75–$7.95 at lunch ($6.95 for the prix-fixe lunch buffet), $9.95–$17.95 at dinner ($6.95–$8.95 for early-bird dinners); Sun brunch buffet $12.95 adults, $5.95 children 5–12. AE, CB, DC, MC, V. Sun–Thurs 11am–10pm, Fri–Sat 11am–11pm (Sun brunch served 11am–3pm). SPANISH.

The most *simpático* spot in Daytona is the boat-filled Halifax Harbor—a complex of water-view restaurants and shops—among them, Columbia, with windowed walls overlooking the marina and an awninged balcony for al fresco dining. Its plant-filled interior, centering on a tiled fountain under a lofty skylight, is simply gorgeous. Everything here is made from scratch. Begin dinner with an assortment of tapas (or compose a meal of them)—perhaps fried calamari, crabmeat quesadillas, and shrimp sautéed with garlic and red chili pepper. Entrées, served with oven-fresh Cuban bread, include a traditional paella, ropa vieja (shredded beef sautéed with onions, green peppers, and tomatoes, served with plantains and rice), and shrimp- and crabmeat-stuffed filet of red snapper baked in parchment and served with yellow rice. It's especially nice—and economical—to come here for early-bird dinners and watch the sun set over the marina. Also popular is happy hour (4 to 7pm weekdays) in the candlelit lounge, featuring complimentary hors d'oeuvres. Lavish lunch and Sunday brunch buffets are also excellent values. Spanish and California wines are featured.

Other dining choices at the marina include **Mangiare,** a casually elegant Italian restaurant open for dinner nightly from 4pm, and **Cha**

Cha Coconuts (see "The Club & Bar Scene" below for details). There's free self- and valet parking at the marina.

INEXPENSIVE

Down the Hatch

4894 Front St., Ponce Inlet. ☎ **904/761-4831.** Call ahead for priority seating (that means you get the first table available when you arrive). Directions: Take Fla. A1A south, make a right on Beach St., and follow the signs. Appetizers $2.75–$5.95; main courses $7.95–$12.95; sandwiches $3.25–$5.25. Reduced prices for children. AE, MC, V. Daily 7am–10pm. Closed Thanksgiving and Christmas. SEAFOOD.

Occupying a half-century-old fish camp on the Halifax River, Down the Hatch is a cozy, candlelit restaurant serving up fresh fish and seafood (note their shrimp boat docked outside). During the day, picture windows provide scenic views of a passing parade of boats and shore birds, and you might even see dolphins frolicking. At night, arrive early to catch the sunset over the river, and also to beat the crowd at this very popular place. Inside, rough-hewn cypress walls are hung with hundreds of photographs of the Daytona Speedway and the old fish camp.

Start your meal with an order of buffalo shrimp in piquant Louisiana hot sauce with chunky homemade bleu cheese dressing. Lightly breaded, deep-fried grouper fingers, served with tartar sauce, are also tasty. Ditto the raw oysters served with cocktail sauce and horseradish. Entrées include fried or broiled fresh fish such as red snapper or grouper, and there's an excellent crab Imperial. If seafood isn't your thing, filet mignon and prime rib are aged on the premises. All entrées are served with hush puppies and a choice of baked potato, salad, cole slaw, or fries. Down the Hatch is also open for breakfasts, including fried fish with eggs.

⑤ Marko's Heritage Inn

5420 S. Ridgewood Ave., at Niver St. ☎ **904/761-9520.** Call ahead for priority seating (that means you get the first table available when you arrive). Appetizers $2.95–$6.95; main courses mostly $8–$13; early-bird lunch $5.99 Mon–Sat, $6.99 Sun; early-bird dinner $5.95–$9.95. Reduced prices for children and seniors. Sun breakfast/brunch buffet $5.95 for adults. $3.50 for children 4–12, free for kids under 4. AE, DC, DISC, MC, V. Dinner Mon–Sat 4:30–9:30pm. Sun 11:30am–9pm (early-bird lunches served daily 11:30am–5pm, early-bird dinners daily 4:30–6pm); buffet breakfast/brunch Sun 8am–2pm. Closed Christmas. SOUTHERN/SEAFOOD.

Like Aunt Catfish's (see above), Marko's is owned by Jim Galbreath. In fact, its 17,000-square-foot warren of cozy dining rooms encompasses the house in which he grew up and his parents' original Daytona Beach restaurant. Off the entrance you'll see large photographs of its 1950s interior, with Jim as a young lad tending the counter. It's all very southern and homelike. Overflow crowds wait for tables on a porch or in an antique-filled Victorian parlor, and there's an old-fashioned candy counter and bakery up front.

This is hearty fare. Your main-course price includes a complimentary bowl of Florida cracker-style fish chowder, salad (go for the fruit with creamy poppyseed dressing), an array of vegetables (coleslaw, stewed apples, stringbeans, pickled beets), potato or scrumptious broccoli casserole, tangerine sherbet between courses, and a basket of fresh-baked oatmeal and cinnamon rolls. My favorite entrée is the grouper Hemingway, sautéed in a crisp sesame crust. Other good choices include smoky barbecued baby back ribs and fried Maryland-style crabcakes. And desserts—such as a first-rate Key lime pie and chocolate peanut-butter pie—are not to be missed. The extensive lunch buffet includes six entrées, salads, vegetables, desserts, and beverages.

EVENING ENTERTAINMENT
The Performing Arts

At the 2,552-seat **Peabody Auditorium,** 600 Auditorium Blvd., between Noble Street and Wild Olive Avenue (☎ 904/255-1314), Daytona Beach's Civic Ballet performs *The Nutcracker* every Christmas and sponsors another ballet every spring. The Daytona Beach Symphony Society arranges a series of six classical concerts between December and April. During the same season, Concert Showcase features pop artists such as Liza Minnelli, Tony Bennett, and Steve Lawrence and Eydie Gorme, as well as full Broadway-cast stage shows. And the London Symphony Orchestra has been performing here for over 25 years during the semiannual Florida International Festival.

Under the same city auspices is the **Oceanfront Bandshell** (☎ 904/258-3169), on the boardwalk next to the Marriott Hotel. The city hosts a series of free Big Band concerts at the Bandshell every Sunday night from early June through Labor Day. It's also the scene of spring-break concerts.

Prices at the Peabody vary with the performances. Bandshell concerts are usually free. Parking is $3 in a lot adjacent to the Peabody.

The Club & Bar Scene
Alexander's Cafe

123 W. Granada Blvd., between N. Ridgewood Ave. and U.S. 1, in Ormond Beach. ☎ **904/673-5312.**

The bar/lounge of this upscale restaurant—very popular with local businesspeople—has a ski-lodgey ambience. It's candlelit and casually elegant. A pianist entertains in the lounge nightly from 7pm. You can order from the extensive wine list, have an appetizer or dessert, try one of the the cafe's many single-malt scotches (I recommend the smoky Lagavulin), cognacs, or draft beers . . . or order up a fine cigar. (The bar is cigar-friendly, but open windows keep the smoke-level down.) Open Monday through Saturday until somewhere between midnight and 2am, depending on the crowd.

Cha Cha Coconuts

125 Basin St. at the Halifax Harbor Marina. ☎ **904/248-8500.** No cover.

The place to be here is on the vast umbrella-tabled deck overlooking the boat-filled marina, listening—or dancing—to music under the stars. Live bands—reggae, rock, top-40, blues, light jazz—perform here nightly, weather permitting, from 4 to 8pm Sunday, 7 to 11pm Monday to Thursday, and 7:30 to 11:30pm Friday and Saturday. Also popular here is Happy Hour, weekdays 4 to 7pm. A full moderately priced menu of tropical fare ranging from a Jamaican jerk burger to peppery grilled lime-garlic grouper Cozumel is served.

Coliseum

176 N. Beach St., at Bay St. ☎ **904/257-9982**. Cover $5–$8.

This upscale Roman-themed dance club occupies a converted movie theater. A DJ plays alternative progressive dance music, with lapses into top-40 tunes; 16 monitors project music and ambience videos; and nightly laser shows are high-tech, utilizing 3-D and sophisticated graphic-arts effects. The crowd is mostly twenty-something with occasional glitterati (Tom Cruise partied here during the filming of *Days of Thunder*), rock musicians, and local athletes in attendance. During spring break there are special events. The Coliseum is open nightly to 3am.

Razzles

611 Seabreeze Blvd., between Grandview and S. Atlantic Aves. ☎ **904/257-6236**. Cover before 10pm, $6–$8 with free drinks; after 10pm, $5 for 18- to 20-year- olds, $3 for those 21 and over.

At this large and popular dance club, a DJ plays top-40 tunes and high-energy music till 3am nightly. The setting is archetypical, with lots of neon tubing, the requisite monitors flashing music videos, and sophisticated lighting effects over the dance floor. A magician frequently entertains in the lobby, there are four pool tables, a blackjack table, and a few video games. The crowd is young—early 20s.

The Spot

176 N. Beach St., at Bay St. ☎ **904/257-9982**.

Under the same ownership as the above-mentioned Coliseum, the Spot shares its address and phone as well. Billing itself as a "premier sports bar," it has large-screen TVs in every corner, which, along with over 30 smaller monitors, air major worldwide sporting events via satellite. This cavernous club centers on a U-shaped Formica-topped bar trimmed in turquoise neon. Amusements include foosball, air hockey, video games, pinball machines, a one-on-one basketball court, eight regulation pool tables, dart boards, and bar games. Light fare (hot wings, good pizza, salads) is available. Monday-night football parties include raffles for tickets to local sporting events, and Tuesday nights grunge videos are shown, beer is $2 a pitcher, and you can engage in a variation of sumo wrestling. Open nightly till 3am.

Waves

In the Marriott Hotel, 100 N. Atlantic Ave., between Earl St. and Auditorium Blvd. ☎ **904/254-8200**. No cover, except during special events.

An elegant bar on the hotel's boardwalk level, Waves airs continuous sporting events (via a four-dish satellite system) on numerous monitors. Its main bar centers on a large aquarium of tropical fish. There are comfy sofas in a quiet alcove with a large-screen TV. A DJ plays music for dancing nightly from 9pm. Other activities here include a pool table and electronic darts. Open nightly till 2am.

Index

$3.00 OFF ADULT ADMISSION
ONE-DAY STUDIO PASS

Regular adult admission price $37.00 (plus tax) Valid for up to 6 people through 12/31/96.
See back of coupon for details.

Thrill to over 400 acres of incredible rides, shows and attractions!

Face the all out attack of JAWS®!

Meet Barney® and friends, Baby Bop™ and BJ™ in their
live sing-along new show.

Face the fury of King Kong. Rocket Back To The Future® on the
greatest ride in history! All of this and more!

Universal Studios Florida® — the only placeon earth where
you can Ride The Movies®!

6183958001991

Avis features GM cars.

Reserve an Avis Intermediate car with request for upgrade at participating Avis locations in the U.S., Canada, Europe, Africa and the Middle East. Then present this coupon at the Avis counter and you can be upgraded one car group... **at no extra charge! An advance reservation with request for upgrade is required.** Subject to complete Terms and Conditions on back. Offer expires December 14, 1996.

Free
Avis Worldwide Upgrade!

For information and reservations, call your travel consultant or an Avis employee-owner toll free at **1-800-831-8000.**

AVIS°
We try harder.

Coupon # UULA008

Save $15

On An Avis Weekly Rental Around The World!

Rent an Intermediate through a Full Size 4-Door car for a week and you can get **$15 off** when you present this coupon at a participating Avis location in the U.S., Canada, Europe, Latin America and the Caribbean. **An advance reservation is required.** Subject to complete Terms and Conditions on back. Offer expires December 14, 1996.

For information and reservations, call your travel consultant or an Avis employee-owner toll free at **1-800-831-8000.**

AVIS°
We try harder.

Coupon # MULA036
Avis features GM cars.

FREE Worldwide Upgrade

Terms and Conditions: Coupon valid for a one-time, one-car-group upgrade at participating Avis locations in the U.S., Canada, Europe, Africa and the Middle East. For legal reasons, this offer does not apply in Germany. In the U.S. and Canada, this offer is valid on an Intermediate (Group C) through a Full Size 4-door (Group E) car. Maximum upgrade to Premium (Group G). Elsewhere, valid on Group A through Group E. Maximum upgrade to Group F. **Offer valid on daily, weekend and weekly rates** only in the U.S. and Canada, and Standard, SuperValue or Discover Europe rates elsewhere. Offer not available during holiday and other blackout periods. If reservation is for a car with automatic transmission, upgrade car will be an automatic. If reservation is for a car with manual transmission, upgrade car will be a manual. Coupon is nontransferable and nonrefundable. Coupon must be surrendered at time of rental; one per rental. Cars and upgrades are subject to availability at time of rental. **An advance reservation with request for upgrade is required.** Renter must meet Avis age, driver and credit requirements. Minimum age is 25 but may vary by location. Offer expires 12/14/96.

Rental Sales Agent Instructions
Automated Locations In The U.S. And Canada. *At Checkout:* • Assign customer a car one group higher than car group reserved. Upgrade to no higher than Group G. Charge for car group reserved. • In CPN, enter **UULA008.**
• Complete this information: RA #_____ Rental Location _____
• Attach to COUPON tape.

Manual Locations In Canada. *At Checkout:* • Assign customer a car one group higher than car group reserved. Upgrade to no higher than Group G. Charge for car group reserved. • Enter **UULA008** in box 15. • Complete this information: RA #_____ Rental Location _____
• Submit COUPON to Marketing Department CHQ.

Automated And Manual Locations In Europe, Africa And The Middle East.
• Assign customer a car one group higher than car group reserved. Upgrade to no higher than Group F. Charge for car group reserved. • In AWD, enter **NO43003.** • Check in normally.

Country HQ Handling Instructions
• Submit COUPON to country Marketing Department. • Renting country must absorb cost of promotion. Chargebacks not allowed. • Complete this information: Rental Location_____
Rental Length _____ Days_____
• Car Group Reserved_____ Date_____

$15 Off A Weekly Rental Worldwide

Terms and Conditions: Coupon valid for $15 off Standard and SuperValue weekly rates at participating Avis locations in the U.S., Canada, Europe, Latin America and the Caribbean. For legal reasons, this offer does not apply in Germany. In the U.S. and Canada, this offer is valid on an Intermediate (Group C) through a Full Size 4-door (Group E) car for a minimum 5-day rental. Elsewhere, valid on Group B through Group E on Standard or SuperValue rates. May not be used in conjunction with any other coupon, promotion or offer. Offer not available during holiday and other blackout periods. Offer may not be available on all rates at all times. Coupon is nontransferable and nonrefundable. Coupon must be surrendered at time of rental; one per rental. Cars subject to availability at time of rental. **An advance reservation is required.** Taxes, local government surcharges and optional items, such as LDW, additional driver fee and refueling, are extra. Renter must meet Avis age, driver and credit requirements. Minimum age is 25 but may vary by location. Offer expires 12/14/96. Offer valid for $15 USD or equivalent in local currency at current Avis exchange rate at time of rental.

Rental Sales Agent Instructions
Automated Locations In The U.S., Canada, Latin America And The Caribbean. *At Checkout:*
• In CPN, enter **MULA036.** • Complete this information: RA #_____
Rental Location _____ • Attach to COUPON tape.

Manual Locations In Canada, Latin America And The Caribbean. *At Checkout:* • Enter **MULA036** in box 15.
• Complete this information: RA #_____
Rental Location _____ • At car return, enter amount to be deducted in box 36. Subtract this amount from the totals of boxes 30 through 35. • Submit COUPON to Marketing Department CHQ.

Automated Locations In Europe. *At Checkout:* • In AWD, enter **NO43007.** • Enter M, followed by monetary value of the coupon in local currency, in the ADJUSTMT field. • Submit Certificate with copy 1 of RA to country HQ.

Manual Locations In Europe. *At Checkout:* • In AWD, enter **NO43007.** • Enter M, followed by monetary value of the coupon in local currency, in the ADJUSTMT box (42). • Submit Certificate with copy 1 of RA to country HQ.

Country HQ Handling Instructions.
• Renting country must absorb the cost of this promotion. Chargebacks not allowed.

**10%
OFF**

DAYS INN

The Best Value Under The Sun.℠

**10%
OFF**

The Best Value Under The Sun Just Got Better!

Now you can save even more at any of more
than 1,600 Days Inns throughout
the United States and internationally.
Just present this coupon upon check-in and
Days Inn will take 10% off your
regular room rate for your entire length of stay!
Advance reservations required, so call now!

1-800-DAYS INN
See details on back.

$3 OFF
REGULAR ROUND TRIP PRICE

Present this coupon to
MEARS MOTOR SHUTTLE BOOTH
for round trip transportation to or from the
HOTEL OF YOUR CHOICE

**COUNTER COLLECTS CASH
gratuity not included.**

For return reservations call
24 hours in advance:
(407) 423-5566

MEARS MOTOR SHUTTLE ✈

**SEE REVERSE FOR BOOTH LOCATIONS
Tickets Must be Purchased at Airport Location for Discount**

The Best Value Under The Sun.℠

- Available at participating properties.
- This coupon cannot be combined with any other special discount offer.
- Limit one coupon per room, per stay.
- Expires December 31, 1996.

1-800-DAYS INN

MEARS MOTOR SHUTTLE BOOTH LOCATIONS

2ND LEVEL

- "A" TERMINAL: Exit through the doors in front of baggage claim carousel #6

- "B" TERMINAL: Exit through the doors in front of Northwest baggage claim carousel #6 or Delta baggage claim carousel #12

THANK YOU FOR USING MEARS TRANSPORTATION

FOR RESERVATIONS CALL:

Sleep 1-800-62-SLEEP

Comfort 1-800-228-5150

Quality 1-800-228-5151

Clarion 1-800-CLARION

Econo Lodge 1-800-55-ECONO

Friendship 1-800-453-4511

RODEWAY 1-800-228-2000

Advance reservations through the toll free number required.
Discounts are based on availability at participating hotels and cannot
be used in conjunction with other discounts or promotions.

Save $2 on admission to

Wet'n Wild®
INTERNATIONAL DRIVE, ORLANDO

Good for up to six people.
Not to be used in
conjunction with any other
offer or afternoon pricing.
Expires 12/31/96.
Macmillan Travel PLU 6A 7C

$1.50 OFF ADULT

$1.00 OFF CHILD

Ripley's
Believe It or Not!®
ORLANDO MUSEUM

8201 International Drive

(407) 363-4418

GOOD FOR UP TO SIX IN PARTY
Not valid with any other offers
Must present coupon prior to check-in. Expires 12-31-96.

AFROM   All Trademarks are owned by Ripley Entertainment Inc.   CFROM

Now Save Money on All Your Travels by Joining

Frommer's
TRAVEL BOOK CLUB

The Advantages of Membership:

1. Your choice of any **TWO FREE BOOKS.**

2. Your own subscription to the **TRIPS & TRAVEL** quarterly newsletter, where you'll discover the best buys in travel, the hottest vacation spots, the latest travel trends, world-class events and festivals, and much more.

3. A **30% DISCOUNT** on any additional books you order through the club.

4. **DOMESTIC TRIP-ROUTING KITS** (available for a small additional fee). We'll send you a detailed map highlighting the most direct or scenic route to your destination, anywhere in North America.

Here's all you have to do to join:

Send in your annual membership fee of $25.00 ($35.00 Canada/Foreign) with your name, address, and selections on the form below. Or call 815/734-1104 to use your credit card.

Send all orders to:

FROMMER'S TRAVEL BOOK CLUB
P.O. Box 473 • Mt. Morris, IL 61054-0473 • ☎ 815/734-1104

YES! I want to take advantage of this opportunity to join Frommer's Travel Book Club.

[ ] My check for $25.00 ($35.00 for Canadian or foreign orders) is enclosed.
   All orders must be prepaid in U.S. funds only. Please make checks payable to Frommer's Travel Book Club.

[ ] Please charge my credit card: [ ] Visa or [ ] Mastercard

   Credit card number: _____

   Expiration date: ___ / ___ / ___

   Signature: _____

   Or call 815/734-1104 to use your credit card by phone.

Name: _____

Address: _____

City: _____ State: _____ Zip code: _____

Phone number (in case we have a question regarding your order): _____

Please indicate your choices for TWO FREE books (*see following pages*):

   Book 1 - Code: _____   Title: _____

   Book 2 - Code: _____   Title: _____

For information on ordering additional titles, see your first issue of the *Trips & Travel* newsletter.

Allow 4–6 weeks for delivery for all items. Prices of books, membership fee, and publication dates are subject to change without notice. All orders are subject to acceptance and availability.   AC1

The following Frommer's guides are available from your favorite bookstore, or you can use the order form on the preceding page to request them as part of your membership in Frommer's Travel Book Club.

FROMMER'S COMPLETE TRAVEL GUIDES

(Comprehensive guides to sightseeing, dining and accommodations, with selections in all price ranges—from deluxe to budget)

FROMMER'S $-A-DAY GUIDES

(Dream Vacations at Down-to-Earth Prices)

FROMMER'S COMPLETE CITY GUIDES
(Comprehensive guides to sightseeing, dining, and accommodations in all price ranges)

FROMMER'S FAMILY GUIDES
(Guides to family-friendly hotels, restaurants, activities, and attractions)

FROMMER'S WALKING TOURS
(Memorable strolls through colorful and historic neighborhoods, accompanied by detailed directions and maps)

FROMMER'S AMERICA ON WHEELS
(Guides for travelers who are exploring the U.S.A. by car, featuring a brand-new rating system for accommodations and full-color road maps)

FROMMER'S SPECIAL-INTEREST TITLES

Arthur Frommer's Branson!	P107	Frommer's Where to	
Arthur Frommer's New World		Stay U.S.A., 11th Ed.	P102
of Travel (avail. 11/95)	P112	National Park Guide, 29th Ed.	P106
Frommer's Caribbean		USA Today Golf	
Hideaways (avail. 9/95)	P110	Tournament Guide	P113
Frommer's America's 100		USA Today Minor League	
Best-Loved State Parks	P109	Baseball Book	P111

FROMMER'S BEST BEACH VACATIONS

(The top places to sun, stroll, shop, stay, play, party, and swim—with each beach rated for beauty, swimming, sand, and amenities)

California (avail. 10/95)	G100	Hawaii (avail. 10/95)	G102
Florida (avail. 10/95)	G101		

FROMMER'S BED & BREAKFAST GUIDES

(Selective guides with four-color photos and full descriptions of the best inns in each region)

California	B100	Hawaii	B105
Caribbean	B101	Pacific Northwest	B106
East Coast	B102	Rockies	B107
Eastern United States	B103	Southwest	B108
Great American Cities	B104		

FROMMER'S IRREVERENT GUIDES

(Wickedly honest guides for sophisticated travelers and those who want to be)

Chicago (avail. 11/95)	I100	New Orleans (avail. 11/95)	I103
London (avail. 11/95)	I101	San Francisco (avail. 11/95)	I104
Manhattan (avail. 11/95)	I102	Virgin Islands (avail. 11/95)	I105

FROMMER'S DRIVING TOURS

(Four-color photos and detailed maps outlining spectacular scenic driving routes)

Australia	Y100	Italy	Y108
Austria	Y101	Mexico	Y109
Britain	Y102	Scandinavia	Y110
Canada	Y103	Scotland	Y111
Florida	Y104	Spain	Y112
France	Y105	Switzerland	Y113
Germany	Y106	U.S.A.	Y114
Ireland	Y107		

FROMMER'S BORN TO SHOP

(The ultimate travel guides for discriminating shoppers—from cut-rate to couture)

Hong Kong (avail. 11/95)	Z100	London (avail. 11/95)	Z101